WILDERNESS VISIONARIES

Leopold

Thoreau

Muir

Olson

Murie

Service

Marshall

Rutstrum

DEDICATION

This edition, for them

NorthWord Press, Inc.
P.O. Box 1360
Minocqua, WI 54548

Cover photograph © Pat O'Hara
Jacket design by Wayne C. Parmley and Kenneth Hey
Book design by Kenneth Hey

Photos and illustrations: Thoreau—Dunshee Ambrotype: courtesy of The Thoreau Society; Muir—courtesy of Bruce Wolfe; Service—courtesy of Public Archives of Canada; Marshall—courtesy of The Wilderness Society; Leopold—courtesy of Nina Bradley/Aldo Leopold Shack Foundation; Murie—by James Marshall/Wilderness Society; Rutstrum—Dr. William Forgey; Olson—courtesy of Barbara Peet.

Printed and bound in U.S.A.

For a free catalog describing NorthWord's line of nature books and gifts, call 1-800-336-5666

Library of Congress Cataloging-in-Publication Data
Wilderness visionaries / by Jim dale Vickery.
  p. cm.
  Includes bibliographical references (p. _____) and index.
ISBN 1-55971-435-2 : $9.95
  1. Naturalists—United States—Biography. 2. Conservationists—
United States—Biography. I. Title.
QH26.V53 1994
508.73'092'2—dc20
[B]   94-20868
                                                                CIP

4/20/95   508.73 Vic   9.95

WILDERNESS VISIONARIES

Leopold

Thoreau

Muir

Olson

Murie

Service

Marshall

Rutstrum

JIM DALE VICKERY

NorthWord
PRESS, INC.

Minocqua, Wi

ACKNOWLEDGMENTS

The author is grateful to the following publishers and persons for permission to quote as follows:

Alfred A. Knopf, Inc., for excerpts from Sigurd F. Olson's books, *Listening Point* (1980), *The Lonely Land* (1961), *Open Horizons* (1969), *Reflections From the North Country* (1976), and *The Singing Wilderness* (1979).

The American Association for the Advancement of Science, for excerpts from Bob Marshall's "The Problem of the Wilderness" in *Scientific Monthly*, Feb. 1930.

Dodd, Mead & Company, Inc., for "The Call of the Wild," from *The Collected Poems of Robert Service*.

Houghton Mifflin Company, for excerpts from William Frederic Bade's *The Life and Letters of John Muir*, 2 vols., 1924.

The University of California Press, for excerpts from Bob Marshall's *Alaska Wilderness: Exploring the Central Brooks Range*, 1970.

The University of Wisconsin Press, for excerpts from Linnie Marsh Wolfe's *John of the Mountains: The Unpublished Journals of John Muir*, 1979; and Linnie Marsh Wolfe's *Son of the Wilderness: The Life of John Muir*, 1978.

The Wilderness Society, for excerpts from Sigurd Olson's "Quetico-Superior Elegy," in *The Living Wilderness*, Spring, 1948.

Mr. William Krasilovsky, Esq., for excerpts from Robert Service's *Ploughman of the Moon: An Adventure Into Memory*, New York, Dodd, Mead & Co., 1945.

It's very sad if our culture only sees wilderness as a place to play. What wilderness should be doing is speaking to our souls and teaching us about being quiet... and respecting the world we live in.

—Bill Mason,
   Canadian artist, filmmaker and wilderness preservationist

Thoreau

Muir

Service

Marshall

Leopold

Murie

Rutstrum

Olson

CONTENTS

PREFACE

March snow falls from a gray sky to settle on a granite ridge as I think of the wilderness visionaries who have led me here with a hunger and craving. People like Henry David Thoreau, Bob Marshall and Sigurd F. Olson. This book, now in a second edition, still written throughout in personal satiation, is about their paths. Their dreams. And the footsteps they took—and we take—to arrive at their deep and abiding visions.

Vision. This is what I hunger for. I seek the composite vision certain men have formed for me, like rivers feeding a sea.

What was it Thoreau, et al., said? How did they live? camp? and canoe? What trails and waterways did they poke down on their own vision quests? Why were they fascinated with wilderness, what did it mean to them, and how did it figure in their philosophy and spirituality? What role did they think wilderness would play in the evolution of North American culture?

Where did my wilderness visionaries toe the line, and what were they willing to die for?

Answers to these questions will help me realize why I have stalked these men for twenty-two years only to end up here on this ridge on the perimeter of northeastern Minnesota's Boundary Waters Canoe Area Wilderness. My tracking has led to this precipice, and I see quite clearly now at midday that the last track is on the edge.

There is nothing left to do but jump. Nothing remains but to leap into the same fires of investigation that lured them, and now us, like moths winging toward light.

I suppose what light there is behind this book began for me in 1967 at Mt. St. Benedict High School in Crookston, Minnesota. The English class I was in was reading aloud passages from Thoreau's *Walden*. When we came to the passage about keeping pace with companions and following a different drummer if one is heard, I was swept with a tide of emotion. I put my head down on my arms on top of my desk. Tears came as I reread the passage, something in my spirit recognizing the words of a man who had given life thought and faced it with a backbone. Sentimental? Yes. But I was at an impressionable age, filled with romance and nonconformity, and I was stung by words like never before. Soon I was studying more Thoreau, natural history, wilderness literature and taking contemplative walks along northwestern Minnesota's Red Lake River.

The tracking of wilderness visionaries—the search—had begun.

Today it is clear from the record that North Americans en masse have undergone a radical transformation in their attitudes toward nature. From the pioneer fear and hatred of nature and wilderness in the sixteenth century there has evolved an appreciation of things natural. From antipathy: empathy. This change in vision has been slow but inexorable.

And perhaps just in the nick of time.

I have chosen to write about the following wilderness visionaries because their greatness is beyond question. Henry David Thoreau, and John Muir, together with Robert Service, Bob Marshall, Calvin Rutstrum, Aldo Leopold, Olaus Johan Murie, and Sigurd F. Olson left big tracks. Each affected the evolution of conservation and wilderness preservation in North America. Their spirit, moreover, remains with us to this day. Muir is mythical among members of the Sierra Club, lovers of California's mountains, and those of us who cherish glad tidings of alpenglow and summit vistas. Poet Robert Service, whose "Call of the Wild" has enticed thousands into the backcountry, is still quoted in pubs and schools. Sigurd F. Olson is identified with northeastern Minnesota's Boundary Waters Canoe Area Wilderness, Superior National Forest, and Quetico Provincial Park in northwestern Ontario. Calvin Rutstrum became one of this century's leading spokesmen on camping and wilderness travel en route to becoming a full-fledged wilderness philosopher.

As for Bob Marshall, I agree with T.H. Watkins, editor of *Wilderness* magazine, when he said one could comfortably argue that Marshall "was personally responsible for the preservation of more wilderness than any individual in history."

In each of my visionaries was a desire to touch—and be touched by—nature and wildness. In each was a hunger to soak up the beauty flooding this third stone from the sun. Each, moreover, helped make people care about wild country beyond mere economic considerations; by doing so, they ensured there would be parks and wilderness areas, wildlife refuges, and wild rivers where people like ourselves can roam without trespassing.

For this we owe them no small debt.

I also believe these visionaries were exceptional outdoorsmen. They learned what they did by placing one foot in front of the other, or by paddling a canoe across lakes whipped with whitecaps or down rock-choked rivers. This too is no small consideration. Wilderness is the primary teacher about wilderness. Consider Thoreau's challenge to confront a natural fact, how he (like Muir later) felt he had to sit down beside it, *camp* beside it if necessary, to *know* it. Reading and talking about wilderness, parks, refuges, and wild rivers leads to an understanding of those things, at least as they relate to human culture, but that understanding must constantly rub up against the real thing.

Vision, let it be said, requires blisters, fatigue, sunburns, grit in our food, thirst, holes in clothes, and broken paddles. Vision demands we kneel on ice, slide down scree, mush across tundra, or sit with our backs against a tree.

Vision demands listening. Demands looking. We must, at times, ache in our search for light.

Wilderness Visionaries, hence, focuses as much as possible on the outdoor experiences of its subjects and how those experiences led to ideas, literature, and movements influencing the evolution of North American vision about wilderness. This book is not a complete history of wilderness preservation. That has been broached elsewhere; I need only cite Roderick Nash's *Wilderness and the American Mind,* Michael Frome's *Battle for the Wilderness* and Stephen Fox's *John Muir and His Legacy : The American Conservation Movement.* Nor is this book a complete roundup of wilderness thinkers of national stature. I chose instead to steer my course from the wilderness movement's most seminal thinkers toward my northern Minnesota home and men I knew. The book's cadence thus jumps from Thoreau and Muir to Rutstrum and Olson, each visionary a note sung at a different pitch yet adding to the harmony of the whole.

Wilderness Visionaries is personal in other ways.

While doing research, I retraced some of the hikes and canoe trips mentioned herein. In 1977 I visited Thoreau's hometown of Concord, Massachusetts, his college town of nearby Cambridge, and his cabin site on Walden Pond before following his footsteps to the summit of New Hampshire's Mt. Washington. I also studied some of Thoreau's original manuscripts at Harvard University's Houghton Library. I met John Muir's spirit on the slopes of Washington's Mt. Ranier in the winter of 1975-76, and again along British Columbia's Inside Passage in 1978. Later that year, while returning from Alaska, I crossed paths with poet Robert Service at his cabin in Dawson City, Yukon Territory.

In 1979, two years after I first met Sigurd and Elizabeth Olson, I coincidentally moved to Burntside Lake on which the Olsons had built their own cabin at Listening Point decades before. I lived on the North Arm of Burntside Lake five years, during which time I canoed some of the same canoe routes in Quetico Provincial Park and the Boundary Waters Canoe Area as Sigurd had. An example is the 250-mile long Pigeon River voyageur route between Lake Superior and International Falls/Fort Frances; Sig canoed the route in 1954 while Ray Niedzielski and I followed in his footsteps in 1984 to celebrate the 75th anniversary of the Quetico-Superior.

Finally, in spring of 1981, I traveled to Marine-on-St. Croix, Minnesota, where I interviewed Calvin Rutstrum a year before his death. Rutstrum had explored by foot and paddle much of northwestern Ontario and northeastern Minnesota in the 1940s. When Ray Niedzielski, Roger Weaver, and I canoed the 170-mile long Big Fork River in May, 1984, following part of the same canoe route Rutstrum had taken on his first canoe trip, we felt Rutstrum's presence. His historical tracks were on, and along, the river.

In tracking the literal and literary footsteps of Rutstrum et al., I approached the precipice where I now sit. All tracks have led to this slice of time.

Other scholars, of course, have written broader biographies of Thoreau and Muir than I have, and I mean to point them out. This is, in part, a guidebook. While condensing lives about which volumes have been written, I lean heavily on my sources, let my subjects speak for themselves, and hope interested readers will continue their search through terrain I have doggedly trod and will likely walk again. Consequently, I have included a rather elaborate section on bibliographical information and source notes. Each note, I hope, functions like a track, a scent on a leaf, or a howl on a distant moonlit ridge, leading the reader forward to progressively deeper views of material presented here.

Besides being a guidebook, *Wilderness Visionaries* includes—as far as I know—the most concise presentation of biographical information about Robert Service and Bob Marshall. The chapter on Sig Olson is the first of its kind, and the chapter on Calvin Rutstrum contains comprehensive biographical material. Inevitably, however, who can say where and when a book begins? Who is its true author? All books rife with history are orchestrated productions, and in bringing this overture to a close I would like to introduce and thank my major musicians:

Dr. Walter Harding of State University College, Geneseo, New York, secretary of the Thoreau Society, author of more than 18 books about Thoreau, and thus Henry David's living authority. Harding patiently answered my letters, supplied me with a photo of Thoreau, and by breaking ground with his exhaustive research, writing and editing made it infinitely easier for me to steer clear of absolute folly. Bruce Wolfe of Piedmont, California, generously allowed me to reproduce his portrait of Muir that originally appeared on a cover of *Sierra* magazine. George Marshall, past president of both the Sierra Club and Wilderness Society, and who now lives in London, England, provided me with working bibliographies about his brother, Bob, in the 1970s; since then he has corrected minor oversights in the manuscript and kept me apprised of new, biographical developments.

With help from Charles Kelly, I was granted access to the Quetico-Superior Papers, specifically the Marshall and Olson folders, at the Minnesota Historical Society Archives. There, too, with kind guidance from reference librarian Dallas Lindgren, and with permission from Mrs. Sigurd F. Olson, I dipped into the Sigurd F. Olson Papers. Mrs. Olson subsequently reviewed my chapter about Sigurd for accuracy and tone.

PREFACE

Bill Langen of Ely, Minnesota, provided background information about Sigurd as a teacher. Much to my pleasure, Barbara Peet of St. Paul granted me permission to reprint a photo of her oil portrait of Sigurd Olson that hangs in the lobby of the Sigurd F. Olson Environmental Institute in Ashland, Wisconsin.

I would also like to thank Lee Schreiber, editor of *Backpacking Journal* and *Camping Journal* in the mid-1970s, for encouraging me to research the lives of great naturalists for his pages. Those profiles—together with several others I wrote for John Viehman and his staff at *Canoe* magazine—eventually formed the living background of *Wilderness Visionaries*. Editor Jim Keough of *Sierra* kindly read portions of this book as its concept germinated. Dr. Bill Forgey and editor Thomas Todd of ICS Books, Inc., together with Roy Becker formerly of ICS Books, did me a great service by believing in this project at the outset and publishing the first edition in 1986. Publisher Tom Klein of NorthWord Press, Minocqua, Wisconsin, carried the ball with this edition. The staffs of Vermilion Community College Library in Ely, and also at the Homer Public Library, Homer, Alaska, helped me find books and related research material from throughout the country.

Finally, I would like to thank Chris Trost for her belief and encouragement as *Wilderness Visionaries* originally congealed (the first edition was dedicated to her). Ginny Hostetter, former senior editor of *Canoe* magazine and an editor with Rodale Publications, helped hone what's in hand by reading most of the manuscript and making editorial suggestions. Bernard Schermetzler, archivist at the University of Wisconsin-Madison Archives, helped find a good photograph of Aldo Leopold. Dr. Giulia Tortora and Wenzi showed me some of Bob Marshall's Adirondack Mountains in October, 1993; Giulia also shared walks and table space as the Leopold and Murie chapters came to fruition. As ever, Dirk Hanson of Ely, author of *The New Alchemists* and *The Incursion*, was at the right place at the right time with a friend's insight and advice.

—Jim dale Vickery
Spring 1994

1

HENRY DAVID THOREAU: ILLUMINATIONS OF A WALKER

"I make it my business to extract from Nature whatever nutriment she can furnish me, though at the risk of endless iteration. I milk the sky and the earth."

—Henry David Thoreau, Nov. 2, 1853

Henry David Thoreau, 29, having changed his name from David Henry Thoreau in an early act of independence, put one foot in front of the other as he—pack on back—left his companions behind on the slopes of Maine's highest peak, Mt. Katahdin, in 1846. He was en route, characteristically alone, to a fog-shrouded summit of realization.

"Perhaps," he noted later about what he experienced on Katahdin, "I most fully realized that this was primeval, untamed, and forever untameable Nature, or whatever else men call it..."

Like *wilderness.*

Thoreau's climb by today's alpine standards was a routine hike in infamous Katahdin weather. Yet at stake and of far more importance than the mere success of his mountain ascent were the ideological insights his climb would bring. Insights about wild country and civilization. Insights about how both wilderness and human culture serve not only to define each other but sustain each other. Little thought had been given to such things. And so it came as a stunning, at least radical, pronouncement when Thoreau, five years after his Katahdin climb, stepped up to a Concord, Massachusetts, podium to say "In wildness is the preservation of the world."

It was a statement indicative of Thoreau's peculiar pilgrimage, and one which eighty-four years later was chosen as the motto of the Wilderness Society. The Society, under the guidance of such men as Bob Marshall and Sigurd F. Olson, accepted the full implications of Thoreau's words. They charged themselves with watchdogging North American wilderness for the sake of both science and the human spirit. It was a responsibility eventually shared in part by the Audubon Society, the National Parks Association, the National Wildlife Federation, the Sierra Club and a variety of offshoot organizations dedicated to specific causes within the overall conservation and wilderness preservation movement. By philosophizing about nature and wilderness, and by spiritualizing his experience of it, Thoreau sowed a volatile seed in the fertile field of 19th- and 20th-century thought. This seed gave rise to a crop of both amateur and professional naturalists who helped shape North America's destiny.

It is because of this irrefutable fact that any discussion of wilderness visionaries together with wild country's inspiriting values must begin with Henry.

Thoreau "led the intellectual revolution that was beginning to invest wilderness with attractive rather than repulsive qualities," Roderick Nash concluded in *Wilderness and the American Mind*. Thoreau, "came to grips with issues which others had only faintly discerned. At the same time he cut the channels in which a large portion of thought about wilderness subsequently flowed."

William O. Douglas, past Justice of the U.S. Supreme Court and prominent wilderness preservationist, traveler, and author of *A Wilderness Bill of Rights*, said as much: "Thoreau lived when men were appraising trees in terms of board feet, not in terms of watershed protection and birds and music. His protests against the narrow outlook were among the first heard on this continent."

Thoreau has been praised by almost every naturalist of note: John Muir, John Burroughs, Theodore Roosevelt, Aldo Leopold, Joseph Wood Krutch, Edward Abbey... the list is endless, so seminal was Thoreau's influence. Writer Leo Tolstoy and social reformer Mahatma Gandhi admired Thoreau's exploration of nonconformity to unjust governments. Thomas Merton, highly acclaimed Trappist monk and contemplative of Gethsemane Abbey, and author of many books on Christian mysticism, followed Thoreau's Walden Pond example by spending time in a forest hermitage. Slice it any way we want, Thoreau's influence has been pervasive and incalculable—a shining glimmer in the warp and woof of American history.

Still, Thoreau remains part myth, part man. On the one hand he is seen as a recluse on a wilderness pond, sailing into intellectual and Oriental bliss on sunny days as flowers and birds filled consciousness with color and melody. On the other hand, Thoreau is viewed as a frustrated quasi-stoic, serious in temperament, a psychological product of sexual complexes and sibling rivalry, or as an intellectual falcon taloned to the historical minutiae of his own relatively short life.

However complex—no matter how warped or right on the mark—our ideas of Thoreau will probably forever remain both stiff and elastic, documented or fantastic, as much the product of research as the creation of our own hearts.

I

In leaping the long trail back to Thoreau we find him born on July 12, 1817, in his maternal grandmother's unpainted farmhouse on Virginia Road among orchards and peat meadows in Concord, Massachusetts. He was the third of John and Cynthia Thoreau's four children. Helen, the oldest, was born five months after her parents married. John Jr., the apple of the community's eye, was born in 1815. After Henry came Sophia—a mediocre artist and businesswoman who edited Henry's writings after his death. The parents, themselves lived a mobile life of debatable compatibility. John, born in Boston in 1787, enjoyed reading classical books, playing the flute and sitting next to the woodstoves of his several stores where he chatted with friends. In time each store failed as an economic venture, due to John's willingness to extend credit.

Mother Cynthia, a full head taller than her husband, was also more assertive than him. She was born May 28, 1787, in New Hampshire, and became (according to biographer Richard Lebeaux) intimidating, liberated for her day, a constant talker, sometimes invective and status-seeking, yet always protecting her family, reforming compassionately and becoming friends with many. She was a member of the Female Charitable Society (which son Henry called the "chattables"), the Bible Society and a founder of the Concord Women's Anti-Slavery Society. Although socially busy, Cynthia took good care of her kids, encouraged their talents and altogether helped them lead childhoods like most others in early 19th-century America.

Son Henry sometimes believed himself the exception. As late as 1851 he thought none of his current experiences compared to those of his boyhood:

My life was ecstasy. In youth, before I lost any of my senses, I can remember that I was alive, and inhabited my body with inexpressible satisfaction; both its weariness and its refreshment were sweet to me. This earth was the most glorious musical instrument, and I was audience to its strains... I can remember how I was astonished. I said to myself—I said to others —'There comes into my mind such an indescribable, infinite, all-absorbing, divine, heavenly pleasure, a sense of elevation and expansion, and I have nought to do with it. I perceive that I am dealt with by superior powers. This is a pleasure, a joy, an existence which I have not procured myself. I speak as a witness on the stand, and tell what I have perceived.' The morning and the evening were sweet to me, and I led a life aloof from society of men. I wonder if a mortal had ever known what I knew. I looked in books for some recognition of a kindred experience, but, strange to say, I found none. Indeed, I was slow to discover that other men had had this experience... The maker of me was improving me. When I detected this interference I was profoundly moved... I was daily intoxicated, and yet no man could call me intemperate. With all your science can you tell how it is, and whence it is, that light comes into the soul?

Henry's boyhood intoxication was spent in rural Concord, Chelmsford, Boston, then Concord again—a series of uprootings mapping out father John's business adventures. March 1824 found the family back in Concord permanently; here Henry had sporadic fainting spells, was kicked by a cow, fell down stairs, smoked dried pond-lily stems, harvested a patch of potatoes in the family garden and chopped off a toe with an ax. He learned the alphabet in Miss Phoebe Wheeler's infant school. Grammar school classmates called him "stupid" because he preferred watching schoolyard games from the sidelines. Later his serious disposition garnered him the nickname "Judge." Intelligent and curious without being precocious, Henry was asked one night by his mother why he couldn't get to sleep; he answered that he was looking through the stars to see if God was behind them.

In 1828, at age 11, Henry with John Jr. enrolled in Phineas Allen's Concord Academy where they studied Virgil, Caesar, Homer, Voltaire and Cicero in the original languages. They also studied history, geography, grammar, astronomy, math, natural history and natural philosophy. Thoreau's essay, *The Seasons*, hinted at the direction his evolving interests took.

Cynthia sensed Henry's bookish and outdoor interests. And, because she wanted one of her children to attend college, she decided Henry should go to Harvard. His education would be funded by increasing profits from the family's new pencil manufacturing business and by donations from Helen and John who taught school. Yet Henry barely passed Harvard's entrance exams. Harvard (in Cambridge across the Charles River from Boston) had an 1833 enrollment of 250 students taught by 35 faculty. The curriculum was best suited for theology. Academic emphasis was on Latin grammar, Greek, history, math, English and philosophy. Thoreau, with his taste for words, took two terms of Spanish, four of French (he was of French ancestry), four of German and five of Italian. His grades were consistently above average except during a long illness his junior year.

Thoreau's response to Harvard was ambivalent. It expanded his intellectual horizons by introducing him to distinguished teachers and current philosophical thought, not to mention the quickening of mind intelligent peers provoke. But it was in Harvard's library that Henry attained his true higher education. He read as many books for personal reasons as for assignments, using the library's 50,000 volumes to fill about 20 notebooks with five to six thousand pages of notes and quotes which he referred to throughout the 1840s for essays and lectures. According to Walter Harding in *The Days of Henry Thoreau*, Henry read most of Chalmers's 21-volume anthology, *The English Poets*, which included work of Goldsmith, Southey, Shakespeare, Chaucer, Milton, Homer, Cowper and Johnson.

Thoreau also read the travel books of Barrow, Back, Hall, McKenney and Brackenridge. The "Judge" was a natural student.

Yet something in Henry ran against the grain. Although he was laying the intellectual and social foundations that later colored his wilderness trips, his participation in bull sessions and general Harvard reverie was at most half-hearted and often nonexistent. Nature called. Henry was becoming fascinated by wildlife, plants and some of nature's intangible values. One winter he visited a weasel's nest in an apple tree every day. Often he hiked alone in the fields and woods around Cambridge and Boston when the spirit moved him: listening, looking, smelling and touching, perhaps watching with a new-found awakening as the then-wild waters of the Charles River slipped by with shards of sunlight toward the wide open sea.

Inevitably, Thoreau at Harvard was quiet—a thinker rather than a player; a walker, rarely a dancer. What he had been thinking about, what he had mulled while being dubbed by some a social bore, became almost dramatically evident on his college graduation day. Here Thoreau manifested a sixth sense of timing that would punctuate the rest of his life. He was asked to speak to an assembly at a ceremonial conference on "The Commercial Spirit of Modern Times, Considered in Its Influence on the Political, Moral, Literary Character of a Nation." Despite the conference's obtuse title, Thoreau came out swinging.

"Let men," he dared say, "true to their natures, cultivate the moral affections, lead manly and independent lives; let them make riches the means and not the end of existence, and we shall hear no more of the commercial spirit. The sea will not stagnate, the earth will be as green as ever, and the air as pure. This curious world which we inhabit is more wonderful than convenient; more beautiful than it is useful; it is more to be admired and enjoyed than used. The order of things should be somewhat reversed; the seventh should be man's day of toil, wherein to earn his living by the sweat of his brow; and the other six his Sabbath of the affections and the soul."

And what did he propose *doing* on these six Sabbaths? Nothing other than what *he* had been doing. Or at least learning to do: "to range this widespread garden, and drink in the soft influences and sublime revelations of nature."

———

Not even fine words helped Thoreau grope for a career from 1837 to 1844, his insecure post-college years. He needed money. He needed a post-Harvard vocation. And he was, of course, given his chance to adapt to the folks back home.

He was given a teaching position at Concord's Center School. Yet two weeks after he started teaching, he was reprimanded for not whipping a few students. Insulted and angry, Thoreau grabbed a couple students, whipped them, then turned in his resignation. He had realized quickly that people back home in Concord had ways of doing things contrary to words in Harvard's library. Anomie set in.

But anomie's severest edges didn't last long, although Thoreau would never flow smoothly in community ways. He helped his father at the pencil factory and improved it by inventing a method of mixing finely ground baked

Bavarian clay into the lead. Plans to travel west with John Jr. collapsed. Then suddenly, in mid-June 1838, hope loomed on Henry's employment horizon. He started his own school in a room of the family home on Concord's Main Street. Two months later he rented Concord's academy building for $5 a quarter. Once John Jr. joined Henry as the academy's preceptor, both taught an enrollment of 25 for two years.

Henry taught Greek, French, physics, natural history, Latin and natural philosophy. Everyone was taken on field trips once a week. Young man Thoreau had a job, social standing and personal direction. It wouldn't last long.

Thoreau's love of the outdoors, pursued during the perennial Sabbaths of his soul, took on new seriousness in 1839 when he and his brother embarked on a river trip that changed Henry's life. The trip was the first of many immersions into wildness and all it evokes. On Saturday, August 31, Henry and John launched the *Musketaquid*, a 15 x 3 ½-foot boat they built the previous spring. Shaped like a fisherman's dory, the boat was painted green below with a border of blue symbolizing "the two elements in which it was to spend its existence." It had wheels in order to be rolled around waterfalls, two sets of oars, several slender poles for shoving in shallow places and two masts.

The brothers rowed down the Concord River to the Merrimack River which they ascended to Nashua, Bedford and Hooksett in New Hampshire. Soon, on foot, they explored the Stone Flume, the Basin, Franconia Notch and Profile Lake in the White Mountains. Finally, after a few days of preparatory mountain climbing, they scaled Mt. Washington, at 6,288 feet the highest peak east of the Mississippi River and north of the Carolinas, and noted for some of the world's worst weather.

The meaning of *Musketaquid*'s voyage fermented with time. In January 1842, as winter snow collected in drifts around the paths and homes of Concord, John nicked his finger while shaving and died suddenly of lockjaw.

Death's lifeless eyesockets stared Henry in the face as mortality spoke to him. He grieved for John. He became sympathetically ill, struggling with some of lockjaw's symptoms. But he surfaced. He decided to expand his Concord and Merrimack River trip notes into a memorial for John and their journey. How to live while reserving enough time to write *A Week on the Concord and Merrimack Rivers* became the focus of Henry's attention.

Walden Pond was the answer.

———— ■ ————

On March 5, 1845, Ellery Channing—Henry's most frequent hiking companion—wrote him, suggesting he build a hut on Ralph Waldo Emerson's property along Walden. "I see nothing for you on this earth," Channing wrote, "but that field I once christened 'Briars'; go out upon that, build yourself a hut, and there begin the grand process of devouring yourself alive. I see no alternative, no other hope for you. Eat yourself up; you will eat nobody else, nor anything else."

Within three months Henry had chopped down pines for a frame, bought used materials from a neighbor's shanty, enlisted help in raising a roof and was "seated" in a $28.13 "wooden inkstand" 10 feet wide by 15 feet long, about a mile and a half south of Concord. The only house he had owned before, if he excepted a boat, was a tent.

Thoreau thought of his Walden cabin as a "crystallization" around him reacting on the builder. It was not so much indoors he saw himself, as "behind a door." He became neighbors to birds "not having imprisoned one, but having caged myself near them."

His cage had a caned bed, table, desk, three chairs, a looking glass three inches in diameter, a pair of tongs and andirons, a kettle, skillet, frying pan, dipper, two knives and forks, a wash bowl, one cup, three plates, one spoon, a jug of oil, a jug of molasses and a japanned lamp. His bathtub and refrigerator were the pond. A nearby spring provided drinking water. Visitors slept on the floor.

"For the first week," he recalled, "whenever I looked out on the pond it impressed me like a tarn high up on the side of a mountain, its bottom far above the surface of other lakes, and, as the sun rose, I saw it throwing off its nightly clothing of mist, and here and there, by degrees, its soft ripples or its smooth reflecting surface was revealed, while the mists, like ghosts, were stealthily withdrawing in every direction into the woods, as at the breaking up of some nocturnal conventicle. The very dew seemed to hang upon the trees later into the day than usual, as on the sides of mountains."

In believing "a broad margin of leisure is as beautiful in a man's life as in a book," he used his free time, Walden's wealth, to work on *A Week* and his journal. He appointed himself Concord's inspector of snowstorms and rainstorms. He rambled daily to identify flowers and birds, to study insects and trees, to make meticulous measurements of snowbanks and pond depths, to collect mosses, bark, beetles and arrowheads. Sometimes he joined Walden's "nocturnal conventicle" by playing the flute in his rowboat adrift in midnight moonlight. He was *inhaling* nature. Perhaps he recalled how he had inhabited his body with such satisfaction as a boy, and how now, senses still open, he could feel something both within and beyond him, something so overwhelming and immutable that only day-to-day absorption of it, *in* it, did it justice.

Regardless, while Thoreau hunkered down along Walden Pond at age 28 he was convinced watching the seasons change was sufficient employment.

The watching and listening was what mattered. The whittling away of energy-sapping distractions. Slowly, one misty dawn after another, the season-watching might, and did, give way to a much more ambitious and still today little-understood objective: to rendezvous with simplicity as bedrock for a quickening of mind and spirit.

"I went to the woods," Thoreau confessed in *Walden*, his second book, "because I wished to live deliberately, to front only the essential facts of life, and see if I could not learn what it had to teach; and not, when I came to die, discover that I had not lived. I did not wish to live what was not life, living is so dear; nor did I wish to practice resignation, unless it was quite necessary. I wanted to live deep and suck out all the marrow of life, to live so sturdily and Spartan-like as to put to rout all that was not life, to cut a broad swath and shave close, to drive life into a corner, and reduce it to its lowest terms."

"Let us settle ourselves," he added six paragraphs later, "and work and wedge our feet downward through the mud and slush of opinion, and prejudice, and tradition, and delusion, and appearance, that alluvian which covers the globe, through Paris and London, through New York and Boston and Concord, through Church and State, through poetry and philosophy and religion, till we come to a hard bottom and rocks in place, which we can call *reality*, and say, This is, and no mistake; and then begin, having a *point d'appui*, below freshet and frost and fire..."

Thoreau's *point d'appui*, his bedrock of belief and action, became at least in part the *present moment*: immediate sensual awareness, and the intuition it feeds. "In any weather, at any hour of the day or night," he wrote, "I have been anxious to improve the nick of time, and notch it on my stick too; to stand on the meeting of two eternities, the past and future, which is precisely the present moment; to toe that line." Here or, rather, *now* his anchor wedged. But before he could fully explore the ramifications of his bedrock, to separate fool's alloy from gold, he had to come to grips with Transcendentalism. He had to burrow downward through the subterrane of his own mind. Through philosophy, rhetoric and speculation.

Enter Emerson.

———

Ralph Waldo Emerson, the same man on whose land Henry squatted next to Walden Pond, moved to Concord in October 1834, when Thoreau was 17. Emerson was riding a wave of interest in Transcendentalism he had generated among New England's most influential minds. He was, in short, already famous and provocative. One of the first things he did in Concord was write his first book; entitled *Nature,* it stuck in Thoreau's mind like a burr.

Thoreau, in turn, clung to Emerson. At least initially. Biographers Harding and Lebeaux believe Emerson was a surrogate father for Henry, whose own father was not intellectual. As Emerson's fame spread, he encouraged Henry's philosophical and writing talents, in part by opening his personal library to him. Emerson also introduced Thoreau to such prominent minds of the time as H.G.O. Blake, Thomas Cholmondeley, Bronson Alcott, Theodore Parker, Rev. George Ripley, Rev. Orestes Brownson, Margaret Fuller and others. They often gathered at Emerson's house for discussions of Hume, Kant, Locke, the tenets of Transcendentalism and Oriental metaphysics. One biographer, Henry Seidel Canby, claims none of Emerson's intellectual peers could so much as eat an apple without thinking of the relation of diet to morals.

Nature as the cornerstone of Transcendentalism underscored what historian Roderick Nash called its core: "The belief that a correspondence or parallelism existed between the higher realm of spiritual truth and the lower one of material objects. For this reason natural objects assumed importance because, if rightly seen, they reflected universal spiritual truths." Ditto for language, which Emerson believed subserved nature. Nature is the vehicle for thought, he wrote, "in a single, double, and three-fold degree:

"1. Words are signs of natural facts.

"2. Particular natural facts are symbols of particular spiritual facts.

"3. Nature is the symbol of spirit."

Parts of speech, he also thought, "are metaphors, because the whole of nature is a metaphor of the human mind."

The noblest ministry of nature for Emerson was "to stand as the apparition of God," for it is the organ "through which the universal spirit speaks to the individual, and strives to lead the individual back to it." The Supreme Being, he wrote, "does not build up nature around us, but puts it through us, as the life of the tree puts forth new branches and leaves through the pores of the old. As a plant upon the earth, so a man rests upon the bosom of God ...". Idealism, in turn, "sees the world in God. It beholds the whole circle of persons and things, of actions and events, of country and religion, not as painfully accumulated, atom after atom, in an aged creeping Past, but as one vast picture which God paints on the instant eternity for the contemplation of the soul."

Prayer, in Emerson's ministerial cosmology, was "a sally of the soul into the unfound infinite." Wisdom was the ability to see "the miraculous in the common." The woods, meanwhile, offered perpetual youth ("the suggestion of an occult relation between man and the vegetable") and was conducive to a powerful mind because it steeped one in that nature which fed allegories, vested thoughts and made man an alembic for art.

Young Man Thoreau—versed in theology at Harvard—was listening.

Transcendentalists, Nash noted, "had a definite conception of man's place in a universe divided between object and essence. His physical existence rooted him to the material portion, like all natural objects, but his soul gave him the potential to *transcend* this condition. Using intuition or imagination (as distinct from rational understanding), man might penetrate to spiritual truths." Because this was especially true in nature, where man's creations didn't sully the world as emblematic of a superior reality, nature and wilderness took on new significance among East Coast intellectuals.

Americans generally had been antipathetic toward nature and wilderness prior to Thoreau's time. Their experiences in the 1600s and 1700s were not those of Concord's comforts (nor those of Emerson and Thoreau, for that matter). Nature posed threats to life and limb. Homes were carved from virgin forests or made of sod—not bought. Homesteads and frontier communities were peopled on the prairie by men and women whose most dreaded danger was Indians. "For whether the settlers had come from the Mohawk Valley," John Madson has written, "or the Dark and Bloody Ground—or from almost anywhere between—there were likely to be victims of Indians somewhere in their own families or among their neighbors. And even if there weren't, they had taken in stories of the red terror with their mothers' milk and had brought the old stories and old fears into the new land."

Too, storms destroyed crops. And there was always the other red terror: fire.

It was easy to feel intimidated by and fearful of nature when one had to fight for a foothold in it. Or had to grub and kill to be self-sufficient, whether on the prairie or in the North Woods. Calluses, not scenic photographs, were symptomatic of wilderness contact.

Hand-in-hand with the pioneer aversion to nature was the Puritan belief that civilization transmitted *the* sacred lifestyle. Like fundamental Christians today, Puritans believed God's kingdom was expanded by taming the wild, the chaotic, the uninhabited wastelands. Theirs was a spirit of conquest, of control, fired with religious zeal and self-righteousness. Didn't the book of Genesis say "be fruitful and multiply, and fill the earth and subdue it"? Christian crosses became symbols of vanishing wilderness: bulldozers of the spirit.

Puritans, Frederick Turner has alleged, saw human existence as a "terrific drama in which God and the devil were joined in struggle toward a divinely appointed resolution. That the resolution was divinely appointed, foredoomed, and foreknown did not lessen one jot the tension of the drama, for uncounted millions had leagued themselves with the Cosmic loser and millions more would yet do so. And at every moment the Devil and his misbegotten minions threatened the sanity and sanctity of the few who fought for God. Here in the New World wilderness, amidst wolves, bleak woods, swamps, and cruel Indians, the drama was more fearsome than it had ever been in those lands from which the Puritans had chosen exile. Here the drama was so stripped to essentials that all could readily sense its presence in the very midst of the workaday round."

Deism, meanwhile, gnawed at pre-Thoreau America's original contempt for wilderness. Deism viewed God as a First Cause—a primordial mover of events manifested in the material world. Deists considered wilderness pure manifestation of God's creative energies, thus, as early as the 1700s, challenging common assumptions that nature was nothing but inert matter.

Finally, Romanticism preceded Transcendentalism in eroding pioneer attitudes toward nature, feeding the tide on which Thoreau's vision would crest. The romantic, with her savory of grand scenery, mystery and solitude sensed in nature spiritual allurements, an undertow that was deliciously inexplicable. Eric Newton in *The Romantic Rebellion* claims the result in the 1600s and 1700s was a radical shift in human self-identity. Instead of viewing themselves at the center of the universe, as Genesis literally interpreted implied, Romantics saw themselves as finite parts of a greater whole. Hope and despair, pain and pleasure, joy and sorrow, life and death existed in kaleidoscopic equilibrium.

Here was immutable wonder and balance.

Here was harmony that could best be glimpsed in nature's grandeur.

Whether in mountains, primeval forest or standing next to the eternal pulse of ocean waves breaking on beaches, 18th century Romantics knew they were not lords of creation. They sat on no thrones.

It wasn't Romanticism, however, nor Deism, or even little-known Primitivism (which claimed earlier cultures were superior to current ones), but Transcendentalism that best systematically painted nature as a prism through which men and women could see reality. In nature's sunsets and moonrises, its flowers and birdsongs, and in its dramas and cycles were intimations of truth and beauty. From beauty came the awe, inspiration and intuitive flashes that elevated common consciousness to spiritual insight. The experience of nature, hence, was believed to expand consciousness, just what Thoreau—who used Transcendentalism as a springboard into deeper inquiry—was looking for.

II

In order for Thoreau to best work "downward through the mud and slush of opinion, and prejudice, and tradition," he found it necessary—at least during his Walden days—for solitude to be his "most companionable companion."

"Like the Hindu," Arthur Christy wrote in *The Orient in American Transcendentalism*, "he [Thoreau] courted solitude for the purpose of spiritual discipline." It was meditation and contemplation, not merely to live cheaply or dearly, that drew Henry to his Walden hermitage. Hadn't Thoreau admitted going to Walden Pond in order "to transact some private business with the fewest obstacles"?

Thoreau confessed in *Walden* to being extremely introspective, addicted to a kind of inward exploration which later colored his walks and wilderness canoe trips:

> Sometimes, in a summer morning, having taken my accustomed bath, I sat in my sunny doorway from sunrise till noon, rapt in revery, amidst the pines and hickories and sumacs, in undisturbed solitude and stillness, while the birds sang around or flitted noiseless through the house, until by the sun falling in my west window, or the noise of some traveler's wagon on the distant highway, I was reminded of the lapse of time. I grew in those seasons like corn in the night, and they were far better than the work of the hands would have been. They were not time subtracted from my life, but so much over and above the usual allowance. I realized what the Orientals mean by contemplation and the forsaking of works.

Thoreau had become familiar with Oriental philosophy, and the interior voyaging it encourages, four years prior to moving to Walden Pond. He had read the *Vedas* (which, he said, contained a "sensible account of God"), the *Mahabharata*, and the *Ramayana*, which included descriptions and rationales of ascetics who had renounced sensual and material enticements to pursue peace and God-consciousness in remote settings. He eventually read the *Laws of Manu* and once admitted to bathing his morning intellect in the "stupendous and cosmogonal philosophy" of the *Bhagavad Gita*. The influence of such books lingered around him "like a fragrance, or as the fog hangs over the earth late into the day."

There is good reason, hence, for some biographers to think Thoreau's ultimate purpose in going to Walden Pond was to give his genius, or spiritual intuition, more freedom to pursue its search for greater intimacy with God and a greater spiritualization of himself. At the time this was best done in solitude. It is important, however, to keep in mind that Thoreau's hunger for solitude grew as much out of his own experience as it did from exposure to Oriental or Occidental systems of spiritual awakening.

Thoreau, in fact, dedicated an entire chapter in *Walden* to solitude. He found it wholesome to be alone most of the time. "To be in company," he said, "even with the best, is soon wearisome and dissipating. I love to be alone."

His nearest neighbor at the pond was a mile away. No house was visible from any place but the hilltops within a half-mile of his own. Regardless, he wanted to know "What sort of space is that which separates a man from his fellows and makes him solitary?" He had found no exertion of legs could bring two minds much nearer to one another.

Thoreau was frank in not desiring nearness. He found society commonly too cheap, meeting "at very short intervals, not having had time to acquire any new value from each other. We eat at meals three times a day, and give each other a new taste of that old musty cheese that we are. We have had to agree on a certain set of rules, called etiquette and politeness, to make this frequent meeting tolerable and that we need not come to open war. We meet at the post-office, and at the sociable, and about the fireside every night; we live thick and are in each other's way, and stumble over one another, and I think that we thus lose some respect for one another."

Was Thoreau ever lonely?

He said in *Walden* he never felt lonesome, nor the least oppressed by a sense of solitude, except once a few weeks after he moved to Walden Pond. For an hour he wondered if neighbors weren't necessary for a healthy life. At the same time, however, he detected a slight insanity in his mood and he began to foresee his recovery. Suddenly, in the midst of a gentle rain, he became sensible of "such sweet and beneficent society in Nature, in the very pattering of the drops, and in every sound and sight around my house, an infinite and unaccounted friendliness all at once like an atmosphere sustaining me, as made the fancied advantages of human neighborhood insignificant, and I have never thought of them since."

He felt every pine needle expand and swell with sympathy, befriending him.

"I was so distinctly made aware of the presence of something kindred to me," he concluded, "even in scenes which we are accustomed to call wild and dreary, and also that the nearest of blood to me and humanest was not a person or a villager, that I thought no place could ever be strange to me again."

Here, perhaps, is part of the crux of Thoreau's Walden vocation. He wanted most to dwell near the perennial source of his life. Next to that source he wanted to "dig his cellar." He admitted he was no more lonely than loons in a pond, dandelions in a pasture, sorrels, brooks, stars or spring thaws.

Yet Thoreau, who has superficially and popularly been thought a recluse, was the first to admit he wasn't a hermit. In his *Walden* chapter, "Visitors," he said he loved society as much as most, and was "ready enough to fasten myself like a bloodsucker for the time to any full-blooded man that comes in my way." He walked to Concord every day or two, and at Walden had more visitors than at any other time in his life. Whatever else Thoreau was trying to do living in woods along a pond, biographer Harding has observed, Thoreau, "was not trying to relive the experience of Robinson Crusoe. When, in Maine, he came across a real hermit, he wondered how the man could endure such separation from humanity."

At Walden, Thoreau once had 25 to 30 souls "with their bodies" beneath his roof. "Yet we often parted without being aware that we had come very near to one another." Drunks dropped in, as did passing farmers, children picking berries, railroad men taking Sunday morning walks in clean shirts, hunters, fishermen, poets, philosophers, all of whom he considered honest pilgrims who left the village behind to seek freedom. These he welcomed, especially those who thought for themselves and who could express an opinion.

An opinion, Henry felt, especially if it was a *good* opinion, was worth walking 10 miles any day to hear.

What Thoreau hated were self-styled reformers. "Men-harriers," he called them. Fortunately Walden's distance from Concord winnowed most of them out. The way Henry looked at it, at Walden he had withdrawn so far within the great ocean of solitude "into which the rivers of society empty, that for the most part, so far as my needs were concerned, only the finest sediment was deposited around me."

Times would change.

III

Although Thoreau confessed in *Walden* to having three chairs—"one for solitude, two for friendship, and three for society"—he abandoned all three, along with work on *A Week*, midway through his pond experience to measure himself against northern Maine's wild Mt. Katahdin.

The mountain, if nothing else, offered Henry a chance to take a hike. He had become addicted to walking, and by 1846 had already elevated it to what John Burroughs aptly described as "religious exercise." Thoreau found walking "sanitive" and "poetic." Nothing so inspired him, he admitted in his journal, "and excites such serene and profitable thought. The objects are elevating. In the street and in society I am almost invariably cheap and dissipated, my life is unspeakably mean... But alone in distant woods or fields, in unpretending sprout-lands or pastures tracked by rabbits, even in a bleak and, to most, cheerless day... when a villager would be thinking of his inn, I come to myself, I once more feel myself grandly related, and that cold and solitude are friends of mine."

He supposed that this value, in his case, was equivalent to what others get by prayer. Or by going to church.

His walking clothes were functional: usually green, brown or Vermont gray for natural camouflage. Henry thought such colors made him look the color of a pasture with patches of withered sweet fern and lechea, and that they helped him get closer to animals. His clothes were tailored to carry a notebook, spyglass, foot rule and surveyor's tape, all gear he used to take measurements and take notes while he was in the field. Later he would expand his penciled notes into full-fledged journal pages. He wore a neckerchief instead of a collar, and he gathered the lining of his hat in midway to make a kind of shelf for flowers and plants, a place where they were kept moist by rising head vapors.

Winter walking required its own special gear, notably boots of three different kinds to be used depending on weather. He wore light boots and India rubbers during thaws and general springlike weather. He wore cowhide boots—kept supple with tallow—for dry snow and bare ground. And he wore rubber boots for slush.

Channing, Thoreau's hiking companion, described Thoreau's hiking gear at length as only a close acquaintance could:

> Before he set out on foot journey, he collected every information as to the routes and the place to which he was going, through the maps and guidebooks... Once he made for himself a knapsack, with partitions for his books and papers,—India rubber cloth, strong and large and spaced (the common knapsacks being unspaced). The partitions were made of stout book-paper. His route being known, he made a list of all he should carry—the sewing materials never forgotten..., the pounds of bread, the sugar, salt, and tea carefully decided on. After trying the merit of cocoa, coffee, water, and the like, tea was put down as the felicity of a walking 'travail,'—tea plenty strong, with enough sugar, made in a tin pint cup; thus it may be said the walker will be refreshed and grow intimate with tea leaves. With him the botany must go too, and the book for pressing flowers (an old 'Primo Flauto' of his father's).

Channing was aware of how anyone who has ever carried a pack up a mountain knows how every fresh ounce tells; yet Thoreau would run up the steepest places as swift as if on flat land, and he was never short of breath. Channing claimed Thoreau advised others to carry with them a heavy plum cake, certainly for its caloric count, possibly for its sugar.

Thoreau felt it was vain to sit down to write if he hadn't stood up to live. He thought the moment his legs began to move, his thoughts began to flow, "as if I had given vent to the streams at the lower end and consequently new foundations flowed into it at the upper." A thousand rills, he said, which had their rise in the sources of thought would burst forth when walking and fertilize his brain.

Another Thoreau acquaintance, Franklin B. Sanborn, once said of Henry that it was his custom to spend a part of each day outside, and he rarely failed. "During many years," Sanborn said of Thoreau, "he used the afternoon for walking, and usually set forth about half-past two, returning at half-past five." Sanborn thought Thoreau didn't walk for medical reasons, exercise, or amusement, but for work. Thoreau wasn't sure why he walked; his reasons, at least, were varied and inconsistent. One moment he is confiding that he cannot preserve his health or spirits unless he spends four hours a day—and often more than that—sauntering through woods, absolutely free from worldly engagements, and later he is saying his walking has nothing to do with exercise. At least, as he put it, not like sick people who take medicine at stated hours. None of that for Henry David. For Thoreau you must walk like a camel "which is said to be the only beast which ruminates while walking." He wanted thoughts to be food for walkers, like wild apples; thoughts that wouldn't be palatable in the house.

In a sense, the secret of Thoreau's sauntering was to have no particular home but to be at home everywhere. He insisted no wealth could buy the necessary leisure, freedom and independence that were the capital of walking. And few people, he swore, knew how to walk well. Few understood its art.

In a late-life essay, *Walking*, Thoreau described how the word "sauntering" is derived from idle people who roved the country during the Middle Ages, asking for charity under the pretense of going a *la Sainte Terre*: to the Holy Land. Children began to point their fingers and yell, "There goes a Sainte-Terrer—a Saunterer, a Holy-Lander." Thoreau admitted walkers who never go to the Holy Land as they pretend are indeed idlers and vagabonds. "But they who do go there are saunterers in the good sense, such as I mean... For every walk is a sort of crusade, preached by some Peter the Hermit in us, to go forth and reconquer this Holy Land from the hands of the Infidels."

His walks in his chosen holy lands were immersions in nature—meandering strolls from one aesthetic focus of fascination to another. The touch of wind on a brown oak leaf salted with frost crystals. The patterns, like veins in a leaf, made by water on the sloping sides of railroad beds. Walden Pond's living bottom seen through inch-thick ice. Or the symmetry of wave prints splayed on Cape Cod seashores. Little escaped his attention, even as he sometimes walked naked upriver with only a hat to shade his head. If meandering didn't suit his purposes, he simply walked in a straight line—what Burroughs called an "air-line."

"In his trips about the country to visit distant parts," Burroughs said in *The Last Harvest*, "he usually took the roads and paths or means of conveyance that other persons took, but now and then he lay down the ruler on his map, draw [sic] a straight line to the point he proposed to visit, and follow that, going through the meadows and gardens and dooryards of the owners of the property in his line of march."

There was a folk story, Burroughs said, that Thoreau and Channing once went through a house where the front and back doors were open.

———————

Thoreau's route to and up Katahdin was far from straight. No "airlines" here. No rangers, either. No guidebooks. Nothing to make the hiking easy for the eager man from Concord.

After traveling by boat and rail to Bangor, Maine, in late August 1846, Thoreau accompanied his cousin, George Thatcher, to Old Town, Lincoln and Mattawamkeag. He found the Mattawamkeag River, although wide, a mere "river's bed," so full of rock and shallows he could almost cross it dry-shod in boots. They took the Houlton road seven miles to Molunkus along which there was only one house, then returned to Mattawamkeag where, because they had no pocket map, they traced Greenleaf's Map of Maine which hung on a wall. The map turned out to be riddled with errors.

The next morning, Thoreau's party—with 15 pounds of hard bread, 10 pounds of pork, a cotton tent, several blankets, and tea—headed up the West Branch of the Penobscot River on foot, crossed Salmon River, by-passed the Penobscot's East Branch, then skirted the West Branch's south shore past a rapids called Rock-Ebeeme. They spent the night with "Uncle George" McCauslin before hiking past Shad Pond to Tom Fowler's. There Henry drank a beer which reminded him of cedar. "A lumberer's drink," he called it, "which would acclimate and naturalize a man at once—which would make him see green, and, if he slept, dream that he heard the wind sough among the pines."

Fowler and McCauslin joined Thoreau, Thatcher, and two loggers for the ascent up the Penobscot in an old, leaky bateau. Once beyond Grand Falls, Thoreau found Quakish Lake handsome and wild; shut in on all sides by forest, the only trace of man was a low logging boom in a distant cove stashed for spring use. Dry lichens hung from spruce and cedar boughs. Scattered ducks flew back and forth. A lone loon laughed and frolicked, sticking out a straight leg for the paddlers, making them laugh. Jo-Mary Mountain came in sight, then a partial view of Katahdin with its summit veiled in clouds. "Like a dark isthmus in that quarter," Thoreau noted of Katahdin's mass, "connecting the heavens with the earth."

Later, while boating to the head of North Twin Lake in the moonlight, Thoreau had the impression he was on a high tableland between the U.S. and Canada, which indeed he was: the northern side was drained by the St. John and Chaudierre rivers, the southern side by the Penobscot and Kennebec rivers. He found no bold mountainous shore, as he half-expected to, but isolated hills and mountains rising irregularly from the plateau. The tableland was, he said, an archipelago of lakes, "the lake country of New England."

One lake was navigated after another until Thoreau and friends reached Aboljacknagesic Stream near the Sowadnehunk deadwater a dozen miles from Katahdin's summit. The next morning at 6 a.m. they steered directly for the base of the highest peak. An afternoon of bushwhacking was rewarded with an awesome view of Katahdin, whose rock rose abruptly from the forest to form a blue barrier like a wall that, Henry thought, looked like it had once bounded the earth in its direction.

They set their compass for a northeast course—the bearing of the southern peak—and plunged back into the woods.

Thoreau found Murch Brook beautiful, but it couldn't contain him that evening. Restless, he left his companions while they set up camp to climb alone above timberline. The climb up a streambed was steep, and soon he reached *krumholz*: compact, stunted black spruce from two-to-twelve feet deep. He walked on the krumholz where he could, then stooped, scrambled, slid and scrambled up some more until he reached an open mountain side at sunset.

Henry—his interest whet—returned to camp.

Everyone headed for Katahdin's summit the next morning. When Thoreau's apparently less enthusiastic companions fell behind, however, he lurched on alone—wrapped in clouds and mist—hopefully to become the fifth or sixth person to put the peak beneath them. He climbed over large, loosely poised rocks for over a mile, edging, he later said, closer and closer to a solid cloudbank which concealed the summit with mist. The entire mountain seemed to be nothing but rocks, as if the skies had *rained* rocks, each rock laying where it had come to rest with many leaning against each other. *Rockingstones*, he called them. Although surrounding skies were sometimes clear, he eventually reached the summit's clouds and walked into them. He wove through this gray cloud for a quarter mile until he reached the summit of the ridge he was on. The ridge was five miles long: a thousand-acre tableland. He could see nothing. Occasionally the wind tore apart surrounding cloud cover as sunlight flooded him, then gray fog and mist returned.

"Sometimes," he recalled, "it seemed as if the summit would be cleared in a few moments and smile in sunshine: but what was gained on one side was lost on another."

The ridge and its cloudy summit were like a chimney while he stood nearby waiting for the smoke to blow away. He began to feel cold, fragile and mortal in an uncanny way. Fear stirred.

"It was vast," he said of Katahdin, "Titanic, and such as man never inhabits. Some part of the beholder, even some vital part, seems to escape through the loose grating of his ribs as he ascends. He is more lone than you can imagine ... His reason is dispersed and shadowy, more thin and subtile like the air ... Nature has got him at a disadvantage, caught him alone, and pilfers him of some of his divine faculty. She does not smile on him as in the plains. She seems to say sternly, why came ye here before your time? This ground is not prepared for you. Is it not enough that I smile in the valleys? I have never made this soil for thy feet, this air for thy breathing, these rocks for they neighbors. I cannot pity nor fondle thee here, but forever relentlessly drive thee hence to where I am kind. Why seek me where I have not called thee, and then complain because you find me but a stepmother? Shouldst thou freeze or starve, or shudder thy life away, here is no shrine, nor altar, nor any access to my ear."

Thoreau had brought his pack and gear to the top of Katahdin for he didn't know if he would be forced back to the river below or toward the settled portion of the state by some other route; for safety he wanted a complete camping outfit with him. The summit, meanwhile evaded him. Its last thousand feet lay beyond his reach. He feared his companions might want to descend to the river and their bateau before dark, and that clouds might shroud the summit for days. Thoreau headed down. Sparrows flitted in front of him like bits of gray rock buffeted by wind. Inside of him, meanwhile, brewed what biographer Sherman Paul describes as the most frenzied passage Thoreau ever wrote:

"What is this Titan that has possession of me?" he asked himself, still stung by how Katahdin made him feel. "Talk of mysteries! Think of our life in nature—daily to be shown matter, to come in contact with it—rocks, trees, wind on our cheeks! the solid earth! the actual world! the *common sense! Contact! Contact! Who* are we? *Where* are we?"

———

Thoreau never forgot Katahdin. It was both literally and figuratively a peak in the evolution of his young vision. If Emerson was right, that particular natural facts are symbols of particular spiritual facts, and that nature is the symbol of spirit, then Thoreau had to begin interpreting Katahdin's—and all of nature's—sometimes frightening actuality. Henry had sensed nature for the first time not as bees buzzing in his Walden cabin's sunny doorway, but on its most indifferent terms: how it could kill him slowly, hypothermically, very untranscendentally.

Gone were words, what he described as the "dinging" in his ears of "man's fair theories and plausible solutions of the universe."

Gone, too, was intellectuality with which Thoreau sometimes became disgusted, and which had caused him to complain that "ever there is no help, and I return again to my shoreless, islandless, ocean, and fathom unceasingly for a bottom that will hold an anchor, that it may not drag."

Now—after Katahdin—he found that which would anchor his cosmology and wean him from Emerson: bare fact, the solid earth: *contact.*

But what about truth? Had Thoreau's legs brought him any nearer to the reality he claimed to hunger for? What sermon had he heard on Maine's highest mountain?

Biographical opinions differ. Garber claims when Thoreau was on Katahdin nature refused to be anything "but its own strange self," and that Henry's habitual leaning toward the figurative was shown to be an irrelevance. William J. Wolf in *Thoreau: Mystic, Prophet, Ecologist* feels Katahdin purified Thoreau of youthful romanticism; religiously, the mountain confirmed Thoreau's suspicion that God was to be found in the human community, wrestling with historic responsibilities, as well as in nature. Inevitably,

Thoreau's climb seems to be reducible to an equation involving man and nature. If the Concord bookworm previously fantasized escaping civilization by heading into virgin wilderness, he now sought balance. A balance of exposure. A blend of civilization and wildness. Here then is Katahdin's bottom line: Thoreau returned to the comparative pastoral ambience of Walden Pond a changed man.

Henry still hungered for nature, solitude, and wilderness, and even commented at the end of his Katahdin essay how remarkable it was that wilderness lay so close to a coastal republic known around the world. Bangor, Maine, where his trip began, was—with its population of 12,000—a "star on the edge of night." Yet a hundred miles away the country was virtually unmapped, unexplored, and there, he said, waved the virgin forests of the New World. He would return to that forest by foot and canoe, but for the moment a rite of initiation was behind him.

Ahead of him, no, *around* him, was a silken web he and his circumstances had woven. Henry called it a personal chrysalis; nymph-like, he hoped to burst forth a more perfect creature.

IV

Although Thoreau left Walden Pond almost one year after climbing Katahdin and exactly two years, two months and two days after moving into his cabin, his vision quest was still quickening by September 6, 1847. He had steeped himself in the philosophies of western civilization and the Orient, and he had spent enough time alone for psychological integration and individuation. Thoreau had even begun to outgrow Emerson whom he ceased to idolize.

As for leaving Walden, Thoreau claimed he had several more lives to live and could not spend more time along the pond. The writer in him, meanwhile, confessed he heard the world squeak to a standstill and its axle needed greasing. The Judge was 30 years old.

Thoreau's Walden experiment had been successful. He finished writing *A Week on the Concord and Merrimack Rivers* in his broad margins of leisure and began circulating it among possible publishers. His journal, which he had begun in 1837 when Emerson asked him *if* he kept a journal, was pregnant with material that would become his most famous book, *Walden*. Living pondside also solidified Henry's fascination with the natural world and forever fixed his walking habits. His expeditions had already become tours that came round again at evening to the old hearth-side from which they set out. "Half the walk," he was convinced, "is but retracing our steps." This was, at least, true for him; each hike seemed to begin and end at his desk. Each walk was an orbit around Concord and, more centrally, his garret, for Thoreau's ultimate goal was a mix of inspiration, description, and publication.

Yet literary success evaded him.

Thoreau's first published item was an obituary of Miss Anna Jones in the November 25, 1837 issue of *Yeoman's Gazette*. His first published essay,

"Aulus Persius Flaccus," and his first poem, "Sympathy," were printed in 1840 in *The Dial*, a Transcendentalist publication associated with Emerson. *The Dial*, during its four-year life ending in 1844, printed much of Thoreau's work: 31 poems, essays and translations. With publication came exposure, encouragement to continue writing and the needed practice to tackle *A Week*. The latter, biographer Wolf has aptly summed, became "an exploration by river into the stream of thought... a highly poetic, tentative grappling with the religious dimension of human existence."

Thoreau fancied otherwise. He thought one peculiarity of *A Week* was its "hypaethral" character in reference to Egyptian temples open to the sky. The book, he said, had little of the atmosphere of the house about it, as if it had been written outside (as in fact most of it was). He hoped it didn't smell of the study or library, or even the poet's attic, but of fields and woods. He wanted it "unroofed," open to the weather, not easily kept on the shelf.

This was wishful thinking. If *A Week* was open to all weather it was also open to severe criticism and, in Henry's lifetime, failure.

Basically the book is the work of a sprouting intellectual outpouring his musings on philosophy and theology, interspersed with asides on Greek mythology, poetry ("mysticism of mankind") and friendship, all wrapped around Henry and John's two-week trip condensed into one. In a sense it is all Harvard momentum, a Thoreau volcano, sheer verbal exuberance, as well as a scorching indictment of Christianity in an embrace of Orientalism. It is young man Thoreau's mind, circa mid-1840s, a montage of mental explorations that he would tighten and caulk, hone and hoe, refine and transcend for the rest of his life.

Throughout *A Week*, whose sentences are—as he liked—concentrated, nutty, expensive and hard as a diamond to swallow, are unconstrained ideals. A book for example, "should contain pure discoveries, glimpses of *terra firma*, though by shipwrecked mariners and not the art of navigation by those who have never been out of sight of land." It should, moreover, be the natural harvest of an author's life. Not something offering a cowering enjoyment, but something whose thoughts are of unusual daring: something that an idle man could not read, a timid man couldn't be entertained by, and that might even make its reader dangerous to existing institutions.

The book is broken into chapters named after each day of the week. Each chapter, in turn, focuses on subjects ranging from fish species, the route's geography and history, Chaucer, a climb of Massachusetts' Saddleback Mountain, government, religion, and spirituality. *A Week*, as biographer Harding has observed, is more typically Transcendental than Thoreau's later work: it explores intuition, for instance, and conscience, not to mention religion. And it was Henry's comments about religion that most alienated his contemporaries by kicking them where it hurt.

"In my Pantheon," Henry teased, "Pan still reigns in his pristine glory, with his ruddy face, his flowing beard, and his shaggy body, his pipe and his crook, his nymph Echo, and his chosen daughter Iambe; for the great God Pan is not dead, as was rumored. Perhaps of all the gods of New England and of ancient Greece, I am most constant at his shrine."

"It is necessary not to be Christian, to appreciate the beauty and significance of the life of Christ. I know that some will have hard thoughts of me, when they hear their Christ named beside my Buddha, yet I am sure that I am willing they should love their Christ more than my Buddha, for the love is the main thing."

"The wisest man preaches no doctrine; he has no scheme; he sees no rafter, not even a cobweb, against the heavens."

"The perfect God in his revelations of himself has never got to the length of one such proposition as you, his prophets, state... Can you put mysteries into words? Do you presume to fable the ineffable? Pray, what geographer are you that speak of heaven's topography? Whose friend are you that speak of God's personality?... Tell me of the height of the mountains of the moon, or of the diameter of space, and I may believe you, but of the secret mystery of the Almighty, and I shall pronounce thee mad."

Finally, and most scathingly, Henry reacted to a minister's scolding when he was seen walking to a mountaintop on the Sabbath, the minister warning him in a "sepulchral tone" of disaster:

> He really thought that a god was at work to trip up those men who followed any secular work on this day, and did not see that it was the evil conscience of the worker that did it. The country is full of this superstition, so that when one enters a village, the church, not only really but from association, is the ugliest looking building in it, because it is the one in which human nature stoops the lowest and is most disgraced.

These confessions won Thoreau few friends. He was sincere. He was honest. And he was relating his own glimpses of what he judged *terra firma*. But he was not discreet, and adding insult to heresy certainly undermined any chance *A Week* had of good sales. The book crashed.

A Week was virtually completed before Thoreau left Walden Pond. It was published in 1849 after being repeatedly rejected by publishers, despite Emerson's generous influence. Henry revised the book after each rejection. Nevertheless, he finally ended up paying $290 to James Munroe and Company of Boston to print an edition of 1,000 copies. *A Week* became, in Harding's words, "one of the most complete failures in literary history." Two out of three reviews were unfavorable. Four years after the book was published, Munroe and Company—in need of its cellar space—sent 706 copies of *A Week* to Henry who gallantly accepted them with graceful aplomb.

"The wares are sent to me at last," he remarked in his journal on Friday, October 28, 1853, "and I have an opportunity to examine my purchase. They are something more substantial than fame, as my back knows, which has borne them up two flights of stairs to a place similar to that to which they trace their origin ... I have now a library of nearly nine hundred volumes, over seven hundred of which I wrote myself ... This is authorship; these are the work of my brain."

Failure, Thoreau wrote to himself moments later, was actually even more inspiring and better for him than if he had sold the thousand copies that had been printed. It affected his privacy less. It left him freer.

Henry knew how to kid himself.

He also knew that despite his difficulties with *A Week*, his fixation on nature—his life's love and subsequent "bride"—remained constant. When concluding *A Week* he had written that men nowhere lived a natural life "round which the vine clings, and which the elm willingly shadows." Man would desecrate nature by his touch, he said, and so the world's beauty remains veiled to him. This would not, could not do. People must not only become spiritualized, but naturalized as well. Here or nowhere, he was convinced, is our heaven: "May we not *see* God? Are we to be put off and amused in this life, as it were with a mere allegory? Is not Nature, rightly read, that of which she is commonly taken to be the symbol merely?" Heady questions these, for a man of 32, a man migrating away from Transcendentalism's symbolism toward pure amazement at what is perceived.

Water, for example, dripping from a deer's mouth among wet riverside bushes following a thundershower. A slate-gray junco hopping up to the heads of grass stems, riding them down, then hopping off to peck seeds on granite.

Walking in and out of the end of a rainbow, as Henry claims to have done, like a porpoise in a sea of color.

The rustle of crisp November oak leaves in gusts of wet wind, sounding like wheels passing on rain-spattered pavement.

Thoreau became fascinated by things in themselves, not merely by what they meant or hinted at. "Let us not underrate the value of a fact," he had written, "it will one day flower into a truth." Now he began to think the flower was inseparable from the truth; the fact *was* the truth.

In early February 1849, Thoreau received a letter from the Boston publishing firm of Ticknor and Fields, saying they were inclined to publish *Walden, or Life in the Woods* (later shortened to *Walden*) at their expense. Ticknor and Fields were at the time publishers of Lowell, Whittier, Longfellow and Hawthorne among others. William Ticknor didn't care for *Walden*, but Fields thought Thoreau brought "a rural fragrance—spicy odors of black birch, hickory buds, and penny-royal—with him from his native fields into the streets and lanes of Boston." Two thousand copies were printed five years later, and out of this first edition all but 256 copies sold the first year.

Walden, unlike the loosely knit *A Week*'s stream of thought, was a tight account of the two years spent along the pond. The book was largely mined from Thoreau's journals. He structured *Walden* around the circle of seasons in a single year: home-building in spring, gardening in summer, pond life in winter, then around again to spring when nature reawakens at thaw. "Economy" describes how Thoreau built his cabin. "Where I Lived and What I Lived For" explains the reasoning behind his pondside experiment. Other chapters discuss solitude, reading, animals and higher laws, the latter a crystallization of his evolving philosophy. Part of that philosophy was

Henry's conviction that it's necessary to free oneself from the trappings of menial labor—one's "quiet life of desperation"—to flush from life its deepest significance. He had, in a sense, explored simplicity and had discerned how to avoid energy-sucking distractions to search within himself, and outside himself in the natural world, for the essence of one's being.

Walden, which is one man's two-year search for reality, fuses wit with wisdom while natural description parallels philosophical insight. Thoreau is at his literary best as words and sentences ignite paragraphs like struck kitchen matches.

Reactions to *Walden* varied, yet most were positive. Daniel Ricketson wrote Thoreau right away, saying the book had "the stamp of a genuine and earnest love for the true philosophy of life... To many, and most, it will appear to be the wild musings of an eccentric and strange mind, though all must recognize your affectionate regard for the gentle denizens of the woods and pond as well as the great love you have shown for what are familiarly called the beauties of Nature." To Ricketson, Thoreau's mind appeared self-possessed and highly cultivated "with a strong vein of common sense." The whole book seemed like a prose poem, yet one as simple as a running brook.

Thoreau's second book netted him $100 in royalties in the next three years but was out of print by 1859 and wasn't reprinted until several weeks before his death. Since then *Walden* has been reprinted over 160 times in almost every language. Sinclair Lewis spoke for many when he called the book one of the four unquestionable classics of American literature.

But what *really* is the book about?

Here historians differ. Here interpretations vary from one biographer and reader to another. Joel Porte, for example, thought the book was a description of Thoreau's dream "to a large extent realized, of perfected self-indulgence and self-possession." Scholar Edward Wagenknecht, meanwhile, refuses to believe *Walden* is a biography or even in a narrower sense a truthful or accurate record of Thoreau's experiences at the pond. "It is instead a fable," he says, "a work of art in which the raw material derived from those experiences has been recreated into art forms which are real but not actual because as they come to us, they existed only in the artist's imagination."

Imagine the truth as we like, the book's success—even in Thoreau's lifetime—indicated his growing influence among East Coast intellectuals. Some *Walden* readers no doubt simply found Thoreau's paean to nature odd. Others must have been intrigued by the book's author: a Harvard graduate claiming he could find no happiness without spending part of each day walking in woods. Taut for the Transcendental flush. Cocked for an infused burst of intuition. Hungry for illuminations.

And young America in general? What did *it* think?

The verdict was not yet in as it mulled over *Walden* and waited for more.

V

In 1853, one year before *Walden* saw the light of day and six years after he left the pond, Thoreau made a second trip to Maine wilderness, reaching Chesuncook by canoe.

Thoreau traveled from Boston to Bangor by steamer on September 13, joined his cousin, George Thatcher, and an Indian guide, Joe Aitteon, then journeyed on to Moosehead Lake via Monson and Greenville. Thoreau fondled a map of the Public Lands of Maine and Massachusetts as they steamed up rough Moosehead, later remarking he saw only three or four houses the whole length of the lake and that the shore was unbroken wilderness of spruce, fir, birch and rock maple. At the north end of the lake, the trio portaged to the Penobscot River where they found a log camp and a large iron pot that lay permanently on the bank for pitching canoes.

"Both Indians and whites use a mixture of rosin and grease for this purpose," Henry later wrote in his chapter, "Chesuncook," in *The Maine Woods*. "Joe took a small brand from the fire, and blowed the heat and flame against the pitch on his birch, and so melted and spread it. Sometimes he put his mouth over the place and sucked, to see if it admitted air, and at one place, where we stopped, he placed his canoe high on crossed stakes, and poured water into it."

The 19½ -foot long, 2½-foot wide, 14-inch deep birchbark canoe, painted green, proved Penobscot-worthy, carrying 575 pounds.

After checking out Lobster Stream coming in from the right (southeast), they returned to the Penobscot which widened to 25 rods and gained speed. Night found them camped at the upper end of an island at the head of Moosehorn Deadwater. Before going to sleep, however, they paddled downstream in the starlight to check out sounds Joe thought were moose. They found instead several "explorers," actually timber cruisers, men who penetrated the Maine-Quebec borderland interior looking for virgin pine to log. Henry envied their freedom and lifestyle, yet forgot them quickly as he paddled a half-mile up a side stream then through light fog while returning to camp.

A large campfire was built at ten, a fire that Thoreau thought burned as much wood as would last a poor family an entire winter with economy and an air-tight stove. He nevertheless relished sleeping next to the fire.

"It was very agreeable," he explained in "Chesuncook," "as well as independent, this lying in the open air, and the fire kept our uncovered extremities warm enough. The Jesuit missionaries used to say, that in their journeys with the Indians in Canada, they lay on a bed which has never been shaken up since the creation, unless by earthquakes. It is surprising with what impunity and comfort one who has always lain in a warm bed in a close apartment, and studiously avoided drafts of air, can lie down on the ground without a shelter, roll himself in a blanket, and sleep before a fire in a frosty autumn night, just after a long rain-storm, and even come soon to enjoy and value the fresh air."

Frost whitened the leaves the next morning, Saturday, September 17, as Joe paddled the party farther down the comparatively smooth Penobscot between Moosehead and Chesuncook. At the mouth of Ragmuff Stream they fished trout. Six miles later they caught their first glimpse of Katahdin and turned up a small stream three or four rods wide coming in on the right from the south. Here on Pine Stream they searched for moose sign, for Joe and George were out to kill moose. Although Thoreau wanted to see a moose close at hand, and to see how an Indian would kill one, he wasn't hunting. He even felt compunctions about being with hunters. He envisioned himself "reporter or chaplain to the hunters—and the chaplain has been known to carry a gun himself." But no, not this time. This time his hands were going to stay clean.

He soon heard a cow and calf in alders, however, directed Joe's attention to them, and ended up measuring the 8-foot, 20-inch length of the dead cow. More exploration followed, together with a dreamy ride to camp in the moonlight. But the moose was back alive in Thoreau's conscience where it charged him through subliminal brush. The moose killing had destroyed the pleasure of his canoe trip. Nor did it help that his companions' ethics irked him. Hunting a moose, he thought, merely for the satisfaction of killing one, not even for the sake of its hide and without making any unusual exertion or running any risk, was too much like "going out by night to some woodside pasture and shooting your neighbor's horses."

Guilt ran rampant as he complained about kinds of wilderness use:

"This afternoon's experience suggested to me how base or coarse are the motives which commonly carry into the wilderness. The explorers and lumberers generally, are all hirelings, paid so much a day for their labor, and as such, they have no more love for wild nature, than wood-sawyers have for forests. Others, white men and Indians, who came here are for the most part hunters, whose object is to slay as many moose and other wild animals as possible. But, pray, could not one spend some weeks or years in the solitude of this vast wilderness with other employments than these—employments perfectly sweet and innocent and ennobling? For one that comes with a pencil to sketch or sing, a thousand come with an axe or rifle... Our life should be lived as tenderly and daintily as one would pluck a flower."

While sitting alone on a fir twig seat by the campfire, Thoreau thought nature looked sternly upon him because of the "murder of the moose." Remorse led to conviction: Every creature is better alive than dead, he thought, whether men, moose, or pines, and anyone who understands this will rather preserve life than destroy it.

It was the poet who made truest use of the pine, he concluded. It was the *living* spirit of the tree, not its spirit of turpentine, that he sympathized with. It healed his cuts.

Henry's conscience continued to bleed as he, Thatcher and Aitteon returned down Pine Stream with a token chunk of moose meat en route to Chesuncook Lake. They entered Chesuncook at its northwest corner, visited a homestead, then paddled back up the Penobscot and out.

Thoreau still simmered in Concord years later. He couldn't forget after two trips in Maine how lumbermen and hunters were apparently ravaging wilderness—what remained of the wild in northern New England. "We shall be reduced to gnaw the very crust of the earth for nutriment," he reflected while writing his essay on the Chesuncook trip. Certainly from time to time a poet must—for strength and beauty—travel the logger's path and Indian's trail "to drink at some new and more bracing fountain of the Muses, far in the recesses of the wilderness." Thoreau was saying there was a nonconsumptive use of wilderness, of nature, that had hardly—if ever—been recognized before. Wilderness had an intangible value, one appealing to one's sense of beauty, to one's soul, which fed the poet. This sentiment, this mood, was not wholly original for here Thoreau echoed emerging genteel tastes in the intellectual East Coast. But what was original was his conclusion: there was a need to preserve, to set aside and not use, parcels of wilderness, places where people could go to drink in natural beauty and flow spiritually where they needed to flow.

"The kings of England," he wrote, "formerly had their forests to hold the king's game, for sport or food, sometimes destroying villages to create or extend them; and I think that they were impelled by a true instinct. Why should not we, who have renounced the king's authority, have our national preserves, where no village need be destroyed, in which the bear and panther, and some even of the hunter race, may still exist, and not be 'civilized off the face of the earth,'—not for idle sport or food, but for inspiration and our own true recreation? or shall we, like villains, grub them all up, poaching on our own national domain?"

VI

Although Thoreau's evaluation of wilderness, first broached in "Chesuncook," was an important part of his mature years, it was in his essay titled "Walking" that he concentrated his strongest remarks about the preservation of wilderness, remarks that were apparently the first of their kind on any shore. "Let me live where I will," he cheered, "on this side is the city, on that the wilderness, and ever I am leaving the city more and more, and withdrawing into the wilderness." In "Walking" he warned what he had to say was extreme and emphatic. Regardless, the result is what John Burroughs later called Thoreau's religion, his "most mature, his most complete and comprehensive statement."

"Walking" was originally a lecture called "The Wild," delivered at the Concord Lyceum on April 23, 1851, culled for the most part from recent journal entries. "I wish to speak a word for nature," he had said at the podium, "for absolute freedom and wildness, as contrasted with a freedom and culture merely civil—to regard man as an inhabitant, or a part and parcel of nature, rather than a member of society." What followed was delivered in lecture form frequently both in 1851 and 1852, and as late as 1857. By 1857, however, he had split his lecture into two parts, the first a gospel on walking, the second on man's need to return periodically to nature and wilderness for nourishment and vigor. Both parts were submitted to the *Atlantic Monthly* by Thoreau on March 11, 1862, where they were published posthumously.

As a walker Thoreau remained a pilgrim, having met but one or two persons in his life who understood the art of walking, who had a genius for sauntering. A true walker, Thoreau said in his essay, requires a direct dispensation from heaven. As for himself, he couldn't at age 34 stay in his chamber for a single day without acquiring some rust. He stressed the importance of being awake to one's senses, and that in his own walks at least he tried to shake off his morning occupations and obligations to society. It wasn't always easy to rid himself of the village, however, for the thought of some work would run in his head and he would not be where his body was. He would be out of his senses. What he wanted to do during his walks was *return* to his senses.

"What business have I in the woods," he asked himself, "if I am thinking of something out of the woods?"

Then abruptly, as if he realized the connection between his sauntering and insight (the latter dependent on the former), he extolled wildness. From it come "the tonics and barks which brace mankind." The best in literature is rooted in the wild, he said, and civilization needs wilderness to keep its strength and proper perspective. He cited the story of Romulus and Remus being suckled by a wolf as not being a meaningless fable but as an allegory of how the founders of any state that rises to eminence are nourished and invigorated by similar wild sources. When an empire loses contact with its wild roots, it falls victim to conquerors who haven't.

Henry wanted friends who were wild men, not tame ones. Hope and the future were not in lawns and cultivated fields, not in towns and cities, but in swamps. These he entered as a sacred place, a *sanctum sanctorum*.

Thoreau: On Man's Relation to Nature

"*To insure health, a man's relation to Nature must come very near to a personal one; he must be conscious of a friendliness in her; when human friends fail or die, she must stand in the gap to him. I cannot conceive of any life which deserves the name, unless there is a certain tender reaction to Nature. This it is which makes winter warm, and supplies society in the desert and wilderness. Unless Nature sympathizes with and speaks to us, as it were, the most fertile and blooming regions are barren and dreary.*"

—*Journal* Jan. 23, 1858

To preserve wild animals, Thoreau realized, generally implies the creation of a forest for them to dwell in. So it is with man. He did not want every man, or every part of a man, cultivated, no more so anyhow than he wanted every acre of earth cultivated; part should be tilled, but the greatest part should be meadow and forest. It was the wildness in man, his naturalness and instinctive oneness with ecosystems, that Thoreau feared was disappearing. Nature informs men when her wild animals are becoming extinct, he said, but not when the wild *man* in her does. He bemoaned how early in life people are weaned from nature, "this vast, savage, howling mother of ours... lying all around, with such beauty, and such affection for her children." Instead, there is only society and culture, an exclusive interaction of man on man, a web of social incest heading for a speedy end.

"Walking," however, ended characteristically with a hop toward hope. All good things, Thoreau concluded, are wild and free, and in wildness is the preservation of the world. There will come a time, moreover, when a "great awakening light, as warm and serene and golden as on a bankside in autumn," will illumine "our minds and hearts."

VII

Thoreau shifted again from the concept of wilderness to wilderness itself in 1857, when he journeyed to Maine's wilderness a final time. He needed the trip. Slavery had become a burning national concern, one that Thoreau had spoken out against at abolitionist meetings. He had met Captain John Brown of Harper's Ferry fame earlier in 1857 and would become not only his friend but public defender. Meanwhile, Thoreau's pacifism was faltering. In his lecture and essay, "A Plea for Captain John Brown," he confessed he didn't want to kill or be killed but he could foresee circumstances when both these things would be unavoidable by him. The Civil War was only four years away.

It was probably with mixed relief and excitement then that Thoreau joined a botanist friend, Edward Hoar, and a Penobscot Indian guide, Joe Polis, for his deepest plunge into lake and river backcountry. At times the distance between houses was 60 miles. Their canoe—made by Polis—was a little over 18 feet long by 2½ feet wide in the middle and weighed about 80 pounds.

"Our baggage," Thoreau recalled in his essay, "The Allagash and East Branch" that became part of *Maine Woods*, weighed about 166 pounds, so that the canoe carried about 600 pounds in all, or the weight of four men. The principal part of the baggage was, as usual, placed in the middle of the broadest part, while we stowed ourselves in the chinks and crannies that were left before and behind it, where there were no room to extend our legs, the loose articles being tucked into the ends. The canoe was thus as closely packed as a market-basket, and might possibly have been upset without spilling any of its contents."

Joe sat on a cross-bar in the stern while Thoreau and Hoar sat flat on the canoe's bottom. Hoar and Thoreau, meanwhile, took turns paddling with Joe.

The trio began their 11-day journey on Moosehead Lake by canoeing across a broad bay opposite the mouth of Moose River to Mt. Kineo, which they climbed. A two-mile portage called the Northeast Carry at the northeast end of Moosehead Lake led to the West Branch of the Penobscot River. Soon they entered Chesuncook Lake, angled northeast into the

Caucomgomoc and Umbazookskus rivers, and made a miserable five-mile portage through swamps to Chamberlain Lake. There they fell asleep on a pebbly shore to the cries of loons.

The next morning they canoed diagonally across Chamberlain to the outlet north, about four miles. Their ostensible purpose? To cruise. To expand geographic consciousness. To get a view of the lakes at the source of the Allagash then return to the Penobscot's east branch via Chamberlain, Telos Lake, Webster Pond and Webster Stream en route to Bangor.

But with Thoreau must come analysis. In seeking to satiate his hunger for wildness he couldn't help noticing the impact Anglo-Americans had had upon his field of wilderness fantasy. He was upset while paddling north into Eagle Lake by the broad belt of dead shoreline trees killed by rising water when loggers had dammed lake outlets. "The Anglo-American," he wailed when lamenting the passing of virgin forests, "can indeed cut down and grub up all this waving forest and make a stump speech and vote for Buchanan on its ruins, but he cannot converse with the spirit of the tree he fells—he cannot read the poetry and mythology which retire as he advances." Americans ignorantly erased mythological tablets, Thoreau believed, in order to print handbills and town meeting warrants on them.

Such ranting was relatively rare in the 140-page Allagash essay. Unlike his Chesuncook experience, Henry's narrative of canoeing in Allagash-Penobscot country skips philosophical asides to concentrate on details about terrain, camping, Indians, insects and weather. He brings the trip alive. The reader smells the hundred-pound moose-hide Joe stashes in the canoe; he or she sees the sheldrakes scuttle across the water in front of the canoe.

"It is all mossy and moosey," Thoreau puns about the East Branch's banks. "In some of those dense fir and spruce woods there is hardly room for the smoke to go up."

At other times: Henry shouts, and taciturn Joe tells him to shut up.

Thoreau sits next to a smoky campfire at night; he wears a head veil and gloves and puts bug dope on for protection from mosquitoes while penciling notes.

Thoreau races Polis down a portage, pots and pans flying from Thoreau's hands. Polis accidentally spits on Thoreau's back, then tells Thoreau—a life-long bachelor—the accident means he will be getting married soon.

But Thoreau wasn't thinking of marriage. There on the Penobscot he was fixated on being comfortable, his comfort reducible to camping techniques described at length in *Maine Woods*.

In choosing a campsite they looked for a clear, hard and flat beach to land on, free from mud, and free from stones that would damage the canoe. One of the campers would check for an open and level space for the camp, preferably in a cool place to cut down on the insects. Sometimes they paddled a mile or more before finding a site suitable to their tastes. Once a site was chosen, the trio unloaded their baggage and pulled the canoe ashore, sometimes turning the canoe over for safety. Joe cut a path to the campsite while Thoreau and Hoar toted up the gear. Birchbark was used to start campfires five or six feet from where they intended to sleep. Someone fetched water in a kettle from the river or lake, and then the pork, bread, coffee and other food stuffs were unwrapped.

Meanwhile, someone cut down the nearest dead rock-maple, or another kind of dry hard wood, and sectioned it into logs to hold a fire during the night. A green stake with a notch or fork in it was also cut to be slanted over the fire; from it a kettle would be hung to heat water or food. Finally, two forked stakes and a pole were cut for the tent. A dozen or more tent stakes were whittled out of moosewood while someone else collected balsam fir, arbor-vitae, or spruce boughs for the floor of the tent, a camping technique now outdated because of its impact on the environment but one accepted at the time.

Water was boiled, pork fried and supper was ready. They ate sitting on the ground or on stumps. Occasionally a large piece of birchbark was used as a table. There they sat: each holding a dipper in one hand and a piece of ship-bread or fried pork in the other, meanwhile shooing-away mosquitoes, or thrusting one's head into the campfire smoke to ward off the bugs. Pipes were lit after supper by those who smoked, veils were donned by those who had them, and Hoar and Thoreau examined and dried plants. Bug dope was smeared on faces and hands prior to bed. And the mosquitoes? Not even Thoreau could transcend them.

The canoe trip continued on July 30 when Thoreau, Polis and Hoar portaged from Webster Pond to the main East Branch of the Penobscot River near Second Lake. There Polis shot a moose. He took the skin, a large sirloin, the upper lip and tongue. Afterwards, the trio paddled on to Grand Lake and a campsite beyond the dam at its southeast end, where some of the East Penobscot's headwaters began. Travel was difficult the next day because of waterfalls and rapids, and they became lost when they couldn't locate themselves on either the "Map of the Public Lands of Maine and Massachusetts" or "Colton's Railroad and Township Map of Maine." Yet water runs true. They could hardly get lost in a dangerous sense. Soon they floated past the mouth of the Seboeis River on the left, and the Wassataquoik River the next day.

By August 3 they had canoed past Mattawamkeag and Lincoln to Old Town.

VIII

After canoeing in Penobscot country, Thoreau continued to broaden his geographical awareness by traveling; from his trips came essays for *Putnam's Magazine*, the new *Atlantic Monthly* and other periodicals.

Four of his trips during the last 13 years of his life were to Cape Cod where he hiked the entire distance from Orleans to Provincetown. In 1850 he toured Quebec, Canada, where he hoped to take "one honest walk... as I might in Concord woods of an afternoon." In 1858 he backpacked to the summit of Mt. Monadnock in southwest New Hampshire, then climbed Mt.

Washington a second time a year later.

Thoreau continued to saunter in the country around Concord between his trips elsewhere, hungry as he was for the ecstasies of Holy Lands. Yet while feeding his addiction to walking he did more than broaden his self-appointment as Concord's surveyor of rainstorms and snowstorms. Something more volcanic was brewing behind his blue-gray eyes. He was becoming politically harried. He was oppressed by the living emergence of social issues he could no longer shirk during woodland walks.

Like slavery.

Not even the wealth of wildness seen during Maine canoe trips could free Thoreau of slavery's mental burr. As early as 1844 he had written a public notice of the anti-slavery "Herald of Freedom" for the *Dial*. A year later he defended Wendell Phillips's right to speak about abolition at Concord's lyceum. He bragged up John Brown. He helped some runaway slaves dodge their way to Canada. Thoreau was even jailed for not paying his taxes—an act of civil disobedience rooted in his inability to justify supporting a government that sanctioned slavery. Henry only spent one night in jail but the experience incited him to write an essay, "Civil Disobedience," against conformity and servitude to unjust governments. Inevitably, the concept and practice of American slavery weighed on the soul of Concord's grown-up "Judge" like a two-ton link of chain. It was an albatross around his spirit, altogether the most salient reason he wanted to wash his hands of both government and religious affairs.

Thoreau longed for peace when Civil War erupted between North and South in 1861, but he was almost too exhausted to care. He had caught a cold on December 3, 1860, while counting tree rings in a snowstorm on Fair Haven Hill near Concord. He lectured in Waterbury, Connecticut, against doctor's orders, and developed bronchitis; this, in turn, irritated tubercular lesions in his lungs which had troubled him during his Harvard days.

Thoreau's doctor—fearing for his patient's life—advised Henry to try a different climate. It was advice which, for once, Thoreau heeded.

In searching for a traveling companion, Thoreau wrote to Harrison Blake (who later edited Thoreau's 7,000-page journal) and explained he had decided against going to the West Indies because of its muggy summer heat. Southern Europe was too expensive in terms both of time and money. So it was to be Minnesota. Around St. Paul. Thoreau figured the inland air might help him or, on the other hand, it might not. Blake declined going along, as did Channing. Hence, on May 11 Thoreau left Concord with Horace Mann, Jr., much younger than Thoreau but a good botanist.

The Minnesota trip was Thoreau's longest and last journey.

Horace and Henry traveled west by rail, stopped at Niagara Falls and Chicago, then continued west to Dunleith, now East Dubuque, Illinois. There they boarded the steamer *Itasca* for St. Paul up the Mississippi River where Thoreau spent several weeks identifying plants and animals around Lake Calhoun with Dr. Charles L. Anderson, state geologist. On June 17, Thoreau rode the steamer *Frank Steele* up the Minnesota River to the Indian

Agency at Redwood where a payment of annuities was to be made to the Sioux. On board were fancy ladies, a German band and Governor Ramsey: "the rich yellow skim"—in the words of the *Minnesota State Atlas*—"from the mottled milk of frontier society." While near Redwood, Thoreau noticed the Sioux's restlessness and dissatisfaction, a cultural uneasiness that erupted into a bloody uprising 14 months later. He walked three miles toward a rumored herd of buffalo but saw none. He watched an Indian powwow, found gophers curious and looked for groves of wild crabapples. But everything seemed empty. Superficial. Ghostly. His heart wasn't in it. His journal: scant. When Thoreau became homesick he convinced Mann to cut their planned Minnesota visit in half.

Thoreau and Mann were back in Concord on July 9; Henry's health had hardly improved.

He accepted his tuberculosis with a touch of finality. As his condition worsened friends and neighbors came to see and speak with him, reminding Thoreau in their own way he hadn't lived in vain. His self-made rattan daybed was placed in the parlor where he often sat visiting with a guest or reading over his papers. His cough was constant; his voice a whisper. But to all who watched him die he seemed to remain at peace with the long night approaching.

Nor did his wit sleep.

When his Aunt Louisa asked him if he had made his peace with God, Thoreau quipped he had "never quarreled with Him." When Parker Pillsbury asked Thoreau about the afterlife, he again responded with a remark as original as its speaker: "One world at a time, please."

It was this one world Thoreau had hungered for throughout his walking days. It was this one world he had climbed toward alone on Mt. Katahdin in 1846, that he had stalked on Walden's shores, and toward which he had paddled on the Penobscot, Chesuncook and Moosehead waterways. Perhaps, then, it was all things wild and real, natural and full of pulsating life that clung in Thoreau like dew to the last.

Death came May 6, 1862. Thoreau asked to be raised upright in his bed so he could smell a bouquet of hyacinths brought over by a friend. "Indian," he said moments later as his breathing grew faint. "Moose."

Outside, spring sun shone.

2

JOHN MUIR:
FOOTLOOSE IN RANGES OF LIGHT

"I only went out for a walk, and finally concluded to stay out till sundown, for going out, I found, was really going in."

—John Muir, *John of the Mountains*

John Muir's reddishbrown beard rippled in a blizzard wind as he gazed apprehensively at an ice bridge before him. He was trapped. Unable to retrace his steps as darkness fell, he had been grimly funneled by glacial walls and impassable crevasses to this critical moment on Taylor Glacier in a land no one knew.

It was a fitting place for this self-made geologist and glaciologist. He had harped and harangued about the glacial history of California's Sierra-Nevada Mountains and about the wonders of wilderness in general, until both coaxed him on a personal expedition to southeastern Alaska in 1880. Here, while studying glaciers, he had walked off with a small dog to check out the glaciated coastal outback. Now camp offered the only protection against a blizzard and certain hypothermic death.

A cold wind thick with snow rasped his hands, his face, and stung his blue eyes squinting in the white. He was at that moment a man with no choice. A rush of warm adrenaline rose in his body like a blush as he fingered the ice field's edge, then shifted his weight out over it. Slowly, each move among the most deliberate, concentrated acts of his life, he eased himself onto the ice bridge and shimmied—like a cowboy astride a horse, or a kid the end of a teeter-totter—across the 70-foot arch. Below him gaped a thousand-foot crevasse. This was Glacier Bay country. And this was Muir at his wildest. Never did cold air taste so good as when he stood on the other side of that crevasse, coaxing the pup to follow. Never did life seem so rich and new and brimming to the lip, so charged with sensation from the whisper of death.

It had been a rugged, aerated road to that whisper for John Muir, yet it was a whisper he had heard time and again on that open, outdoor road. It came with the terrain of being a mountaineer at a time when the Pacific Northwest was peppered with unclimbed peaks. It also came with the turf of being a self-educated botanist and glaciologist as well as a writer of magazine articles and books, who was convinced the clearest way into the universe was through a forest wilderness.

So adamant was he about this that at times he sounded like a wilderness messiah, a John the Baptist of wild places, places he explored and wished to preserve. His fight to preserve such wildernesses as the Grand Canyon, Yosemite National Park, and Kings Canyon National Park inevitably earned him the sobriquet of Father of the National Park Service in the United States. In 1892 he founded the Sierra Club, which today is one of the continent's major environmental organizations with a membership of over 300,000. Muir numbered among his close friends such exceptional philosophers, naturalists, and politicians of his time as John Burroughs, Asa Gray, Theodore Roosevelt, and Ralph Waldo Emerson. Men like these, and such women as Jeanne Carr who so often took Muir under her confidential, encouraging wing, recognized in Muir a greatness knocking on the western door of North American history. They wouldn't—like Roosevelt during the Hetch Hetchy controversy—always agree with him, but they admitted to themselves, if not one another, that he was worth listening to. That he had seen wildness, lived in wilderness, and had listened and looked while there with insight unlocked by zeal.

It was zeal that led Muir late in life to brag that he could have become a millionaire, but instead became a tramp.

And tramp he did. His impassioned, now legendary ramblings in what in retrospect was virgin wilderness makes walker Thoreau appear almost urban in comparison. Muir's footsteps ranged from southern Canada to southern Florida, from California's Sierra Mountains with which he is most identified to Washington state's Mount Rainier. There were the San Joaquin and Minarets peaks. There was Mount Shasta and Mount Ritter, and then southeastern Alaska's ice-choked fjords where, in time, a glacier was named after him. In Wisconsin where he grew up there would be a Muir Lake and Muir Knoll. There would be, on Mount Rainier, a Camp Muir. In California he is named in the state nomenclature more than anyone else: Muir Woods National Monument in Marin County, *Mt.* Muir in Tulare County, Muir *Peak* in Los Angeles County, Muir *Gorge* in Yosemite, Muir *Pass* in Kings Canyon, Muir *Crest* in Sequoia, and the John Muir Trail among Sierra peaks. Always something natural, wild, and remote for good reason. Is it surprising cities made Muir feel weak and dislocated? that there he felt poisoned by industrial plumes and the pale palsied hands of chronically indoor people? He knew the reward for tramping was a peculiar freedom flowered at times by alpine slopes daubed with shell-pink sunrises. He knew the voices of cold mountain streams. He knew as well as anyone the rigors and exultations of extended backcountry trips. Nothing could hold this man back. Not writing. Not women. Not even the scholars of great public stature he held in rare respect.

"Climb the mountains and get their good tidings," he preached in words now postered on thousands of city walls. "Nature's peace will flow into you as sunshine flows into trees. The winds will blow their own freshness into you, and the storms their energy, while cares will drop off like autumn leaves."

Exactly. This is exactly what Muir wanted to impress upon Emerson when New England's Big Mind ventured to Yosemite in 1871. Yosemite was already a tourist attraction drawing about 2,000 people a summer. Muir, by then enthralled with the region, felt Emerson of all men would be the quickest to "see the mountains and sing them," so he wanted to escort Emerson, 68, into the mountains where they could camp and cavort intellectually. Yet it was a young man's romantic wish. When Emerson and his entourage of twelve arrived at the meager Yosemite accommodations, Muir hung back on the edges of evening crowds that gathered around Emerson. Muir, after all, was still in the morning of his career at age 33; he was a part-time sawyer of dubious reputation, a curiosity, eccentric but harmless. Who else thereabouts headed off alone into surrounding hills to return by moonlight with arms full of plants, thoughts tipsy with inspiration?

As Stephen Fox tells it in *John Muir and His Legacy*, Muir didn't spur himself out of bashfulness until he heard rumors Emerson was due to leave Yosemite. Muir left him this note:

> Do not thus drift away with the mob while the spirits of these rocks and waters hail you after long waiting as their kinsman and persuade you to closer communion ... I invite you to join me in a month's worship with Nature in the high temples of the great Sierra Crown beyond our holy Yosemite. It will cost you nothing save the time and very little of that for you will be mostly in eternity ... In the name of a hundred cascades that barbarous visitors never see ... in the name of all the spirit creatures of these rocks and of this whole spiritual atmosphere Do [sic] not leave us *now*. With most cordial regards I am yours in Nature, John Muir.

Emerson had been told about Muir by a mutual acquaintance, so in the morning he rode over to the sawmill where Muir had built a small room below the mill's gable. There Muir, when not cutting fallen yellow pine, lived above a stream and could see both South Dome and the mountain valley to the west. Rocks and plants were scattered throughout Muir's nest, no doubt piquing Emerson's interest, for Emerson owned a substantial frame house with library, dining room and flowering lawn hedges in Concord,

Massachusetts. Muir again asked Emerson to accompany him into the backcountry, but was told his friends wouldn't allow it for fear he would catch cold.

"The shadows were growing long," Muir later recalled, "and he leaned on his friends. His party, full of indoor philosophy, failed to see the natural beauty and fullness of promise of my wild plan, and laughed at it in good-natured ignorance, as if it were necessarily amusing to imagine that Boston people might be led to accept Sierra manifestations of God at the price of rough camping."

A few days later Muir was invited to ride with Emerson, et al., to the sequoias of Mariposa Grove, which he agreed to do if Emerson would camp there. Emerson indicated he would. But once they got near Mariposa Emerson's friends again refused to hear of it. Muir tried all the angles: he argued that colds were caught in homes and hotels, not in the Sierra; he described a large "climate-changing" campfire he would build and the fragrant beauty of sequoia flame; he described how the giant trees would stand transfigured in the purple light with stars looking down between their lofty domes; he wanted to make "an immortal Emerson night of it." But "carpet dust" and "unknowable reeks" were preferred. Muir *again* tried convincing Emerson the next day when they rode horseback in Mariposa, but England's minister of literature and Thoreau's mentor "was past his prime, and was now as a child in the hands of his affectionate but sadly civilized friends." Muir was not one to let opportunity slip through his fingers, yet here he failed. He had overestimated Emerson's hunger for wildness. With sadness he watched Emerson ride off with his friends then turn around on his saddle and wave good-bye with his hat from Wawona Ridge.

Muir would never see Emerson again.

Muir, for the first time ever, felt lonely among the sequoias. He sauntered back into the heart of Mariposa, made a bed of sequoia plumes and ferns near a stream, gathered firewood, then walked around until sundown. Soon he was alone next to a warm campfire. Shadows leapt among tree trunks, boughs and mounds of needle duff. His thoughts, too, must have leapt as he tried to digest what had happened. He couldn't understand—certainly never would empathize with such sheepishness from the man and mind behind *Nature*. Writing about nature in the abstract was one thing; experiencing wilderness next to a campfire was another. Muir continued to correspond with Emerson over the years, and late in life kept a photo of him (and one of Thoreau) on the mantel of his study, but Muir never bridged the gulf between himself and Emerson. The latter would write Muir and tease him about his "probation and sequestration in the solitudes and snows" in the Sierra-Nevada Mountains, and invite Muir to New England's intellectual culture and rich American history.

But Muir resisted. Always. He had unfinished business—the roots and dimensions of which now licked and tongued at Muir's blue eyes as he stared into sequoia flames in Mariposa Grove.

I

Dunbar, Scotland, where Muir was born on April 21, 1838, must have seemed like a dream, so different was it from the wild forest life he had come to know in California. He was the first boy and third child of Ann and Daniel Muir (*Muir* in Scottish meant "moor," or a "wild stretch of wasteland," not unlike original meanings of "wilderness.") Young John found no lack of wildness near the stormy North Seas. His first country walks, at age three, were taken with Grandfather Gilrye, who later taught him the alphabet from shop signs across High Street from father Daniel's food-and-grain store. Later "with red-blooded playmates," he recalled, "wild as myself, I loved to wander in the fields to hear the birds sing, and along the seashore to gaze and wonder at the shells and seaweeds, eels and crabs in the pools among the rocks when the tide was low." Best of all were the waves that thundered against the craggy headlands and ruins of Dunbar Castle when the sea, sky, waves and clouds fused into one wild song of motion. Muir was ordered to stay in the backyard and garden, but every Saturday and on every school vacation except Sundays he would sneak off to the seacoast, regardless of inevitable punishment.

A natural inherited wildness ran in his blood, biographer Edwin Way Teale has written, "true on its glorious course, as invincible and unstoppable as stars."

Muir was a climber from the start. He and boyhood friends would see who could climb the highest on the crumbling peaks and crags around Dunbar Castle, where they took chances he thought later no cautious mountaineer would try. At other times he and his brother David would attempt to outdo one another at night by performing stunts out their second floor bedroom dormer window. One night John hung himself out over the slates, holding onto the sill, while the wind made a balloon of his nightgown; later he performed the stunt with one arm, then one finger. He became so proud of his climbing skills that when a servant girl told him about hell, which he imagined as a sooty pit with stone walls like those of a castle, he was certain he could climb out of it.

Such cocksureness led to bloody fist fights on most school days, sometimes half a dozen in a single day. Not that Muir was a bully. He and friends were steeped in stories about Robert the Bruce and William Wallace, the great Scottish fighters; they and each boy wanted to grow up to be soldiers. They waged snowball fights, grass-sod fights, or filled their blue bonnets with sand and snow to use as cannonballs. They were typical boys in many ways, their young blood alive with knights and kings and heroism.

Fortitude in their scheme of things was a virtue. Showing pain brought mockery. One of the school yard games was for two boys to make whips with saplings, square off, then thrash one another on the legs until one gave in to pain. Homemade guns were made and fired with real gunpowder. Trees were climbed; garden walls scaled. Bird nests were counted. Running matches, often of 10 to 20 miles, were organized in winter. And, for John, there were

Bible verses to memorize; by age 11 he knew three-fourths of the Old Testament and all of the New "by heart and by sore flesh." Whippings were common during recitation mistakes, for, as Muir put it, "the grand, simple, all-sufficing Scottish discovery had been made that there was a close connection between the skin and the memory, and that irritating the skin excited the memory to any required degree." Herein lay partly the secret to boyhood fights and school-versus-school battles. The way Muir viewed it, he and friends couldn't believe it was fair their teachers and fathers could thrash them so industriously for their own good while begrudging them the pleasure of *thrashing each other* for their own good. Fortitude to pain would serve Muir well in the future as he left bloody trails on sharp North American ice peaks to see the wonders of the world.

First came Wisconsin.

"Bairns," father Daniel announced to his boys and their grandfather on February 18, 1849, "you needna learn your lessons the nicht, for we're gan to America the morn!"

The words were, Muir remembered, the most glorious and wonderful that the boys ever heard. One minute he was studying school lessons and the next his head was full of visions of a New Land. Hawks. Eagles. Sugar trees growing in ground full of gold. Millions of bird's nests. No gamekeepers. Only Grandfather Gilrye was sad. He mumbled something to the boys about hard work while inside he suddenly waxed lonely, old, deserted. John, 11, ran out into the night streets to tell his friends about his trip to "Amaraka." "Weel," he said when they doubted him, "just you see if I am at the skule the morn!"

Muir wasn't at school in the morning. He was on his way to New York Harbor, reached from Scotland in six weeks. It was April 5. With John and his father were sister Sarah, 13, and David, 9. The rest of the family—mom, three girls, and a boy were scheduled to rendezvous with Daniel and kids when they had a house built in the New Land. Daniel wasn't quite sure *where* to build that new house at first. He left Scotland, which was land poor when it came to someone of his social standing, with the intention of settling on land in the backwoods of Upper Canada. Ship talk about land had been frequent, however, and by the time he reached the United States he was convinced Wisconsin or Michigan was the place to go. They ended up in south-central Wisconsin, about 40 miles north of Madison. The result: Fountain Lake Farm, 80 acres of sunny open woods on the side of a lake not far from the Fox River. The farm was veined with springs.

The site was intoxicating at first for young John and David, for they were still too young and too small to be good for little else but play. Muir described the homesteading's first months as a "plash into pure wilderness." Nature streamed into them, he recalled, "wooingly teaching her wonderful lessons, so unlike the dismal grammar ashes and cinders so long thrashed into us. Here without knowing it we still were at school; every wild lesson a love lesson, not whipped but charmed into us... Everything new and pure in the very prime of the spring when Nature's pulses were beating highest and mysteriously keeping time with our own! Young hearts, young leaves, flowers, animals, the winds and the streams and the sparkling lake, all wildly, gladly rejoicing together!" Not far away was Portage and Packwaukee Lake with an Indian trail. There were brown thrushes on the topmost sprays of oak trees. Robins were some of the bird "people" he never would forget, like the nuthatches locals called Devil-downheads. There were bobwhites, bluebirds, and chickadees, Canada geese, and swarming clouds of passenger pigeons from horizon to horizon. Too, there were loons, including one he captured, brought into the house, and which he watched as it nailed the family cat between the eyes with its long sharp bill. Fountain Lake Farm was a glorious, youthful place for Muir, and later a locus of boyhood stories. But Grandfather Gilrye eventually proved right. Wisconsin, at least under the authority of Daniel Muir, meant work.

For son John: slavery.

Muir's father, it turned out, chose poor land with thin, organically lean, sandy loam that could barely sustain the family. He nevertheless bought another 40 acres and, in 1855, an entirely new farm six miles away subsequently named Hickory Hill Farm. Hardwood trees at each place had to be cut down, sawed into logs, and moved. Stumps had to be torn loose from the soil, and their roots grubbed out. Boulders and rocks had to be weeded from the loam. Much of the work fell on John's shoulders. He was the oldest son and as such driven dawn to dark. The birds he once hailed as a boy were now seen through films of sweat. His hands became callused to the soft petals of flowers. In cold weather he had to put on wet socks and squeeze his feet into frozen boots. It is a wonder Muir didn't—like most pioneers—begin to hate wilderness: to despise its constant mind-numbing work, endless chores, and the stress coming from both farm failure and family.

Eight years of this.

Yet there seemed to be some sanctuary in young John, some interior refuge that sustained him through a hellish puberty that damaged or wrecked the wills and minds of his brothers and sisters. Perhaps the work wouldn't have been so bad if father Daniel hadn't taken his Calvinism to the limit of insanity. Sometimes even across its fine line. He had no patience for what he perceived an imperfection. He watched everything his sons said, did, or didn't do but should have. And he remained quick to grab the switch. "I want you to be like Paul the Apostle," he would tell John, "who said that he desired to know nothing among men but Christ and Him crucified." Such grim religious passions have a way of becoming all-encompassing with age; as Daniel grew old he became more religious and did less work, for he was convinced the word of the Lord according to a sect known as the Disciples of Christ was sometimes reducible to rural crucifixion. He no longer whipped John every evening whether or not he deserved it, but he certainly had no qualms about teaching him hard lessons.

Like digging a well by hand.

When the Muir family moved to Hickory Hill Farm, Daniel tried to dynamite out a well but failed. He decided instead to have John chip almost *90 feet* down into hard sandstone with a hammer and chisel until he hit water. At 80 feet John almost died of chokedamp: carbonic acid that had settled to the bottom of a self-made hell not even scooter John could climb out of. One of his last glances prior to collapsing unconscious into the windlassed hoist bucket was of a bur oak tree branch at the top of the well shaft. A day or two later his father lowered him back down, and the work continued. It had taken months. John eventually struck water but not perhaps without reaching a new depth of disdain for his father, his father's farming, and his father's religion that somehow justified it all.

What his father's religion *didn't* justify, at least at first, was John's penchant for monkeying with machines, a penchant rooted in his love of reading. When 15 years old, John recalled, he "began to relish good literature with enthusiasm, and smack my lips over favorite lines." But there was no time to read; Daniel saw to that and at night after worship when John tried to steal a few minutes to read next to a candle, his Pa would inevitably scold him and shame him. One night he slipped. He told John if he really wanted to read he could get up in the morning before work and read then. John did. Instead of rising an hour or two before dawn, however, he starting getting up at one o'clock. Reading was avoided during winter because it required a fire in mid-winter's zero-degree weather, and John feared Daniel's wrath for burning firewood that took time to chop. No matter that indomitable John would have chopped all the wood the home needed, and more; Daniel wasn't reasonable about such things. So John decided to head for the cellar where it was warmer at night and where there were some tools. He began building a self-setting sawmill later operated by the waterpower of a dammed stream.

Such tinkering was just a beginning.

By sleeping only five hours a night instead of ten, Muir's stolen moments erupted into a flurry of inventions: a fire-lighter, hygrometers, a barometer, a machine for feeding horses at any required hour, a bed that would tilt him and set him on his feet at any set time, a thermometer three-feet long that could be read from a distance while plowing fields, and a large "town" clock with four dials and time figures so large neighbors could read them; the side of the clock facing the house, meanwhile, also indicated weekday and month.

John wanted to put the big clock on the barn. Daniel, fearing curious onlookers, said no. Then John wanted to put it on top of an oak tree. Who, Daniel asked, "ever heard of anything so queer as a big clock on the top of a tree?"

John trashed the clock. It was time—he could tell—to leave Hickory Hill and his "all-Bible" book-spreading and freelance Sunday-preaching father.

———————————

Muir's first destination was Madison, Wisconsin. The wild coastal scenes of Scotland's Firth of Forth and the primeval richness of Wisconsin's lush vegetation and wildlife simmered below consciousness like a bubbling

Fountain Lake spring, but Muir, still unable to intuit his later obsession with nature, wanted to become a doctor. Machines would point the way. Medical studies were expensive, he reasoned, so he would find a job at a machine shop where he would cache a nest egg by inventing machines.

First stop was the 1860 Wisconsin State Fair; here, farm friends had advised, he would find admirers of his work, which proved true. Everyone who saw his baggage on the way to Madison was fascinated with his wooden clocks, thermometer, and morning-rising gadgets. At the fair, doors were opened as fast as he could knock on them. His inventions stole the show, particularly because Muir had invented his time pieces without having ever seen the inside of a commercial clock. He was hired after the fair by a fellow from Prairie du Chien who was designing an iceboat for winter navigation on the Mississippi River. When the iceboat failed, and when Muir didn't get his promised education, he returned to Madison and enrolled at the university.

Reading now became a lifestyle instead of minutes snatched in Daniel Muir's cold kitchen.

Muir was at the university off-and-on for almost three years. He studied botany, geology, mathematics, Latin, Greek and physics. Meanwhile, as if hounded by time, he kept on perfecting his efficiency machines. The same winter he supplemented his income by teaching at a school 10 miles south of Madison he astonished everyone by contriving a machine that lit the school's wood stove at a set time, so the schoolroom was warm when he and students arrived. He also perfected the mechanical bed that set him on his feet every morning at a determined hour, a kind of bed-flipping alarm clock, but now he added attachments. Not only did the machine light lamps, but after several minutes were allowed for dressing it pushed a book on to a desk where it was to be studied, opened it, then closed it and replaced it with another when allotted study time was up. Understandably, Muir's room became a showcase for university professors, and once even a laboratory used by an instructor.

Everyone was certain Muir's future held no limits. He was a mechanical genius.

Few people knew, however, that back at Hickory Hill Farm during summers Muir had begun using his lunch break and midnights to study plants. He had become friends with Ezra Carr, a University of Wisconsin professor of natural history and chemistry, and a generous man who opened up his library to Muir; there John had begun to study the works of Thoreau, Emerson, geologist Louis Agassiz, and botanist Alexander von Humboldt. A fellow student named Milton S. Griswold, meanwhile, had opened Muir's mind to the living intricacies of plant life. Plants, Muir realized, were organic machines with working parts, but rather than being mere mechanical coincidences of creation, they were amazing individual manifestations of a harmonious whole. Each plant was different and perfect in itself. Yet each had roots in a creative energy, some nonmaterial, divine shoot underlying every atom of plant beauty.

In the meantime, Ezra Carr's wife, Jeanne—a native of Vermont who was passionately devoted to plant study—began to coax Muir away from machines toward what he later called the "University of the Wilderness."

It was a large university, this wilderness was, one open to all students willing to walk "pathless ways," as Muir biographer Michael Cohen put it. Muir was restless in 1864 as the Civil War drew to a close. He saw trouble ahead for himself if he devoted his energies entirely to machinery, but he couldn't see any viable alternatives. Farming was out of the question although Daniel was willing to give him part of the farm; John wanted no dark shadows cast on his budding enthusiasm. Becoming a doctor was out, too. He had nothing left to do but roam.

This he did with a knapsack, a single change of underclothing, and a notebook and pencil, which he toted on foot across Michigan until he reached the lakes, bogs, and meadows between lakes Erie and Huron. There he studied bushes, trees and flowers for months, a migrant Audubon of the plant world, a romantic lad in the footsteps of von Humboldt and Linnaeus. He was willing "to whirl... like a leaf in every eddy, dance compliance to any wind." When winter forced him out of the woods he began work at a broom handle factory near Meaford, Ontario, where, under contract, he agreed to improve or invent machines for the production of 12,000 rakes and 30,000 broom handles in exchange for half the profits. This he accomplished by February 1866. The following month the plant and storage buildings, together with Muir's notebooks, burned to the ground.

But something had happened to Muir in Ontario's backwoods that never would be destroyed, something he later ranked as one of the two highlights of his life. He had a natural mystical experience—a union of yearning emotion with natural beauty.

As biographer Fox describes it, one day in June of 1864 Muir was pushing his way through dense swamps in late afternoon, when—already taut with loneliness—he became concerned about where he would spend the night. Suddenly on a stream bank he found two white flowers, the rare orchid *Calypso borealis*, against a background of yellow moss. "They were alone," he explained later. "I never before saw a plant so full of life; so perfectly spiritual, it seemed pure enough for the throne of its Creator. I felt as if I were in the presence of superior beings who loved me and beckoned me to come. I sat down beside them and wept for joy."

Muir later found a place to sleep but he never forgot how his loneliness was assuaged by *Calypso*, how the plant, alone like him, was useful despite its remoteness, and how the world could possibly suffer by the destruction of a single plant. One plant, one person coming together in time, united by an intuitive leap of light. Without the plant, what then of Muir's enlightenment on that late spring day?

"I am captive," Muir wrote, integrated by his vision. "I am bound. Love of pure unblemished Nature seems to overmaster and blur out of sight all other objects and considerations."

He nevertheless left Meaford country for Indianapolis, where he resumed inventing production machinery, this time for Osgood, Smith and Company, makers of spokes, hubs and various carriage wheel parts. He rose quickly in the company. Eagerly he eyed promotions and money coming his way. Success seemed so near, so within sight until fate struck like a javelin in March 1867. As Muir unlaced a belt-joining with the sharp end of a file, the file slipped and flew up into his right eye, piercing the cornea; ophthalmic fluid dripped into his hand.

"My right eye gone," he muttered. "Closed forever on God's beauty."

His other eye went into shock. He became blind. Muir lay for a month in total darkness, with time to mull his past, his dark future, and to meditate on the wonder of light: how it illumined *Calypso* in auras of moss-gold; how the rosy reds of passenger pigeons changed to emerald-green and rich crimson along their sides. Never would he take light or, as he put it, Light, for granted again. He dreamt long hours of color and sight, and he resolved that, should his vision come back, he would "study the things of God rather than those of men." Within him was a new urgency to pursue what he loved... what most brought him joy.

To hell with clocks, then! He wanted the natural freedom of eternity. Nature was what he wanted. But not nature for mere recreation. He would stalk nothing less than the law governing relationships between human beings and nature. Hadn't he glimpsed an aesthetic connection necessary to wholesome living? But what was that connection? How could he stay attuned to it? What would happen if he aimed his head and heart at it full-time?

This then is what he would do: he would be his own nurse while wilderness doctored his body and soul.

II

When Muir's eyesight returned he began a thousand-mile walk from Louisville, Kentucky, to the Gulf of Mexico. It would be a hard, transforming journey. Strapped to his belt was his notebook; on its inside cover was written his new geographical identity: "John Muir, Earth-planet, Universe."

In his pack was a comb, brush, towel, soap, change of underwear and three books—a small New Testament, a copy of Robert Burns's poems and Milton's *Paradise Lost*. Muir covered about 25 miles a day as he roamed through the backwoods of Tennessee, the southeastern edge of North Carolina, Georgia, and parts of Florida. His original plan was to keep going by boat and foot until he reached the tropical jungles of South America along the Andes; there he would latch on to a tributary of the Amazon, which he would float down on a raft or skiff to the Atlantic. He wanted to botanize and immerse himself in wilderness, but paradise lost was not paradise easily found. His biggest problem was food.

"Oftentimes," he recalled in *A Thousand-Mile Walk to the Gulf* (which bridges his life periods found in *The Story of My Boyhood and Youth* and *My First Summer in the Sierra*), "I had to sleep out without blankets, and also without supper or breakfast. But usually I had no great difficulty in finding a loaf of bread in the widely scattered clearings of the farmers. With one of these big backwoods loaves I was able to wander many a long, wild mile, free as the winds in the glorious forests and bogs, gathering plants and feeding on God's abounding, inexhaustible spiritual beauty bread."

He sometimes covered 40 miles in a day without lunch or dinner. While camping among the tombs of Bonaventure Cemetery near Savannah, Georgia, and waiting for money to be forwarded by his brother, he became so famished living on three or four cents a day he grew giddy. He also staggered while walking. His worst hours coupled hunger with horrid camping conditions. Near the Savannah River, he used an earth mound for a pillow while sleeping beneath an oak; large, prickly-footed beetles crept across his hands and face, mosquitoes stung him, and when he awoke he learned his pillow was a grave. Later, in a Florida swamp he was caught groping in the dark for a place to camp; when his feet stopped splashing in water, he would feel the ground with his hands, find a relatively dry spot, eat a chunk of bread, drink some brown water from a nearby pool, then lie down. He often had to grope for slimy pools in the grass for drinking water, meanwhile fearing alligators. He frequently awoke cold and wet with dew, and would set out without breakfast.

Muir had never been sick before, so when he began to feel ill in Florida's Cedar Keys he tried to ignore it. But his condition worsened. He fell down unconscious on a narrow trail among dwarf palmettos. He rose, staggered, then fell again he knew not how many times in "delirious bewilderment, gasping and throbbing with only moments of consciousness." He was eventually found unconscious in a heap of sawdust at a lodging house. Malaria turned to typhoid fever. Muir was laid up for three months. When it was all over, he was born again for the second time in two years.

His thoughts turned to religion. As biographers often point out, it is in his *Thousand-mile Walk* journal that Muir turned his back on the orthodox Christianity of his time—his father's faith—and began to arrive at his own spiritual ideas. Foremost were conclusions about death, which he had faced so squarely in Florida. "On no subject are our ideas more warped and pitiable," he penned. "Instead of the sympathy, the friendly union, of life and death so apparent in Nature, we are taught that death is an accident, a deplorable punishment for the oldest sin, the arch-enemy of life, etc." Death caused groans and tears, morbid exultation, and led to black-boxed burials in ill-omened places of haunt and gloom. "But let children walk with Nature, let them see the beautiful blendings and communions of death and life, their joyous inseparable unity, as taught in woods and meadows, plains and mountains and streams of our blessed star, and they will learn that death is stingless indeed, and as beautiful as life, and that the grave has no victory for it never fights. All is divine harmony."

Ideas of and attitudes toward death led naturally to thoughts of God. Here Muir broke with his past. "The world," Muir said we are told, "was made especially for man—a presumption not supported by all the facts. A numerous class of men are painfully astonished whenever they find anything, living or dead, in all God's universe, which they cannot eat or render in some way what they call useful to themselves." Their god, Muir added, was comparable to a heathen idol. "He is regarded as a civilized, law-abiding gentleman in favor of either a republican form of government or of a limited monarchy; believes in the literature and language of England; is a warm supporter of the English constitution and Sunday schools and missionary societies; and is as purely a manufactured article as any puppet of a half-penny theater." Such manufactured views, Muir thought, led to erroneous ideas of the creation, notably that everything was made for man. But why did water drown Lord Man? Why do minerals poison people? Alligators eat them? Why is the Lord of creation subject to the same laws of life as lions and tigers "which smack their lips over raw man"? To say that plants and animals are not immortal but perish unlike man was, Muir reasoned, something we know nothing about.

Strong words, these. *Heresy*, in fact.

But Muir had seen through his own wanderings and struggle with death an inescapable truth: the Creator had made *Homo sapiens* from the same dust of the earth, the "common elementary fund," as he had made every other creature "however noxious and insignificant to us."

"Now," Muir concluded, "it never seems to occur [to most Christians] that Nature's object in making animals and plants might possibly be first of all the happiness of each one of them, not the creation of all for the happiness of one. Why should man value himself as more than a small part of the one great unit of creation? And what creature of all that the Lord has taken the pains to make is not essential to the completeness of that unit—the cosmos? The universe would be incomplete without man; but it would also be incomplete without the smallest transmicroscopic creature that dwells beyond our conceitful eyes and knowledge."

Just as Muir had invented clocks in Wisconsin without ever having seen the inside of a marketed timepiece, he now independently realized a biocentric truth which shaped his philosophy, theology and wilderness preservation struggles later on—a truth rediscovered time and again since by thousands of others in the footsteps of Muir's awakening. Traditional Christianity, which North Americans and Europeans believed in, was human-centric. But biocentrism shifted the axle to the rim in a system of thought that viewed all species as equal. They shared both center and circumference of reality. As biographer Fox has noted, Muir—after his hike to Florida and by the time he reached California—viewed animals, plants and perhaps even minerals—as being possibly endowed with a divine spark of sensation "that Christian man in his overweening hubris could not appreciate." This was, Fox said, the central insight of Muir's life, "the philosophical basis of his subsequent career in conservation."

III

Muir's life following malaria and rebirth was a matter of boot on rock, for he abandoned plans to go to South America. Instead he visited Cuba and

New York City, then booked passage for California. Uncannily, a psychic friend of Mrs. Carr's had told her that her friend Muir would end up near California's Yosemite Valley, a prophecy Muir had shrugged off in skepticism although he had seen a folder of the region when he was a boy. Yet now here he was, landing in San Francisco, asking the first person he saw on Market Street which direction was the fastest way to any place wild. An Oakland ferry, a hike past San Jose and across the Santa Clara Valley, a jaunt east through Pacheco Pass, a sojourn across the San Joaquin Valley ... onward, step after step, to mountain foothills, then up the divide between the Tuolumne and Merced rivers. Finally, Muir set eyes on his home for the next four years: Yosemite.

Here, in the ancestral home of Ahwahneechee Indians whose tribal leaders had claimed kinship with Uzamaiti, the grizzly bear, where miners and soldiers laid claim to the region's gold in 1851, where the federal government saw fit in 1864 to give the land to the state of California as the nation's first wilderness park—here Muir came to rest, made home, and re-made himself into a mountaineer and nationally respected glaciologist.

At first he took odd jobs: harvest hand, mustang breaker, ferry operator, shepherd, and the small sawmill operator position he had when Emerson showed up. Such jobs, T.H. Watkins explains in *John Muir's America*, gave him his first mountain experiences, particularly shepherding, which brought him back to the divide between the Tuolumne and Merced rivers, to a camp north of Yosemite Valley, then to the forests north of Tuolumne Meadows. A new nuance of mysticism began to crackle in his blood. "Now we are fairly into the mountains," he wrote in his journal, "and they are into us. What bright seething white fire enthusiasm is bred in us—without our help or knowledge a perfect influx into every pore and cell of us fusing, vaporizing, by its heat until the boundary walls of our heavy flesh tabernacle seem taken down and we flow out diffuse into the very air." He said he was converted—no longer a shepherd with a few bruised beans and crackers in his stomach and wrapped in a woolen blanket—"but a free bit of everything."

His focus of interest swept the valley like a young man in love, which he was.

True, he had semi-romantic run-ins with such women as Mrs. Therese Yelverton and Mrs. Elvira James Hutchings, but these could not be his true love. He avoided emotional trappings like serious sickness. He was too full of rock and light and nature-infatuation now, too engrossed with heady camping trips, too fascinated by storms among sequoias and dizzying free-falling waterfalls. His book that grew out of this period, *My First Summer in the Sierra*, tells of bee pastures, watching leaf shadows on rock, shepherding, sleeping on mossy boulders, Indians, life with and without bread, bears, flies, and a hackle-raising glance down a half-mile waterfall of Yosemite Creek. His description of climbing to the lip of Yosemite Falls evinces in many eyes Muir's reckless abandon to wilderness's extreme experiences, the elbow-rubbing with death which, when defied, leaves the climber, the canoeist, the explorer elevated with adrenaline intoxication and closer to a peculiar immutable truth:

> I took off my shoes and stockings and worked my way cautiously down alongside the rushing flood. keeping my feet and hands pressed firmly on the polished rock. The booming, roaring water, rushing past close to my head, was very exciting. I had expected that the sloping apron would terminate with the perpendicular wall of the valley, and that from the foot of it, where it is less steeply inclined, I should be able to lean far enough out to see the forms and behavior of the fall all the way down to the bottom. But I found that there was yet another small brow over which I could not see, and which appeared to be too steep for mortal feet. Scanning it keenly, I discovered a narrow shelf about three inches wide on the very brink, just wide enough for a rest of one's heels. But there seemed to be no way of reaching it over so steep a brow. At length, after careful scrutiny of the surface, I found an irregular edge of a flake of the rock some distance back from the margin of the torrent. If I was to get down to the brink at all that rough edge, which might offer slight fingerholds, was the only way. But the slope beside it looked dangerously smooth and steep, and the swift roaring flood beneath, overhead, and beside me was very nerve-trying. I therefore concluded not to venture further, but did nevertheless. Tufts of artemisia were growing in clefts of the rock near by, and I filled my mouth with the bitter leaves, hoping they might help to prevent giddiness. Then, with a caution not known in ordinary circumstances, crept down safely to the little edge, got my heels well planted on it, then, shuffled in a horizontal direction twenty or thirty feet until close to the out-plunging current, which, by the time it had descended thus far, was already white. Here I obtained a perfectly free view down into the heart of the snowy, chanting throng of comet-like streamers, into which the body of the fall soon separates.

Gazing down a 2,600-foot drop dizzy with white watery motion, the air misty with spray. Barefoot. Chewing artemisia to keep stomach and mind steady. Muir's risky boyhood feats in Dunbar window dormers now served him well. What better apostle could have been sent to Yosemite to extol its wildness and beauty? What better way to get to know its extremes? *On the brink? Fascination willing to endanger life?*

It is certainly not surprising that Muir—by 1870 on a fast track to Yosemite knowledge—come to know the region better than anyone else. Better anyhow than his periodic boss, Jim Hutchings, the Yosemite hotel pioneer and sawmill owner who jealously guarded the dissemination of park information. Better even than Josiah Dwight Whitney, California's official state geologist who, in a controversial rebuttal of Muir's evolving glaciological theories contrary to his own, scorned Muir as a mere "shepherd," and "ignoramus." Biographers like to dwell on the Muir-Whitney affair and for good reason. Besides being a visionary of wilderness values, Muir was a glaciologist, albeit a self-educated one, yet a man who tested book theories by scrambling in ravines and up ridges until his knuckles were red with blood. He wasn't afraid to confront authority diplomatically but steadfastly if he was certain about his ideas. Particularly ideas derived from hands-on experience.

This was precisely the case between 1870 and 1872 when Whitney propounded his theories publicly, and young Muir—clothes torn and beard unbrushed—dissented.

As William Frederic Bade explained it in *The Life and Letters of John Muir*, Whitney was a man of much social stature throughout the late 1860s and early 1870s. In 1865 he was a professor of geology at Harvard and had the backing of the leading geologists of his day. With assistants, Whitney conducted a six-volume topographical, geological and natural history survey of California, titled *Geological Survey of California*. In 1869, Whitney published *The Yosemite Guide-Book*, thereby becoming the foremost scientific authority on subjects pertaining to Yosemite Valley. What irked Muir was that Whitney insisted Yosemite was created not by glacial activity or "ordinary denudation," but due to the caving-in of the valley floor. In other words, the valley's bottom sank to an unknown depth when its support was withdrawn during the region's convulsive creative moments, or shortly thereafter.

"There is no reason to suppose," Whitney averred, "or at least no proof, that glaciers have ever occupied the Valley or any portion of it ... so that this theory [of glacial erosion], based on entire ignorance of the whole subject, may be dropped without wasting any more time on it."

Yet Muir, who had in Madison studied the work of Swiss geologist Louis Agassiz, had seen during his first summer in the Sierra signs of glacial activity. By 1870, he was convinced glaciers, not valley subsidence, had carved out Yosemite. That same year he traveled with geologist Joseph Le Conte (from the University of California) from the crest of the Sierra to Mono Lake, convincing him en route "that the Valley has been wholly formed by causes still in operation in the Sierra—that the Merced Glacier and the Merced River and its branches ... have done the whole work."

Yosemite glaciation obsessed Muir's consciousness for the next four years, and intermittently until 1879, allowing him to say in truth he had spent 10 years studying the origins of Yosemite. "You would not find in me one unglacial thought," he wrote Jeanne Carr in the autumn of 1871. His thoughts were all "ice."

Earlier he had written the "grandeur of [Yosemite's] forces and their glorious results overpower me, and inhabit my whole being. Waking or sleeping I have no rest. In dreams I read blurred sheets of glacial writing or follow lines of cleavage or struggle with the difficulties of some extraordinary rock form." In early October 1872 he climbed more than 24,000 feet in 10 days while studying glaciers, his studies becoming more minute, replete with stakes, ribbons, strings, and measurements of ice movement down to three-sixteenths of an inch. In time Muir discovered more than 65 small glaciers in the Sierra, simultaneously attracting the attention and companionship of notable geologists and scientists of related disciplines: John Daniel Runkle, president of the Massachusetts Institute of Technology (MIT), with whom he traveled in the canyons of Yosemite; Dr. Clinton L. Merriam of the Smithsonian Institution; Professor Samuel Kneeland of MIT; botanist Asa Gray; and Emerson. In 1872, Louis Agassiz responded to one of Muir's letters by saying Muir was "the first man who had any adequate conception of glacial action." Muir inevitably defeated Whitney in what turned out to be a public scientific debate, but so stubborn was Whitney that 10 years after Muir began publishing his glaciological discoveries, Whitney still denied the existence of *any* glaciers in the Sierra-Nevada.

Muir believed the secret to glaciological knowledge was not in books. True, he read current literature on natural history, geology and evolution but hands-on experience is literally what he subscribed to—a preference he later applied to wilderness insight in general. While studying Yosemite's geology he had lived in "so haunting, hovering, floating a way, that it seem[ed] strange to cast any kind of anchor." So he didn't. As far as his ice work was concerned, it was purely physical. All depended on the goodness of one's eyes.

"No scientific book in the world can tell me how this Yosemite granite is put together, or how it has been taken down," he wrote Carr. "Patient observation and constant brooding over the rocks, lying upon them for years as the ice did, is the way to arrive at the truths which are graven so lavishly upon them."

His method of study, he one day told professors of the American Association for the Advancement of Science, was to drift from rock to rock, stream to stream, and to camp wherever night found him. "When I discovered a new plant, I sat down beside it for a minute or a day, to make its acquaintance and hear what it had to tell. When I came to moraines, or ice-scratches upon the rocks, I traced them back, learning what I could of the glaciers that made them."

We live with our heels, he once said, as well as our heads, and most of our pleasure comes in that way.

Muir once slid down an incline on his stomach, letting himself down with his hands—wetted with his tongue and struck flatly upon the rock to make them stick by atmospheric pressure—to feel how ice would have moved downhill with gravity. Such gut-on-rock contact remained the alpha and omega of Muir's cosmology throughout the rest of the nineteenth century.

———————————

Muir's glaciological studies, together with his concomitant and subsequent mountaineering accomplishments, are all the more remarkable in light of how little he used to assist him to reach great heights. Unlike today's mountaineers and wilderness campers, he didn't have the lightweight equipment and proven climbing and camping techniques handed down through a hundred years of trial and error. Nylon tents, down or fiberfill sleeping bags, crampons, small cook stoves, pocket guidebooks and topographic maps were unknown to Muir. In some instances he went without equipment to concentrate on vigor and endurance. At other times he tested what worked for him. And what didn't. His was a personal exploration of possibilities and limitations, a series of brave rediscoveries of what leads to injury and death. And what doesn't.

Biographer Fox has written one of the best, albeit brief, analyses of Muir's camping equipment and techniques, although a full study has yet to be done. When possible, Muir loaded a pony with gear: eight to 10 pounds of bread (his favorite food) or crackers; a few pounds of oatmeal and tea; a pair of thick blankets for sleeping; and two tin cans with wire handles for cooking. Everything was packed in strong canvas bags. Camping clothes, sometimes "tough grey ... the color of granite," consisted of loose-fitting pants of duck or blue denim, a woolen shirt, a broad-brimmed hat, and a vest with pockets filled with instruments—barometer, watch, hand lens and thermometer. Occasionally he carried a clinometer, a tool for measuring angles of slope. Muir rarely wore a coat camping because it cramped his arms, flapped in wind, and snagged on rocks and bushes. He once reached the summit of a 14,000-foot peak at 11 o'clock at night only to end up dancing most of the time until morning because he was cold in his shirtsleeves. Temperature: 22 below.

Muir preferred shoes instead of boots, because boots shrank and expanded when wet without any way of adjusting them, unlike shoes which could be retied. His shoes, moreover, were low with thick soles and round-headed hobnails tied over both instep and ankle with buckskin strings. The sole of such a tight-fitting shoe, Muir thought, acted like an extension of the foot "and we can tell exactly in making a leap where the foot will strike."

If his bread or crackers were smashed while camping, Muir simply ate the crumbs with pinched fingers or like granola. Or, as with his oatmeal, it could be wetted and fried on hot stones into cakes. Tea needn't be steeped: it could be chewed like tobacco, or diluted in the mouth with cold water. At least once he ate venison broiled on coals, for he would eat meat on camping trips if it was provided by someone else. He was not a hunter, although on an early Yosemite trip he shot an owl, which he and a friend ate. (Muir also shot his friend in an accident on the same trip, injuring him slightly.)

It was not unusual for Muir to go 24 hours or more without food. In 1877, on a long trip in the Sierra-Nevadas, he ate only one meal in four days "coupled with the most difficult, nerve-trying work," yet he felt little exhaustion. There didn't seem to be any limit to his endurance. His pack in those early years felt as light as a squirrel's tail; his health was so good he "knew nothing about it." Companions, meanwhile, often had difficulty keeping up with Muir although he seldom ran. He has been described as walking with a long loping stride and with bowed head, searching the ground for plants; when finding one he liked he studied it with a lens, often sitting to conserve his strength, never standing still for long.

Muir enjoyed walking. Sometimes it seemed to him he was walking on "living rock where a distinct electric flash" shot out from each step. Mossy bogs felt soothing and soft to the foot. Night posed no danger to walking. Sometimes he walked with no apparent aim, particularly on short walks, when "adrift on currents gentle and invisible," but most of his saunters had a goal: a mountain, lake, glacier or belt of woods. As a mountaineer he was described as a "human spider."

The steep country above timberline posed its own problems, the first being that Muir had to leave his packhorse behind. Freedom of movement and freedom of extra weight was critical; he was known to strip to his undershorts for ultimate agility. He often left his blankets behind even though he was more than a day's hike from the summit, preferring instead to build nests of branches, boughs and brush near which he would build campfires. He slept little at such bivouacs, freezing on one side and baking on the other, but he eked what rest he could while concentrating on loftier ambitions. He camped as late in the day as possible, and arose with dawn's first light, shortening cold nights at both ends. The idea was to get up and down a mountain's peak in one heady rush. A summit thrust. He was willing to wallow in snow armpit-deep to do this. To go without food. To go alone if necessary (sometimes by preference). Even to place his life in God's hands when his techniques—tested as they were—collided with overwhelming nature.

The closest Muir ever came to a mountaineer's death was probably on California's Mount Shasta. As early as 1874 Shasta had been unkind to Muir, trapping him at timberline in a blizzard for five days. He had climbed the mountain alone, sinking frequently in snow to his shoulders between buried blocks of loose lava, but generally only to his knees. "When tired with walking," he recalled in *Steep Trails*, "I still wallowed slowly upward on all fours." He made the summit, stayed there for two hours, but headed down when wind and clouds made him cold. He reached his coat and camp about dusk, and there hollowed a strip of loose ground in the lee of boulders where firewood was abundant, rolled himself in his blankets, and slept. As the storm roared day after day he contented himself writing in his notebooks, studying the movement of trees when taking snow, watching squirrels and mountain sheep, and examining snow crystals with his hand lens. Never was he uncomfortable or in danger, so it was with mixed feelings that he allowed a guide with horses from the lowlands to "rescue" him after friends below became concerned.

A Shasta death knocked more heartily on Muir's door a year later.

On April 28 he led a survey team to the summit, then two days later climbed back up with one companion, Jerome Fay. A storm hit them on the summit. First came hail, then snow, then the temperature dropped 22 degrees in several minutes to below zero. Lightning flashed in growing darkness. Thunder growled as they hiked a dangerous ridge for a mile. Muir wanted to descend to camp but Fay, who knew less about mountain weather, feared going on. They argued, both were adamant, but Muir refused to leave Fay because he felt responsible for Fay's peril.

Fay—"wavering and struggling to resist being carried away" by the wind "as if he were fording a rapid stream"—led the way back to the summit's hot springs. The idea was to bivouac at the hot springs using its heat to stay as warm as possible. Muir worried about the spring's acid gases and how they would make it back to camp with soaked clothes once the storm was over.

Snow fell two feet deep in several hours.

The duo, bonded by fate, lay on their backs during the storm to present as little body surface as possible to the wind and to let the snow drift over them. Soon the snow froze stiff. As skies cleared the men were doomed to spend the night.

"When the heat became unendurable," Muir recalled, "on some spot where steam was escaping through the sludge, we tried to stop it with snow and mud, or shifted a little at a time by shoving with our heels; for to stand in blank exposure to the fearful wind in our frozen-and-broiled condition seemed certain death. The acrid incrustations sublimed from the escaping gases frequently gave way, opening new vents to scald us; and, fearing that if at any time the wind should fail, carbonic acid, which often formed a considerable portion of the gaseous exhalation of volcanoes, might collect in sufficient quantities to cause sleep and death, I warned Jerome against forgetting himself for a single moment, even should his sufferings admit of such a thing."

With life but a dim fire within them, they called to each other throughout the night. Hours dragged on. In dreamy stupors they imagined themselves surrounded by resinous logs perfect for campfires. Their bodies—except for the eyes—seemed dead, so encrusted and immovable were they by ice. Thirteen, then 14 hours passed. Suddenly sun appeared, its light creeping up Shasta's slope, promising life. When the sunlight reached them, Muir despite frozen feet and a numb arm lurched down the mountain with Fay behind him. It was May 1. Soon they met mounted help sent from a nearby hotel. There was hot sun in the lowlands. No snow.

Muir, who had been helped onto his horse, was now helped into a bed to recuperate. As he lay there gazing through windows and poplar leaves at snow-coned Shasta, the hotel keeper's children brought him spruce boughs for his pillow and handfuls of lilies to scatter across his bed. Muir healed and soon felt radiant, but not without thawing to a resurrected sense of life as gift.

IV

Ironically, wilderness contact provided grist for Muir's emerging literary mill. It was a mill he denied at first, later publicly denounced, yet one which nevertheless became so absorbing—the writing and selling and publishing of words—it became his chief occupation as a wilderness preservationist. So immersed in writing did he become that in 1899 when he was invited on an expenses-paid trip to Alaska, he nearly turned it down because he was busy writing a book about national parks. Surely he had by then recognized the power of the pen: how it could educate, inspire, preserve, and arouse public opinion.

He went to Alaska, preferring glaciers to grammar, but not without knowing full well he would one day write about what he learned there. Which he did.

Muir, who had sent rhymed letters and poems to young friends as a boy, developed a facility for words by the time he wrote his *Thousand-mile Walk* journal. The journal offers glimpses of the alliterative beauty, the rolling of vowels and letters off the literary tongue, arrived at by a writer only through practice, much reading and the almost unconscious habit of putting experiences into words whether or not they are actually written down. When Muir reached the Gulf of Mexico, for example, he was reminded of the "dulse and tangle, long-winged gulls, the Bass Rock in the Firth of Forth, and the old castle, schools churches, and long country rambles..." The surf on the shores of Cuba was "one great song sounding forever all around the white-blooming shores of the world." Shortly thereafter, during his first summer in the Sierra, his journal notes included the vivid Yosemite Falls incident. He was also writing voluminous letters to Jeanne Carr once or twice a month (as he had been since his solitary ramblings in Ontario), letters home, letters to Catharine Merrill and letters to scientists. Letters seemed to focus Muir's thoughts, define his ambitions and character, and condense his journal jottings into nuggets, albeit weighty, of what he was doing, learning and wishing.

Regardless of where Muir's writing is actually taprooted, it blossomed into publication in 1871 on the heels of his glacier studies. "Some of my friends," he wrote Carr on September 8, "are badgering me to write for some of the magazines, and I am almost tempted to try it." He was afraid, however, that magazine writing would distract him from his main work even more so than the "depressing labor of the mill or guiding [tourists, which he sometimes did]." He nevertheless supposed that perhaps what he should do is "give some of the journals my first thoughts about this glacier work," then later gather them together into a book "for the Boston wise." It was an optimistic approach yet, as it turned out, a realistic one. His first article, "Yosemite Glaciers," was published in the prestigious *New York Tribune* the following December. Two more articles followed in the same journal. The indefatigable Jeanne Carr made arrangements the following spring for Muir to write a series of glacier articles for the *Overland Monthly*: ditto for *Atlantic Monthly*. He didn't seem to know what a rejection slip was as he earned $150 to $200 checks. "My life work is now before me plain enough," he wrote in September 1872, referring to his writing. Soon writing about his glacier studies was the most important thing in his life. He visited Oakland for 10 months, returned to Yosemite for a long backcountry trip, then settled down with Mary and John Swett in San Francisco—a kind of base camp for the next four years.

Muir continued to struggle with his writing. He always would. But now the difficulty of working with words seemed especially acute. He strove for perfection and was pained for it. He complained of having a limited vocabulary, of writing slowly, and of the sticky nature of words themselves. Words sometimes seemed dead, bony, and rattling in his teeth: "Can't get a reasonably likely picture off my hands. Everything is so inseparably united. As soon as one begins to describe a flower or a tree or a storm or an Indian or a chipmunk, up jumps the whole heaven and earth and God himself..." Most

English words, he lamented, were made of mud for muddy purposes, "while those invented to contain spiritual matter are doubtful and unfixed in capacity and form, as wind-ridden mist-rags." He nevertheless persisted, scratching out and rewriting, chipping toward polished prose with the same determination he once summoned to chisel the Hickory Hill Farm well.

It took a month, Muir complained, to write a chapter someone could read in an hour.

Muir finished his glacier articles in September 1874; they appeared first in the *Overland Monthly*, then later in a book, *Studies in the Sierra*. This was the magnum opus of his Yosemite years, says biographer Michael Cohen: Muir's first and last attempt to write a scientific book. En route Muir realized something about writing he couldn't have learned another way: if he was going to write—and he wanted to, and would—he would do it "only to entice people to look at Nature's loveliness. My own special self is nothing."

Wind-ridden mist-rag words would have to do.

———————

Muir's life changed drastically after his Yosemite novitiate. While living with the Swetts in San Francisco he began making adjustments, albeit begrudgingly, to city life. There were social gatherings. French cooking. Good wines. Even the best tobacco. Civilization set its hooks in him with increasing firmness until, as biographer T.H. Watkins has noted, "he was like a great, fighting salmon, running the line to its limits but never again free." Periodic forays into new wilderness areas helped relieve the transition. In May 1877 he toured Utah's Wasatch Range before dropping down to Great Salt Lake's valley. He visited Lake Tahoe, southern California's San Gabriel Mountains and the Santa Cruz Mountains where he inventoried what was happening to coastal redwoods. That fall he floated down the Merced and San Joaquin rivers in a rowboat until reaching the confluence of the Sacramento River with the San Joaquin. The following summer was spent with a U.S. Coast and Geodetic Survey team in Nevada.

He was moving willy-nilly, never knowing from one month to the next where he was going to end up.

Beneath Muir's physical restlessness was new ideological thunder, a foreboding recognition that the wilderness he loved—Yosemite, Hetch Hetchy Valley, the groves of coastal redwoods—was being changed irrevocably by man. Not only couldn't he forecast his own movements but he was beginning to wonder what he should *believe*. How should he respond to attacks on his sacred areas? Why should he *care*? What—for him, and for everyone—was being lost?

Perhaps he recalled the freedom and joy, almost rapture, he had felt in the wide open spaces of Wisconsin and now in the Sierras and neighboring wild ranges. Perhaps he recalled how one June day in the mountains his body had felt like a "flesh-and-bone tabernacle ... transparent as glass" to the beauty around him "as if truly an inseparable part of it, thrilling with the air and trees, streams and rocks, in the waves of the sun,—a part of all nature, neither old nor young, sick nor well, but immortal." Country air was clean; city air comparatively foul. In the mountains was ease of movement; in cities were gates, walls, curbs, fences, *No Trespassing* signs, and people—desperate for time and status—groveling for money everywhere. Nature offered freedom from schedules, customs, mores, fashion, expectations; it presented opportunity to find oneself crystallized and brimming with colors, scents, motions and the fluidity of unclocked day/night/day. Did not God pervade such joy? Wasn't the pulsating energy in sequoia, bear, butterfly and bee buzzing with love in receptive souls?

Muir felt earth change. Perpetually. It flowed like a river.

"This grand show is eternal," he cheered. "It is always sunrise somewhere; the dew is never all dried at once; a shower is forever falling; vapor is ever rising. Eternal sunrise, eternal sunset, eternal dawn and gloaming, on sea and continents and islands, each in its turn, as the round earth rolls."

Muir, whether he admitted it or not, had learned how to write. And when he was aware of the round earth rolling, of this eternal grand show forever rising—when he sensed and intuited it most intensely—it flooded him like a wave. Nature, he said, *fountained*. It gushed up in him. It streamed outward within him from some mysterious core to wash receptive senses and gather them into exquisite feelings. Like a tidal surge returning to the sea. The fountainhead itself? It was loaded with aesthetic silt. Throughout all was fluid natural beauty—Muir's synonym for God. How could he ever reduce beauty/God to words? Yet his spirit would be dead without it.

He suspected the same of everyone.

Vision, hence, coupled with the joy evoked by beauty, is what Muir lost as some of his favorite haunts were overrun by sheep. "Hoofed locusts," he called sheep. They destroyed flowered meadows as if sweeping them with fire. Elsewhere, sequoia were being clean cut: North America's oldest living things razed for lumber by a march of loggers, and the consumers behind them, who believed—as did some of the leading scientists of the time—that such trees were destined for mankind's ax. What had happened in America's East, the logging, plowing, mining and developing, now knocked on the door of the Pacific Coast, where some of the continent's last forest sanctuaries soughed in eternal winds.

"The great wilds of our country," Muir cried in *Steep Trails*, "once held to be boundless and inexhaustible, are being rapidly invaded and overrun in every direction, and everything destructible in them is being destroyed. How far destruction may go it is not easy to guess."

But he did guess, and what he feared most was man's attitude. The unquestioning self-righteousness, the intellectually ensconced manifest destiny, the assumption, for Christ's sake, that nature was adorned to fall to Lord Man, and that wildernesses like Yosemite were created for his taming. Pastoralism had become the American ideal whether landscapes were industrial with factories or rural with cattle. Where were people who appreciated nature for its own sake? They were few. This terrified Muir whose ground of being, nature, was being raped.

If wild areas were to be saved from Lord Man's saw and sheep in favor of aesthetic stimulation and psychological wholeness, then cultural assumptions would have to change. This, Muir realized, might be done in two ways: 1) Entice people, as he already knew, to recreate (almost compulsorily) out-doors, and 2) coax government via the media to manage—if possible pre-serve—natural areas. This, biographer Cohen noted, was "institutionalized "stewardship," but what else would work? Shouldn't places like Mount Shasta, Muir asked, be set apart like Yellowstone and Yosemite as national parks "for the welfare and benefit of all mankind, preserving its fountains and forests, and all its glad life in primeval beauty?... No private right or interest need suffer, and thousands yet unborn would come from far and near and bless the country for its wise and benevolent forethought."

V

Just as Muir's program for preservation began to become clear there came another tug on the line on which he salmoned. He had fallen in love. Matchmaker Jeanne Carr, who already had introduced Muir to most of his best friends, had introduced him to a Dr. and Mrs. John Theophile Strentzel, and their daughter, Louie (Louisiana) Wanda, in 1874. But Muir, always wary of romance, had relegated his social instincts to Louie's parents, notably Dr. John. He was from Poland, was educated in horticulture and medicine, and had emigrated to North America to avoid being drafted into the Russian army. He and his Texan wife moved to California in 1849, where they became large land owners and fruit-raisers in Contra Costa County. Muir held an active correspondence with both of Louie's parents; only slowly did he begin to court their daughter.

After writing to Jeanne Carr about an early visit to the Strentzel ranch, Carr responded by asking him if he had seen anyone besides Dr. John. "Well, yes," Muir replied, "there was a young lady in the house." The young lady had dark hair and gray eyes, and was nine years younger than Muir. She was the Strentzels' only child. A homebody, she rarely traveled, content to visit San Francisco occasionally but happiest beneath the parental umbrella of her father's Martinez ranch. She had, however, graduated from Miss Atkins' Young Ladies' Seminary at Benicia (Mills College at Oakland) where she had become an exceptionally good pianist. Friends advised her to become pro-fessional. No way, she said. Home was too precious. There she could bask in the aura of her millionaire father and her mother who, in reading some of Muir's articles before meeting him, wrote in her journal:

"How I should love to become acquainted with a person who writes as he does. What is wealth compared to a mind like his!"

Not until 1877 did Muir take the Strentzels up on their three-year-old invitation to visit. He was on a roll of trips, that Utah-Nevada-coastal California loop cited earlier which led him to the San Joaquin River. Rivers, he believed, made "the most charming of travels. As the life-blood of the landscapes, the best of the wilderness comes to their banks and not one dull passage is found in all their eventful histories." His first descent of a California river was down the Sacramento in a skiff called "Snagjumper," a trip of five days spent rowing and drifting. Later that year, after hiking in Kings River mountain country, he built a small boat out of gnarled, sun-twisted fencing, nails, and a stone hammer. This he launched into the Merced River. He floated to, then down, the San Joaquin.

Muir's destination?

Martinez and the Strentzel ranch.

It took him two weeks to cover the 250 miles of the San Joaquin but the end result, besides familiarity with new country, was a "pure white bed" and "fruity table." His compass was leaning a few degrees toward romance. Talks, walks and gifts were shared with Louie.

Late one night in 1879, just before his first trip to Alaska, Muir met with Louie to ask a question big as gold. The elder Strentzels, having welcomed him "home" after being in a series of controversial glacier lectures, went to bed early. About midnight, after Louie met with Muir, she knelt beside her mother's bed. Her mother, restless, heard her daughter whisper: "All's well, Mother. All's well, and I'm so happy."

Muir was 42 when he married Louie Wanda in 1880, an event which continues to divide biographers as to its reasons and results. He was that year, in his own words, "the happiest man I ever saw." Fox says Muir married not for love but for stability, children (he would have two daughters), and a permanent home. Having $5,000 in his savings account, Muir didn't need Louie's likely inheritance, so financial interests seem moot. He wasn't looking for a travel partner; his sole trip to Yosemite or any place wild with Louie cost $500, an investment he never again duplicated. Records show Muir had felt guilty for remaining single; Mormon wives in Utah had teased him for not having children, and often, while living with friends such as Swetts, he felt like everyone's stepbrother.

Yet something deeper than social comfort propelled Muir toward and through his only marriage. He had found a soul mate. Not only would Louie critique everything he wrote, she would encourage him in his glacier studies and wilderness wanderings. His trips, particularly when she was pregnant the first time, pained her, but never did her apparent love seek to hold him back, to tie him down on her couch, piano bench, or in her flower gardens. She even refused to play her beloved piano if Muir was upstairs writing. Louie came to know Muir better than anyone, and it was she who spearheaded the end of his ranch work when, after 10 years of it, it began to rot his health.

It's hard to tell just what Muir was trying to prove at the Strentzel ranch. He wanted to make a living for his wife and daughters, and he wanted to make money, but the fury with which he threw himself into ranching indicates some less obvious compulsions. There was the challenge of working with plants; as a ranch manager, Muir supervised 15-40 people, and he also grafted Dr. Strentzel's experimental pears and grapes with Bartletts and Tokays, which instantly increased ranch profits. There was, perhaps, the excitement of having a home... a base camp, he wrote Asa Gray, where he could store burs and grass. There was the novelty of a loving wife, and daughters to take on walks through flowering orchards. His life now had an axis. Thoreau would have called it an anchor. Still, why the work and strain to exhaustion?

Muir rose at six o'clock during the busiest time of the orchard seasons, worked through the day, then went to bed at nine when he would read until midnight. He was turning down an editor's request for articles in 1883, claiming he was "lost and choked in agricultural needs." From 1885 to 1888 he didn't step foot in wild country. He developed nervous indigestion and a bronchial cough. His weight dropped to 100 pounds, frighteningly low for a man five feet, ten inches tall. Muir the mountaineer became Muir the coughing driven rancher. Some dawns found him driving a buggy to the Martinez bank where he brought a large white bag marked "Laundry." He was, of course, feeding a savings account. But why one so large? Why several? One account of $50,000 he wouldn't touch in his lifetime. (For 21 years he sent $100 annually back to his native city of Dunbar, Scotland, for the poor.) Other accounts totaled $100,000 to $250,000 in 10 years. Muir, the orchard perfectionist, insisted every acre produce as much as possible, yet slowly he was really perfecting what amounted to a beeline to wealthy mortality.

What kept him going?

Alaska. The Great Land. His few trips to Alaska in the early and late 1880s kept his health and enthusiasm for wildness alive. This, for John Muir, made all the difference in the world.

———— ——

Muir eventually made five trips to Alaska to study its coastal glaciers. There, where he became known as the "Great Ice Chief" by natives, he was the first white man to see much of what today is prime tourism country, places like the glacial fjords of Glacier Bay National Park in southeastern Alaska (where Muir Glacier is today named after him).

Alaska meant other adventures for Muir. In 1880, on his second trip to Alaska, he told two prospectors where he thought gold could be found based on the region's geology. Joe Juneau and Joe Harris took Muir's advice, and several years later the boomtown of Juneau was making headline news. In 1881, Muir joined the crew of the *Thomas Corwin* to the Arctic Circle to search for the *Jeanette* which, with 33 men, had left in 1879 to find the North Pole. The *Thomas Corwin* never did find the Jeannette, for it had sunk and most of its crew perished during an on-land search for help. Yet Muir, during the Corwin's trip, became one of the first men to step foot on Wrangel Island. Much of Muir's first three Alaska trips was spent shipboard, but occasionally he abandoned steamship and company comforts to feel again nature's wildness and danger as with the dog Stickeen on Taylor Glacier in 1880.

A new side of Muir's personality began to emerge during these Alaskan trips. He began taking what his companions thought were unnecessary risks. He felt, however, that there was a benevolent spirit with him, one which intuitively warned him to back off if he was in imminent peril. Call it a sixth sense. Muir had it all his life.

Once in Yosemite he felt the presence of one of his old Madison professors, Dr. Butler; the next day Muir hiked down from the heights to find and surprise his old teacher. In 1885 when John's father died, he had had a premonition his father wasn't well. John journeyed home and was at Daniel's bedside—his father's "wanderer" come home—when the old apostle died. Muir also had premonitions of his mother's death. And once, when suffering up a mountain peak for two days, he felt near the peak that he mustn't continue upward. That he must turn back. So strong was the sensation he didn't question it and for once he failed to make a summit. Again, on Mt. Ritter, he had felt instinct or spirit come to his aid when he was caught on a granite cliff; his senses had been heightened and clarified, and he scurried out of his trapped situation with a skill and surety he hadn't known before.

Good luck, Muir felt, always traveled with him. Things worked in his favor. Still it was rarely easy for him to convince wilderness companions they need fear nothing when the going got tough.

His 1879 trip to Alaska is an excellent case in point. His journey included a month canoe expedition with southeastern Alaska Indians to and from Glacier Bay country. With Muir was an Indian chief, Toyatte, who rode stern, gave directions and chose campsites with an old-timer's practiced eye. Muir, however, often tried to override Toyatte's decision, and when he succeeded he often led the canoe crew into close escapes. Once they almost wrecked the boat on a rock, thinking it was the back of a whale. Soon thereafter, they nearly capsized on a sandbar. Both incidents could have been prevented if Muir would have heeded the chief's choice of campsites.

Muir's stubbornness and good luck reached a crescendo near Cape Fanshawe, when he again ignored Toyatte's advice to pull over and camp; soon wind and waves were propelling the canoe toward a storm-lashed reef.

Toyatte wanted to go around, or at least try to.

"Go across, go across!" Muir yelled.

"Very well," came Toyatte's irritated reply. "If we die, you die too."

Just when the canoe reached the reef a large wave lifted them up and over past danger. Muir had been right, but the old chief still gave him hell. Not only did Toyatte think Muir must be a witch to seek knowledge in glacier country in miserable weather, but he was convinced Muir was wrong in risking the lives of others.

Such adventures nevertheless brought Muir's spirit back to life, resurrecting it from ranching. At times in Alaska he was too thrilled to sleep at night. A letter to Louie written while journeying on the *Corwin* in 1881 indicates well how wildness revitalized Muir's writing, and how beauty burst in upon him to soak his eyes with veils of light:

> The Storm King of the North is again up and doing, rolling white, comb-

ing waves through the jagged straits between this marvelous chain of islands [near Unalaska], circling them about with beaten, updashing foam, and piling yet more and more snow on the clustering cloud-wrapped peaks. But we are safe and snug in this land-locked haven enjoying the distant storm-roar of wave and wind ... It is snowing still and the deep base of the gale is sounding on through the mountains. How weird and wild and fascinating all this hearty work of the storm is for me. I feel a strange love of it all, as I gaze shivering up the dim white slopes as through a veil darkly, becoming fainter and fainter as the flakes thicken and at length hide all the land.

Louie Wanda had the wonderful sense to recognize what wilderness adventure did to her husband.

"A ranch," she wrote her husband while he was gone, "that needs and takes the sacrifice of a noble life, or work, ought to be flung away beyond all reach and power for harm. The Alaska book and the Yosemite book, dear John, must be written, and you need to be your own self, well and strong, to make them worthy of you."

Nothing, she felt, was more important than Muir's writing and the experiences which gave him vision and strength. Nothing but the welfare of their children. Muir's squirreling away of money—enough for his family and their travels for the rest of their lives—took care of that.

VI

In realizing how wild nature revitalized his health and spirit, and by believing it had similar effects on other people, Muir was ready to begin work to preserve wild areas in 1889. The concept of wilderness preservation, although still novel in America, was familiar to Muir. He had read in Thoreau's *Maine Woods* almost 20 years earlier of Thoreau's envisioned national reserves of wilderness. Shortly after leaving Wisconsin, Muir tried to persuade his brother-in-law to set aside *carex* meadows on the old Muir farm as a kind of miniature personal reserve of Wisconsin wilderness flora. But now Muir was ripe to work on a national scale. The redwoods, too big to saw, were being dynamited to the ground, much of the wood lost as waste. Elsewhere sheep were foraging through virgin mountain meadows. Where horseback riders once rode their steeds belly-deep in flowers, now was little but stubble and rock; this allowed rain—once held back by dense vegetation—to flow fast and erosive into streams and rivers.

Wild America, even on the mountainous shores of the Pacific, faced eventual destruction. Muir took it personally.

The key to Muir's most effective wilderness preservation work came, not surprisingly, from the East in the person of Robert Underwood Johnson. As editor of *Century* magazine (successor to *Scribner's* for which Muir had written in the 1870s), Johnson relaunched Muir on a literary career while simultaneously making him a national celebrity. Johnson was of that rare breed most content editing and publishing. He cultivated, coaxed and cajoled many of the best minds of his day: Walt Whitman, John Burroughs, Nikola Tesla,

Mark Twain and Theodore Roosevelt. Under Johnson and his boss, Richard Watson Gilder, *Century* boasted a circulation of over 200,000. It also paid top-dollar to its writers. When Johnson journeyed to California in 1889 to solicit manuscripts about the state's gold rush, he inadvertently ran into Muir. Muir, in turn, became Johnson's "great discovery."

"Johnson, Johnson, where are you?" Muir called down the corridors of San Francisco's Palace Hotel when they had arranged to meet.

Although late, Muir let loose a characteristic stream of verbiage when he found Johnson's room.

"I can't make my way through these confounded artificial canyons," he explained, playing up his role of wilderness personality. "There is nothing here to tell you where to go. Now, if you were up in the Sierra, every tree and mound and scratch on the cliff would give you your directions. Everything there is as plain as a signpost, but here, how is one to know?"

Johnson might have chuckled at Muir's humor, perhaps even found it crude by eastern genteel standards, but he allowed Muir to guide him on a trip of several days into Yosemite. With three burros and a cook, they traveled in June to Soda Springs in Tuolumne Meadows and Wawona Ridge, where Muir had parted with Emerson. Muir showered Johnson with "little attentions" at night, tucking him in his blankets around the campfire where they lay and talked revealing, Johnson noted, their "inmost selves." It became apparent to Johnson that Muir loved the region "as a mother loves her child," and during their time together Muir began to seem larger than life. Johnson remembered him looking like "John the Baptist, as portrayed in bronze by Donatello and others of the Renaissance sculptors. He was spare of frame, full-bearded, hardy, keen of eye and visage, and on the march eager of movement. It was difficult for an untrained walker to keep up with him as he leaped from rock to rock as surely as a mountain goat, or skimmed along the surface of the ground... If he ever became tired nobody knew it." John the Mountain Baptist must have looked the wild part in the campfire glow beneath redwood boughs crowned beyond with stars, a soft plant hum breezing through the loftiest sequoia branches, yet it was a role Muir was game to play. In part the role was true. In part magnified. Maybe Muir realized exaggeration and imagination were sometimes more effective than straight-line reality in getting a point across. His point was coming, as was Johnson's, as each studied the other on Muir's home turf.

"No weather," Johnson continued in his autobiography, *Remembered Yesterdays*, "no condition of wilderness, no absence of animal life could make Muir lonely ... To some, beauty seems but an accident of creation; to Muir it was the very smile of God ... The love of nature was his religion."

With these romantic responses to Muir's visage stirring in Johnson like sequoia coals, the point of their trip and friendship ignited into the light of day. Johnson, like Muir, wanted to create a Yosemite National Park patterned after Yellowstone National Park, which Congress had established in 1872. Johnson's strategy was simple. He wanted Muir to write two articles for *Century*, the first on "The Treasures of Yosemite" to attract general attention, the second on "The Proposed Yosemite National Park," outlining boundaries.

With these articles in hand, together with illustrations, Johnson intended to advocate the park's establishment before the committee on Public Lands.

Muir wrote the articles after persistent persuasion on Johnson's part, Johnson followed through with Washington legwork, and the park became a reality on October 1, 1890. The duo pulled off a double-header 15 years later when they successfully fought to return Yosemite Valley to the federal government, to be included in the Park. Unlike Yellowstone National Park, which had originally been set aside as a kind of freak show of curious natural phenomena like boiling springs and geysers, Yosemite became the first preserve deliberately set aside to protect wilderness. Muir's sense of beauty, his love of light, and the prose with which he strained to explain and share it had provoked at least eastern sensibilities to take stock of nature's intangible values.

It was a small beginning for wilderness preservation. But a beginning nevertheless.

Trees, together with the magnificent forests of the Pacific slope, filled Muir's mind in the early 1890s as he continued to broaden his travels and backcountry experiences. He was a lover of plants, a botanist at heart, and nothing better appealed to his sense of beauty than trees: the climax of the botanical world. He watched trees sway like temple pillars above him as he lay on his back. He climbed trees in storms to sense their motion, life and orbits. He slept in the hollowed trunks of them, watched them glow like orange iron bars on hillsides after forest fires, and he made pilgrimages to them in Wisconsin, Florida, Ontario, Nevada, and throughout California. Even in 1911, when he fulfilled a lifelong dream by going to South America, he went 500 miles out of his way looking for the monkey-puzzle tree (*Araucaria imbricata*); near the snow line of the Andes he found a forest of them, where he camped in a grove with the strange, gangly trees surrounding him on all sides. Two companions slept in a tent and Muir, 73, slept under the stars to be with the trees. There was magic in that Andes forest— a snow line satiation.

Didn't he believe the "clearest way into the Universe was through a forest wilderness"? Not desert wilderness. Not lake country wilderness. Not even glacier wilderness. Tree country. And when it came to tree country, Muir reasoned (despite his night in the Andes), America's virgin forests were second to none.

It was with special interest, therefore, that Muir witnessed the birth of the U.S. Forest Service, a birth that was slow in coming and in which Muir would play an influential role. The ball began rolling in 1891 when president Benjamin Harrison used the Forest Reserve Act to set aside 15 forest reserves totaling 13 million acres. Muir had promoted such a scheme as early as 1875 after seeing much waste and too much cutting and running, but he realized legislation protecting forests would be long in coming. As late as 1895 he still felt government protection "should be thrown around every wild grove and forest on the mountains, as it is around every private orchard, and the trees in public parks. To say nothing of their value as fountains of timber, they are worth infinitely more than all the gardens and parks of towns." Partly due to Muir's media instigation, and due in part to the influence of Gifford Pinchot, Charles S. Sargent, and *Century*'s Johnson, a National Forestry Commission was appointed in 1896 to survey the timber reserves of the nation and to recommend a program of forest management to Congress. Muir was made an ex-officio member and traveled with the commission through much of the West.

Perhaps Muir couldn't foresee what was happening within the commission's ranks as they toured Montana, Wyoming, Washington, Oregon, Arizona, and several other southwestern states. As for himself, he thought his role with the commission gave him an opportunity to formulate a policy to preserve American wilderness; yet, he also began to sense another group sentiment favoring forest and wilderness use. Pinchot, the nation's first trained forester and destined to head the U.S. Forest Service in 1905, was already championing forests as resources. Forests as crops. He and his associates were interested in the economic value of timber stands and only secondarily their aesthetic value. Muir, meanwhile, championed beauty. Aesthetics was his middle name. And as he and Sargent began to discern the Pinchot school's monetary motives, a gap was clearly growing among conservationists themselves: some wanted to conserve forests for sustained yields while others, such as Muir, felt there was an equal if not higher value: preserve forest beauty for sustained *aesthetic* yields.

The commission's report was issued in 1897 and, although divided on aims and forest use, made four salient recommendations to Congress:

—repeal and/or modify various timber and mining laws detrimental to the nation's forest;

—create 13 new forest reserves in eight states;

—manage those forests to maintain a sustained yield;

—and create two new national parks, the Grand Canyon and Mt. Rainier.

Muir was supposedly responsible for the report's position forbidding grazing on reserve land, which prior to the report was the primary commercial use of the forests.

Muir: On Saving Trees

"Any fool can destroy trees," Muir wrote during the national brouhaha surrounding the Forestry Commission's recommendation to establish forest reserves. "They cannot run away; and if they could, they would still be destroyed,—chased and hunted down as long as fun or a dollar could be got out of their bark hides, branching horns, or magnificent bole backbones. Few that fell trees plant them; nor would planting avail much

> *towards getting back anything like the noble primeval forests.*
> *During a man's life only saplings can be grown, in the place of*
> *the old trees—tens of centuries old—that have been destroyed. It*
> *took more than three thousand years to make some of the trees*
> *in these Western woods,—trees that are still standing in perfect*
> *strength and beauty, waving and singing in the mighty forest*
> *of the Sierra... Through all the wonderful, eventful centuries...*
> *God has cared for these trees, saved them from drought, disease,*
> *avalanches, and a thousand straining, leveling tempests and*
> *floods; but he cannot save them from fools,—only Uncle Sam*
> *can do that."*
>
> —*Our National Parks*

President Grover Cleveland followed up on the Commission's recommendation in 1897 by creating the 13 reserves of 21 million acres, but the embers of legislative forest fires were just beginning to be fanned by controversial winds.

Pinchot had signed the report grudgingly and began immediately to correct politically what he viewed as report errors. Help came from the new President, McKinley, who suppressed the report, and also by the McCrae-Pettigrew Bill, which sought to open the reserves to grazing. Pinchot approved of the McCrae-Pettigrew Bill and with his support the bill passed Congress. He had, after all, fallen out with Muir when in the summer of 1897 they had both been embarrassed in an incident at a Seattle hotel. Apparently Pinchot had told the Seattle press grazing should be allowed in the national forests; seeing Pinchot in a hotel lobby, Muir walked up to him and shook a newspaper in his face.

"Are you correctly quoted here?" Muir asked sternly.

When Pinchot admitted guilt, Muir said he wanted nothing more to do with him. A year earlier Pinchot had agreed with Muir that, yes, sheep *did* do much harm to forest meadows.

Muir biographers are well aware that here, in a quarrel over forest grazing, much more was at stake than a friendship. The incident manifested an inevitable crack among conservationists, a break in the way they viewed nature: use versus preservation. The same division had become apparent in the Forestry Commission, and to some extent Thoreau had sensed it 40 years earlier. But what was once a crack in the weave of conservation now became an irreparable rent. Muir had admitted in the mid-1890s that the national forests would be used to produce timber "selectively cut," but he now was beginning to realize that wilderness was not compatible with the economic, scientific management of forests. You either have a natural meadow filled with indigenous wildflowers, or you have an ecologically changed meadow pocked with sheep dung and peppered with second-growth flora. On the one hand you have 300-foot virgin sequoias, or you have chin-high saplings. As historian Nash says, "Forestry seemed so much of an improvement on unregulated lumbering practices that he [Muir] did not immediately see its incompatibility with wilderness preservation." Now he did.

His old feeling that a forest was so complete in itself that it seemed almost sacrilegious to move a dead limb or log now returned to taunt him. Muir had long vacillated between utilitarian conservation and preservation; now he chose the latter. He had appealed all along to something deeper than board feet and pocketbooks. Something deeper than glorified farming. So, in 1897 when Congress passed the Forest Management Act, which mandated that reserves would be used to furnish the nation with a continuous supply of timber, it was clear to Muir that what he wanted to protect lay—at least temporarily—outside the scope of the forest reserves he had fought for. He now had nowhere to turn to implement his mature ideology except to his books, and back to the nation's gestating national park system.

VII

Although Muir was swept up in the forestry issue throughout most of the 1890s, he was also busy with other matters. In 1892, in the wake of some coaxing by the *Century*'s Johnson, Muir helped organize the Sierra Club. The club was dedicated to the exploration, enjoyment, and preservation of the Sierra-Nevada Mountains, and it elected Muir its first president, a position he kept for 22 years until his death. The Sierra Club remained small during Muir's reign despite its popular outings program, but it would continue to grow as a result of his ideals and inspiration throughout the twentieth century until its membership topped 300,000. By the mid-1980s, the club was a major lobbying force in every important wilderness and environmental battle in America, from the Forest Service roadless area regulations to wolf protection to the National Alaska Lands bill. In the beginning, however, the club restricted itself to pressing Sierra-Nevada wilderness issues and to disseminating information about the mountain regions of the Pacific Coast.

In 1893 Muir ventured East, first to Boston and New York then to Scotland. While in New England he and Johnson made a pilgrimage to the graves of Emerson and Thoreau near Concord, Massachusetts. There Muir—who late in life found Thoreau's writings wisest of all his favorite writers—was impressed not only by the graveyard where he laid flowers on Thoreau's and Emerson's graves but also by Walden Pond. The pond, he wrote home to Louie, was like a "bright dark eye in wooded hills... No wonder Thoreau lived here two years. I could have enjoyed living here 200 years or 2,000."

On Emerson's grave was a large boulder of white quartz, and there perhaps Muir recalled Emerson at Yosemite's Mariposa Grove, how he had stopped on his horse to turn and wave farewell, his body now lying beneath a rugged, angular tombstone as if dropped there by a glacier.

Soon afterwards Muir was visiting the living: Sargent, the botanist; Nikola Tesla, Mark Twain, Rudyard Kipling, Gifford Pinchot's father, and then a man with whom he would often be compared: John Burroughs.

Burroughs—sometimes called the "Seer of Slabsides" based on the name of one of his cabin retreats—was nationally known as a literary naturalist when Muir knocked on his door. He was born in 1837, one year before Muir, and was 25 when Thoreau died. ("I'm not worthy to tie Thoreau's shoes," Burroughs penned in 1910; he also felt *Walden* was the best book of its kind in English literature.) New York's Hudson River and Catskill Mountains were home to Burroughs like the Sierra-Nevadas were home to Muir. But Burroughs liked to "import the world" rather than leave his home territory to roam the ranges. Not only did he believe "a rolling stone gathers no moss, and a little moss is a good thing on a man" giving him flavor and coloring, but he thought nature would *come to him*; that is, he didn't go to nature to be taught, but liked to learn about it passively, almost unconsciously while camping, fishing or being idle for "all things come to those who wait, because all things are on the move, and are sure sooner or later to come your way."

Burroughs, however, had more than regional moss. He could write. When his essay, "Expression," was mistaken for the work of Emerson in 1860, his literary career was launched.

When Muir met Burroughs, the latter already had eight of his eventual 20 books published including *Wake Robin* (1871), *Winter Sunshine* (1875), *Birds and Poets* (1877), *Fresh Fields* (1884) and *Indoor Studies* (1889). Burroughs was a lifelong friend of poet Walt Whitman with whom he had often camped in secluded coves. In fact, it was after attending a Walt Whitman Club dinner that Burroughs met Muir. Burroughs had a slight hangover so neither man impressed the other, although Burroughs noted in his journal that Muir seemed to have "the Western look upon him."

Burroughs elaborated on Muir later that month and again in 1896:

> A very interesting man; a little prolix at times. You must not be in a hurry, or have any pressing duty, when you start his stream of talk and adventure. Ask him to tell you his famous dog story (Stickeen) and you get the whole theory of glaciation thrown in. He is a poet, and almost a seer; something ancient and far-away in the look of his eyes. He could not sit down in a corner of the landscape, as Thoreau did; he must have a continent for his playground. He starts off for a walk, after graduation, and is not back home in 18 years! In California he starts out one morning for a stroll; his landlady asks him if he will be back to dinner; probably not, he says. He is back in 7 days; walks 100 miles around Mt. Shasta, and goes two and a half days without food. He has done many foolish, foolhardy things... (but is) probably the truest lover of Nature, as she appears in woods, mountains, glaciers, we have yet had.

Both men would travel together in 1899 on the Harriman Alaska Expedition, a classy tour on the *George W. Elder* with 124 other naturalists, scientists, and artists at magnate Edward Henry Harriman's expense, but there their differences—Burroughs the somewhat seasick bookworm, Muir the vigorous, if not braggart, adventurer—became paramount. They traveled together again in 1909 to the Grand Canyon and Yosemite country, but there Muir continued to tease Burroughs relentlessly.

"I puttered around here for ten years," Muir scolded Burroughs in Yosemite, "but you expect to see and do everything in four days! You come here, then excuse yourself to God, who has kept these glories waiting for you, by saying 'I've got to get back to Slabsides' or 'We want to go to Honolulu.' "

When Burroughs complained once of needing sleep, Muir cried "sleepy, Johnnie! Why, lad, there'll be time to sleep when you get back to Slabsides, or at least in the grave."

Such chiding was tiring to Burroughs, as Muir appeared to wax macho in the role of ageless, robust mountaineer. Speaking with Muir became too much like a sparring match. Muir, Burroughs noted, "liked to get in the first cut and follow it up. It delights him to see you wince... He likes to walk over the flesh of his fellow men with spurs in his soles." Burroughs figured Muir had too much of the "rough, bruising experience in life" which made him callous. Regardless, Burroughs wished sometimes he could punch Muir or "thrash the ground with him," yet in a letter he confessed his love for Muir and added: "I have my laugh at your expense—when you are not around."

No doubt Muir viewed his friendship with Burroughs differently, for Muir was never deliberately cruel. He simply loved to talk and make fun. Nor was he blind to the real differences between them.

—Burroughs, for example, was anti-Christian and claimed that "joy in the universe, and keen curiosity about it all" was his religion. (His philosophical theology, such as in *The Light of Day* (1900), shared much with Oriental spiritual concepts.) Muir, meanwhile, equated natural beauty with God—never cutting himself off totally from his Christian upbringing.

—Burroughs doubted the extent glaciers played in geologically shaping Yosemite, a position anathema to Muir. (When Burroughs once asked Muir how petrified wood was created, Muir—disinclined to answer direct questions—quipped: "Oh, get a primer of geology, Johnnie!")

—Burroughs was often accompanied by women; Muir usually wandered alone.

—According to Clara Barrus, whose *Life and Letters of John Burroughs* portrays the two Johns at the Grand Canyon so well, Burroughs needed adequate food and sleep to do his best work, to enjoy anything, even to get along with others; Muir was insensible to fatigue, indifferent to food, and scoffed at sleep.

—Muir's love for new scenes was practically insatiable; Burroughs became homesick in strange surroundings, which Muir couldn't understand.

Nor, finally, could Muir—whose independence let him leave Louie for Alaska immediately before and after their marriage—understand Burrough's innate homebodiness, his perpetual questioning of traveling "just to see things" when he could see "the constellations every night from my doorstep." This being stationary, regardless of rationale, was a foreign language to Muir. While chatting for that June hour in 1893, with the taste of rich living clinging to Burroughs's hungover lips, Muir told his new friend *Century* was willing to pay him $500 to go with him to Europe.

Would he go?

Burroughs told him "circumstances" wouldn't allow it. Wild-eyed Muir knew the circumstances barring Burroughs's way was his wife.

———

Muir's writing life reached its prime at the turn of the century as he put his best years spent outdoors behind him. In 1894 he came out with *The Mountains of California*, a reshaping under editor Johnson's guidance of earlier magazine articles. Subjects included animals, storms, hikes and climbs in his beloved Sierras. A first printing of 1,500 copies sold out quickly. The book, biographer Wolfe says, "rallied and solidified the conservation sentiment of the entire nation," due to Muir's uplifting prose together with his unmitigated praise for nature primeval. Another 9,000 copies of The *Mountains of California* quickly reached public hands, helping to create a demand for the Forestry Commission's study, and launching Muir into his second book, *Our National Parks*.

Muir minced no words about the purpose of his second book. He wanted to encourage people to visit the nation's parks and enjoy them "and get them into their hearts, that so at length their preservation and right use might be made sure." Because there were only several national parks in 1901, Muir focused on Yellowstone and Yosemite, especially the latter. He wrote of Yosemite's flowers, animals, birds and streams. A short chapter described Sequoia and General Grant national parks. Yet, the book's main strength is its material on American forests. Here he reworked ideas originally expressed in the *Atlantic Monthly* in what appeared to be blatant ignorance of 1897's Forestry Management Act. The use of forest reserves, as far as Muir was concerned, was still up for grabs. They should, he said, be kept in their natural condition, or under wise management—"keeping out destructive sheep, preventing fires, selecting the trees that should be cut for lumber, and preserving the young ones and the shrubs and sod of herbaceous vegetation"—they could be made to be a "never failing fountain of wealth and beauty."

A page later, nevertheless, he claimed the dawn of a new day in forestry was breaking.

"The wonderful advance made in the last few years," he wrote, "in creating four national parks in the West, and thirty forestry reservations, embracing nearly forty million acres; and in the planting of borders of streets and highways and spacious parks in all the great cities, to satisfy the natural taste and hunger for landscape beauty and righteousness that God has put, in some measure, into every human being and animal, shows the trend of awakening public opinion."

Our National Parks enjoyed a dozen printings and continued to establish Muir as a major literary voice in the young wilderness preservation movement. The 382-page book included black-and-white photos and an appendix of parks, monuments, and details about the national forests. It was a guidebook, a yellow pages to where the conservation and preservation movement stood. And where Muir felt it should go.

Muir still suffered as a word craftsman despite success. Writing was hard work. Its solitariness irked him. He was tense when writing and easily distracted by sound. It remained strange to him that a paper, which read smoothly and could be read in 10 minutes, should require months to write. Fortunately, fan letters helped ease the pain, helped show "that even nature writing is not altogether useless." Still it was a grind. While writing in the 1890s he rose early to work at his desk until around 10, ate breakfast with his family, read Louie his morning's work, then returned to writing for one or two more sessions during the day.

While working on *Our National Parks* he complained of a "slow, sadly interrupted pen," but a year after the book was published Muir yearned to write much more.

In a letter of January 1902 to Walter Hines Page, Muir outlined the books he still wanted to write. The first would be a small one titled *Yosemite and Other Yosemites*. There would be a guidebook to California trees and shrubs. There would be an illustrated mountaineering book about camping, climbing and walking, another book on Alaska's glaciers, forests, and his travels, and still another book focusing on landscape-shaping forces: glaciers, earthquakes and the distribution of animals and plants. Finally, there would be an autobiography, a book requested 10 years earlier but humbly declined by Muir "in the midst of so much that is infinitely more important."

The outline of books sent to Page was a wish list, for Muir was beginning to see what all aging writers must inevitably see. The handwriting was on the chronological wall. Muir was 64. At best he had time to write two or three more books. What remained after that would have to be scratched out, if possible, by someone else.

Someone in his footsteps.

VIII

Muir's reputation as a writer and woodsman was widely known by 1903 when President Theodore Roosevelt, also a naturalist, sent him a compelling note: "I do not want anyone with me but you," he wrote, "and I want to drop politics absolutely for four days, and just be out in the open with you."

"Out in the open" meant Yosemite where Roosevelt wanted to camp with Muir. Tap his tongue. It was an historic invitation, one Muir couldn't decline despite plans to leave on a round-world trip with Sargent. It was an honor when a President requested the sole presence of someone under any circumstances, let alone a wilderness trip, and secondly Muir hoped he could do some "forest good" while talking with Roosevelt in the shining intimacy of campfire light.

The trip materialized in mid-May as Roosevelt wished. He and Muir with two cooks spent three nights in the Yosemite backcountry, first in Mariposa Grove, then behind Glacier Point followed by a night in Bridal Veil Meadow. Roosevelt was already a friend of the forest reserve concept, had even advocated keeping sheep and cattle out of the reserves, but Muir pummeled him with the preservation view anyhow.

One night it snowed four inches, which Roosevelt found "bully." Snow or not, he came away from the trip a rejuvenated defender of national forests.

"As regards some of the trees," he told a Sacramento audience after leaving Muir, "I want them preserved because they are the only things of their kind in the worl ... I ask for the preservation of other forests on grounds of wise and farsighted economic policy. I do not ask that lumbering be stopped... only that the forests be so used that not only shall we here, this generation, get the benefit for the next few years, but that our children and our children's children shall get the benefit.

"We are not building this country of ours for a day. It is to last through the ages."

Roosevelt and Muir would not always see eye-to-eye, because Roosevelt eventually turned the nation's forestry affairs over to utilitarian Pinchot in the Department of Agriculture's new Forest Service. Roosevelt would also support the side of developers during the bitter battle over damming Hetch Hetchy *within* Yosemite National Park, hurting Muir deeply in the process. The two nevertheless remained friends for life, as their 1903 trip together had far-reaching results. If nothing else it justified Roosevelt's conservation tendencies. By the time he left office, he had added 150 million acres of forests to the national forest system, doubled the national parks from 5 to 10, established 16 national monuments including, on Muir's recommendation, Grand Canyon (which subsequently became a national park), and he increased the number of wildlife refuges from one to 51.

Roosevelt, as a Muir-influenced politician, did what no legislator had done before him. He protected by law what had previously existed only in naturalistic sentiment.

Theodore Roosevelt's Craving for Wild Country

When Theodore Roosevelt (1858-1919) camped with John Muir in Yosemite in 1903, he had already become one of his generation's most accomplished naturalists. He was a naturalist with a wilderness vision, moreover, for as President his public land policy went beyond wise management of natural resources to include other values of undeveloped land. "No nation," he once wrote, "facing the unhealthy softening and relaxation of fibre that tends to accompany civilization can afford to neglect anything that will develop hardihood, resolution, and the scorn of discomfort and danger."

Roosevelt thought wild land could instill in Americans frontier personality characteristics which, on a collective scale, could keep the nation strong. Wilderness experience, moreover, fought cowardice and exposed men and women to the "silent places: the wide waste places of earth, unworn of man, and changed only by the slow change of the ages ... through time everlasting." Roosevelt's own experience of wilderness began in western North Dakota's Badlands where, in 1883, he established the Maltese Cross Ranch with 400 cattle.

His plans to be an absentee rancher, however, were shattered the following February when his wife, Alice Lee, and his mother died during a single night. Roosevelt returned to the Badlands (today's Theodore Roosevelt National Park) the following summer seeking peace, solitude, consolation and the simplicity of life lived close to the land. He bought another ranch and built his herd into the fourth largest in the county. He struck an uncanny figure in cowboy country. Born to one of New York's richest families, and educated at Harvard, Roosevelt's thick glasses and clean-shaven, short-haired fondness for books coaxed cowhands into nicknaming him "Four Eyes" and "Storm Windows." Undaunted, he learned to ride horses, brand steers, rope cows and rear calves, a lifestyle he cultivated almost full-time for three years.

"It was a land of vast silent spaces," Roosevelt wrote later of the Badlands, "of lonely rivers, and of plains where the wild game stared at passing horsemen... In that land we led a free and hardy life, with horse and with rifle. We worked under the scorching sun, when the wide plains shimmered and wavered in the heat... In the soft springtime the stars were glorious in our eyes each night before we fell asleep; and in the winter we rode through blinding blizzards, when the driven snow-dust burnt our faces....

"We knew toil and hardship and hunger and thirst; and we saw men die violent deaths as they worked among the horses and cattle, or fought in evil feuds with one another; but we felt the beat of hardy life in our veins, and ours was the glory of work and the joy of living."

Roosevelt's joy of outdoor living took a criminal turn in 1886, when three thieves stole the only boat he kept on the Elkhorn Ranch's waterfront. He took the law into his own hands. He and two cowhands built a flat-bottomed scow and headed downriver. Three days later they arrested the thieves and brought them to jail.

One old-timer—with the grit of frontier life in his veins—criticized T.R. for "all this fuss instead of hanging 'em offhand."

Roosevelt craved wild country even as the nation's top executive from 1901 to 1909. According to naturalist John Burroughs, Roosevelt craved the "wild and the aboriginal," a hunger that seemed to overcome him at least once a year. Roosevelt camped in

Yellowstone with Burroughs in 1903, the same year he rode horseback into Yosemite backcountry with Muir.

T.R.'s yearning for hardihood (he had asthma as a boy) and wildness reached a climax after his presidency. From 1909 to 1910 he ventured to Africa on a hunting expedition to gather animal, ornithological, and botanical specimens for the Smithsonian Institution and the American Museum of Natural History, his sponsors. Returning to America he wrote and published African Game Trails, *which sold more copies than any of his other 20-plus books. He also wrote articles for* The Outlook, Metropolitan Magazine, Scribner's *and his own* An Autobiography.

Roosevelt led a canoe expedition three years later down Brazil's River of Doubt. His explicit reason for the South American trip was identical to the African one: collect specimens for American museums. Once in South America, however, Colonel Candido Mariano da Silva Rondon of the Brazilian Telegraphic Commission convinced Roosevelt to explore the unmapped River of Doubt—a 1,000-mile tributary of Brazil's Amazon. The expedition lost one man and five of seven canoes in 48 days while mapping the unexplored route. Even Roosevelt became a casualty. He injured his leg while rescuing a provision-laden canoe. He had to be carried. Malaria complicated his condition, and the group stopped when he became too sick to move. Food ran low. Roosevelt—the hard-nosed Badlands graduate—heroically asked everyone leave without him.

They didn't, of course, but the upshot was evident: Here was a man who had self-composure (he once gave an hour-long speech with a bullet in his body). Here was the man whom Muir had fairly fallen "in love with," for never prior to camping with Roosevelt in Yosemite had he "a more interesting, hearty, and manly companion." And here was a man who, despite vast political responsibilities, wrote 150,000 letters during his life, the last one a congratulatory note to naturalist William Beebe who had recently published a monograph on pheasants.

Muir's personal life continued to spiral onward in the early 1900s. His round-the-world trip with Sargent took him to Scotland, Russia, Egypt, Australia, New Zealand, and Japan, en route expanding his botanical collection until it became one of the most comprehensive private collections in the world. Muir stopped writing for more than a year when Louie died of lung cancer in 1905; his grief was so deep he wouldn't allow anyone to move anything in his home because he wanted it left precisely where Louie's hand had placed it.

From 1908 to 1913, Muir fought gallantly to prevent damming of the Hetch Hetchy Valley, a battle he lost to the detriment of both his health and spirit. Muir was willing "to sacrifice his own family for the preservation of beauty," San Francisco's mayor, James D. Phelan, had said. "He considers human life very cheap, and he considers the works of God superior." No and yes. No, he had never considered life cheap, human nor animal. Yes, he considered the works of God superior to those of men when people insisted on sacrificing beauty to mammon. It was common knowledge during the Hetch Hetchy fight that San Francisco could get its water from somewhere other than a scenic valley second only to Yosemite. The developers had nevertheless been adamant in what amounted to almost a personal battle against Muir and the whole concept of wilderness preservation. The bottom line was money. Muir felt if Hetch Hetchy was dammed the nation may as well dam "for water tanks the people's cathedrals and temples, for no holier temple has ever been consecrated by the heart of man." An irreplaceable geographical gem in western America's wilderness legacy was being stolen from future generations by "wealthy wicked."

Bitter words, yet words nevertheless reflecting Muir's long view.

"They will see what I meant in time," he wrote Bailey Millard when the taste of Hetch Hetchy defeat numbed his lips. "There must be places for human beings to satisfy their souls. Food and drink is not all. There is the spiritual. In some it is only a germ, of course, but the germ will grow!"

Truth and right *would* prevail, he thought. The important thing was to be true to one's vision.

The day would come when the National Park Service, established in 1916, would preserve some of the natural beauty Muir so loved, so needed, and for which he so ardently lived. And the nation would see the hour when even portions of the national forests would be set aside in a Wilderness Preservation System to protect their natural values. But this Muir only sensed. This he hoped. For by 1914 he was again writing 12 to 16 hours a day. Life was a candle burning at both ends. At least he now held an angle of vision sharpened by experience and old age.

And it had been vision—and the light making it possible—*which had fascinated Muir*. It alone had most dazzled his emotions and mind since the factory file accident nearly eclipsed his sight. *Light*: He knew not a single word fine enough for it. "Its currents pour," he noted in his journal, "but it is a heavy material word not applicable to holy, beamless, bodiless, inaudible floods of Light." Never, in the shadow of the file, had he taken light and sight for granted again. In the mid-1880s he recalled in a letter to Janet Moores the beauty he had seen over the years: "The richest sun-gold flooding these California valleys, the spiritual alpenglow steeping the high peaks, silver light on the sea, the white glancing sun-spangles on rivers and lakes, light on the myriad stars of the snow, light sifting through the angles of sun-beaten icebergs, light in glacier caves, irised spray wafting from white waterfalls, and the light of calm starry nights beheld from mountain-tops dipping deep into the clear air."

It was pure wild light Muir had been obsessed with. More than sound, more than smell, taste, and touch, it was the illuminated beauty in mountain ranges and forests he could not let people destroy. It was fitting, therefore, that Muir's last piece of writing in his final book, *Travels in Alaska*, was about light. In his chapter "Alaskan Auroras," he recalled how in 1880 on a solo canoe trip in southeastern Alaska he had watched from his bouldery bed how magnificent upright bars of light "in bright prismatic colors suddenly appeared, marching swiftly in close succession along the northern horizon from west to east." Yet three days later when he had returned to a cabin, he watched the most dazzling "supreme, serene supernatural light show of all. A glowing silver bow spanned Muir Inlet in an arch whose ends rested on top opposite mountain walls. It was like a rainbow of stars, he said, raked into a windrow. Soon a band of "fluffy, pale-gray, quivering ringlets" arose over the eastern mountaintop to glide up and down the bow to the opposite mountain wall. The ringlets remained vertical all the way across and slipped along swiftly as if suspended like a curtain on rings. Muir guessed there must have been hundreds of miles of ringlets which he watched skirt the arch for an hour. He returned to his cabin when the white arch faded, stoked his fire, then decided to take one last look at the sky before going to sleep.

A new bow of light was developing, Muir forgot sleep, ran back to the cabin, grabbed his blankets and lay down on the glacial moraine to watch the skies until daybreak. Like the boy afresh in Wisconsin fields he once was, and like the young man stumbling into virgin Yosemite meadows, Muir now lay bug-eyed and breathless "that none of the sky wonders of this glorious night within reach of my eyes might be lost."

Linnie Marsh Wolfe, in *Son of the Wilderness: The Life of John Muir*, recounts a strange impulse on Muir's part shortly before he died. He cleaned his Martinez home, built new bookcases, bought rugs and curtains, and installed electricity. All were remarkable changes by someone who had demanded all things be left alone since his wife's death. Muir had presentiments of his parents' deaths years earlier, so perhaps now he intuited his own. In December 1914 he traveled to Daggett on the Mojave Desert to visit his daughter, Helen. But he wasn't well. He had been exhausted and weak throughout the Hetch Hetchy fight, and chronic coughs and headaches had returned to plague him. He reached Daggett in the middle of the night and caught cold. The next night, after working on *Travels in Alaska* next to a fire, he stood and staggered from faintness.

He had pneumonia. Muir was rushed to a Los Angeles hospital where his health appeared to improve, where a new peak rose in sight, before death suddenly descended like an avalanche. Spread out on Muir's bed was his chapter on Alaskan auroras. The boy from Dunbar's moors had been a writer to the last. In his heart, perhaps, were friends like Louie and Emerson, Fay and Toyatte, visionaries like Humboldt and Thoreau. Muir had witnessed much death in his life and had thought about it deeply. Now, while believing death separates, he also thought it ironically unites.

"The sense of loneliness," he once wrote with an eagle quill, "grows less and less as we become accustomed to the new light, communing with those who have gone on ahead in spirit, and feeling their influence as if again present in the flesh."

3

ROBERT W. SERVICE:
THE WILD TRANSFORMATION

Have you gazed on naked grandeur where there's nothing else to gaze on,
   Set pieces and drop-curtain scenes galore.
Big mountains heaved to heaven, which the blinding sunsets blazon,
   Black canyons where the rapids rip and roar?
Have you swept the visioned valleys with the green stream streaking through it,
   Searched the Vastness for a something you have lost?
Have you strung your soul to silence? Then for God's sake go and do it;
   Hear the challenge, learn the lesson, pay the cost.

Have you wandered in the wilderness, the sagebrush desolation,
   The bunch-grass levels where the cattle graze?
Have you whistled bits of rag-time at the end of all creation,
   And learned to know the desert's little ways?
Have you camped upon the foothills, have you galloped o'er the ranges,
   Have you roamed the air sun-lands through and through?
Have you chummed up with the mesa? Do you know its moods and changes?
   Then listen to the Wild—it's calling you.

Have you known the Great White Silence, not a snow-gemmed twig aquiver?
   (Eternal truths that shame our soothing lies.)
Have you broken trail on snowshoes? mushed your huskies up the river,
   Dared unknown, led the way, and clutched the prize?
Have you marked the map's void spaces, mingled with the mongrel races,

Felt the savage strength of brute in every thew?
And though grim as hell the worst is, can you round it off with curses?
Then hearken to the Wild—it's wanting you.

Have you suffered, starved, and triumphed, groveled down, yet grasped at glory,
Grown bigger in the bigness of the whole?
'Done things' just for the doing, letting babblers tell the story,
Seeing through the nice veneer the naked soul?
Have you seen God in His splendors, heard the text that nature renders?
(You'll never hear it in the family pew.)
The simple things, the true things, the silent men who do things
Then listen to the Wild—it's calling you.

They have cradled you in custom, they have primed you with their preaching,
They have soaked you in convention through and through;
They have put you in a showcase; you're a credit to their teaching—
But can't you hear the Wild?—it's calling you.
Let us probe the silent places, let us seek what luck betide us;
Let us journey to a lonely land I know.
There's a whisper on the night-wind, there's a star agleam to guide us,
And the Wild is calling, calling ... let us go.

—Robert Service, *The Call of the Wild*

In 1911—the same year John Muir published *The Mountains of California* and journeyed to South America's Amazon River—the call of the wild tugged at Robert Service's soul as he paddled his birchbark canoe down the calm waters of the Yukon Territory's Porcupine River. Here, in pants cut off at the knees and shirtsleeves cut off at the shoulders, his face tan and whiskered, was a poet who would immortalize the Klondike Gold Rush of 1898. Here was the author of such humorous ballads as "The Shooting of Dan McGrew" and "The Cremation of Sam McGee." Here, too, was the scribe of "The Spell of the Yukon" and "The Call of the Wild": two haunting poems that would inspire untold thousands of outdoor enthusiasts to seek wildness, to seek that immutable something—call it mystery, perhaps—which lay locked yet waiting long beyond the ranges. Behind Service in his canoe were a thousand miles of water travel, some of the hardest and most bizarre work of his life.

Yet ahead of him loomed an even graver challenge.

Jake Skilly, Service's temporary canoe partner, had threatened to kill him. And it didn't do Service an ounce of good to have his loaded rifle up front with him in the bow.

"Seems to me," Skilly said, "you're all fixed up to fire that there gun of yours." "Might see a bear on the bank," Service said, his back toward Jake. "I've got an ax here," Skilly reminded Service, "might be useful if we saw...

a bear. I'm a good man at thrown' an ax."

It was a foul fix for a famous bard but Service (1874-1958) had asked for it. He had believed throughout life that experience was gold grist for the mill of "inkslinging" success. His most famous poetry books—*The Spell of the Yukon, Ballads of a Cheechako,* and *Rhymes of a Rolling Stone*—were based in part on immersing himself in the spirit of backcountry travel, in wilderness, and in the milieu of the Far North's most eccentric characters and tales. Service, however, was hardly a Dangerous Dan McGrew. He didn't chase women, play poker or get drunk regularly on hooch. Service was a writer, not a fighter; a banker, not a gold-digger. Despite his rhymed Klondike bravado, chances are, had he actually been there, Service would have died portaging up Chilkoot Pass.

Which was precisely part of the problem.

The man who is today associated with Yukon Jack, "the black sheep of Canadian liquors," could not measure up to the women and men who people his books. At least not throughout his early years. By emulating "Men of the High North" and "Lords of the Wilderness," Service had inadvertently established standards for himself that were impossible to keep.

In 1910, for example, he decided to test his grit by walking—a la Muir— from New York City to New Orleans. But after three weeks of walking in the rain, sometimes 20 miles a day, he trashed his hiking plans and bought a rail car ticket for destinations beyond Philadelphia.

Enter: Self-reproach.

Again later that year he tried to walk from Cuba's Havana to Santiago. He wanted to become acquainted with the hinterlands, with the pub rather than the pew. The heat, however, together with humid rain and low-life filth proved too much. Service bailed out, this time to the chic Hotel Madrid, where good food and sleep put six pounds on his beltline in three weeks.

More guilt and reproach convinced Service that he detested what was happening to him. He had become, according to the laws of the North, a pup—not a man. He recalled former days when physical fitness enabled him to snowshoe from dawn to dusk in Yukon mountains. Days when he took baths in cold water and rubbed his skin with ice. Nights when he walked tirelessly beneath stars and northern lights while lyrics leapt alive in his mind. Slowly, Service realized what many successful people must face. Money had softened him.

He still had, nevertheless, one option: Design a trip that, if completed, would inflate his self image, bolster his public image, bless him with pride, and enhance both the face and depth of his poetry.

A canoe trip in the Yukon Territory with its wild rivers and nameless valleys was the answer.

Service's resulting itinerary—the 2,000-mile old Edmonton trail, mapped his most ambitious outdoor adventure. He would descend the Athabasca River by steamer, scow and canoe to Lake Athabasca, then continue down the mighty Mackenzie River before paddling up the Rat River to a little-known mountain pass. From there he would ride whitewater, slicks and calm water of the Bell and Porcupine rivers to the Yukon River.

His geographical goal?

Famous Dawson City, Yukon Territory, frontier town with gold-nugget ladies and men-of-the-knife. There Service wanted to write his third book of poems: *Rhymes of a Rolling Stone*.

His canoe trip companions? None. As far as he knew.

———

Certainly Service had time while paddling toward his destiny on the Rat and Porcupine rivers to reflect upon the long road that had led to a pinnacle in his uncanny career. Born in Scotland, he had emigrated on a tramp steamer to Canada in 1896 at the age of 22. A train carried him with nothing but spare change in his pockets to a ranch near Duncan, British Columbia, where he became a cowhand or, in his words, a "cowjuice jerker." Soon he was wandering along North America's West Coast—Vancouver Island, Seattle, and San Francisco. He picked oranges for needed money, helped build a railroad tunnel, and worked—supposedly unknowingly—as a caretaker for a San Diego whorehouse.

In his pockets and pants were poetry books. For if Robert W. Service was anything he was a lover of poetry. Robert Burns was partly to blame.

"My great-grandfather," Service claimed late in life, "had been a crony of Robert Burns and claimed him as a second cousin. One of our parlour chairs had often been warmed by the rump of the bard."

There were other poets, too: Tennyson, Browning, Thackeray, Hood, Patmore, Poe, and Owen Meredith. Service took his poetry with him everywhere: To the Stobcross branch of the Commercial Bank of Scotland where he worked. To the bank's St. Vincent branch. To stores. Even to the toilet. Only slowly did he become familiar with other fields as he turned to literature by Jack London, Rudyard Kipling, Robert Louis Stevenson, Thoreau, and George Borrow. These were young Service's tracks, the ones he followed. Meanwhile, he became intrigued with what he called the "gift of vagrancy," low life, and vagabondage, all things in a son any good father might fear.

Service's father, Robert Sr., had been a character in his own right. History records him as an amateur cobbler who lived off his wife's inheritance. He drank almost precisely 10 days a year. He realized his mastery over his kids was over when they turned 16; from then on, each got a latchkey and could stay out until midnight. He forced his children to go to church. He never went. Robert Sr. ironically gave son Robert a Bible as a parting gift when they said farewell on the Atlantic dock in 1896.

"I'm sorry to say I never read it," Service quipped in his first autobiography, *Ploughman of the Moon*, "Yet I kept it sentimentally for many years; and, in wild camps of thieves and vagabonds, that was the one possession no one ever tried to steal."

One small job led to another in the American Southwest as Service bummed through Arizona, Colorado, and Nevada around 1898. But gone was wandering's romance. Service felt like he belonged to the "Great Unfit" and that in the "fight for survival I must be trampled under."

He didn't taste hope until one day he scanned an old newspaper on a train. A ton of gold had been found in the Klondike country. "Another gold rush like that of forty-nine," the story read. "Maybe it will have its dramatic aspects. No doubt another Bret Harte will arise and sing of it in colourful verse."

Something hard and cold broke in Service's disenchantment. He always knew his destiny would evolve around his pen, but now there was a surge of clarity. Perhaps his poetic pen should check out the Klondike. Fate seemed to nudge him in the ribs with its elbow.

Fate eventually punched Service outright, as it always does. Between October 10, 1903 and November 8, 1904, he held three consecutive bank jobs, the last one in Whitehorse, Yukon Territory. Here and in Dawson City to the north lay his payload.

But it was Stroller White, editor of the *Whitehorse Star*, and not any need of Service's to express himself that got the pen rolling.

"Why don't you write a poem [sic] for it," White asked Service, 32, referring to an upcoming local church concert in 1906. "Give us something about our own bit of earth ... There's a rich paystreak waiting for someone to work. Why don't you go in and stake it?"

Service had written over 100 poems for Glasgow weeklies back in Scotland. He had published poems in the *Whitehorse Star*. And he had written poems for himself. But what now? What for the public? How could he relate poetry to the Yukon? Suddenly, with a single line in mind, a shot rang out. Service had just walked past a local bar where music and human riproar had given him an idea for his poem's first sentence: "A bunch of the boys were whooping it up at the Malamute Saloon." But when he stepped inside the bank to finish the poem at his teller's cage, a guard mistook him for a burglar, gripped his pistol and fired. The guard missed, but the gunshot and sensation of a bullet whizzing past Service's head put him in a perfect mood to write "The Shooting of Dan McGrew."

"McGrew" was a popular ballad about a gunfight triggered by romantic revenge. In it, Service hoped, was the "power of music to stir the subconscious and awaken dormant passions," effects he hadn't intended when he wrote the poem. All he had wanted to do was create a dramatic monologue— for the church concert. Inevitably, he didn't even recite the poem. He had put in a few cuss words and didn't want to take them out.

A month later, after listening to a miner's story about a man who cremated his pal, Service wrote "The Cremation of Sam McGee." This tale of an arctic man who never felt warm until sitting in his own crematorium, a blazing wrecked ship, became the keystone of Service's success. The heights of

Miles Canyon soon inspired him to write "The Call of the Wild," another of his poetic gems, for it manifested (like little poetry and prose since) the subtle, almost immutable allure of wild places and the suffering people endure to taste it. Back-to-back poems made Service feel like a "solitary pedestrian pounding out his rhymes from the intense gusto of living."

And so a redeeming career began.

First came *The Spell of the Yukon* (Songs of a Sourdough in Canada), which surprisingly reached the public eye through his father. The elder Service had emigrated to Toronto from Scotland, and in 1907 he received his son's $100 Christmas bonus and a drawer full of his Yukon poems. Mission: Please bring them to a publisher. Pa Service brought the poems to William Briggs who was connected with Ryerson Press. Son Service, meanwhile, was back in Whitehorse whipping himself psychologically for having vainly mailed his poems to be put in print.

He could have spared the whip. Briggs's men in the press's typesetting room started spouting off bits of Service's poems to one another. *The Spell of the Yukon* was printed, bound and packaged in record time. Briggs became suspicious. But when he looked closely at what had inspired his typesetters and pressmen to work so feverishly he began selling copies immediately. Almost 2,000 copies sold from galley proofs alone. Service chucked his vanity like a bad thought when Briggs sent him a $170 check and a letter asking him to sign a contract giving him 10 percent royalty on a book selling for one dollar. Service signed. Although encouraged by what had happened, little could he know that 36 editions of the book would be printed in the next 10 years.

The implacable dreamer's career was launched.

The Yukon's new bard was transferred on April 4, 1908 to Dawson City, locus of the Territory's historic gold rush, the same place he had read about in that railcar newspaper. Gold production had dropped, and Dawson's population was down 4,000, but it was in Dawson City that Service—still a bank clerk—celebrated publication of his second book of poems: *Ballads of a Cheechako*. Scruffy characters like Windy Ike, Muckluck Meg, Pious Pete and Claw-fingered Kitty came alive in verse. There was the Dago Kid, Gun-boot Ben and Hard Luck Henry. No bizarre brawl or strange story escaped Service's pen. He talked to old-timers, mining them for grisly tales. Sin, not sanity, was his want.

"Vice," Service said, explaining his preferences, "seemed to me a more vital subject than virtue, more colourful, more dramatic, so I specialized in the Red Light atmosphere.

"Verse, not poetry, is what I was after—something the man in the street would take notice of and the sweet old lady would paste in her album; something the school boy would spout and the fellow in the pub would quote."

Service was quoted all the way to the bank. *The Spell of the Yukon* alone brought him the then fantastic sum of $4,000 a year. Ballads doubled his income. When he reached his savings goal of $5,000 he started thinking of his account as a "pool being constantly fed by small streams." Service resigned from the bank when he began making more money than the bank's president.

"I envied no one on earth," Service said as his fantasies came true. "I leapt to high heaven and came down clutching handfuls of stars."

One star was a self-imposed lifestyle in a rented log cabin on a hill overlooking Dawson City and the Yukon River. There he installed a telephone, double windows, and painted interior cabin walls blue. He added a door with a window. Heat came from burning wood he bought but chopped himself. Water for tea was heated on the stove; meals were eaten at downtown cafes. The sitting-room, his office, had two chairs and a small table with a Blickensderfer No. 5 typewriter on it for polishing drafts of manuscripts. On one wall was a framed reminder: "Rebuffs are only rungs in the ladder of success." Pinned to other walls sometimes were course rolls of paper on which he wrote with charcoal; he would pace back and forth in front of his words, studying them from a distance, trying to make them appealing to both eye and ear. The bedroom had a double bed with good springs, which he sometimes shared with a Siberian bear hound and a cat he had rescued as a kitten on a frozen trail.

And time? Service had all he wanted for two years as summer's midnight sun and winter's dimly lit afternoons swung seasonally back and forth in the shadow of the Pole.

Service wrote full-time. But full-time for Service meant something like this: He slept until noon, napped about 5 p.m., and ate supper about 10 p.m. Nights were his. As Dawson City slept, Service wrote. Despite winter nights of 72° below zero and times when his bedroom would get so cold the blankets around his head would become sheathed with ice from his breath, he managed to finish his first novel, *The Trail of Ninety-Eight*, in five months.

It was this book—hot with revisions and destined to become a movie in 1928—that Service brought to New York publishers before setting out on foot for New Orleans. Within a year, stung with reproach, he was nosing his canoe up the Rat River. Heeding the call of the wild.

"There was a whisper on the night wind, a star agleam to guide him," as Service changed from poet and author to canoe voyageur. Fortunately the change came slowly. He rode stage for two ways, from Edmonton to Athabasca Landing, where he began a three-day canoe trip with four others to catch up with some Hudson Bay Company barges.

He soon learned paddling was a "vigorous activity," although sitting in the bow of a canoe slipping down a strange stream was a joy hard to match. This was especially true if the river had a good current, was narrow and deep, and turned corners every few hundred yards. The voyageur looked ahead with expectation and excitement.

Once on a Hudson Bay Company barge, however, Service turned to more dramatic canoeing excitement, antics he later called "a needless bit of bravado."

"The only exciting spot on the [barge] trip," he explained in *Ploughman of the Moon*, "was the descent of a series of rapids. The Engineer [a traveling companion heading for the Coppermine country to prospect] suggested we get out a canoe and run them ... I felt I must take part. So I sat in the bow as we tackled the tossing river. I loosened the laces of my high boots and when we reached the danger point I prudently slipped them off. The Engineer gave me a contemptuous look, but he happened to be wearing moccasins. I saw he had no confidence in me. He warned me to sit still and leave everything to him; but when a big boulder suddenly shot up I poked it out of the way. We slid sideways, half turned over, and it looked nasty. However, a canoe takes a lot of upsetting, and before I had time to be scared we were in smooth water. Behind us was a swirling, tossing welter of white foam and brown boulders."

One of the barges was less fortunate than Service's canoe. It broached on a rock and had to be hauled off. "The steersman," Service added, "said he was so distracted by our adventure he could not concentrate on his own job. The accident was blamed on our canoe and from then on we were forbidden to do these silly stunts."

Silly stunts. An ex-parson at Fort McMurray had different words for Service's antics.

"You're not going alone?" he asked Service about his crossing of the Richardson Mountains.

"I'll need guides to cross the divide," Service said airily, "but once I get to the Yukon watershed it should be smooth sailing."

"Young man," said the ex-parson, shaking his head solemnly, "you're going to your *doom*."

Farther down the Athabasca River another "Churchman," a priest with a long silvery beard, took Service into his confidence. "Whatever you do," this "ideal shepherd of the Wild" said, "don't go alone: To travel by oneself in the Arctic is to court death. I know, because I've lived here all my life. A single slip and you are lost."

Service was prepared to risk his life. Although his conscience had chided him as a "fake pathfinder" and a "phony explorer"—someone who could be lounging in a lobby with cigar and cocktail—he nevertheless accepted a fifty-fifty chance of survival. Wasn't he young, strong and active? *the bard of the Yukon?*

Later he admitted he hadn't enough sense to be scared.

So ignorance, often a good friend of youth, fed Service's Arctic bliss. He continued by barge down the Athabasca and Slave rivers to Great Slave Lake, where he bought the finest birchbark canoe he could find; it was built by an old Indian considered the best canoe-maker of his tribe.

"He judged it his masterpiece," Service wrote, "and truly it was like a flame upon the water. A gaudy patchwork of purple, scarlet, primrose and silver, it danced on the ripple as lightly as a leaf. The old man sighed as he parted with it. He had gone far to select the bark. He had sewn it with wood fiber and lashed it with willow wands. There was not a nut or a nail anywhere. It had taken him a year to fashion, and now he looked at it with the sadness of an artist who sees his finest work being sold. With reluctance he took the twenty-five dollars I offered him."

Service christened the canoe *Coquette*. Although it was "as nervous as a thoroughbred," he soon mastered it by paddling up and down parts of the upper Mackenzie until it felt a part of him, until nothing would upset him on the lure of the lone trail.

The best laid plans of poets, however, are bound to go astray, particularly in a land where strange things are done beneath the midnight sun. Service's will had weakened, and he was almost ready to spend winter in the Arctic rather than attempt the mountain divide alone, when he ran into a group of three with a half-ton scow going, incredibly, to Dawson City. The trio was led by Captain McTosh, a big man with a fiery beard and bold belly. With him was his petite comely wife and Jake Skilly, a "rat-grey little man" with a perpetual grouch. Both McTosh and Skilly hated the Hudson Bay Company. They wouldn't sell a pelt to it for any price. But it was Skilly who riveted Service's attention. Here was a "fine type of Arctic adventurer"—the embodiment of Service's wildest ballads.

Skilly had a cadaverous face like a wolf, Service said, and was "one of half a dozen white men who thought nothing of going off alone into the winter wild, of building an ice house in the blizzard, of living on raw fish so rotten he poked a hole in the skin and sucked out the substance." Jake had traplines on the Mackenzie Delta where his white fox skins ran into hundreds. His highest claim to fame, however, was that he and Arctic explorer Stefansson were the only two men in the Far North who could truly live off the land.

When *Ophelia's* crew asked Service to join them in crossing the Richardson Mountains, he thought his troubles were over. Little did he dream they were just beginning.

Service's first challenge was physical. He was able to paddle *Coquette* up a short stretch of the Peel River to the mouth of the Rat "where the canoe leapt eagerly forward," but soon the current became too strong. He loaded the canoe on the scow and began to fight upstream every inch of the way. Shallow waters of the upper Rat forced the entire crew to harness themselves to a tow rope, a job, wrote Service, which "made a Volga boatman look like a slacker." Never had Service worked so hard. He tugged, strained, grunted and drooled at the mouth. He pulled in water waist-deep, sometimes 12 hours a day to cover a half mile. Once he was dragged under water downstream, his back bumping over boulders, but luck, brandy and the "ministrations" of Mrs. McTosh brought him around.

A typical Rat River scene, Service said, went like this:

"We have come to where the valley opens out, and the river forks in a dozen channels. We select the likeliest stream and explore it. It is only a few inches deep and studded with boulders. How I curse that unwieldy scow! How I hate these fur men and their stubbornness! Why couldn't they have a stout canoe for the job? Blast and dam *Ophelia*! Well, we will have to get the old bitch over somehow. So first we unload her and portage the stuff half-a-mile. Then we proceed to boost her over the boulders, scraping her bottom all the way. At one place we deepen the channel, at another build a wing dam. Often we have to get under the scow and heft her on."

Service remained undaunted. He had, in fact, never felt better. He smiled. He laughed. He bluffed playing a lusty, enjoyable game. Whether squatting on a sand bar and swallowing his spittle while watching bannock bake, or smoking his after-supper pipe before sleeping "like a hound after the hunt," Service played his Arctic bard role to the hilt.

What *didn't* help were sounds in the night.

As the orange glow of a cigarette shone from Jake's tent, Service, also unable to sleep, could hear the McToshes make love. They were on a belated honeymoon. Service, in the land "that god forgot," was not.

———————

Service was ready to "string his soul to silence in black canyons, where rapids rip and roar," by the time he reached a small, vicious stream flowing downhill to the Bell River. It was a mile portage across the pass. On the last of four trips he carried his canoe "in the Indian way": he crossed his paddles as a "back brace" or yoke, and from the thwarts he slung a band around his head. The muskeg footing was hell; a hundred times he fell to struggle up again, and often he was waist-deep in icy slime. Finally he reached a small headwater lake where he put his canoe in the water and began to sing.

He still sang the next day: a nervous song "about Maggie and when she and I were young." It was the kind of song people sing when one foot is in hell, the other toeing a fine line between exultation and death.

The stream he had anticipated for so long, the one which would bring him to the Porcupine and Yukon rivers via the Bell, now seized *Coquette* "with a giant hand" to shake her "as a terrier does a rat." The stream descended in a series of rapids varied by small cascades, so that Service—often waist-deep in foam—had to get out and line the canoe. Once he was dragged into a deep hole and had to swim. Other times he feared his birchbark canoe would be smashed like an eggshell.

"Sometimes," he reminisced, "it would be gripped by fang-like boulders and held clear out of the water. Often it tilted till the water came over the thwarts, but always it righted itself. I fought desperately to steer and clear it, for I was alone now and realized what it would mean if I upset and lost my grub."

Service left the *Ophelia* and its crew to feel new lighthearted life on the bosom of the Bell. Turbulent waters became tranquil. Verdant green banks framed mirror-surfaced currents. Often he would lie full-length in the canoe and let its crystal clear water carry him along. He ate bacon, blueberries, and bannock. He swam. He made shoreline pots of tea. At night, perhaps following sunsets "on naked grandeur where there's nothing else to gaze on," he slept on dry ground fragrant with crushed pine cones.

"And I was really, truly alone," he said. "I felt that if I had drawn a hundred mile circle around me there would not have been a human soul in its compass. As I hugged my fire of an evening I gloated over my solitude. As I dawdled downstream I felt so free and careless I was in no hurry for company. After two hundred miles of the Bell I would come on the Porcupine, but I was in no rush to reach it. I wanted this beautiful stream to unwind forever."

It might have, if not for the likes of Jake Skilly. For soon, on the Porcupine's placid brown water, the *Ophelia* and its quarrelsome crew caught up with Service. Murder was in the air.

Skilly, a nicotine fiend, needed rolling papers for his cigarettes. His jaw muscles twitched. His fingers jerked habitually as if he were rolling a smoke. And he had grown to hate Captain McTosh. His hatred was rooted, in part, in the trip's hardships, and in his growing passion for Mrs. McTosh, but mostly in the fact his rolling papers—pages from an *Argosy* magazine torn in half—were almost gone.

Here was a man who smoked through meals and at intervals during the night. While paddling with Service early in the trip, Jake would stop every 15 minutes to roll a fresh cigarette as Service hung on to a shoreline branch. He inhaled the strong smoke deep into his lungs (a pipe was too weak). Then, after about 10 minutes without, as Service put it, "a coffin nail," a wild look came into Skilly's eyes as he began to tremble violently.

Skilly was ready to tear Captain McTosh apart with his bare hands when Service met them on the Porcupine. Service had begun to feel guilty about leaving the crew, so he was ripe bait for the lovely Mrs. McTosh when she begged him to take Jake with him in *Coquette*. The plan was for Jake and Service to push ahead to Rampart House where Jake could get paper.

Any paper would do. Jake had been in a similar position once before when the only paper he owned was a Bible his beloved mother had given him.

"I carried that there Bible everywhere," Jake told Service as they paddled toward Rampart House. "I never read it, but jest liked to have it with me, thinkin' it might come in useful. Well, it did—mighty useful. For I smoked it through from Genesis to Revelation. Damn poor smokin' at that, but it saved my life. Yes sir, that Bible saved me from a bullet in the bean."

Skilly was already threatening Service with insane actions when they reached Rampart, so it was with grave disappointment they were told they couldn't land there. The village was plagued with smallpox. A doctor handed them a note saying they hadn't stepped ashore and weren't contaminated, something the doctor felt would ease their journey downstream when they met folk aware of the disease. The duo—wedded in a sullen, bizarre fate—had to go on. Jake wanted to roll a cigarette with the doctor's note. The bard said no.

It was there on the Arctic's Porcupine River where Service "grew bigger in the bigness of the whole." As Jake glared at his back in "murderous hate," Service readied his gun in the bow for whatever improbable pitch fate might throw him. It was a scene straight out of one of his books. Crazy Skilly, meanwhile, clutched his ax like a starving malamute snarling over an untouchable mildewed bone.

Fortunately for the Yukon's best-known poet, a launch—replete with rolling paper—swung around a bend of the Porcupine as Service knelt on a gravel bar sucking the seams of his canoe in search of a leak. Skilly immediately became a changed man: barely a shadow of the self who, a few years later, would blow his head off in a lonely cabin on the Arctic Ocean.

Meanwhile Service strutted his stuff.

In *Ploughman of the Moon*, which he wrote at age 70 in 1945, Service recalled the moment he met and boarded a sternwheel steamer chugging up the Yukon River for Dawson City, trip's end:

"As we materialized from out of the blue a score of eyes were on us. At the sight of *Coquette*, dancing daintily on the wave, there were shouts of admiration. She was as gay and colourful as when I first bought her. Now she shot forward with an air of saucy triumph... A dozen people were regarding the shapely craft as its owner, a bronzed and bearded individual, leapt lightly ashore. He looked like a scarecrow spewed out of the wild... Lean as a greyhound, sinewy as a panther...."

Service walked the streets back in Dawson City a changed man. Not only did his body bear "the stamp of the Wild" but he saw himself in the same romantic light he shone on his poetry's most remarkable characters. He bragged about the greatness of the Mackenzie Valley compared to the Yukon. He spoke casually about "dropping in from Edmonton." Certainly Service had shed his self-reproach like a snake sheds skin.

Best of all, Service embodied his own ballad. And from it he sang.

"I was of the North," he crowed, "its lover, its living voice. Dawson was my home; I had no thought of ever deserting it."

But desert Dawson City he would. For the next year, however, he plunged back into his poetry with a gusto and freshness transcending his earlier work. *The Spell of the Yukon* had been written with no thought of publication. *Ballads of a Cheechako* was a "tour de force" written in four months between midnight and 3 a.m. Yet now in *Rhymes of a Rolling Stone* he embarked on a "leisured and pleasant job spread out over most of a year," the results of which inundate readers with images based not on what Service heard in Yukon villages, then embellished, but partly on what he had done in the Yukon's backcountry. His references to rivers, wilderness travel in general, and canoeing in particular come vitally alive. One senses that not only has Service experienced his subject, or at least its setting, but he also feels it. It still stings in open cuts. It busts blisters. There is a proud joy in the telling, a richness of detail that comes only from an author who's been there.

Take "The Nostomaniac," for example. This 85-line poem is written in the first person. Service is "dreaming to-night in the fire-glow, alone in my study tower" with books "battalioned" around him and a copy of Rudyard

Kipling on his lap. The nostomaniac is haunted by the call of the North and slips into a daydream:

> And I'm daring a rampageous river that runs the devil knows where;
> My hand is athrill on the paddle, the birch-bark bounds like a bird.
> Hark to the rumble of rapids! Here in my morris chair
> Eager and tense I'm straining—isn't it most absurd?
> Now in the churn and the lather, foam that hisses and stings,
> Leap I, keyed for the struggle, fury and fume and roar;
> Rocks are spitting like hell-cats—Oh, it's a sport for kings,
> Life on a twist of the paddle... there's my 'Kim' on the floor.

The falling of Kipling's book on the floor is symbolic of how the nosto-maniac—probably Service in an autobiographical sense— wishes to exchange the "enervate life of the pen" for the manly bravado of rugged wilderness life.

Elsewhere in *Rhymes,* Service salts his poems with references to canoe travel. In "The Land Beyond," he writes about a land "that dreams at the gates of the day" that is reachable by "saddle and pack, by paddle and track." In "Sunshine" he dreams of "How sweet in slim canoe to glide, And dream, and let the world go by!"—which is precisely how he had felt on the Bell River. In "The Song of the Camp-Fire" he explores the relationship of risk, death and canoeing:

> And because you hold death lightly, so by death shall you be spared...
> On the roaring Arkilinik in a leaky bark canoe.

Service apparently preferred such danger over city life. In "I'm Scared of It All," perhaps written in New York City in 1910 before his long canoe trip the following spring, he confesses he's frightened "of the terrible town" and wants to go back to "My rivers that flash into foam." Too, he wishes he was up "where the Coppermine flows to the kick of my little canoe."

He still has a "little light canoe" in "The Squaw Man," but this time it is like a "flame upon the water" in a land "All river-veined and patterned with the pine."

Finally, in "While the Bannock Bakes," Service asks his reader to sit awhile with him where the "river is a-flop with fish, and rippled silver-clear." No longer is he thinking, as he did in his first book, of how wild rivers drown weak men like rats; nor, as in "To the Man of the High North" in *Ballads of a Cheechako,* of how "nameless men who nameless rivers travel... greet strange deaths alone." Rather, by the time Service wrote *Rhymes* there was "no doctor like the Wild." He and the reader—while bannock baked—were "fine specimens of manhood."

Why?

> It's the tracking and the packing and the poling in the sun;
> It's the sleeping in the open, it's the rugged, unfaked food;
> It's the snow-shoe and the paddle, and the camp-fire and the gun,
> And when I think of what I was, I know that it is good."

Service eventually became a world traveler, novelist and resident of Paris for 15 years. He worked in Hollywood, wrote a second autobiography covering his last 35 years (*Harper of Heaven*), then returned to France with his wife, Germaine Bourgoin. He continued writing verse in France at his seacoast cottage, *Dream Haven*, near Lanceiux. He never returned to Dawson City.

Yet the Yukon hung on in his heart.

"Of all my life," he admitted when an old man, "the eight years I spent there are the ones I would most like to live over."

Indeed, it was there—"In the land where the mountains are nameless, and the rivers all run God knows where"—that he staked a poetic paystreak that made him a millionaire. It was there he learned the power of gold. And it was there, in answering the call of the wild, that he found in vastness something he had lost.

4

BOB MARSHALL:
FROM KNOLLWOOD TO
ALASKA'S KOYUKUK

"To countless people the wilderness provides the ultimate delight because it combines the thrills of jeopardy and beauty. It is the last stand for that glorious adventure into the physically unknown that was commonplace in the lives of our ancestors, and has always constituted a major factor in the happiness of many exploratory souls."

—Robert Marshall

It was snowing hard on the North Fork of the Koyukuk River in Alaska's Brooks Range as Bob Marshall helped Ernie Johnson, Jesse Allen and Kenneth Harvey load their boat. For days they had tried to climb Mt. Doonerak but had been pushed back each time by bad weather. Now they had given up for the year. It had snowed in the mountains during the night, bringing snowline down to within 500 feet of the valley, so the group had decided to make an easy day of it by floating four miles down the North Fork to Fish Creek.

Marshall knew the north branch of Fish Creek rose in igneous mountains that had never known the foot of man. There lay Robert Service's vastness. There lay wilderness which on Marshall's map—and all maps—was blank. Bob had been haunted by blank spaces on maps since boyhood, since he was old enough to daydream about the explorations of Lewis and Clark, so it was with an intense sense of sustained excitement that he headed toward more *terra incognito* wilderness in Koyukuk country.

But the river, now flooding, had changed. Its current was dangerously fast, a full 15 miles per hour, and they noticed the river's main channel had shifted 2,000 feet from the western side of the river to the eastern side. Ernie casually mentioned pulling over and pitching camp.

Then they saw it.

"All at once," Marshall recalled in *Alaska Wilderness,* "we saw that what had appeared to be an innocuous gravel bank, about 40 feet high and no different from hundreds of others along the side of the river, was not along the side of the river at all but overhanging it. The tremendous floods which had changed the course of the river by 2,000 feet pounded with full, gigantic power against the gravel bank. The force of this terrific impact had washed away the gravel from the floodline. The drop in water since the flood crest, had left a gravel bank about one foot above the river and overhanging it. The main current shot straight under this overhang, and then turned and tore right *through* the gravel bank, tunneling underneath in a 30-foot-wide passage whose end we could not see."

The boat, with a sickening sound of crunching wood, slipped beneath the overhanging bank. Marshall was immediately dunked in cold black water. Death seemed imminent.

There was no way for Marshall to know if the water would carry him through the tunnel, pin him in a narrow cave, or slam his head against a rock or log suspended from the overhang's ceiling. He recalled Ernie's words about keeping his head above the water in a capsize, floating with the current—saving one's strength to escape the river's grasp on whatever side was best. Marshall thought of how easy it would be to die, how he would simply run out of breath then gasp for air only to suck in eternity instead. He also thought of how he wished he had time, before dying, to review his life's adventurous highlights.

These thoughts weren't orderly or logical. They were the flashback musings of a man choking on apparent peril.

Suddenly bright light filled the darkness. The Koyukuk had carried Marshall through the gravel bank as it short-circuited a bend in the river. Marshall, on the left side of the current, found slack water in the eddy of an uprooted spruce and waded easily to shore. He looked around, spotted Ernie and the damaged boat, and saw Kenneth and Jesse on the other side of the river. No one was hurt seriously. But it was snowing, the temperature in the low 30s, and everyone was shivering. Two fires were lit, one on each side of the river. There the men stood wringing out their clothes at their respective sentinels, heating their bodies, and certainly, like Muir on Taylor Glacier, feeling renewed if not keenly alive. Spared death by a pocketful of luck.

I

Bob Marshall had known—and would continue to know—his share of luck as one of the most influential Americans in the evolution of wilderness preservation. Besides being the first white person to explore much of Alaska's Central Brooks Range, he authored *The People's Forests, Arctic Village, Alaska Wilderness,* and almost 100 periodical articles on subjects ranging from scientific forestry to wilderness recreation. He was friends with many of the leading conservationists and preservationists of his time, took an active role in advising the Quetico-Superior Council in the early 1930s and spearheaded general U.S. Forest Service thought about wilderness. He also founded the Wilderness Society.

Robert Sterling Yard once aptly called Marshall "the most efficient weapon of preservation in existence."

For William O. Douglas, Bob Marshall "did as much, if not more than, any American to sound the alarm against inroads on our wilderness and to promote long-range scientific programs for its preservation." Stephen R. Fox, who believed it was under Marshall's guidance that the concept of wilderness took on a more permanent status both within government and the private sector, described Bob as "the first mountaineer in the conservation movement since Muir to approach his combination of firsthand experience, scientific interests, and writing skill."

"As to Bob's character," Sigurd F. Olson wrote me in 1978, "he had an indomitable urge to do the impossible, physically and mentally, because of a deep love of wild places."

Marshall was legendary as a hiker. His brother and chief biographer, George Marshall, said Bob—who hiked with tennis shoes because they were light and dried fast—made over 200 day hikes of 30 miles each and many 40-mile day hikes. One of his lifetime goals was to walk 30 miles in a day in every state. In 1936, he hiked *70* miles through Arizona's Fort Apache reservation in *one day*, then, after going sleepless for 34 hours, he attended a meeting. Paul Schaefer, past vice president of the Association for the Protection of the Adirondacks, recalled in a 1966 article in *The Living Wilderness* how Marshall decided on returning from an Alaskan trip to see how many high Adirondack peaks he could climb in a single day, and how many vertical feet he could achieve while doing it. Starting at 3:30 a.m. on July 15, 1932, Marshall climbed 14 peaks totaling 13,600 feet by 10:00 at night.

Such peripatetic love of wild places began for Marshall in New York's Adirondacks where his father, Louis (1856-1929), and mother, Florence Lowenstein Marshall (1873-1916), owned a summer home called "Knollwood" on Lower Saranac Lake. Its green and brown buildings overlooked a fleet of islands, while in the southeast were the high peaks of the Adirondacks. There young Bob—following his birth in the family's brownstone house in New York City on January 2, 1902—spent 21 consecutive summers.

"As a little boy," James Marshall wrote me of his brother, "he was shy, reticent, liked to be alone, composed poetry after he went to bed at night and, long before he could write, dictated it to our mother in the morning. He was afraid of the dark and made himself, when quite young, walk in the woods at

Knollwood at night without a light. He told me once that he felt that this helped him learn to be alone in the forest."

Bob's father cast a tall figure into his son's budding vision. Louis, the son of German immigrants (the name was *Marschall* in Germany), was a well-known constitutional lawyer, conservationist, and friend of Theodore Roosevelt and Woodrow Wilson. He was among delegates at the New York State constitutional convention of 1894 who, George Marshall has written, placed in the constitution the section that provides that New York's great Forest Preserve shall be "kept forever as wild forest lands." Louis continued to fight year after year against its being amended and against desecration of the Forest Preserve. Schaefer claimed the archives of the Association for the Protection of the Adirondacks are filled with letters and accounts of Louis Marshall's work with governors, legislators and members of constitutional conventions who sought his counsel. Louis was also a leader in Jewish affairs, a humanitarian and a defender of minority rights.

Young Bob, meanwhile, had already begun hungering for adventure. While he was bedridden with pneumonia, someone read him *Pioneer Boys of the Great Northwest* by Captain Ralph Bonehill, a book Bob re-read one to three times every year for the next 10 years. An ideology resulted that was, he wrote later, "definitely formed on a Lewis and Clark pattern, and for a time I really felt that while life might still be pleasant, it could never be the great adventure it might have been if I had only been born in time to join the Lewis and Clark Expedition."

Sometimes his Lewis and Clark daydreams ended in depression when he imagined he had been born a century too late.

Regardless, Marshall—when not playing baseball (130 games in eight years)—was hoofing around Knollwood's backyard: Lower Saranac Lake, Fish Creek, Forest Home Road and up surrounding peaks. As biographer Jim Glover tells it, one day while Bob was rummaging through a bookcase at Knollwood he found four dusty volumes of Verplanck Colvin's Adirondack topographical and land survey reports of the 1870s and 1880s. Colvin claimed some of the Adirondack ranges had never known the foot of man. Bob read all four reports, then read T. Morris Longstreth's *The Adirondacks*. Bob told his younger brother, George, about his readings and convinced him they should follow in Colvin's footsteps by hiking the high peaks of the neighborhood. Fortunately for the two boys, father Louis and Mother Florence had hired a family guide in 1906 by the name of Herb Clark. Clark was a wiry man of 50, well known for his fishing and rowing skills. It was Clark who taught the Marshall boys how to navigate in the woods with compass and map; it was he who led them to the top of Mt. Ampersand (3,352-feet), Bob's first peak, on August 15, 1916.

"He was the fastest man I have ever known in the pathless woods," Bob said of Clark. "Furthermore, he could take one glance at a mountain from some distant point, then not be able to see anything 200 feet from where he was walking for several hours, and emerge on the summit by what almost always would be the fastest and easiest route."

After Ampersand, mountains were in the threesome's blood. The trio climbed their first 4,000-footer, Whiteface (4,867-feet), in 1918, and then set out during the next six years to become the first climbers to scale 42 of the 46 peaks in the Adirondacks above 4,000 feet. (They climbed the other four peaks in the next four years.) In 1921 alone they scaled 23 peaks; 18 of them didn't have trails, and as far as anyone knew seven of the mountains hadn't been climbed before.

Adirondack mountain climbing was, in Bob's words, "our greatest joy in life" from 1918 to 1924. The best view, he thought, was from the summit of Haystack Mountain because it "was one of the few places east of the Rockies where a person could look over miles of territory without seeing civilization." Note-taker Bob published a booklet in 1922 about their climbs entitled *High Peaks of the Adirondacks.*

Marshall decided to become a forester in his teens, although he didn't have the remotest idea what forestry was. Instead, he had "vague notions of thrilling adventures with bad men, of lassoing infuriated grizzlies, and of riding down unknown canyons in Alaska." By his junior year in high school he knew he would hate to spend the greater part of his lifetime "in a stuffy office in a crowded city." He loved woods and solitude. Hence he enrolled in Columbia College for one year after graduating from Manhattan's Ethical Culture High School; after Columbia he spent four years at New York's State College of Forestry in Syracuse. In 1923, a year before getting his B.A. in forestry, he participated in a New York State Conservation Commission plot study in the Adirondacks. Following a summer working for the U.S. Forest Service in Washington State, he enrolled at Harvard Forest, Petersham, Massachusetts, where he received a Master of Forestry degree; his thesis was on the effect increased light has on hemlock growth when a forest's upper story is removed.

He was intoxicated with education from 1925 to 1928. He worked first as a junior forester, then as an assistant silviculturist, at the Northern Rocky Mountain Forest Experiment Station with headquarters in Missoula, Montana ("my best loved city"). Weekends here were spent hiking in Lewis and Clark and Flathead national forests, the same region known today as the Bob Marshall Wilderness Area.

In an article titled "Impressions From the Wilderness," Marshall described how a separate hike in the Selway National Forest of Idaho was at this time cementing his love of the wild. Friends had noticed his enthusiasm for backcountry experiences, and some were beginning to think he had gone overboard, that he was "taking an abnormally long time to outgrow the romanticism of childhood." Others implied he was chronically unbalanced. But, Marshall thought, certain doors of sensation were entirely shut to such critics: "They never felt the need of the unique esthetic stimulations which the wilderness alone can provide. They never sensed the value of being entirely independent physically. They never discerned that a person might die spiritually if he could not sometimes forsake all contact with his gregarious fellow-men, and the machines which they had created, and retire to an environment where there was no remote trace of humanity."

For himself "and for thousands with similar inclinations," however, Marshall already knew very well that the most important passion of life was "the overpowering desire to escape periodically from the strangling clutch of mechanistic civilization. To us the enjoyment of solitude, complete independence, and the beauty of undefiled panoramas is absolutely essential to happiness."

He felt this need for wilderness was as genuine as the more conventional yearnings for knowledge and love.

Marshall used the rest of "Impressions From the Wilderness" to describe two hikes in the Selway National Forest, one on the Lolo Trail, the other in Grave Peak country. The article is filled with vivid, if not sweet descriptions, for he wanted readers to gain an understanding of how someone could lust the primeval. Notably himself.

In 1928, the same year Bob enrolled at the Laboratory of Plant Physiology, Johns Hopkins University in Baltimore, Maryland, where he later earned a Ph.D. degree, he published another article, this time in *Forest Service Bulletin*; in it he tried to drum up support for preserving pristine sections of national forests. Primeval wilderness was beginning to stick to his mind like a wet tongue on cold steel.

II

Certainly it was a euphoric moment for Marshall, with his confessed fascination for "blank spaces on maps," when the wheels of Noel Qien's Hamilton airplane touched down at Wiseman, Alaska, on July 12, 1929. Wiseman's 77 whites, 44 Eskimos and six Indians were hunkered down on the Koyukuk River 200 miles from the nearest pavement, auto, railroad and, as Bob put it, "the closest electric light at Fairbanks."

It was the *terra incognito* mountain ranges to the north, however, which lured Marshall like a moth toward light.

Of particular interest to him was the Central Brooks Range, part of a vast mountain range stretching 600 miles east-to-west and 150 miles north-to-south, an area he felt was the most unknown part of Alaska. Half the Dall sheep of the world lived there, along with grizzlies, moose, wolves, and a million caribou. The Brooks Range consisted of a half-dozen mountain chains, including the Endicotts and Romanzofs, and was named after Dr. Alfred Brooks, an authority on Alaska and director of the U.S. Geological Survey.

Bob teamed up with Al Retzlaf, a prospector, miner, and woodsman for a trip up the North Fork of the Koyukuk River by foot with two packhorses. They passed between Boreal Mountain and Frigid Crags (the "Gates of the Arctic"), climbed Slatepile Mountain, then explored Ernie Creek where Bob pursued the explicit purpose of his first Alaskan trip: to study tree growth at northern timberline. Much of the area had never been visited by white *or* Eskimo. On the way back to Wiseman, Bob came face-to-face with a grizzly, and he and Retzlaf almost got cut off from reaching Wiseman by rain-swollen flooding rivers.

Marshall's baptismal plunge into the Brooks Range was a headspin of wilderness magic, heightened moreover in February of the following year when his article, "The Problem of the Wilderness," was printed in *Scientific Monthly*. Originally titled "Wilderness Areas," the piece was rejected five times before it was accepted. Marshall was 28. Benton MacKaye, father of the Appalachian Trail, called the article the "Magna Carta of the wilderness preservation movement." As a concise statement of the psychological and aesthetic values of wilderness, MacKaye said, and as a call for its preservation, the article was unprecedented. Nor has it been matched since.

"The Problem of the Wilderness" had four salient themes: 1) the disappearance of American wilderness, and the need to decide the fate of our last wilderness by "deliberate rationality"; 2) the benefits of wilderness—physical, mental and aesthetic; 3) the *rapidly* disappearing wilderness; and 4) the need to preserve it.

Throughout Marshall's discussion, and in fact throughout the rest of his life, he used the word *wilderness* to denote "a region which contains no permanent inhabitants, possesses no possibility of conveyance by any mechanical means and is sufficiently spacious that a person in crossing it must have the experience of sleeping out." Wilderness, moreover, required anyone who existed in it to depend exclusively on their own effort for survival. Marshall thought all roads, settlements and power transportation should be barred from wilderness to preserve "as nearly as possible the primitive environment." Trails and temporary shelters, however, which were common long before the coming of white men, were permissible.

When going into greater detail, Bob described the physical benefit of wilderness as being reducible to health—not only the obvious clean air, clean water and quiet, but the physical challenge of carrying heavy packs, snowshoeing in blizzards and climbing difficult peaks. Wilderness offered opportunities for complete self-sufficiency when camping safely was based on skills, something he felt was important as long as Americans prized individuality and competence. There was also the factor of man's quest for adventure, "breaking into unpenetrated ground, venturing beyond the boundary of normal aptitude, extending oneself to the limit of capacity, courageously facing peril."

Marshall distilled the mental benefits of wilderness experiences down to their ability to incite independent thought requiring an "objectivity and perspective seldom possible in the distracting propinquity of one's fellow men." He cited as examples Thoreau and Muir, Thomas Jefferson, and William James. Repose, too, was a vital mental benefit of wilderness; many people who lived stressful urban lives depended upon the possibility of convalescing in the silence and privacy of sylvan places to help them cope with modern life.

Marshall's explanation of wilderness's aesthetic values was especially graphic and insightful, as pertinent today when defending wild country's intangible worth as it was a half-century ago.

For one thing, of the many kinds of world beauty only natural phenomena like wilderness are detached from all temporal relationships. Everything else—Egypt's temples, paintings of the Renaissance—are "anchored in the historic stream." As Bob put it, the "silent wanderer crawling up the rocky shore of the turbulent river could be a savage from some prehistoric epic or a fugitive from twentieth century mechanization." He also felt the sheer stupendousness of the wilderness gives it a quality of intangibility unknown in ordinary manifestations of ocular beauty. Wilderness vistas sometimes caused "a certain giddy sensation that there are no distances, no measures, simply unrelated matter rising and falling without any analogy to the banal geometry of breadth, thickness and height."

The size of wilderness, he argued, also has a physical ambience that most forms of beauty lack. And because Marshall explored that ambience so well, leading the reader nearer and nearer to the essence of his argument, it is appropriate to quote him at length:

> One looks from outside at works of art and architecture, listens from outside to music or poetry. But when one looks at and listens to the wilderness he is encompassed by his experiences of beauty, lives in the midst of his esthetic universe.
>
> A fourth peculiarity about the wilderness is that it exhibits a dynamic beauty. A Beethoven symphony or a Shakespearean drama, a landscape by Corot or a Gothic cathedral, once they are finished become virtually static. But the wilderness is in constant flux. A seed germinates, and a stunted seedling battles for decades against the dense shade of the virgin forest. Then some ancient tree blows down and the long-suppressed plant suddenly enters into the full vigor of delayed youth, grows rapidly from sapling to maturity, declines into the conky senility of many centuries, dropping millions of seeds to start a new forest upon the rotting debris of its own ancestors, and eventually topples over to admit the sunlight which ripens another woodland generation.
>
> Another singular aspect of the wilderness is that it gratifies every one of the senses. There is unanimity in venerating the sights and sounds of the forest. But what are generally esteemed to be the minor senses should not be slighted. No one who has ever strolled in springtime through seas of blooming violets, or lain at night on boughs of fresh balsam, or walked across dank holms in early morning can omit odor from the joys of the primordial environment. No one who has felt the stiff wind of mountaintops or the softness of untrodden sphagnum will forget the exhilaration experienced through touch. "Nothing ever tastes as good as when it's cooked in the woods" is a tribute to another sense. Even equilibrium causes a blithe exultation during many a river crossing on tenuous foot log and many a perilous conquest of precipice. Finally, it is well to reflect that the wilderness furnishes perhaps the best opportunity for pure esthetic enjoyment. This requires that beauty be observed as a unity, and that for the brief duration of any pure esthetic experience the cognition of the observed object must completely fill the spectator's cosmos. There can be no extraneous thoughts—no question about the creator of the phenomenon, its structure, what it resembles or what vanity in the beholder it gratifies. "The purely esthetic observer has for the moment forgotten his own soul"; he has only one sensation left and that is exquisiteness. In the wilderness, with its entire freedom from the manifestations of

human will, that perfect objectivity which is essential for pure esthetic rapture can probably be achieved more readily than among any other forms of beauty.

Marshall's "Magna Carta" also outlined several disadvantages of wilderness areas and how to resolve them, at least in part, but it was his article's conclusion that rang the chimes of wilderness preservation at the time. He felt a thorough study should be done immediately to determine the probable wilderness needs of the country. Exigency was required because 1) it's easy to turn a natural area to "industrial or motor usage," but practically impossible to reverse the process, 2) the population of wilderness enthusiasts was growing, and 3) modern standards of living would enable people to gratify previously weak yearnings for wilderness recreation. Once the study was done, Bob called for immediate steps to preserve enough wild country "to ensure everyone who hungers for it a generous opportunity of enjoying wilderness isolation."

To carry out this program, he concluded, "it is exigent that all friends of the wilderness ideal should unite. If they do not present the urgency of their viewpoint the other side will certainly capture popular support. Then it will only be a few years until the last escape from society will be barricaded. If that day arrives there will be countless souls born to live in strangulation, countless human beings who will be crushed under the artificial edifice raised by man. There is just one hope of repulsing the tyrannical ambition of civilization to conquer every niche on the whole earth. That hope is the organization of spirited people who will fight for the freedom of the wilderness."

Strong words, these, for a 28-year-old. No matter. Their author, whom the Eskimos at Wiseman named *Oomik Polluk* ("Big Whiskers"), was busy chasing related dreams. The ink of "The Problem of the Wilderness" was barely dry in *Scientific Monthly* when Marshall received his doctorate degree from Johns Hopkins in plant physiology. He was, furthermore, getting ready for a 13-month stay in Wiseman.

———————

Marshall's reasons for going to Wiseman, or anywhere in the Alaskan bush for that matter, were changing by August 1930. As a scientific forester he was still interested in studying northern Alaska's timberline, but he had left Wiseman in 1929 with the vivid impression that the region's whites and Eskimos were on the whole the happiest folk he had ever met. Hence, he decided to combine two objectives: study Wiseman's eclectic frontier community, and continue exploring the headwaters of the North Fork of the Koyukuk River.

These goals were at least the ones he told inquiring friends and associates.

Yet Marshall had other reasons for returning to wild Alaska, the most important being that he wanted to gain "the absolutely unassessable thrill of just looking at superb natural beauty." He was beginning to realize that the justification for exploration in modern times was found in what it contributes to the personal happiness of the explorer, not in what it might add to the well-being of the human race. And as far as he was concerned, he wanted the thrill of "that most glorious of all pastimes": setting foot where no one had ever walked before.

Once in Alaska, Bob's first trip—again with Retzlaf—took him back up the North Fork of the Koyukuk to Ernie Creek country; it included exploration of Kenunga Creek and Ernie Pass. The return trip via Jack Delay Pass led Marshall and Retzlaf into sedge tussock terrain for which the Brooks Range is notorious. The tussocks were so high and grew so close together that walking between them was almost impossible. "But it was also impossible to walk on top of them for any distance," Bob recalled in *Alaska Wilderness*, "because they would roll over, plunging us off into muck. This would happen about once in every twenty steps and as we took about two thousand steps to the mile I think it conservative to say that at least a hundred times in each of three miles we would find ourselves sitting on the ground, a 65-pound pack anchoring us firmly in the mud, with an overhanging cliff of sedge formation nearly waist-high towering above us. We would grit our teeth, gather energy, and pull ourselves up the necessary three feet—only to do it all over again within the next twenty paces." They began the trip with horses but returned by pack, altogether covering 216 miles. They made 170 miles of side trips with light packs, climbed six unscaled peaks (three on the Arctic Divide), visited three major unexplored valleys and six minor valleys, gulches, and chasms, and mapped 42 miles of previously untraversed valleys. Reaching Wiseman, Al returned to Fairbanks while Bob settled in a 16- by 18-foot rented log cabin near the roadhouse for the winter.

What followed was the fulfillment of Marshall's wildest exploration fantasies. He had scant time to read his cache of 66 books as he alternated social binges with wilderness trips.

In October he went on a four-day shake-down dog sled trip. A few weeks later, he, Jesse Allen and Kenneth Harvey mushed for 10 days to get eight cached sheep near the head of the Dietrich River. In March, following a debate whether Clear River headed against the Arctic Divide, Bob and Ernie Johnson explored Clear River's headwaters; they rounded out their trip with a sally over to Wild Lake country then returned to Wiseman through Bettles.

It was on the Clear River trip that Bob experienced what he called "the supreme exultation of which a person is capable" when he and Ernie stood in the pass between Clear and Hammond rivers. There Marshall gazed "into the winter-buried mystery of the Arctic, where great, barren peaks rose into the deep blue of the northern sky, where valleys, devoid even of willows, led far off into unknown canyons. Below me lay a chasm so many hundreds of feet deep it seemed no sunlight could ever penetrate its depths. From its upper reaches, bathed in sunshine, a white pinnacle rose into the air for almost a mile...." Earlier he had been stunned by the rugged terrain around Karillyukpuk Creek, the largest fork of Clear River, where nature seemed so grand, so splendid that all other life seemed trivial in its presence.

Almost as a postscript, Bob added that part of his joy in Clear River country was the knowledge that mankind, despite its mechanical power, could never duplicate what lay before him.

Marshall's lifestyle back in Wiseman manifested his wide, cultivated tastes in literature and music. The books he read included *The Magic Mountain*, *Anna Karenina*, *Plays of Euripides*, *The Decline of the West*, *The Sexual Life of Savages*, *Social Psychology*, *Physics of the Air*, and *Medical Biometry* and *Statistics*, and *Thermodynamics*. In the evening after one of Wiseman's many dances, he would walk home in the crisp, freezing air while northern lights rolled brightly overhead. Reaching his cabin he would read or, if tired, turn on some music while preparing for bed. He might play the *Hungarian Rhapsody*, the *Gymnopedie*, or Schubert's *Unfinished Symphony*. He always put on the last record just before getting into bed. There he would listen to the music. When the record player would click off, he would usually fall asleep within 30 seconds—a man, for the moment, at perfect peace.

He and Ernie Johnson made another trip together in July and August of 1931, before Bob had to return to the lower 48 states. It was a trip of 50 days by motorboat and foot, with the explicit purpose of exploring 4,500 square miles of unknown wilderness, an area the size of Connecticut bounded on the south by the main Koyukuk River and lower Alatna River, on the north by the Arctic Divide, on the east by the John River, and on the west by the Alatna River and one of it tributaries, the Unakserak. While sojourning on the John, Bob and Ernie climbed Cairn Mountain where they absorbed a Brooks Range panorama of black summits and green slopes tumbling in a wild confusion as far as they could see. Marshall thought the mountains seemed to be falling and rising like giant ocean waves frozen in motion. It was an extremely pleasant sensation, one which Marshall carried with him to fireside his and Ernie's last night out.

Johnson had cooked a perfect lamb stew. Both men sat together on a log by the fire as stars came out. "We didn't say very much sitting there," Bob recalled. "You don't when it is your last camp with a companion who had shared the most perfect summer of a lifetime. We just sat, with a feeling warmer than the crackling fire, exulting in the sharp-edged pattern which the mountain walls cut against the northern sky; listening to the peaceful turmoil of the arctic river with its infinite variation in rhythm and tone; smelling the luxuriance of untainted arctic valleys; feeling the wholesome cleanliness of arctic breezes blowing on cheeks and hair."

Gone were the Adirondacks. Gone were the nights when young Bob groped around Knollwood's darkness to squelch fears of the unknown.

III

Marshall began working on three literary projects when he returned to Washington, D.C. and New York from Alaska in 1931. He wasn't, as his brother George has ably documented, a stranger to the pen. A bibliography of Bob's writings totals at least 104 published works on wilderness theory and policy, wilderness travel, sociology, technical forestry, Alaskan policy, the Adirondacks and general national forest policy. It was the latter he addressed in 1932, when collaborating with the U.S. Forest Service in the Copeland Report, *A National Plan for American Forestry*, the most comprehensive report on forestry at the time. Bob wrote the sections on national parks, wilderness and recreation.

It was in 1933, however, the same year he was appointed Director of Forestry of the Office of Indian Affairs (now the Bureau of Indian Affairs), that his writing career blossomed. Two of his three major books, *Arctic Village* and *The People's Forests*, were published.

Arctic Village was, some people believe, Bob's most important book: a 399-page study of whites and Eskimos flourishing in the upper reaches of the Koyukuk during his Wiseman experiences in 1930-31. Chapters cover geography, climate, history, roadhouse activities, food, clothing, shelter, the quest for gold, sex life, philosophy and even conversation, of which Marshall—an inveterate record keeper—recorded 5,016 minutes.

"The fact that plans for more than three months in advance only occupied ten minutes out of more than five thousand minutes of conversation," he noted, "is typical of one of the most distinctive Koyukuk traits. People live and think emphatically in the present, enjoy life while it is passing without dreaming constantly about some future happiness, and do not spend their time in futile worry about what will probably never occur."

Overall, he found the inhabitants of the Koyukuk region "would rather eat beans with liberty, burn candles with independence, and mush dogs with adventure than to have the luxury and the restrictions of the outside world."

Outside—in the lower 48 states—*Arctic Village* became a bestseller and a Literary Guild selection. It was reviewed in at least 100 publications. *Forum* called it "an unusually interesting and valuable sociological document, fit to join the works of Malinowsky and Margaret Mead, but more humanly appealing than either." Few people realized Bob shared his royalties from *Arctic Village* with Wiseman's residents: about $18 each.

The People's Forests, meanwhile, was a small book of 48,000 words written on the heels of *A National Plan for American Forestry* and George P. Ahern's *Deforested America*. It examined the use and abuse of American forests. After systematically describing the devastation of forests sweeping the country, Bob analyzed the economic and aesthetic values of forests and wilderness. In 1931, he noted, there were 246,900,000 visitors to forests, parks and monuments; in 15 years park use had increased 750 percent, forest use 920 percent, evincing the "enormous popularity which recreational forest use [had] attained in America."

"There can be no doubt," he added, "that the greatest attraction of the forests is their natural beauty. As society becomes more and more mechanized, it will be more and more difficult for many people to stand the nervous strain, the high pressure, and the drabness of their lives. To escape these abominations, constantly growing numbers will seek the primitive for the finest features in life."

The most important values of forest recreation, Marshall argued, are not reducible to monetary terms. They are concerned with inspiration, gains in understanding and aesthetic enjoyments. It was no more valid to rate them in terms of dollars and cents than it was to rate the value of a telephone pole in terms of the inspiration it gives. The common denominator of both commodity and recreational values of forests was the human happiness derived from each use.

There are many reasons why people seek wilderness, he wrote, in what amounts to a recapitulation of "The Problem of the Wilderness": health, physical exhilaration, beauty and communion with nature.

"For many people," he explained, "there is a significance, as vital and as satisfying as that which any communicant ever derives from feeling his spirit one with God, in feeling themselves to be one with nature, in cutting all bonds of habit and drifting into the timeless continuity of the primeval."

Bob cited how some people crave other values in wilderness: contemplation, scientific knowledge, self-sufficiency, even escape. Again he elaborated how wilderness is infused with dynamic beauty, how it offers the best opportunity for pure aesthetic enjoyment, and that in wilderness, beauty can be experienced as an all encompassing unity. Redundant? Yes. But Marshall was hammering at a point.

He didn't mince words in *The People's Forests*.

"What we are after," he said, "is human happiness."

The challenge for everyone was to figure out how to manage the national forests in order to realize their highest potentialities for mankind's well-being. As far as recreation and wilderness preservation were concerned, people's needs varied along an entire spectrum of use which, in turn, required designation and management of different *types* of forest. These types entailed distinct standards of beauty, size and administration.

He therefore proposed area definitions: "Superlative" areas, he said, are those regions of such astounding beauty—the Grand Canyon, the Tetons, Crater Lake, etc.—that the obvious necessity to protect them was practically beyond dispute.

—"Primeval" areas are those with virgin timber where human activities haven't upset nature's normal processes. They preserve virginal growth conditions. The two major values of primeval areas are: 1) scientific study for comparison purposes, and 2) the ability of primeval areas to inspire people with beauty. Marshall recommended a half-dozen primeval areas of at least 5,000 acres be set aside in every forest type.

—"Wilderness" areas were defined identically to the definition used in "The Problem of the Wilderness." At least 200,000 acres seemed to be about the smallest size a designated wilderness could be. The basic difference between a primeval area and wilderness area, he explained, was that the former exhibits primitive conditions of growth, while wilderness areas exhibit *primitive methods of transportation*. Wilderness areas could contain primeval areas, but their chief function "is not to make possible contact with the virgin forest but rather to make it possible to retire completely from the modes of transportation and the living conditions of the twentieth century."

At the time—1933—Marshall estimated there were only nine areas of 1,000,000 acres or more, 18 areas of 500,000 acres or more, and 38 areas of 200,000 acres or more that would qualify as wilderness without interfering with highway plans, mining and fire protection. He proposed setting aside 20 million acres as wilderness that, together with additional acreage for superlative, primeval, roadside, campsite, residence and outing areas totaled 55 million acres of land. This was 11 percent of the total 506 million acres of commercial timber land then in the United States.

The upshot of *The People's Forests*, however, was not the value of recreation per se, but the need for the public to wrest control of its forest resources then being devastated (about 1 million acres a year) under private ownership. He urged the public to purchase at least 562 million acres out of the then 670 million acres of potential forest land. Our woods do not belong to lumbermen, he concluded. Every acre of woodland in the country—and perhaps here he stretched the point—is rightly a part of the people's forests.

Marshall's obligations as director of forestry in the Office of Indian affairs in the Interior Department didn't quiet his growing concern for the need of some kind of agency or organization to watchdog American wilderness. He was already convinced that wilderness areas were vanishing so quickly that it was hard for most people "to reorient themselves to the viewpoint that the once all-pervading wilderness has become almost extinct." He thought a "Wilderness Planning Board" should perhaps be appointed, and that wilderness areas should be set aside by an Act of Congress, like national parks (thus prefiguring the Wilderness Act of 1964 which authorized Congress to do precisely this).

The only thing *not* being planned, he complained to Dr. Rexford G. Tugwell of the Department of the Interior in a letter of February 27, 1934, "is the preservation of natural conditions." At that time "not a single preserve of even 5,000 acres [had] yet been set aside where timber cutting and grazing will be barred."

Two of Marshall's friends, meanwhile, Benton MacKaye, a forester and regional planner then employed by the Tennessee Valley Authority, and Harold Anderson, the founder of the Potomac Appalachian Trail Club, were discussing the same problem. Anderson was encouraging like-minded folks to band together to give a united expression of their views. This nucleus of wilderness preservationists, together with a half-dozen others, organized a petition in October 1934 to form the Wilderness Society. The group's explicit purpose was to hold wild areas sound-proof as well as sight-proof from the continent's increasingly mechanized life.

Marshall: One Man's Reaction

"His eyes reflected a great joy for living, and his face was deeply tanned and ruddy with health. He was dressed in a

> *light, well-worn, plaid shirt, blue denims, and sneakers... He*
> *exuded a restless, dynamic strength of purpose... He seemed to*
> *personify all that we saw before us: the limitless sweep of moun-*
> *tains rolling on and on to far horizons, the ancient rocks, the*
> *deep gorges, the unbroken forests, the scores of glacial lakes*
> *sparkling in the sunlight, and the rivers threading their way*
> *down lovely valleys. There was about him the essence of a wild*
> *freedom and an utter determination to preserve wilderness for*
> *generations to come."*
>
> —Marshall, as described by Paul Schaefer,
> after they met in New York's Adirondacks in 1932

The group had nine principles, some of them reflecting Marshall's maturing wilderness philosophy as much as anything else. The first principle described wilderness—"the environment of solitude"—as a "natural mental resource having the same basic relation to man's ultimate thought and culture as coal, timber, and other physical resources have to his material needs." Secondly, the time had come to recognize wilderness as a serious human need, rather than a plaything or luxury. This need, furthermore, was being destroyed by motor roads and radios.

Two other Society principles focused on how, because wilderness was vanishing, what wild areas remained are "all-precious" and their preservation constituted a vital necessity. Too, any encroachment on any single American wilderness area was an "attack upon the whole," therefore creating an issue of national importance and not one for local action alone.

In a November 1934 letter to Ernest Oberholtzer, a landscape architect but also the prime mover behind the Quetico-Superior wilderness of northeastern Minnesota and northwestern Ontario, Marshall said he didn't want any "straddlers" to join the Wilderness Society, "for in the past they have surrendered too much good wilderness and primeval areas which should never have been lost." In another letter to Oberholtzer, Marshall said he had been asked to be president of the Society but had refused due to possible conflicts of interest as head of Interior's Indian Affairs. He wanted Aldo Leopold to be president, partly because Leopold's article, "The Last Stand of the Wilderness" in the October 1925 issue of *American Forests*, had proposed setting aside extensive wilderness areas for the first time, at least since Thoreau's era. MacKaye, meanwhile, should be vice-president.

Oberholtzer, who approved of Marshall's recommendations, had originally refused to sign the Wilderness Society's credo because he was overworked with Quetico-Superior affairs. He endorsed the Society's principles, but he didn't have the funds, energy or health to become involved with wilderness matters outside his home region. He later changed his mind and signed the credo.

When Leopold, like Marshall, declined the Society's presidency, it was offered to Robert Sterling Yard who accepted it. Yard was 74, oldest of the

Society's founders; for almost 20 years he had been administrative head of the National Parks Association. The Society was officially launched in 1935 with a $1,000 donation from Marshall. Thereafter, until his death, Marshall nevertheless controlled the Society, partly by his donations of $2,500 to $3,000 a year, and partly by his dominating presence.

"He was so magnificently informed, and yet so humble about it," Harvey Broome, a fellow Society founder and Knoxville lawyer, has said about Bob. "He dominated our meetings without our realizing it."

Marshall set up a self-perpetuating Society council with members on it, such as his brother, George, and wilderness biologist Olaus Murie, who believed in the Society's principles. Five of the 13 councilors were, or had been, associated with the Forest Service. The council was supposed to guide Society policy but when Bob died Yard confessed that "instead of the ideas of one man, we shall have those of thirteen."

Leopold: On Wilderness

"*Right here I had better explain that motor roads, cottages, and launches do not necessarily destroy hunting and fishing, but they destroy the wilderness, which to certain tastes is quite as important.... [W]ilderness can not be re-created when the need for it is determined by hindsight. The need for it must be determined by foresight, and the necessary areas segregated and preserved.*"

—Aldo Leopold

So staunch was Marshall in refusing to compromise his—and the Society's—wilderness values, that even as a professional forester he couldn't condone so-called "improvements" in wilderness areas. In June 1935, he wrote Ferdinand Silcox, Chief of the U.S. Forest Service, from the Consolidated Chippewa Agency in Cass Lake, Minnesota, after a brief tour in the Ely-Buyck area on the perimeter of the Quetico-Superior. Marshall had recently been appointed by the Interior Department to serve on the President's Committee for the Quetico-Superior, so he held special interest in the region. He complained to Silcox of a half-dozen winter roads branching off from the Ely-Buyck Road (now Echo Trail) to threaten adjacent roadless areas. He also cited unnatural trails, burn spots, cleared brush, dirt pits and elevated trails.

"To me," he wrote, "one of the finest features in a real wilderness trail is traveling for miles through the acid flora of the virgin forest... The Wisconsin lake country is almost as artificial as Central Park. Most of the Minnesota lake country has been devastated and opened up by all manner of roads. There is just one little bit of really primitive wilderness in the whole of the lake states; Along [sic] the border lakes in Minnesota and extending a short distance south... There are still great wilderness valleys left in the Quetico-Superior country but if the present CCC program is continued they will be seriously depleted.

"My God, Sil, I cannot conceive how increasing the growth of black spruce or jackpine [by thinning] for ten years or giving a little better underfooting to a man packing supplies to a lookout possibly balance the damage caused to primitive wilderness of this type remaining in the United States."

Marshall's mission became clear.

"The preservation of our few remaining wilderness areas," he confessed to Silcox, "seems more important to me at the present moment than anything else which is possible in a conservation way."

IV

The year 1937 was a banner year for Marshall as a writer, bureaucrat, wilderness traveler and what *National Geographic* author Mike Edwards called "hot-gospeler of the primeval."

In April he published "The Universe of the Wilderness is Vanishing" in *Nature Magazine*. It was a clarion exposition of his wilderness philosophy, a new and updated crystallization of how wilderness areas were vanishing, "melting away like the last snowbank on some south-facing mountainside during a hot afternoon in June." He responded to the growing number of critics who claimed it was childish to hold on to the days of Lewis and Clark, and that doing so in terms of preserving wild land was an unnecessary luxury the nation couldn't afford.

Yet for Bob the nation could afford to sacrifice *almost any other value* to retain something of the primitive.

"To countless people," he explained, "the wilderness provides the ultimate delight because it combines the thrills of jeopardy and beauty. It is the last stand for that glorious adventure into the physically unknown that was commonplace in the lives of our ancestors, and has always constituted a major factor in the happiness of many exploratory souls. It is also the perfect esthetic experience because it appeals to all the senses. It is vast panoramas, full of height and depth and glowing color, on a scale so overwhelming as to wipe out the ordinary meaning of dimensions. It is the song of the hermit thrush at twilight and the lapping of waves against the shoreline and the melody of the wind in the trees. It is the unique odor of balsams and of freshly-turned humus and of mist rising from mountain meadows. It is the feel of spruce needles under foot and sunshine on your face and wind blowing through your hair. It is all of these at the same time, blended into a unity that can only be appreciated with leisure and which is ruined by artificiality."

Throughout the 1930s, as even today, one of the major arguments against wilderness preservation was Gifford Pinchot's dictum of "multiple use," that forests should be used to reap the greatest good for the greatest number of people. Bob rebutted this by saying the relationship between goods and people doesn't have to take place on *every* acre.

"If it did, we would be forced to change our metropolitan art galleries into metropolitan bowling alleys. Our state universities, which are used by a minor fraction of the population, would be converted into state circuses where hundreds could be exhilarated for every one person who may be either exhilarated or depressed now. The Library of Congress would become a national hot dog stand, and the new Supreme Court building would be converted into a gigantic garage where it could house a thousand people's autos instead of Nine Gentlemen of the Law."

There are many things, he said, that depend for their value on the *total* impression they have on the senses. Parts of their unity meant nothing. He explained how the Mona Lisa had thrilled many people, but if it was cut into inch-square pieces and distributed to art galleries around the world, where millions could see it rather than hundreds, then neither the millions nor the hundreds would derive any genuine value.

Regarding land, *volume* of use should not be management's objective.

"Quality as well as quantity," he reasoned, "must enter into any evaluation of competing types of recreation, because one really deep experience may be worth an infinite number of ordinary experiences."

Marshall admitted that nonprimitive and motorized forms of recreation would continue to bring joy to multitudes with no taste for wilderness. Nevertheless this didn't mean the minority who do enjoy "the far greater elation of wilderness travel" should be shortchanged by having their relatively few wilderness areas destroyed by transportation routes. Each group, he concluded, should be tolerant enough to respect the variety of pleasure others enjoy. Available lands should be divided accordingly.

Bob ended "The Universe of the Wilderness is Vanishing" by analyzing the threats posed to wild regions by waterpower projects, grazing, inefficient forestry, needless road projects and truck trails. He felt these would have to be fought by well-organized groups willing to battle with legislators in public arenas.

His own roles in the public arena expanded in May 1937, when Silcox appointed him to head the Forest Service's Division of Recreation and Lands, a position practically created especially for Marshall. A year earlier, Bob had prepared—along with Althea Dobbins—a map at his own expense, inventorying all the roadless areas of 300,000 acres or more left in the United States. Thirty-two of the 46 areas were in western national forests. At the time he had sent each area's regional forester a copy of his inventory, along with management recommendations, but now as Chief of Recreation and Lands he planned a series of field trips to inspect potential wilderness areas.

This was, he admitted again in a letter to Oberholtzer, the work he was most interested in.

———————

By June, Oberholtzer was helping Marshall plan a canoe trip along the boundary waters of Superior National Forest in northeastern Minnesota. "Ober," as he was known to friends, suggested Bob motor to the Basswood

River than canoe via Crooked Lake and Lac la Croix to Crane Lake "making some short side trips into tributaries along the way." In the same letter, Oberholtzer told Marshall that Sig Olson—a Quetico-Superior guide, preservationist, author and dean of Ely Junior College on the perimeter of the boundary waters—recommended Marshall take several trips by plane to get "a bird's view of the lakeland." Ober hoped to canoe with Marshall and Olson, and if so a fourth man would go along as cook. If Ober couldn't go, Marshall and Olson would go alone. Which is exactly how the trip ended up.

The canoe trip was historic in that it brought two of the century's most influential wilderness preservationists together in the backcountry. As for Bob, he wanted to go in paddling and come out the same way.

"No launches," he penned Olson, "no planes, no mechanized transportation of any kind. I want to see that wilderness the way the voyageurs saw it and travel the way they did."

Marshall and Olson began their five-day trip on a clear day in August, with fair winds on Fall Lake, east of Ely. They shared a kettle of tea at Newton Falls, then paddled swiftly down Newton Lake, portaged around Pipestone Falls, and cruised through the rocky, pine-covered islands of Basswood Lake's Pipestone Bay. Their first camp was along the Canadian side of Basswood River.

"The blue skies," Olson recalled in an article titled "Quetico-Superior Elegy" in *The Living Wilderness*, "had disappeared and it was misting and dark. As we made that last carry, we could see the river swirling down below us. On a shelf of rock just above the stream and commanding a full view of the rapids were the tattered remains of an Indian teepee, just a few old poles and a roll of torn birchbark, stacked together."

Marshall wanted to camp there. The spot had tradition, he told Olson, and the voyageurs had probably camped there. Olson was convinced. Besides, it was dark and raining hard. They set up their tent. As the rain poured they ate beans, hardtack, drank coffee and capped dinner off with dried fruit. Before sleeping, Olson showed Marshall how to catch a northern pike with a hook and line he carried with him on all canoe trips.

They canoed down Basswood River the next day, visited pictographs on Crooked Lake, then paddled across the international boundary into Ontario's Quetico Provincial Park. Olson wanted to show Marshall how the canoe routes from Lake Superior and Superior National Forest continued into the north, how the whole region was a single geographical unit, "not an area split by a political boundary line." It was also important for Marshall to see how the canoe routes were part of a much larger wilderness canoe system, and how important it was that both areas receive similar management. Bob and Sig eventually canoed Robinson Lake, Sarah, McIntyre, Brent and Cone lakes. They sometimes portaged into small lakes off the main canoe route to see what they were like. Their third night was spent at Curtain Falls, outlet of Crooked Lake, and the next day they paddled through Iron Lake and portaged into Lac la Croix.

They heard the motor just south of Lac la Croix's Shortiss Island. They hadn't seen anyone yet, had heard no motors, but now they stopped paddling to watch the Forest Service's ChrisCraft motorboat bear down on them.

"Your voyageur days are over," Olson quipped to Marshall. "From now on this is an official tour of inspection."

Once the motorboat had swung alongside Olson's and Marshall's wood-canvas canoe, the ranger asked if Marshall was one of the party. Yep. He then told Marshall the motorboat was at his disposal if he wanted to use it.

Marshall looked at Olson and grinned.

"No thanks," Marshall said to the ranger. "We've still got some exploring to do with the canoe, but tell the gang at the ranger station we'll see them for supper tonight."

Later that night, at the American ranger station above the mouth of Boulder River on Lac la Croix, Marshall told several Forest Service officers he hoped the whole Rainy Lake watershed, which comprised much of the Quetico-Superior, would be made into an international forest to be preserved and managed by both American and Canadian agencies as wilderness canoe country. Wilderness canoeing was the region's most important recreational aspect, he said, and without it the area would lose its color and charm.

Marshall continued to impress Olson the next morning when he turned down a plane ride back to Ely. Instead, he wanted to paddle out on Boulder River, Agnes and Nina-Moose lakes, then up Moose River until he and Sig reached the Echo Trail.

Olson later described Marshall as "one of the best wilderness travelers on the continent." He didn't know where Bob got his tremendous enthusiasm for covering distance, for he seemed to be born "with a love of wide open country in his blood." Four walls, moreover, seemed to cramp him as did all small, confining situations.

Marshall: On Wilderness Values

"The most glorious value of the wilderness is that in it a person may be completely disassociated from the mechanical and dated age of the twentieth century, and bury himself in the timeless oblivion of nature. Its enjoyment depends on a very delicate psychological adjustment... You have got to be immersed in a region where you know that mechanization is really absent, and where you are thrown entirely on the glorious necessity of depending on your own powers.

—Bob Marshall, "The Wilderness on Trial,"
Outdoor America, March 1938

Sig felt Marshall's wild free spirit only found release and satisfaction on wilderness trails, and he used to tease him of wearing "seven-league boots" and would ask him how he survived life in the big towns.

V

Marshall, too, must have wondered how he survived life in the big towns, for in 1938, one year after his canoe trip with Olson, he was again haunted by Alaska.

Restless, he wrote Ernie Johnson:

"I keep thinking constantly of those glorious 76 days we spent together out in the wilds of the Koyukuk drainage. I have never spent happier days in my life. In many ways the greatest one day I have spent was the day we snowshoed up the very head of the Clear River and looked down over the top into the Hammond River watershed."

Bob wanted now to return to Alaska to climb Mt. Doonerak, and to explore the headwaters of the Anaktuvuk River which, via the Colville River, empties north into the Arctic Ocean.

Marshall was assailed by Alaskan reporters on his way to Wiseman in August. They wanted to know if he was afraid of being lynched by villagers because of his candid publicizing of Wiseman in *Arctic Village* five years earlier. Yes, he was nervous, but he needn't have been. He was greeted with open arms.

"Of course, Bob," George Eaton, 77, told him, "when I was saying how I'd slept with more women than any other man in Alaska, I didn't expect you to put it in a book, but I'm a-telling you, it's true."

Wiseman had changed much since he had been there last. Two or three planes arrived each week instead of about 13 a year. There were now 150 tourists a year instead of one. Almost all of the old residents had left or died. A car worked the six-mile road between Wiseman and Nolan Creek. Change had come quickly, surprising Marshall, yet he was pleased to see there were no "unpleasant remarks about *Arctic Village*, in spite of the described 'improprieties' in terms of Outside customs."

Marshall, Johnson, Jesse Allen and Kenneth Harvey voyaged up the North Fork of the Koyukuk River on August 10 in a 30-foot long, 1,200-pound boat with 1,300 pounds of food and gear, and 700 pounds of men and dogs. They explored Pyramid Creek for the next two weeks while base-camped near Ernie Creek. They climbed the Arctic Divide. And as they hoped, they explored the upper reaches of the Anaktuvuk.

"Everything we looked upon was unknown to human gaze," Bob wrote in a journal (later edited by his brother, George, and published in *Alaska Wilderness*). "The nearest humans were a hundred and twenty-five miles away, and the civilization of which they constituted the very fringe—a civilization remote from nature, artificial, dominated by the exploitation of man by man—seemed unreal, unbelievable. Our present situation seemed also unreal, but that was the unreality of a freshness beyond experience. It was the unreality of a remoteness which made it seem as if we had landed miraculously on another planet which throughout all passage of time had been without life. There was also the unreality of countless needle pinnacles, jutting around us through the fog, alternately appearing and disappearing as the atmosphere thinned and thickened."

Rain for 27 of the trip's 29 days prevented them from climbing Doonerak. It also caused rivers and creeks to flood, including the Koyukuk's North Fork that had slammed the group's boat against a gravel bank and sent Marshall through a tunnel beneath ground which could have killed him. Instead he burst into the light of day on the other side of the bank. The boat was wrecked, so the group hiked 75 miles back to Wiseman in three days. They were told later that the rains and floods were the worst recorded since the arrival of white people to the Koyukuk region in 1899.

Marshall returned to the Brooks Range nine months later in June 1939 for the fourth and last time. It was another strenuous trip, this one of 24 days. They backpacked the entire route between Wiseman and Doonerak with 55-pound loads. With Bob were one-armed Jesse Allen, Kenneth Harvey, three dogs, and an Eskimo, Natirwik, whose name meant "blizzard." Marshall failed again to climb Doonerak, although he made first ascents of Apoon, Amawk, North Doonerak and Alhamblar mountains. From their summits he finished mapping 15,000 square miles of Koyukuk country, of which 12,000 had been a total cartographic blank. He climbed 28 peaks during his total of 210 days in the Brooks Range, and he named at least 160 geographic areas.

The spirit of Lewis and Clark was alive.

"Bob probably was the last explorer and mapper of a large region," George Marshall has noted, "who traveled on foot and by boat with no contact with the outside world during his wilderness trips, and who did his mapping along rivers and on mountains with relatively crude instruments... Views from summits were deep spiritual experiences. His joy was complete when, standing on some peak never before climbed, he beheld the magnificence of a wild timeless world extending to the limit of sight filled with countless mountains and deep valleys previously unmapped, unnamed, and unknown."

Alaska and exploration continued to singe Marshall's thoughts and dreams through 1939. He had written Melville B. Grosvenor of the National Geographic Society that the thrill of adventure and exploration ("the greatest aesthetic experience a human being can know") and the possibility for them, should be prolonged as much as possible. Northern Alaska seemed the logical place for such activity. Bob's comments on the Report of Alaska's Recreational Resources and Facilities, for the U.S. National Resource Committee's *Alaska—Its Resources and Development*, bore the final stamp of his mind:

> Because the unique recreational value of Alaska lies in its frontier character, it would seem desirable to establish a really sizable area, free from roads and industries, where frontier conditions will be preserved. Fortunately, this is peculiarly possible in northern Alaska, for economic

and social reasons. Economically, the population is so scattered that airplane transportation is the only feasible means of mechanical conveyance, and auto roads could not possibly justify their great cost. At the same time, the country is far too remote from markets for successful industry. Sociologically, the country of northern Alaska is inhabited chiefly by native populations which would be much happier, if United States is any criterion, without either roads or industries. Therefore, I would like to recommend that all of Alaska north of the Yukon River, with the exception of a small area immediately adjacent to Nome, should be zoned as a region where the federal government will contribute no funds for road building, and permit no leases for industrial development. Alaska is unique among all recreational areas belonging to the United States because Alaska is yet largely a wilderness. In the name of a balanced use of American resources, let's keep northern Alaska largely a wilderness!

Suddenly, on November 11, 1939, five months after Marshall's eyes had drunk in the beauty of the Brooks Range's Mt. Doonerak, he was dead at the age of 38. He had been aware of a congenital heart lesion but he hadn't let it slow him down. In September, in Washington's Cascade Mountains, he had become sick. "Sunstroke," he called it. Now, in his berth on a Pullman railroad car bound from Washington, D.C. to New York City, where he planned to visit his brother, James, he was found dead of heart failure. (An autopsy found an anemic blood count and heart damage.) After initial shock and sorrow, public praise for Bob Marshall rose up like Brooks Range winds.

Gifford Pinchot, leading mind behind the U.S. Forest Service, called Bob "one of the greatest woodsmen and mountainmen of his time."

Secretary of Agriculture Henry A. Wallace cited Marshall in the Washington, D.C. *Evening Star* as "one of the nation's leading exponents of maintaining forest recreation values in our national life."

Marshall's Enduring Legal Legacy

Not only were Bob Marshall's ideas seminal to America's wilderness preservation movement, but his intergovernmental efforts to protect actual wilderness—in retrospect—bore fruit:

In October 1937, 16 wilderness reserves on Indian reservations recommended by Marshall were approved.

While with the Forest Service, he proposed all roadless areas of more than 100,000 acres be given "primitive" classification. He was the prime mover behind the Forest Service's Wilderness Area and Wild Area classifications (U-1 and U-2) of 1939, which strengthened the protection of wild areas and provided the public an opportunity for much-needed channels of participation in the wilderness classification process. The "U" regulations eventually extended wilderness

127

status to more than 14 million acres in the West. Several of the nation's greatest forest wildernesses—the Three Sisters and Pasayten in Washington's Cascades, and the Selway-Bitterroot in the Rockies—were established under Marshall's influence.

Bob helped defeat a proposed New York state constitutional amendment in the 1930s that would have permitted cabin colonies anywhere on state land in New York's Adirondack Wilderness. He also resisted the building of truck trails for alleged fire protection in the same area.

When President Jimmy Carter signed the Alaska National Interest Lands Conservation Act on December 2, 1980, more of Marshall's vision materialized. Not only did the act triple the size of the National Wilderness Preservation System, and double the size of the National Park System, but it set aside much of Marshall's Koyukuk River stomping grounds in the 7.9 million-acre Gates of the Arctic National Park and Preserve.

Finally, the National Wilderness Preservation System, which was established in 1964 due, in large part, to the efforts of the Wilderness Society (which Marshall founded), now encompasses over 88 million acres.

Oberholtzer, who was still neck-deep in Quetico-Superior preservation efforts, enthused in *Outdoor America* that "no man in the country knew the whole scene of the American wilderness so well" as Marshall. Oberholtzer was aware that Bob had never needed to work; he had been independently wealthy throughout life, and at death left behind an estate of $1.5 million. A fourth of his estate was willed (dated July 1938) to the Wilderness Society, to be used "to increase the knowledge of the citizens of the United States of America as to the importance and necessity of maintaining wilderness conditions in outdoor America for future generations"; the rest went toward advancement of civil liberties and promotion of an economic system in the U.S. "based upon the theory of production for use and not for profit." Oberholtzer thought there was no one too lowly for Marshall's sympathetic understanding "and no cause for the advancement of human happiness to which he was not eager to lend a helping hand. He wanted nothing for himself that was not equally available to all."

Sig Olson, meanwhile, whose own torch was beginning to flame in the Quetico-Superior region, eulogized in *The Living Wilderness* that with Marshall's death the cause of wilderness preservation lost "one of its greatest champions, a man whose love of the wilds was deep and sincere, a man [and this was of utmost importance to Olson] who had the courage to fight for what he believed."

5

ALDO LEOPOLD: WITNESS AT THE BREAK OF DAY

"It is only the scholar who appreciates that all history consists of successive excursions from a single starting-point, to which man returns again and again to organize yet another search for a durable scale of values. It is only the scholar who understands why the raw wilderness gives definition and meaning to the human enterprise."

—Aldo Leopold
"Wilderness"
A Sand County Almanac

Certainly there came a dawn, come autumn, come freeze-up, when Aldo Leopold—father of wildlife management and a land ethic, a defender of American wilderness, and author of *A Sand County Almanac*—sat among the pines he had planted on his 120 acres of land in the sand country of central Wisconsin, specifically Sauk County, to look and listen from a special perch of upwelling gratitude. Leopold never quite wrote explicitly about such a dawn, a mere thirty miles west of where John Muir grew up; yet it is easy to imagine him at a point in time and space, among his beloved pines, in the peak of his career, watching night's last stars meld into the unfolding sunlight of day.

Day breaking.

It might be three-thirty in the morning, or four o'clock, but he would be there: alone, alert, adding to his knowledge of wild nature as if it had no end. As if, as Muir said, everything was connected to everything else. Leopold knew this was true. What fascinated him most, though, besides what he observed, was how wild nature, indivisible, flowed up through gradients into human cultures. People, in turn, left signatures on wild nature. With technology, this could be disastrous or, applied in the full purview of biotic ecology, could help nature absorb the impact of people, even allow them to flourish.

A symbiosis was called for. A balance and harmony.

Maybe it was this again he was thankful to see: the natural balance, the pervasive beauty, the evolving mystery: as much present in the little things of nature as in the great earth-shaping forces.

With him, we know from *A Sand County Almanac*, would be his "emblems of sovereignty": his customary coffee pot, Zeiss binoculars, notebook, and a light-intensity meter to correlate candlepower of sunlight with bird songs. He would set the pot next to him, take a cup from his shirt front, get out his watch, pour coffee, and lay his notebook on his knee. He was there, after all, to perceive and take note, to witness; and the more he sensed and understood, the finer the ecological intricacies became.

Here was insight and, for a mind like his, corresponding pleasure.

Questions arose naturally.

Would geese, on this morning, fly in, riding a north wind, or wait until a later day?

When would dawn's first chickadee, perhaps #65290, one he had banded, break its nocturnal silence? Too large to be an insect, yet too small to be considered by owls and hawks as meat, was the chickadee prepared for the explosion of life ahead?

And what of the marsh's mallards? Were they among the duckweeds? What—and here he might have jotted a note—of bluebills? Shouldn't they pitch pondward soon, tearing "the dark silk of heaven in one long rending nose-dive"?

Or might a white-tail buck walk by, pausing next to a stout jackpine?

Leopold, uncannily inquisitive, asked himself such questions and many more. They were a part of his journey. His whole life was a continuum of questions asked and answered, a movement forward like a river current, leading the way—on this day like so many others—clearly into the essence of who he had become.

And this he now knew: All along the way, his becoming, his growth, had brought him into relationships with land. Land was his core, his constant, his harbor. He loved all kinds. Yet the healthiest, and this he had to admit, was wilderness.

Wilderness like the Mogollon Mountains and Gila River country of the Southwest where, in formal respects, his career began. He had known other wild places: Arizona's White Mountain and Escudilla with its last grizzly, and New Mexico's Sangre de Cristos and the San Juan Mountains. There was northern Mexico's Sierra Madres, the Delta of the Colorado, and the singing waters of the Rio Gavilan. There was Manitoba's Clandeboye Marsh with its grebes and pelicans, Minnesota and Ontario's Quetico-Superior canoe country, and Wisconsin's Flambeau River.

As healthy and beautiful as these places were, however, and no matter how alluringly they called to Leopold along his lifelong journey, it was the sand country of central Wisconsin that most appealed to him. It was here he made his most intimate contact with the earth. It was here he felt the power of mutual transformation. And it was here, in moments of uncertainty, that he could turn to pines, birds, and morning sunshine to find his home of promise.

I

To understand how Leopold became so attached to mountainless, relatively nondescript central Wisconsin, where wildness was found in secret places or, as with the geese and cranes, in passing migrations, it's necessary to understand the twists and turns, the circling around, of his boyhood and career.

Born Rand Aldo on January 11, 1887, in Burlington, Iowa, Leopold was the first child of Carl L. Leopold and Clara Starker, first cousins, married eleven months earlier. (His birth was commemorated by the planting of a red oak in front of the family mansion on Prospect Hill, a limestone bluff overlooking the Mississippi River.) Leopold's father, of German ancestry, was a respected manufacturer of quality oak, walnut, and cherry rolltop desks, a business employing a hundred men. Aldo's mother was a petite, attractive, energetic woman, the apple of a private education with a blush of German romanticism who loved gardening, cooking, piano, and opera. It was from Clara that Aldo seemed to get his esthetic sensibilities, while from his reserved father he learned independence, common sense, steadfastness of character, and a love of the outdoors.

The Mississippi River area near Burlington was the migratory pathway for a quarter of America's ducks and geese and, not surprisingly, became Leopold's backyard classroom. He was good in school, almost a model student, but he preferred going with his father on walks, waterfowl hunts, picnics, and fishing excursions. By age sixteen, with help from Frank M. Chapman's *Handbook of Birds of North America* (given him by his folks, his avowed best friends), he could identify 261 bird species. Some he saw while exploring the Mississippi's bluffs, others while skinny-dipping Flint Creek and hunting near Eagle Swamp of Crystal Lake.

"From the beginning," Curt Meine says of Leopold in his definitive biography, *Aldo Leopold: His Life and Work*, "hunting was more than a simple issue of killing versus not killing. It was complex activity, attended by the whole range of human attitudes from outright greed to sport to communion."

Communion with nature, as with any naturalist, would be a long time coming, yet Leopold fueled it, in part, with literature: first the adventures of Daniel Boone and Hiawatha, then with Jack London, Thoreau, Theodore Roosevelt, Stewart Edward White, and Ernest Thompson Seton. He did some of his reading at a resort in Les Cheneaux Islands of Lake Huron where the family had a membership and where, for six weeks each summer, Leopold explored, fished, camped, sailed, and canoed as his sandy hair tossed in wind and his blue-green eyes gazed toward water and sky.

A recurrent dream? Canoe north to Hudson Bay.

Leopold, unlike Olaus Murie and Sigurd Olson, would never make it to Hudson Bay, but he could not know this when, in 1904, he was sent to Lawrenceville Preparatory School in New Jersey. There, age 17, he studied English, history, algebra (never good at it), geometry, speech, Cicero, and composition. After school, he took so many walks despite rain or snow that his friends nicknamed him "the naturalist."

"Dressed in his knee boots," Meine says, "and winter coat, bandanna around his head, plant collection box slung over his shoulder, walking stick in hand, Aldo set forth on tramps to Princeton, Washington's Crossing, Trenton...Over his year-and-a-half career at Lawrenceville he came to know every field and stream and woodland within a ten-mile radius of the school, and to his study of birds he added an equally eager study of the local plant life."

Leopold's mother, missing her favorite child, encouraged him to write home frequently. He did, sometimes writing four or five letters a week. The first letters were rich with enthusiasm, listing birds, plants, and describing his tramps; but even at the tender age of eighteen, Leopold the philosopher was awakening.

People can describe botanical and ornithological specifics, he once wrote Clara, "but who can write the great things, the deep changes, the wonderful nameless things, which are the real object of study of any kind?"

His academic studies, meanwhile, were the required regimen—math, English, science—as he worked his way through the Sheffield Scientific School at Yale University, then Yale's Forest School. Educationally, it was a challenging time for Leopold. Socially, fancy shoes, suits, and tailored shirts replaced his boots and bandanna as he began dating and participating in the East Coast's nightlife. Slipping grades brought scolding from his father, tactful but clear. To Leopold's credit, he caught himself, persisted, improved his grades, and, in 1909, was awarded a master's degree in forestry.

There was never a question as to what to do next. Careers in the young United States Forest Service never looked better. From 1903-1907, President Roosevelt had doubled the size of the national forests from 63 million acres to 150 million acres. All of it needed management, preferably by Yale-educated foresters. Leopold knocked, and the door snapped open.

———

The aroma of pinion, juniper, and sage became a part of Leopold's life in 1909 when he reported for work as forest assistant in the year-old Apache National Forest of Arizona. It was a wonderful country for a young man who wanted to work in the outdoors. Baldy Peak, at 11,590 feet, loomed over a forest of aspen, fir, spruce, cottonwood, and pine, oh pine, a fragrance fusing with the smell of juniper and sage morning, noon and night. Up on Baldy there was big sky, snow, cold, alpine plants. Below: mountain sheep, antelope, whitetail deer, ducks, geese, doves, even a few grizzlies, mountain lions, and wolves.

Leopold saw and learned much on the Apache, but it was the wolf that taught him one of the most lasting ecological lessons of this life.

"We were eating lunch on a high rimrock," he explained later in *A Sand County Almanac*, "at the foot of which a turbulent river elbowed its way. We saw what we thought was a doe fording the torrent, her breast awash in white water. When she climbed the bank toward us and shook out her tail, we realized our error: it was a wolf. A half-dozen others, evidently grown pups, sprang from the willows and all joined in a welcoming melee of wagging tails and playful maulings. What was literally a pile of wolves writhed and tumbled in the center of an open flat at the foot of our rimrock.

"In those days we had never heard of passing up a chance to kill a wolf. In a second we were pumping lead into the pack, but with more excitement than accuracy: how to aim a steep downhill shot is always confusing. When our rifles were empty, the old wolf was down, and a pup was dragging a leg into impassable slide-rocks."

Although in the *Almanac* Leopold simply says, "We reached the old wolf in time to watch a fierce green fire dying in her eyes," it wasn't—based on separate file notes—quite that simple. Apparently Leopold walked up to the old wolf, which couldn't move, and held his rifle out towards it. The wolf gnashed at the rifle, grabbing it in its teeth, and the men backed off. It was then the wolf with its wildness, its fierce green eyes, its natural hunger for life among pups, all sustained by deer, it was then the wolf died, rightfully branding Leopold's conscience.

"I realized," he added in the *Almanac*, "and have known ever since, that there was something new to me in those eyes—something known only to her and the mountain. I was young then, and full of trigger-itch; I thought that because fewer wolves meant more deer, that no wolves would mean hunters' paradise."

He was wrong, of course, as were the other trigger-itchy foresters who had been with him. Like Leopold, those who lived long enough would sadly see wolfless mountains raked by mazes of deer trails as deer populations, untrimmed by wolves, grew to such numbers they browsed themselves into starvation. Deer died en masse. Where they died, by sage or pine, the putrid smell of rotting carcass rode the noon breeze.

It wasn't just what happened to the deer that would come to haunt Leopold, however, nor what an overabundance of deer did to the land; for with the loss of wolves, as with the extermination of grizzlies and mountain lions, the landscape suffered a corresponding loss of richness of spirit.

It lost the "something new" Leopold had glimpsed in the wolf's green eyes on the banks of an Arizona river.

———————

Leopold, apparently on a fast track to Forest Service success, was promoted in 1911 to deputy supervisor of the million-acre Carson National Forest in northern New Mexico. The Carson, albeit beautiful with the San Juan Mountains and Sangre de Cristos, was one of the most heavily used units of the young Forest Service system. Over 600 homesteads were scattered through the forest while a guesstimated 200,000 cattle and almost two million sheep roamed the ranges. With a salary of $1,400 a year, it was a good place for the new guy from the Apache to learn range politics and, as it turns out, fall in love.

Her name was Maria "Estella" Bergere, and Leopold met her soon after starting on the Carson. He romanced her with letters, nudged aside another suitor, proposed to her four months after first looking into her brown eyes, and, on October 9, 1912, married her in Santa Fe. He would never regret it. Estella, to whom he would dedicate *A Sand County Almanac*, was the daughter of a prominent Spanish-American land grant family and a woman whose interests, needs, and values complemented his. She would support Leopold's work all her life even as he nurtured hers. Together they would have five children (Starker, 1913; Luna, 1915; Nina, 1917; Carl, 1919; and Estella, 1927) and, until that fatal day at the Shack, remain best friends.

It became customary for them to spend evenings with one another. Sometimes they just sat, talked, listened to music, held hands, whatever: the sweet stuff. Or they read out loud to each other, sharing books and magazine features. In the middle of their marriage, they both took up archery; they would sequester themselves in the basement making arrows as arrowheads, nocks, feathers, and shafts became part of their mutual language. Leopold's interest was in bow hunting, Estella's in competition. She eventually shot her way up to state woman champion.

Although close, their first trial as a couple came quickly back up the Carson. In April 1913, while on a horseback trip into the Jicarilla district, Leopold was caught in a snowstorm and forced to spend several nights in a wet bedroll. His body began to swell. By the time he reached Chama, his knees were so swollen he had to cut his boots. A Chama doctor diagnosed rheumatism. Nope. Leopold continued onward by train to Santa Fe where, nearly dead, another doctor correctly diagnosed acute nephritis: Bright's disease. His kidneys had failed, and his body tissues had accumulated lymph and toxins. Leopold was twenty-six.

He now faced sixteen months of rest and recuperation. Work and strenuous activity were forbidden.

Leopold spent much of his convalescence back in Burlington, Iowa, where he coped with misfortune as best he could. Flat on his back much of the time—through summer, his beloved autumn, winter with its snows, and spring's goose music—he visited friends, family, wrote letters, and read whenever he could. Among his favorite books were Stewart Edward White's

The Cabin and Thoreau's journals, but it was William Temple Hornaday's *Our Vanishing Wildlife* that struck the loudest chord. Slowly, one page at a time, perhaps pausing to look out the window at the river flowing by, he began wondering what it would be like for the great Mississippi waterway and country everywhere to lose its ducks, geese, pheasants, and deer.

Wouldn't country without wildlife be a barren land?

———

Leopold returned to work in October 1914, assisting John Kerr in the Forest Service's District Office of Grazing, Albuquerque. It was a bureaucratic paper-pushing job. Still, work was work, he was feeling better, and he needed the distraction.

In December, his father died. Three days later, John Muir died. Leopold hadn't met Muir but had read his books, shared his love of nature, and felt the passing of a great man.

The job with the Office of Grazing (handling claims, applications, complaints) soon grew into a new one involving Forest Service recreation, publicity, and, he was pleased to see, wildlife protection. It gave him an agency footing to work with while he simultaneously stepped outside with his wildlife zeal to work on his own. He joined a group of other citizens in New Mexico to form a game protective organization. Their goals were straightforward: reform state game and fish administration, provide better wildlife law enforcement, create game refuges, and, as Leopold later regretted, eradicate predators. The New Mexico Game Protective Association became the first U.S. conservation organization with a paid staff.

It also had a quarterly newspaper, *The Pine Cone*, which Leopold helped write, edit, publish, and circulate. Although designed to further NMGPA's program, its overall purpose—as Leopold wrote in an early issue—was to promote "the protection and enjoyment of wild things...may it scatter the seeds of wisdom and understanding among men, to the end that every citizen may learn to hold the lives of harmless wild creatures as a public trust for human good, against the abuse of which he stands personally responsible."

Once Leopold's literary career stirred, it flourished.

From 1915 to 1920, he wrote for a variety of publications, each essay marking a shift in his wildlife focus and concern. In "Game Conservation: A Warning, Also an Opportunity" in *Arizona*, he described the Southwest's shrinking game populations and how to improve them through law enforcement and refuges. In "Make Stinking Lake a Game Refuge," in *Outers' Book*, he suggested the 2,000 acre marsh near the New Mexico-Colorado border be managed for maximum waterfowl, but not by leasing it to private hunting clubs which would, in effect, wield a monopoly over it. In "Turkey Hunt in Datil National Forest," in *Wildlife*, he again argued for game refuges but, in what became more typical of some of his essays, he mixed personal anecdote with natural history data. It was a literary and scientific approach he soon used with blacktail deer and the doves and ducks of the Rio Grande Valley. He had become interested in *detail*, the specifics of hard wildlife science, and so when he shot something, he also weighed it and studied the contents of its stomach. He then plugged this information into his essay. It didn't do much for the flow of his narratives, but it *was* specific, *was* the results of hard science, and what increasingly concerned him was when he went looking for comparable data elsewhere, he wasn't finding it.

Wildlife science, he realized, didn't exist except in the most fragmentary of stages. How Americans were treating their animals and birds was based on myth as much as anything else.

Leopold took a hard look at his own agency in this regard and, by 1918, decided to broadside it in *The Journal of Forestry*. In his essay, "Forestry and Game Conservation," he reminded the Forest Service that game management, with its implied attendant science, was, or at least should be, as much a function of the Forest Service as timber and range management. While they were at it, moreover, they should bear in mind the ultimate game management goal was "the perpetuation of every indigenous species." Not only was variety in game as important as quantity, but exterminating a species— or, the implication was, allowing it to disappear—"would be a sin against future generations."

A region's native coyotes and wolves, in other words, like its songbirds, ranked with board feet and cows. All should be nurtured. It was near anathema.

Leopold was shooting from his young literary hip, of course, yet he fired one more salvo before temporarily holding his peace.

In the *Bulletin of the AGPA*, he said he had noticed two kinds of game managers: "wildlifers" and "game farmers." Wildlifers represented a new, important viewpoint by regarding game "not as meat, not as sport, nor yet as a set of zoological specimens, but rather as a source of democratic recreation, a human source, a social asset." Whereas game farmers just wanted to produce something to shoot, the wildlifer sought to preserve a sample of all wildlife, game and non-game, with the preservation of native species "an end in itself, equal if not greater in importance than the perpetuation of 'something to shoot'." This, he said, was more ethical. As for public land and water, it "must and will be preserved and developed at public expense," not only for free hunting but, with closed seasons and special refuges, to protect native species with weak recuperative capacity.

When it came to wildlife, and what it might need for the long haul, Leopold was toeing a new ideological line.

II

While Leopold wrote his essays and rattled bureaucratic cages, he grew increasingly frustrated with the Forest Service's sliding wartime interest in wildlife issues. Soon the status of the nation's supply of sawlogs was not enough, despite his persistent commitment, to keep him at his post. When he was offered the job of secretary of the Albuquerque Chamber of Commerce in 1918, he took it, thinking he could use the position to keep on pushing wildlife protection, at least in the Southwest.

He wasn't, however, cut out to be a secretary or civic booster. Luncheons, meetings, and a chamber of commerce's constant promotion of commercialism were not his forte. His heart and mind were elsewhere. Although he did well with the chamber, it was a detour, and he returned to federal service in 1919 as Assistant District Forester in Charge of Operations.

The new position, occupying him until 1924, involved responsibility for personnel, finances, roads, trails, and fire control on 20 million acres of national forest land in the Southwest. Leopold was also supposed to promote recreation and, given the land management climate of the time, for good reason.

The Forest Service, in the Department of Agriculture, was wary about losing some of its land to the National Park Service in the Department of Interior. Since its establishment in 1916, and thanks in part to John Muir's publicizing and the dynamic leadership of Stephen T. Mather, the Park Service had caught the country's attention by boasting about its parks as recreation meccas. Perhaps, talk went, there should be *more* parks? more places of great beauty where people could get outdoors into wild country without running into cattle and tree stumps? And where were there vast holdings of land already in the public domain? The national forests.

Recreation, walk or drive, became the buzzword as the two agencies, now rivals, coveted land.

The Forest Service, fighting back out of its silvicultural corner, upped the ante by pushing its own scenery, open space and opportunities for outdoor recreation. It was a new agency emphasis underscored in 1917 by a study made by landscape architect Frank A. Waugh. In his summary, *Recreation Uses On The National Forests*, Waugh claimed the forests had "notable beauty" and "enticing wildness," both of "direct human value." He suggested hiking, sightseeing, and camping be considered equal to any other economic criteria when evaluating how forests should be used.

Leopold, whose personal values ran parallel to Waugh's professional recommendations, was listening. He was also the right man within the Forest Service, given his new job, to carry the torch.

On December 6, 1919, Leopold met with another landscape architect, Arthur Carhart, in Denver, a meeting which became a flashpoint in wilderness thought. Carhart, then 27, also from Iowa, had just been hired by the Forest Service as its first recreational engineer and had, the previous summer, conducted a survey at Trappers Lake, Colorado, to help determine the best location for vacation homes on the lake. He was so impressed by the beauty of the lake, however, he recommended it be protected for wilderness recreation.

When Leopold met with Carhart, they discussed Carhart's reasoning, and Leopold asked for a follow-up memo.

"The problem spoken of in [our] conversation," Carhart subsequently wrote, "was how far shall the Forest Service carry or allow to be carried manmade improvements in scenic territories, and whether there is not a definite point where all such developments, with the exception perhaps of lines of travel and necessary sign boards, shall stop...There's a limit to the number of lands of shoreline on the lakes; there is a limit to the number of lakes in existence; there is a limit to the mountainous areas of the world, and in each one of these situations there are portions of natural scenic beauty which are God-made, and the beauties of which of a right should be the property of all people."

Such areas, Carhart added, were valuable not only to America but the world, and should be protected from the "marring features of man-made constructions."

The question wasn't *whether* to do this but how it best could be done.

Carhart's memo resonated with Leopold who, albeit quiet about actual wilderness preservation, had been interested in it as early as 1913 Having met Carhart the concept seemed to accelerate into new articulation. It was time for Leopold to step fully out of the closet, and time, he knew, to begin new work with his pencil.

Although Leopold eventually wrote three books, 500 published articles, reports and newsletters, and another 500 unpublished essays, speeches and policy papers, he rarely wrote about himself. Hence it's difficult to know how his prose flowed, how his manner of literary composition evolved, en route to publishing "The Wilderness and Its Place in Forest Recreation Policy."

This essay, published in the November 1921, issue of *Journal of Forestry*, became one of the seminal statements of the wilderness preservation movement, what Meine describes as a "fulcrum point in the 150-year history of America's public domain, and in American civilization's shifting view of its land, its development, and its own values." Although various state lands, including New York's Adirondacks, had already been set aside, and despite recent designation of several national parks, the concept of wilderness, especially as it applied to the nation's forests, remained undefined.

Leopold wanted to give it definite form.

He agreed, he said in the essay, with Gifford Pinchot's dictum that the highest use of national forests had to do with the greatest good to the greatest number of people, a "guiding principle by which democracies handle their resources," yet the principle didn't necessarily apply to *every* instance but might even "demand that representative portions of some forests be preserved as wilderness." He defined wilderness as a "continuous stretch of country preserved in its natural state, open to lawful hunting and fishing, big enough to absorb a two weeks' pack trip, and kept devoid of roads, artificial trails, cottages, or other works of man." Several assumptions, he said, could be made without argument: "First, such wilderness areas should occupy only a small fraction of the total National Forest area—probably not to exceed one in each state. Second, only areas naturally difficult for ordinary industrial development should be chosen. Third, each area should be representative of some type of country of distinctive recreational value, or afford some distinctive type of outdoor life, opportunity for which might disappear on other forests lands open to industrial development."

Leopold realized most people wanted some form of development, whether roads, hotels, or graded trails, but the needs and desires of the minority not wanting this should also be met.

Foresight was necessary.

"It will be much easier to keep wilderness areas than to create them...Right here is the whole reason for forehandedness in the proposed wilderness area policy."

Yes, he said, there will always be "patches of rough country," relatively wild, for camping, but "the man who wants a wilderness trip wants not only scenery, hunting, fishing, isolation, etc.—all of which can be found within a mile of paved auto highway—but also the horses, packing, riding, daily movement and variety found only in a trip through a big stretch of wild country." Hunting *shouldn't* be allowed in national parks, he added, and roads and trails were "right and proper," but Forest Service wilderness areas were different. He went on to suggest a half-million acres of Gila National Forest be preserved, specifically the region encompassing the headwaters of Gila River. It was topographically isolated by mountain ranges and box canyons and, as the "last typical wilderness in Southwest mountain," its highest use demanded protection.

To Leopold's pleasure, critical acclaim for his essay included positive bureaucratic response. District Forester Frank C. W. Pooler asked him to inspect the Gila and its proposed wilderness area the following spring and summer. Soon Forest Supervisor Frederic Winn helped Leopold draft a wilderness protection policy. With everything in order, including support from sportsmen's groups, loggers, and livestock grazers (their activities would be allowed to continue), Pooler—on June 3, 1924—designated 574,000 acres of Gila National Forest as wilderness.

It was the first official wilderness area in American history.

"Here was a sign of cultural foresight, a willingness to let a wild place be," Meine says when elaborating on the significance of the Gila Wilderness. In the wide scope of time, its creation was "a quiet act of national magnanimity... No European nation ever could, or ever would, proclaim such a wilderness."

While Leopold's first wilderness essay was brought to fruition by the Forest Service, his career as an administrator—developing forest inspection methods, refining fire control procedures, smoothing-out personnel practices, and promoting recreation—inched forward.

In a 1922 evaluation, Assistant Forester Roy Headley commented on Leopold's eagerness to scientifically determine things, his tireless working habits, and his ability to learn quickly. His interest in wildlife was unsurpassed. He had even pioneered soil erosion studies in reference to watersheds, publishing a mimeograph, *Watershed Handbook*, in 1923. Animals; birds; cattle; predators; water; wind; wilderness; it all was flowing together more comprehensively for Leopold when fate tossed him a curve ball.

The Forest Service, impressed by his administrative skills, asked him to accept the position of associate director of the agency's Forest Products Laboratory in Madison, Wisconsin. They hinted he might become director within a year. Leopold, who had already turned down at least five other promotions during his fifteen years in the Southwest, reluctantly accepted.

The results of his decision were bittersweet. Estella and four of the five children were uprooted from their birth country and relatives. The director Leopold had a high likelihood of replacing didn't resign. And Leopold's hopeful work—encouraging better relations between the laboratory and individual national forests, spurring genetic research and better use of waste wood, steering the logging industry toward "inferior" tree species, and coordinating the laboratory's mission with forest conservation, all projects he was initially led to believe he could spearhead—was lost to administrative paper shuffling and the agency's myopic focus on the economics of industry.

If Leopold's administrative ambitions were stifled, however, his inner growth, wilderness vision, and its literary expression were not.

As if by some convoluted, compensatory process, his interest in wilderness and its preservation blossomed incrementally, each unfolding bringing him down a path of what he had to say. In 1924-25 alone, and perhaps spurred on by his success with the Gila, Leopold wrote no less than six articles on the values of wild country. American recreational needs remained important to his outlook, but he began to broach cultural, esthetic and, sometimes, intangible values.

His shift toward intangible values is particularly clear in an obscure essay, "The River of the Mother of God." Written in 1924, the essay was submitted to *Yale Review*. Leopold wanted to explore the relationship of wilderness to the human psychological need for the mystery of unknown places. At the outset, in a rare moment of personal candor, he confesses a debt to South America, not because of its rubber for tires "which have carried me to lonely places on the face of Mother Earth where all her ways are pleasantness, and all her paths are peace," nor even for its rare woods, fruits, medicines, and coffee brewed over memorable campfires "with the dawn-wind rustling in autumnal trees," but for the River of the Mother of God. He couldn't recall when or how he first heard of the river but he remembered the story of how a Spanish Captain, exploring a remote Andean height, sent word back to his people that he had discovered a great river disappearing into trackless, Amazonian wilderness.

"He had named it el Rio Madre de Dios," Leopold explained. "The Spanish Captain never came back. Like the river, he disappeared. But ever since some maps of South America have shown a short heavy line running eastward beyond the Andes, a river without beginning and without end, and labeled it the River of the Mother of God."

The line became a symbol for Leopold of the "Unknown Places" of the earth. It also represented the Spanish Conquest, and conquest in general, reducing unknown places "one by one, until now there are none left."

"Speaking geographically," he lamented, "the end of the Unknown is at hand. Is it to be expected that it shall be lost from human experience without something likewise being lost from human character?"

He didn't think so. Blank spots on maps had always been important to the human spirit as foci of daydream, wonder and lure. Exploration, he said, was almost as much a racial instinct as hunting, hence contemporary trips into the backcountry by thousands of people: "little expeditions, afoot, by pack train, or by canoe, into the odd bits of wilderness which commerce and 'development' have regretfully and temporarily left us here and there." Yet whereas hunting, as a racial instinct, could be superimposed on farm and forest, the experience of wilderness, the geographic unknown, "cannot be superimposed on anything." Quite simply, wilderness was a bedrock of spiritual and physical welfare that couldn't be created, and if it was going to be protected from roads and the "Great God Motor," that is, perpetuated, it had to be done in areas exclusively dedicated to wilderness. It was a question of humans, unique among species, creating their own environment through self-control. Urgency was needed. People had to act quickly and vigorously before the last vestiges of wild country were gone. Such areas, he explained, needed to be owned and held for the public by the Government which should, in effect, "draw a line around each one and say: 'This is wilderness, and wilderness it shall remain'...Such a policy would not subtract even a fraction of one percent from our economic wealth, but would preserve a fraction of what has, since first the flight of years began, been wealth to the human spirit."

Wasn't it logical to suppose, he asked, that something that had sustained humans and their psychological needs would help preserve the same in the future?

Leopold was edging toward the abstract, the ineffable: perhaps what Robert Service poetically termed the call of the wild. And because Leopold equated the lure of wilderness to the immemorial tendency of humans—whether Hanno, Ulysses, or Columbus—to explore unknown places, he was drawing untrodden parallels beyond the comfortable editorial ken at *Yale Review.*

They rejected "The River of the Mother of God." Leopold cached the essay in his desk, what he called his "cooler," where, fading, the essay went unpublished in his lifetime.

It is clear from the chronological record of Leopold's writing and publishing, however, that after finishing an essay he didn't wait around for an editorial pat on the back. He either wrote back-to-back essays or worked on several at the same time.

This was proven true in 1925 when he published thirteen different items, five of them pertaining to wilderness. As Leopold biographer Susan Flader and wilderness historian Roderick Nash say, the flurry of literary output was in response, at least in part, to the failure of the previous year's National Conference on Outdoor Recreation, called by President Calvin Coolidge, to explicitly address America's need for wilderness. True, a program photograph showed people camping in wild country, and Coolidge underscored how "the physical vigor, moral strength, and clean simplicity of mind of the

American people can be immeasurably furthered by the properly developed opportunities for life in the open," but wilderness preservation per se was ignored.

This irked Leopold who raised the issue on several fronts.

In "Conserving the Covered Wagon," published in the March 1925 issue of Sunset Magazine, he criticized America's current Good Roads Movement as "mania" and pleurisy. While he admitted some roads were good (giving ranchers access to cities, and city-dwellers access to outdoor recreation areas) it wasn't good to punch roads into every remaining patch of wilderness "cutting off, irrevocably and forever, our national contact with the Covered Wagon days." He claimed Americans had an instinctive craving for wilderness, based on their cultural—if not genetic—heritage, proven by the plethora of published outdoor experiences where the authors, whether in Alaska or, taking needs to British Columbia or Africa, momentarily re-created for themselves the challenges of pioneers. As Leopold had argued previously about hunting, it was vital not to allow adventure travel to become the lone realm of the rich. Common Americans, wishing to touch the same risk and adventure that had shaped them culturally, needed wilderness areas nearby where they could find the storms, wildwater, vast open spaces swept with wind, the loneliness, and the other physical and emotional challenges their forebears knew, surmounted, and wove inadvertently into national character.

Americans would, in this way, remain rooted to their past and, as a result, retain awareness of how they came to be: a people connected to, and nourished by, wild country.

"Is it," he asked in reference to this quest, "unreasonable or visionary to ask the Forest Service to preserve...unmotorized wilderness for those who prefer that sort of place?

"Would it be unreasonable or visionary to ask the Government to set aside...remnants of wilderness here and there throughout the National Forests and National Parks? Say one such area, if possible, in each State?"

It was foolish, he added, to think that just because a few foresters had tentatively formulated a wilderness policy that wilderness areas were assured. No way. Commercial boosterism and the development of roads were a "steam roller," and once the last tracts of wild country were penetrated a "correct wilderness policy" was useless. What was needed to stop the steamroller was the mandate "of an organized, fighting, and voting body of far-seeing Americans" who would defend the wilderness idea.

All of Leopold's wilderness essays in the 1920s presented essentially the same argument although cast, as Flader notes, "in a distinctly different tone and vocabulary, carefully crafted to persuade its target audience." Leopold's audience, three months after "Conserving the Covered Wagon" appeared in print, was none other than his Forest Service colleagues.

In "The Pig in the Parlor," in a mimeographed U.S. Forest Service Bulletin, he remarks on an earlier Bulletin item downplaying the fervor wildlife enthusiasts were showing about the invasion of wilderness by roads, indicating the wilderness "idea" was anti-road. This assumption, Leopold insisted, was wrong, and he encouraged foresters to acquire a "rudimentary understanding" of the wilderness idea before they condemned it.

He put it this way:

"I do not know of a single 'enthusiast' for wilderness areas who denies the need for more forest roads. It is not a question of how many roads, but a question of distribution of roads. The wilderness idea simply affirms that a well-balanced plan for the highest use of National Forests will exclude roads from certain areas so that the unmotorized forms of public recreation will not be left high and dry, just as summer homes are excluded from certain areas so that the camper will not be left high and dry. The only difference is that where a public campground requires a forty, a public wilderness area requires a few townships."

Roads were like pigs, he said, alluding to his tongue-in-cheek title. People might realize bacon is good to eat but that doesn't mean pigs are welcome always and everywhere.

The parlor, of course, was wilderness.

———

Although Leopold published two other pro-wilderness essays in 1925, "The Last Stand of the Wilderness" in *American Forests and Forest Life* (which brought him to Bob Marshall's attention) and "A Plea for Wilderness Hunting Grounds" in *Outdoor Life*, it is his October 1925 essay, "Wilderness as a Form of Land Use," that solidified his reputation as the decade's foremost spokesman for the preservation of wild country.

The essay, published in *The Journal of Land and Public Utility Economics*, formally, systematically, and comprehensively presented Leopold's thoughts on wilderness preservation as a component of American land use. En route, he reiterated some of his old themes in order to graduate beyond to the specifics of language, wilderness locations, and the dynamics of actual wilderness management.

The essay, slanted to a scholarly audience, was the last time Leopold wrote about wilderness for ten years.

"From the earliest times," he began, "one of the principal criteria of civilization has been the ability to conquer the wilderness and convert it to economic use. To deny the validity of this criterion would be to deny history. But because the conquest of wilderness has produced beneficial reactions on social, political, and economic development, we have set up, more or less unconsciously, the converse assumption that the ultimate social, political, and economic development will be produced by conquering the wilderness entirely—that is, by eliminating it from our environment.

"My purpose is to challenge the validity of such an assumption and to show how it is inconsistent with certain cultural ideas which we regard as most distinctly American."

When considering land use, he explained, it was important not to mistake sound tendencies for ultimatums which, essentially, might be foolish. It was good for a city to grow but not wise to cover the entire city with buildings. It was good to harvest trees for lumber but foolish to use up all the wood. Agriculture could be productive but not if it led to overproduction. As for wilderness, was it wise to go beyond necessary conquest to eradicate it altogether?

Here was a new question in the American mind, partly because the continent had always had an abundance of wilderness. But what now as its last remnants disappeared?

There wasn't even a functional language for discussion.

The rest of the essay is divided into six sections, each with a theme. In the first, "What is a Wilderness Area?" he proposes some ideas and definitions. He defines wilderness differently than he did four years earlier, this time as a "wild, roadless area where those who are so inclined may enjoy primitive modes of travel and subsistence, such as exploration trips by pack-train or canoe," bearing in mind four ideas about wild country:

First, it's a resource, both physically and, as a distinctive environment, an area that can yield social values.

Secondly, its value varies with location; if too remote, the value is negligible: people can't get to it.

Third, wilderness is both nonreproducible (it can't be created) and reproducible, that is, it can be used indefinitely "and still be as good as ever...The practical point is that if we want wilderness, we must foresee our want and preserve the proper areas against the encroachment of inimical uses."

Fourth, and this would come to have greater importance in Leopold's later years, wild country is a relative condition existing in all degrees: "from the little accidental wild spot at the head of a ravine in a Corn Belt woodlot to vast expanses of virgin country." In this capacity wilderness had to be flexible, adjusting to other uses of land, becoming a part of the whole mosaic of land functions. Size could vary from a few acres "to wild, roadless regions approaching in size a whole national forest or a whole national park." He made clear, however, he was not talking about a new kind of public land reservation but of designations within presently existing forests and parks "to be duly correlated with dedications to the other uses which that system is already obligated to accommodate."

No new land lock-ups, he was saying. He also wanted to exclude from consideration any wild country so absolute and remote it was beyond fire protection or lawful patrols.

"What kind of case, then," he asked, "can be made for wilderness as a form of land use?"

Wilderness preservation was a reversal of economic tendency, running against predominant cultural momentum, yet the time had come to consider what wilderness had contributed to American culture. It was a matter of balancing opposing tendencies and, here again, he cites how the environment, once an adversary to progress, inadvertently shaped the development of Americans. Could it be Americans were just as much a product of the impress of wilderness as of racial stocks?

And what of the relationship between wild environments and American institutions?

"If we have any such thing as an American culture," he wrote, "its distinguishing marks are a certain vigorous individualism combined with ability to organize, a certain intellectual curiosity bent to practical ends, a lack of subservience to stiff social forms, and an intolerance of drones, all of which are the distinctive characteristics of successful pioneers. These, if anything, are the indigenous part of an Americanism, the qualities that set it apart as a new rather than an imitative contribution to civilization. Many observers see these qualities not only bred into our people, but built into our institutions. Is it not a bit beside the point for us to be solicitous about preserving those institutions without giving so much as a thought to preserving the environment which produced them and which may now be one of our effective means of keeping them alive?"

Under the section, "Wilderness Locations," Leopold presented a cursory overview of remaining wilderness. Large areas of half a million acres or more were disappearing rapidly, thanks to roads (what Flader calls Leopold's "bête noir"). From 1910 to 1925, five of six roadless areas in Arizona and New Mexico had been compromised by roads. Only two of ten large areas in California remained. Motorboats threatened northern Minnesota's canoe country and adjacent Ontario (where Leopold had paddled for two weeks the previous summer). The outlook appeared grim. Except for areas in northwestern United States, Leopold thought all of the other wild areas in the U.S. would be invaded by motors within ten years.

He could understand the "spirit of enterprise" in backcountry communities as they tried to attract tourists, and he didn't mean to criticize their attempts to build roads with public money, nor was he arguing that roads lacked economic use. What he was saying, and he expressed this clearly, was that road systems pushed into wild country rarely yielded "a return sufficient to amortize the public investment," and even when they did "their construction is not necessarily in the public interest, any more than obtaining an economic return from the last vacant lot in a parkless city."

Wasn't it true, too, that with the development of motor-oriented tourism outdoor recreational tastes were being standardized?

Before bringing "Wilderness as a Form of Land Use" to a close, Leopold turned his attention to the practical aspects of establishing wilderness areas. Costs, he thought, would be minimal because wilderness required no improvements. Costs for fire patrol and administrative patrols shouldn't, he guessed, exceed two or three cents an acre annually, and some of these costs were already part of park and forest budgets. In some cases, as in the Lake states, lands might need to be purchased, but they required this anyhow to "round out" park and forest units. The end result would be a system of designated wild lands on existing federal lands, creating a "healthy variety into the wilderness idea itself."

Wild areas in the national forests could be "public hunting grounds," in the national parks they could be wildlife sanctuaries, yet in both cases they would remain "public playgrounds in which the wilderness environments and modes of travel may be preserved and enjoyed."

So many words. So little time.

Leopold ended his essay with lament and appeal. He feared the day when canoe travel consisted of paddling in the wake of noisy motorboats and portaging through the backyard of cabins: "When that day comes, canoe travel will be dead." He feared the day when pack-trains had to meander up graveled highways and pasture near summer hotels; the spirit of Jim Bridger and Kit Carson would no longer be known. Even hunting and fishing, if America lost its wild country, would be Europeanized: nights would be spent in lodges, food would be catered, the entire challenge reduced to killing rather than the additional challenges, still found in America, of hard travel, camping, and surviving under wilderness conditions.

Let us look at ourselves, he was saying. Let us see if we cannot create a homeland that has room enough for both the civilized and wild.

There was still time for Americans to direct their evolution.

"Wilderness as a form of land use," he concluded, "is, of course, premised on a qualitative conception of progress. It is premised on the assumption that enlarging the range of individual experience is as important as enlarging the number of individuals; that the expansion of commerce is a means, not an end; that the environment of the American pioneers had values of its own, and was not merely a punishment which they endured in order that we might ride in motors. It is premised on the assumption that the rocks and rills and templed hills of this America are something more than economic materials, and should not be dedicated exclusively to economic use.

"The vanguard of American thought on the use of land has already recognized all this, in theory. Are we too poor in spirit, in pocket, or in idle acres to recognize it likewise in fact?"

Certainly, if Bob Marshall's 1930 article, "The Problem of the Wilderness," was—as Benton MacKaye claimed—the Magna Carta of the wilderness preservation movement, then Leopold's "Wilderness as a Form of Land Use," published five years earlier, was a rough draft.

III

Leopold was the U.S. Forest Service's foremost spokesman for wilderness preservation in the mid-1920s, yet he must have felt new stirrings, a subtle need for fresh direction, as he puffed on his pipe in private moments or spoke confidentially with Estella. He had become disenchanted.

Not only was he weary with his agency's myopic foot-dragging when it came to sociological issues of forestry, but its slow handling of the wilderness "idea" prompted him to wonder if the Forest Service would merely become "a federal bureau which executes laws," or would it, in fact, evolve into a "national enterprise which makes history?"

He had his doubts. He also had grown increasingly disappointed with his work at the Forest Products Laboratory in Madison.

It was time for change.

In June 1928, after nineteen years with the Forest Service, Leopold accepted a new position with the Sporting Arms and Ammunitions Manufacturers' Institute. It was an odd venue for Leopold, and his association with SAAMI would later draw brief fire from Bob Marshall, yet the new work—directing a national survey of game—allowed him to change focus from wood products to the living pulse of the land: to the ducks and geese of the sky, to the grouse, woodcocks, and pheasants of lowlands, to songbirds, predators, and the elusive whitetail deer. As a hunter, Leopold had always enjoyed the pursuit of prey as a reminder of the human dependency on the soil-plant-animal-man food chain; his interest, however, went beyond the visceral to the esthetic and, increasingly over time, to the scientific, for he began to see animals as an ecosystem's expression of health.

But what, really, was the status of game or, as it came to be called, wildlife?

How should it be managed?

What factors affect populations?

What about sustained yield?

As Leopold had discovered, little scientific research of wildlife and habitat had been done to answer these questions. SAAMI wanted to hasten answering them for the sake of the sporting industry. Leopold, for his own mosaic of reasons, also wanted to know.

During the next two years, from July 1928 to January 1930, Leopold traveled through nine northcentral states (Wisconsin, Indiana, Iowa, Missouri, Mississippi, Ohio, Illinois, Michigan, and Minnesota) conducting his surveys. He studied environmental factors influencing game productivity as well as social factors: game laws, hunter behavior, and farming practices. Inevitably, he spent two weeks to two months in each state, visited over 300 areas, and met with over 600 hunters, local officials, and scientists. It was an immense project for Leopold, brought together—replete with charts and maps—in 1931 with publication of his book-length *Report on a Game Survey of the North Central States*.

Many wildlife enthusiasts and field biologists, including Olaus Murie, read the report. Murie, then knee-deep in his Wyoming elk studies following years spent surveying Alaskan caribou, wrote Leopold saying the report seemed fair, particularly its defense of predators. Leopold responded suggesting he and Murie meet.

Leopold's star, after all, was rising in a new field. Just as he had become a leader in American reflection on wilderness values, he began to emerge at the forefront of national thinking on game management. He used this stature to accomplish what he could. While doing his surveys and report, he helped establish game research fellowships at five universities and lectured about game management at the University of Wisconsin. More importantly, he served as chairman and chief draftsman of the Game Policy Committee of the American Game Conference in 1930, spearheading a new national game policy shifting management emphasis from laws, refuges, artificial propagation and hunter control to a fostering of wildlife from the ground up. Habitat improvement by landowners, whether public or private, was the key: an exercising of husbandry by applying perception of ecological processes to land management.

The new national game policy also called for acceleration of scientific study of species and habitat, rooted in field research, and urged creation of game management as an academic profession.

While working on the national game policy, Leopold recognized, and progressively voiced, conceptual shifts. In a speech at the 1930 conference, he said the public, not just sportsmen, own game, and that nongame species should be given just as much study and protection as game species. In other words, robins and loons were as important as deer: a bold idea dished to America's venison-eating public. Game restoration, he added, was just a part of conservation as an integrated whole. True conservation, what he defined as "harmony between men and land," had to conform to what was discovered about evolution and ecology or, as he later put it in *A Sand County Almanac*, what became known about the natural processes "by which the land and the living things upon it have achieved their characteristic forms...and by which they maintain their existence."

As for predators, and here Murie ideologically applauded, people needed to accept the results of research indicating predators had a vital role in the dynamics of stable wildlife populations. By culling the weak and old, predators not only kept prey populations vigorous but limited the effect overpopulations had on vegetation and, hence, the land's other chains of life.

This was important. Leopold had read P. D. Ouspensky's *Tertium Organum* and tended to agree, in a kind of preview of today's Gaia Hypothesis, that all land—integrated globally—formed a living organism of countless species in associated pyramids of indigenous food chains. These were rooted in vegetation, soil, and the climatological forces of rain, wind, snow, and drought. It all flowed together, ebbing and fluxing, almost breathing, as predator and prey balanced each other in the current of evolution.

Every species—sparrow, whale, or wolf—had its place.

Leopold: Earth as a Living Being

"*Possibly, in our intuitive perceptions, which may be truer than our science and less impeded by words than our philosophies, we realize the indivisibility of the earth—its soil, mountains, rivers, forests, climate, plants, and animals, and respect it collectively not only as a useful servant but as a living being, vastly less alive than ourselves in degree, but vastly greater than ourselves in time and space—a being that was old when the*

*morning stars sang together, and when the last of us has been
gathered unto his fathers, will still be young.*

—Leopold, "Some Fundamentals of
Conservation in the Southwest"

As Leopold enlarged his thoughts on wildlife over the next few years, he
came to view some predators as actual noumenon, or species representative
of ecosystems, embodying their essence and, as Flader and Callicott say,
manifesting their health, without which the ecosystem lacked wholeness
and integrity.

"Is a wolfless north woods any north woods at all?" he would ask.

———

Just as Leopold began to develop such farsighted, ecologically charged,
notions, however, his personal income—floating his game studies and home-
life—was jerked out from beneath him in 1931 by the wake of the American
Depression. His SAMMI funds dried up.

Out of paid work, he sideslipped toward a personal dark zone wondering
how he would support Estella, the kids, and their modest but comfortable
Madison lifestyle. And how was he going to continue his own most important work, the expansion of perception and writing, if he didn't have any
money? Help came in the form of a few freelanced game survey assignments
in Iowa and Wisconsin, and a two-month tour of erosion control work with
the Civilian Conservation Corps in the Southwest, but it wasn't until 1933
that Leopold got the career break he needed.

He was hired for five years (eventually lifelong) by the University of
Wisconsin to begin a game management program in the Department of
Agricultural Economics. There he became the nation's first professor of
game management.

He had done his homework.

Back in 1931, while unemployed, Leopold used his natural tenacity to
begin writing a textbook, *Game Management*, for a scholarly field that he
would essentially establish himself. For material, he drew on his *Report on a
Game Survey of the North Central States*, on writing he had done about
southwestern game, and on notes from the lectures he gave at the university
that eventually hired him. The book, of course, was targeted at a wildlife and
science audience but wasn't as straight-forward as it could have been. Besides
incorporating, thus publicizing, the theories of British ecologist Charles
Elton (including the concept of ecological niche as an organism's function in
the larger community of life), Leopold couldn't resist spicing *Game
Management* with philosophical asides. After all, he wrote, the hope of the
future "lies not in curbing the influence of human occupancy—it is already
too late for that—but in creating a better understanding of the extent of the
influence and a new ethic for it governance."

If hope was a question of understanding, Leopold figured, certainly wildlife management, like any science, needed to anchor itself in the broadest evolutionary view of the world. Philosophy—which often led science by the hand—was part of this.

So why shy away from it?

As for the "new ethic," he was thinking about it and would, when the time was ripe, speak out.

Leopold was nicknamed "the professor" at the University of Wisconsin, where *Game Management* became a classic, and with his serious demeanor, glasses, and pipe, he fit the role. He became known for his periods of intense concentration, sometimes forgetting to shift gears in his car. He lectured eloquently. He nurtured gifted students yet expected all of them, by writing popular articles and appearing on radio programs, to be effective, not merely knowledgeable, people. Apparently a Ph.D. didn't impress him. His focus was on the quality of the person.

For these reasons, and others, students took notice.

"He was one of the great teachers we had at this institution," Joe Hickey, Professor Emeritus at the University of Wisconsin, recalled of Leopold in a 1980 videotape interview. "He had a love for young people, and particularly a fascination for new and young ideas. Here was a man with a youthful mind...bubbling with enthusiasm about the natural world. And he was a very humble man who never thought of himself as a prophet or seer."

People like Bob Marshall, however, were thinking otherwise.

———————— ■ ————————

In October 1934, as Leopold was getting his game management program off the ground, he received a letter from Marshall who, since an earlier exchange of letters, had become an increasingly nervous man.

Marshall originally thought of Leopold as the "Commanding General of the Wilderness Battle." Now, having become the general himself while Leopold focused on wildlife, he wanted Leopold to join a dozen other Americans to form a new organization to fight aggressively for wilderness.

It was time to recruit, equip, and engage.

"We want no straddlers," Marshall wrote, as he would a month later to Ernest Oberholtzer, "for in the past they have surrendered too much good wilderness and primeval areas which should never have been lost...The time has come, with the brutalizing pressure of spreading metropolitan civilization, to recognize this wilderness environment as a serious human need rather than a luxury and plaything."

Marshall was psyched. Just before writing Leopold, he had networked with Benton MacKaye, Bernard Frank, and Harvey Broome in Tennessee at a forestry convention. Talk turned to wilderness. Roads were threatening remote regions of the Smokey Mountains and Shenandoah National Parks and, in fact, still threatened wild country throughout America. If they formed a core group of wilderness defenders, as they intended, who would be among the guiding elite? They discussed Leopold. Marshall wasn't impressed with Leopold's old gun company associations, but he still respected his literary contribution to wilderness protection.

Truth is, Marshall confided to a friend, "[Leopold] has done some of the most effective work yet done to save various areas from mechanical invasion."

Leopold, although burdened with responsibilities, agreed to help out with the new Wilderness Society but, when asked by Marshall, turned the presidency down. He became instead the Society's senior advisor, representative, and, as Meine says, its "intellectual statesman." From the beginning he was an important contributor to the Society's publication, *The Living Wilderness.*

"We do not yet understand," he reminded readers of the first issue, "and cannot yet control the long-time interrelations of animals, plants, and mother earth." If so little was known, what justification was there for the "biotic arrogance of homo americanus?" He called for an "intelligent humility toward man's place in nature" and, as far as he was concerned, the Wilderness Society would be one of the "focal points" of the new attitude.

IV

Leopold's words about man's place in nature must have held special resonance for him when he finally saw them in print, for, earlier in 1935, he landed himself in the country. All his trails, whether as wilderness preservationist, professor of wildlife management, or writer, had led through a forest of ideas. Perhaps it was inevitable that they circle around to center on one geographical spot.

He called it "the Shack."

Leopold had always wanted a place in the country, a kind of combination hunting camp and Walden refuge: a touch-the-earth locus where he could test his theories and, hopefully, nurture new ones. Living in a residential area of Madison wasn't enough. Periodic visits to wild places weren't enough. There was always the yearning for a place to anchor himself, develop long-term intimacy with a landscape, and to expand perception.

On January 12, one day after his forty-eighth birthday, he found it.

He was driving along the Baraboo Hills of Sauk County, Wisconsin, with friend Ed Ochsner, touring the countryside bordering Wisconsin River, when they came across an abandoned farm. Walking around, they noticed how the corned-out farm field was turning to panic grass, sand burs, and, to the west, bare sand. The farmhouse had burned down leaving only its fieldstone foundation. A nearby marsh had also burned. The river island was logged. Nothing was left, it seemed, but sky, scrubby vegetation, and, off to the side, a chicken coop last used as a cowshed.

Leopold should have been dismayed, yet, as he glanced around, he must have felt the sleeping power of the place. Although beat up, it was still alive and could heal. All of America's history lay in its wounds. Perhaps now, with the intelligent application of human care, the place could rise up again, bloom with beauty, and arrive at a semblance of its original vibrancy.

Despite the ecological trauma, Leopold saw promise.

He asked Ochsner to arrange a lease. By May, however, with ducks in the marsh, the river flowing, and with birds singing dawn songs, he wanted no less than full ownership. He bought the farm.

Thus began Leopold's most profound association with a landscape. For the family, the place was a getaway. Everyone threw themselves at projects. They cleaned the manure out of the chicken coop, built a fireplace inside, and fixed the shack's roof for a home-away-from-home. They built a fire pit outside for cooking. They built birdhouses, benches, cut firewood, and planted prairie grass and trees.

Of all trees, though, Leopold would favor the pine: whites and reds. Give him a choice between a birch and white pine and he would go for the pine every time.

It was, he admitted, an *a prior* bias.

Why?

He wasn't sure. If he had planted the pine, he later wrote in the *Almanac*, his bias was possibly paternal. Yet there were other factors: Birches were abundant in his township; pines were scarce. Birches lived fifty years; pines lived a century. Birches dropped their leaves in October; pines stayed green all winter. A bottle gentian might grow beneath a birch but beneath a white pine there could be pyrola, twin flower, or Indian pipe. Birches would host hairy woodpeckers: pines would attract the more rare pileated. And in April, the birch would rattle naked branches while wind sung in the pine.

"These possible reasons for my bias carry weight," he admitted, "but why? Does the pine stimulate my imagination and my hopes more deeply than the birch does? If so, is the difference in the trees, or in me?

"The only conclusion I have ever reached is that I love all trees, but I am in love with pines."

They also—when he sensed them at dusk—filled him with courage.

Over the years, Leopold, Estella, and the children planted over 30,000 pines, other trees, prairie plants, flowers, and shrubs on their property. There were new projects: a woodbox to build, walls to chink, a table to make, more birdhouses to hammer together. More importantly, there was the land to learn. Aldo and Estella learned to identify every flower. They walked, sat by the river, or enjoyed campfires in front of the Shack. Bitterns and cranes called from the marsh. Woodcocks "sky danced" spring evenings. Geese, honking heavily, passed in front of the moon.

One fascination led to another as, some years, Leopold spent almost every weekend at the Shack.

Friends saw a new spring in Leopold's steps while Estella, spared domestic chores in the country, noticed her husband begin a new journal. Like his hunting journal, which he started in 1917, the Shack journal took on a life of its own. From its earliest notations of planting food patches for wildlife to, ten years later, the lists of bird-song times, the journal became a repository of Shack activity, field data, and all kinds of related phenological observations.

Here, in three volumes over time, was Leopold the scientist, ever reluctant to explore his rich personal life. Yet here, too, was Leopold the writer, the witness, leaving sign of what he saw, heard and felt as the sand counties of Wisconsin deepened their spell.

Perhaps it's not surprising, given Leopold's new adventure, that he began the most productive period of his life. Besides his teaching, which took on new depth and flair, he served on—or advised—two dozen agencies, committees, and organizations. He helped establish the Wildlife Society. There was also the work with the Wilderness Society which, along with two trips, lured Leopold's understanding of wilderness into new territory.

The trips were antipodal.

In autumn 1935, Leopold joined a group of scientists on a two-and-a-half month trip, sponsored by the Oberlander Trust and Carl Schurz fellowships, to Germany. Although the journey strained his and Estella's marriage, he was able to meet Bob Marshall en route and, as was the group's purpose, study wildlife management and forestry in a country where, in its own artificial way, it had been practiced for centuries. Leopold saw the famed Black Forest, spoke with German foresters and gamekeepers, but he wasn't impressed.

Something was missing.

Wildness.

Where were the wolves and other great predators?

"We Americans," he soon crabbed in "Naturschutz in Germany," "have not yet experienced a bearless, wolfless, eagleless, catless woods. We yearn for more deer and more pines, and we shall probably get them. But do we realize that to get them, as the Germans have, at the expense of their wild environment and their wild enemies, is to get very little indeed?"

Besides the lack of wildness, the forested areas in Germany appeared relatively unhealthy: weakened in their ability to renew vigor following storm and disease. They were, in short, over-managed as the hand of people lay heavy upon the land.

The extent of German land management and, in comparison, much of America's, didn't become fully clear to Leopold until the next year when he made the first of two wilderness pack trips into the Sierra Madres of northern Mexico. There he discovered the guacamaja, or Thickbilled Parrot, as well as the clear waters of the Rio Gavilan, and a population of deer and wolves living in harmony with the land. All the ancient ecological processes, washing forward wave by wave, seemed unmarred. Even the few people who had lived in the region did so in a way that left it unimpaired.

Until the Sierra Madres, Leopold later confessed in an aborted *Almanac* introduction, he had seen "only sick land, whereas here was a biota still in perfect aboriginal health. The term 'unspoiled wilderness' took on new meaning."

The comparison between the Sierra Madres and Germany, between wild and inhabited country, intrigued him. Not only were they antipodes but only by knowing both extremes could he understand both. The one, left alone, protected by its own remoteness, was vibrant with biodiversity and health while the other, bearing a hard human imprint, was losing—or had lost—innate richness. Predators were gone. A monoculture of pines and spruce had funneled other mammals and birds up a tottering food chain or led over the edge of regional extinction altogether. For Leopold, it was the land comparison, the juxtaposition creating distinction, that suddenly mattered.

Could it be, he asked himself, that wilderness had "unexpected importance" as a touchstone for problems of land health?

Yes.

It took several years but his explanation, on a single page, appeared in The Living Wilderness under the title "Wilderness as a Land Laboratory." It was one of his last essays on wilderness values to appear in a periodical. After discussing examples of "derangement in the land-organism," such as erosion, animal irruptions, and micro-flora, he said it was important to keep in mind that prevailing conservation practices were treating "biotic pain," or symptoms, and not necessarily leading to cures. For that, a science of land health was needed which, in turn, required a "base datum of normality, a picture of how healthy land maintains itself as an organism."

There were two available norms:

"One is found where land physiology remains largely normal despite centuries of human occupation...The other and most perfect norm is wilderness."

If wilderness areas were going to function as norms for a true land science, however, it would no longer be sufficient to cut one out of each American state's cloth, as he proposed years earlier. Each "biotic province," rather, should have its own representative wilderness area for comparative study. No wilderness area was too small. None too large. All had value.

"The important thing," he concluded, "is to realize that recreation is not their only or even their principal utility."

———

For some writers, the congealing of experience and awareness occurs near the end of life as time simultaneously enlarges and compresses expression. This was true of Leopold who, in the 1940s, found himself working early mornings at the university on a collection of essays called *Great Possessions,* later retitled *A Sand County Almanac.* It would become Leopold's magnum opus and, long after his death, a classic of environmental literature.

"There are some who can live without wild things," he began, "and some who cannot. These essays are the delights and dilemmas of one who cannot."

The essays did not come easily. As Dennis Ribbens explains in "The Making of A Sand County Almanac," Leopold—unlike Muir and Thoreau—did not have the luxury of extracting from journals for his essays. His journals were factual and quantitative, not thematic. Instead, he would simply draft his remarks, writing longhand with pencil on a yellow legal pad, and enlarge his theme as he went along. He used few preparatory notes. He would cut, paste, and revise as needed, occasionally revising an essay a half-dozen times. He might delete sections, or add others, and when in doubt about a number or technical term, he would leave a blank space and fill it in later.

If he were interrupted, or the essay needed time to "cool," he would slip it into his walnut desk then retrieve it in a week or month.

At first, Leopold thought he could just collect his favorite essays, flesh them out, and add a few more then publish the results: a common literary ploy. Such looseness gave him publishing trouble from the start. In 1944, the Macmillan Publishing Company, to whom Leopold submitted his book proposal, found his attempt at fusing lyrical prose with philosophical essays too confusing; the book seemed to lack a unifying theme and they rejected it. Harold Strauss, of Alfred A. Knopf Publishers, came close to accepting the book, coaxing Leopold forward in the mid-1940s; but Strauss, too, declined. Just as the structural problem seemed insurmountable, help ironically came from still another rejection letter. An editor at the University of Minnesota Press suggested he introduce more of himself into what he was writing, stop holding back, and let his personal experience become "the thread on which the essays are strung."

This was the same thing Leopold's friends, with whom he shared material, had begun telling him.

Didn't his experience, whether in Mexico or at the Shack, actually bolster his ideas—grounding them? Why did his prose seem to leap alive when he described what it was like to sit next to a dawn marsh or, way back when, to shoot that wolf? What about all his Shack experiences? Were they not now pivotal to his sense of land, place, and philosophical vision?

Leopold saw the point and, although it ran against his usual sense of privacy, the point was him.

By the time Oxford University Press accepted Leopold's book in 1948, two weeks before his death, then published it a year later, all the contents of what became *A Sand County Almanac* had slipped into place. Part I consisted of a series of monthly oriented vignettes, such as "January Thaw," "Sky Dance," and "Axe-in-Hand," centered on activities at the Shack where the family sought, and found, "meat from God." Part II was a collection of episodes and adventures, ranging from Wisconsin and Iowa to the Sierra Madres and Manitoba, evoking Leopold's experiences with different landscapes and what he learned form them.

Part III, "The Upshot," contained his most distilled remarks on conservation's salient themes.

In "The Land Ethic," for example, he brought together his final thoughts on the human-land relation, reducing it to morals. Ethics, he said, were possibly "a kind of community instinct-in-the-making," evolutionary like biology; just as ethics originally arose to deal with relations between individuals, then between individuals and society, now ethics had come to bear on human relation to land. The old, and still prevailing, economic relation was no longer sufficient. People had to assume a new obligation of care, a respect for nonhuman nature, based on the realization people are only a part of the land-community: rooted in it, dependent on its health, and not its conqueror but plain member. *We live or die together.* An enlargement of loyalties, convictions, affections, values, and conscience was involved.

Leopold: On Giving

"*Every living thing represents an equation of give and take. Man or mouse, oak or orchid, we take a livelihood from our land and our fellows, and give in return an endless succession of acts and thoughts, each of which changes us, our fellows, our land, and its capacity to yield us a further living. Ultimately we give ourselves.*"

—Leopold

And how are people, when it comes to treatment of land, supposed to know what is wrong or right?

"A thing is right when it tends to preserve the integrity, stability, and beauty of the biotic community," he said. "It is wrong when it tends otherwise."

The second section of the *Almanac*'s "Upshot" focused on wilderness in what amounts to a summary of his previous wilderness essays. He discusses wilderness remnants, the importance of wilderness for recreation (especially the "more virile and primitive skills in pioneering travel and subsistence"), the value of wilderness as a land laboratory, to wildlife, and the need for wilderness defenders. The essay, in its own way, was a map of Leopold's personal growth, a sketch of his discoveries in reference to wilderness values. And there were many.

The *Almanac*'s final chapter, "Conservation Esthetic," brought everything back to one of his original Forest Service concerns: outdoor recreation. "We seek contacts with nature," he said, "because we derive pleasure from them." Over the years he had witnessed the mass exodus of people from cities to countrysides, hastened by motors and roads. There were hunters, photographers, and people involved with nature study, each gradient of recreationist consuming less of the resource base. Opportunities for solitude, meanwhile, or the "feeling of isolation in nature," were being diluted.

Which led him to his point:

"Recreation is not the outdoors, but our reaction to it."

Recreation was as much an *opening up* as a going out.

It was, inevitably, a question of perception: the looking, listening, feeling, and learning that mattered. It was the witnessing of the plant and animal community. It was the ability to see "the swoop of a hawk...as the drama of evolution." It was the awe one felt when looking at stars. This and all more: everything connected, nurturing itself, moving forward through evolution and the dynamics of ecology into the mystery of Being.

"Let no man jump to the conclusion," he explained, "that Babbitt must take his Ph.D in ecology before he can 'see' his country. On the contrary, the Ph.D may become as callous as an undertaker to the mysteries at which he officiates. Like all real treasures of the mind, perception can be split into infinitely small fractions without losing its quality. The weeds in a city lot [or pines and prairie plants near a shack, perhaps?] convey the same lesson as the redwoods; the farmer may see in his cow-pasture what may not be vouchsafed to the scientist adventuring in the South Seas. Perception, in short, cannot be purchased with either learned degrees or dollars; it grows at home as well as abroad, and he who has a little may use it to as good advantage as he who has much."

No, he concluded, recreational development wasn't a job of "building roads into lovely country, but of building receptivity into the still unlovely human mind."

In the end, as in the beginning along his boyhood Mississippi River, it was perception that Leopold hungered, as if—no matter where he went or what he saw—he could keep expanding his perception with its reciprocal understanding and, through teaching, lecturing, and writing, express it and give it to the world. It was his gift to his kind, and a persistent yet gentle tug for others less inclined to follow.

He did this not for his own sake, but for all people, healthy land, and wild beauty.

"And when the dawn-wind stirs through the ancient cottonwoods," he asked in some of his finest prose, "and the gray light steals down from the hills over the old river sliding softly past its wide brown sandbars—what if there be no more goose music?"

He had always preferred not thinking about such silence. He had preferred instead to live in the direction of his hope, his dream, not his fear.

And so, while finishing the *Almanac*, he had continued his work which, besides Estella, the children, and his constant hunger for nature, was what he loved. It was a full life. He continued teaching despite developing tic douloureux, or trigeminal neuralgia, a painful inflammation near the main facial nerve requiring surgery at the Mayo Clinic. He was elected president of the Ecological Society of America. He recommended policies for, it seemed, countless agencies, committees, and professional organizations. He spoke in public on behalf of ecological conscience and against unnecessary dams on rivers.

Leopold seemed to be everywhere, his influence pervasive, as he and Estella returned, for the last time together, to the Shack.

It was April 20, 1948. Spring. Hundreds of geese flew north overhead. Leopold cleared a trail, planted a hundred pines, then canoed with Estella up a slough. He wrote in the Shack journal in the evening. The next morning, at the break of day, he was back outside beneath clear sky. Light coming. He counted over 800 geese fly by: a new dawn record and, in retropect, a farewell.

Around 10:30 a.m., he and Estella smelled smoke. Dry marsh grass and alders on a neighbor's land had caught fire. It swept toward the Shack with its groves of young pines. Leopold, knowing full well the power of wildfire, sent Estella off for help, grabbed a water pump, then headed to the front of advancing flames. There, alone, his heart gave out. He apparently had lain down on a patch of unburned grass where, as he died or soon afterwards, fire licked lightly at his body.

In his pocket, unscathed by fire, was the plaid-covered notebook that had been his constant dawn companion.

Lilac shoots, Leopold last wrote, 2" long.

The words were as tight and succinct as pine seeds.

6

OLAUS JOHAN MURIE:
EMBRACING THE WILD PULSE OF LIFE

"Whether it be a wide unspoiled landscape that inspires us, or the beauty of the humble little wildflower at our feet, the fact remains that we need inspiration to go forward."

—Olaus Murie

It was Olaus Murie's embrace of the wild pulse of life that found him tracking caribou in Alaska on April 24, 1923. As Aldo Leopold, far to the south, put the finishing touches on his *Watershed Handbook*, and as Sigurd Olson began guiding in Minnesota and Ontario's Quetico-Superior canoe country, Murie—forever the biologist and lover of wild Alaska—stood with his brother Adolph at the divide between Twelvemile and McManus creeks northeast of Fairbanks. Murie had spent all winter dogsledding in search of scientific information about caribou, and now, only thirty-four years old with spring in the air, one of the great moments of his life arrived with the clicking of hooves.

As Murie gazed across the hills, long single files of caribou wound through a small valley, crossed a hilltop, then continued onward to another hill. The caribou gathered so thickly it looked to Murie like the hill's snowy slope was covered with black spruce. Excited, he and Adolph counted 2,500 animals: the largest caribou herd Murie would ever see.

He would never forget how they pulsated across the hilly tundra in a migratory sweep of sinew and instinct. He would never forget how, in their own indomitable way, they were stitching together his life, his love, his dream.

It was a dream that would guide Murie over the next forty years to many other parts of wild Alaska, including today's Arctic National Wildlife Refuge which he and his wife, Mardy, would fight to create. It would bring him to Wyoming's Teton Mountains and elk ranges, to New Zealand's fjords on a scientific expedition, and into the thick of wilderness battles throughout America as the director of the Wilderness Society. Along the way, he became known and loved in America as an explorer, a gifted writer, an accomplished artist, and as a naturalist who, having woven his life with wildness, embodied a life of integrity that drew nothing but praise in the end.

"He was the one person who best personified wilderness in our culture," Howard Zahniser said of Murie in a 1963 eulogy. "His life and living were in and from the wilderness, and in his personality the concept of wilderness had a noble and compelling expression."

I

The origins of Murie's wilderness career or, as Zahniser put it, his "compelling expression," are rooted in the woods once banking the Red River of the North near Moorhead, Minnesota, where Olaus was born March 1, 1889. He was the first son of two Norwegian immigrants, Joachim D. and Marie (Frimanslund) Murie. Marie, who loved to pick bouquets of wild flowers, spent girlhood summers tending cows in the high mountain pastures of Norway. Her husband, trained in Norway as an army officer, draftsman, and surveyor, became a farmer in America where they immigrated a year before Olaus's birth. Olaus was seven years old when Joachim died of tuberculosis. His mother remarried, had another son, Adolph, then grieved again when her second husband also died of tuberculosis.

Keeping the name of her first marriage, Mrs. Murie was left penniless with a small house, one cow, and three sons. (Martin, from her first marriage, was three years younger than Olaus.) Olaus did what he could to help make ends meet. He delivered pails of milk before and after school, helped furnish the house with firewood by dragging it home from the forest on a small sled, and worked, albeit only eight years old, on truck farms and gardens earning vegetables for pay, then coins, and eventually a dollar a day.

While helping to support the household and completing a grade and high school education, Olaus headed outdoors to the wooded banks of the Red River whenever possible. He and his brothers called the woods "the wilderness," put up a teepee, and built a canoe using barrel hoops for ribs with a covering of sturdy wheat sacks. They paddled the canoe upriver for miles: fishing for needed food and watching raccoons, mink, red foxes and prairie chickens. In quiet moments, perhaps under a solitary cottonwood, he read the writings of Ernest Thompson Seton given him by his fourth-grade teacher.

"As I look back now," Murie said late in life, "I am thrilled by the thought of the open air farm life we led...We were living the wilderness type of life in rural areas."

Despite her frugality, Mrs. Murie dreamt of an education for her sons. She must have been pleased when Olaus won a scholarship to Fargo College across the river in Fargo, North Dakota. There he became close friends with Arthur M. Bean, a biology professor, who took him under his wing. When Bean transferred to Pacific University in Forest Grove, Oregon, he asked Olaus to come along. With nothing but a few clothes and a paper sack of lunch, Olaus headed west, passed through the Rocky Mountains and, as he once phrased it, "got through college." They were busy years. He worked part-time in the biology department, washed dishes for spare cash, played football despite weighing only 135 pounds, ran for the cross-country team, participated in debating societies, and, somehow, found time to study well enough to get a Bachelor of Arts degree in 1912.

Murie spent the next two years working for the Oregon State Game Commission under William Finley. He collected wildlife specimens, photographed various animals, and made slides. He felt stifled, however, so in 1914 capitalized on an opportunity to join ornithologist W. E. Clyde Todd on an expedition to Hudson Bay in northern Canada as a collector of museum specimens for the Carnegie Museum of Pittsburgh.

"Another man had been hired for the job," Murie once explained, "but he decided it was too dangerous. He was married and had a family. I was free."

The expedition, with two Ojibwa guides, journeyed by canoe from Cochrane, Ontario, to Rupert House, East Main, Fort George, and Great Whale River on the east shore of James Bay. They returned on the steamer *Inenew* to Moosonee, then paddled the last 180 miles back to Cochrane.

Murie, however, was too inspired by the far north to make the expedition's last leg to Cochrane. He stayed in Moosonee for the winter. Although technically unemployed, he made arrangements to continue collecting wildlife specimens while also studying the subarctic life of Cree Indians and Eskimos. Through it all ran a river of simple allure.

"The north had appealed to me—its freedom and its beauty," he confessed in *Journeys to the Far North*. "I had given much thought to it. I didn't have definite plans but I just wanted to be there. I wanted more."

Winter days in Moosonee grew short and cold, but not without beauty. Two days after Christmas he found himself on a walk that only deepened his love for where he was and what he was doing. Afterwards, with a young writer's exuberance, he turned to his journal.

"I went along the 'Northwest Path'," he wrote. "The trees stood around me—masses of spruce, a rich, soft black, the spire tops outlined against the bright, moonlit sky and here and there silvered over with a coating of snow. As I walked, I looked through openings or lanes among the trees, where the soft but clear moonshadows stretched across, and rounded snow mounds and snow-covered logs were outlined by their delicate shadows. On the level snow and over the snow-sprinkled trees sparkled the 'diamonds,' and over all, high in the sky, shone a clear moon. I walked along the path, here gazing up at the wonderful moonlit trees, there looking in among the trunks into a little opening flooded with light, or along a lane where the delicate shadows mingled wonderfully. Small bushes seemed frosted over and sparkled. Everything seemed crystalline, yet strangely mellow. There was a feeling of purity about the whole thing, as if I were in a holy place—so much so that when I heard someone shout to his dogs in the distance it felt painful, like a discordant note in music.

"I finally came to the river bank out at the back of the island, and here was another scene. The wide, smooth expanse of the river was bounded by the distant, dark shores of the islands. I crossed over to Charles Island and wandered about on a diminutive lake, and finally turned back as a thin, cloudy haze began to dim the shadows and obscure the wonderful purity of moonlight. In such surroundings a man feels elated, no task seems too big, and all evil thoughts disappear."

Later that winter, Murie traveled by dogsled with Willie Morrison, a mail-carrier, to Rupert-House then, with Cree Indians, to East Main, Fort George, and Great Whale River: the "real beginning of Eskimo land." Still wanting to get further north, he joined two Eskimos on a trip to their summer hunting grounds at the mouth of the Nastapoka River in late April 1915. He then journeyed by canoe when the ice went out to Port Harrison and the Revillon Freres Company trading post near Portland Promontory. From day to day, hour to hour, as the miles passed beneath him, Murie kept at his work: taking scientific notes, expanding his journal, and preparing bird specimens he hoped to sell to the Carnegie Museum later in the year.

The Eskimos noticed Murie collecting and preserving small birds and quickly named him *Kopinua angoraka*, "little-bird white man."

Murie's zeal, which brought him back to Great Whale River and, by October, Moose Factory and Cochrane, paid off. In May of 1917 he joined ornithologist Todd on another expedition, this time to the relatively unexplored interior of northern Labrador. The objective was to learn what birds lived in interior Labrador and to expand the collections and knowledge of the Carnegie Museum. With three nineteen-foot Peterborough freight canoes, the team of three white man and five Indians traveled from Clark City near St. Lawrence Gulf up across the 4,000-foot irregular plateau of interior Labrador with its lakes, streams, hills, and waterfalls to Fort Chimo on Ungava Bay off Hudson Strait.

To the south was forest. To the north: barren ground and sea.

The expedition ended in October and headed homeward on the *S. S. Nascaupie*. There were reasons for joy. Besides the expedition's scientific success it was the first known group of people to traverse Labrador's 700 miles south to north.

II

Murie's career leapt forward like a struck match in 1920.

After serving as a balloon observer in World War I, he was hired by the U.S. Biological Survey (now the Fish and Wildlife Service) to study the life history and migrations of Alaska-Yukon caribou. He worked on the caribou project from July 1920, to December 1923, and on three subsequent summer trips and a short winter trip. He visited all principal caribou ranges, studied several domestic reindeer herds for comparative purposes, and gathered information about caribou from travelers, hunters, prospectors, Indians, Eskimos, and his own inevitable fieldwork. Much time was spent afoot, sometimes with pack dogs, yet most of Murie's summer travel—occasionally going forty-eight hours without food or sleep—was done by motorboat or poling boat.

In winter, he traveled by dogsled.

Dogsledding held a special fascination for Murie who, over the years, loved to talk and write about his dogs and their mode of travel. It seemed to epitomize life in the North. The dogs liked to be active, "eager to be up and doing, to go somewhere, to pull the sled." They had a "primeval truculence...a real joy in the fight." His lead dog, Snook, would "sail into a mass of fighting dogs with what appeared to be a smile on its face." Despite such feistiness, there were also moments of special peace along the dog team trail.

"It was still and clear," Murie would recall of a memorable night near Rainy Pass of the Alaska Range, "and close to forty degrees below zero. I knew it would not storm on such a night. I fed the dogs some ptarmigan meat and ate a little of the moose heart myself [the moose heart was given to him by an Indian he met on the trail; he and the dogs lived on it for several days when his dog food supply became so low he had to ration his own food with the dogs]. I didn't bother to put up the tent but simply spread out my sleeping bag, took off my boots, and crawled in, parka and all... As I lay there, cozy and warm in the sleeping bag, the four dogs curled up close around the edges of my bed, life seemed good."

One of Murie's longest dogsled trips studying caribou was with his brother, Adolph, who joined him for eighteen months as an assistant. Beginning on November 24, 1922, in Fairbanks, they journeyed on the Yukon and Koyukuk rivers into the Brooks Range, then returned to Fairbanks via the Chandalar and Yukon river valleys. The trip covered 1,500 miles, slid through temperatures reaching -68 degrees Fahrenheit, and ended on April 26, 1923, two days after they saw the herd of 2,500 caribou on the divide between Twelvemile and McManus creeks.

There were moments, of course, of despair. Sleds overturned. Dogs fought. The cold, short arctic days with their "blue and gray and white with an accent of black in the strips of forest" were physically and emotionally chilling. Still, at other times, they anticipated the arctic days ahead, explored new valleys, and all the little adventures added up to neutralize the cold and loneliness, bringing, instead, fulfillment and joy.

"I seemed to want to roam over these plains myself, like the caribou," Murie said of the tundra portion of the trip, "and feed on lichens, face the winds, and travel on and on."

By March, shortly before trip's end, the Muries mushed through Wiseman, visiting the remote Arctic village six years before Bob Marshall.

Although the caribou project took most of four years, Murie nevertheless found time to study waterfowl in the Hooper Bay region of Alaska and brown bears on the Alaska Peninsula. Among his field trips was a five-month, 800-mile journey to the treeless shores of the Bering Sea where he supervised a large party from Fairbanks in a study of native birds. Murie enjoyed the eiders, jaegers, emperor geese and Alaskan longspurs, but his heart, sometimes, had a new ache.

He had fallen in love with Margaret E. Thomas.

Olaus first met Margaret (or Mardy, as she is known to friends) in Fairbanks in June 1921, while working on his caribou study. Mardy, born in Seattle on August 18, 1902, had moved to Fairbanks with her family in 1911 at the age of nine. There she stayed, growing up among rows of log cabins on the bank of Chena slough, offshoot of the Tanana River, until she headed off for Oregon's Reed College. She was back in Fairbanks for the summer after her sophomore year when she intersected with Olaus.

The first thing Mardy noticed was Olaus's pleasant voice and blue eyes. Soon they were walking each other home, talking, beneath a rosy sky.

"All I can remember," Mardy wrote in *Two in the Far North*, "is that we agreed we didn't care to live in cities. He did not say: 'When may I see you again?' as all the rest of them did. He was not *like* any of the rest of them, and it took me quite a while to learn this. But in a few days we went on a trip upriver with Jess and Clara [Rust, who introduced Olaus to Mardy] in their motorboat, and at one place in the quiet water of Moose Creek, Jess cut the motor and we heard a great horned owl hoot far off in the forest. Olaus answered him. Again the owl spoke, a bit closer this time. Olaus hooted again, and so it went, until suddenly out of nowhere the dark soft shape floated into a treetop right above us on the riverbank and sat silhouetted against the golden sky. What kind of magic did this man have? And when we made a camp later that evening he took out his notebook and made me a sketch of that owl. So he was an artist too? He did all this quietly with a few words."

Slowly, inexorably, Olaus and Mardy called each other closer just as Olaus had called the owl.

They exchanged letters the following winter when Mardy was studying at Simmons College in Boston, then really blew wind on the fire the following summer and fall. Mardy was back home in Fairbanks to attend the University of Alaska where she would become its first woman graduate. Olaus and Adolph were sharing a cabin a block from Mardy's as they waited for snow prior to their 1922-23 dogsled trip into the Brooks Range. But Olaus didn't just wait for snow. He was tracking Mardy, moving more deeply into her heart. She taught him to dance. He helped her with college math. Then they slipped apart, Olaus to the dogsled trail, Mardy to class.

"We really came to know each other," Mardy wrote me in December, 1978, about her courtship with Olaus, "through the letters we both wrote during that long winter when he and Adolph were up in the Arctic and he was sending letters back from every little village and every mailman he met on the dog team trail—-we talked in those letters about all the things which meant most to us in thinking about Life. And I think it is still true as it was then, that a period of absence in the midst of a romance enables one to sort everything out. By the time Olaus returned in late April I had a pretty firm idea about his inner strengths, his great appreciation of life and its opportunities, his marvelous sense of humor, and his great tenderness."

Olaus and Mardy waited a little over a year before marrying at three o'clock in the morning on August 19, 1924, in Anvik, Alaska.

Olaus, returning from his field trip to the Bering Sea, journeyed up the Yukon River to meet nervous Mardy who, with cake and entourage, traveled downstream.

At night, red Mars, closer to Earth than usual, shone on starlit water.

"What are you marrying that fellow for?" a friend of Olaus's in Fairbanks had asked Mardy before the wedding. "He's half caribou: you'll never keep up with him."

"Well," Mardy replied, "Maybe I can keep about fifty feet behind."

And she did.

Their honeymoon was characteristic of the future. From Anvik, the dearly beloved took a three-week boat trip to Bettles where, in a small cabin, they set up house and awaited freeze-up. It was a quaint place: nights meant lit lamps, a crackling fire, and wind banging at the stovepipe as a yellow moon cast yellow sparkles on the black, still unfrozen, water of the Koyukuk River.

Soon Olaus taught Mardy how to catalogue and label mammal specimens which, that winter, meant mice.

"Each mouse label," she explained, "had to contain the date and location of the catch, the Latin name of the animal, and its sex; then the conventional scientific data without which it would not be a specimen: total length, length of tail, and length of hind foot. And all this then had to be entered in the proper columns in the catalogue, a hard-covered blank book in which the notes for Olaus's mammal collection now amounted to some 1,940 entries."

Such tedious tasks, essential to Olaus's work, slowly surrendered to more winter, a frozen river, and snow for the dogsled trail. They headed into the Endicott Mountains for six weeks. Instead of a snug cabin, home became a canvas tent with Yukon wood stove and a bed of spruce boughs. Come twilight, Olaus gathered and split wood as Mardy, kneeling, cooked meat over an outside fire.

Daytimes were given over to covering ground.

"It was a fairyland," Mardy wrote of one stretch of particularly nice country, "this highland, skyland, on a glorious blue and gold day. Our seven dogs, the two of us, alone up there, sliding along on top of the world. Out there above the tableland's edge were the tops of white mountains that seemed to rise out of nowhere."

Mushing in remote Alaskan mountains.

Surrounded by snow and sky as the sled dogs, sometimes gracefully, other times ornery, padded on towards day's end for the two young lovers.

It was the stuff of fantasy: the motion, day by night, of wild Alaskan dream.

———

Two years later, after a six-month separation as Olaus studied brown bears of the Alaskan Peninsula, Olaus and Mardy regrouped for a four-month goose-banding expedition to the headwaters of the Old Crow River in northwestern Yukon Territory. They traveled by motorboat and poling boat on the Tanana River, the Porcupine, then the Old Crow with its rapids, molting geese, bears and horrendous mosquitoes. Tough going, with parallel dangers, yet Mardy had discovered being with Olaus was "more important than safety."

With them this time, however, beneath stars, during rosy dawns, or as wolves howled, was their ten-month old son, Martin. His powdered milk was diluted with the closest river water.

III

Elk.

Murie's career as a rambling father, husband and federal biologist headed south in 1926 to Jackson Hole, Wyoming, where he was destined to do with elk what he had done with caribou: get to know them better than anyone. Elk, or *wapiti*, had vanished from most of their original range and a special Elk Commission was created by the President's Committee on Outdoor Recreation to find out why. The Elk Commission, in turn, asked the U.S. Biological Survey to make a comprehensive study of the life history of elk to be used as a basis for efficient elk management. Murie was assigned the study and, because the largest herd of elk in the world, some 20,000 animals, lived near Jackson Hole, he had to turn his back on Alaska and go Outside.

Jackson Hole, with its adjacent village of Moose, became Murie's study headquarters. It also became home.

Beginning in July 1927, Murie spent more than five years studying North American elk. Although he and Mardy built a stucco house in Jackson Hole, summers meant a family migration to the Teton backcountry where they lived out of a tent; Olaus needed to be close to his work. Field trips were made on foot and by horseback such as Olaus's 1928 horseback trip, again with Adolph, from the south entrance of Yellowstone National Park, through the upper Yellowstone and Thorofare country, over Two Ocean Pass, around to Pacific and Whetstone creeks in Teton National Forest, then back to Moran. Murie analyzed habitat, elk migration patterns, life zones, elk physiology, reproduction, natural enemies, parasites, food habits, and populations. It was a life of tracking sign. More elk study brought Murie to Washington, Idaho, California, Montana, Oklahoma, Canada, and Alaska. In those rare moments when Murie sat still, he reviewed over 320 literary items about elk.

It was, for the entire Murie family, elk madness.

There were boiled elk skulls in the house, a shoe box filled with elk teeth, and elk antlers scattered throughout the autumn living room. It was elk this, elk that, as Olaus—even called "Mr. Elk"—discovered why so many were dying: necrotic stomatitis, like calf diphtheria, infecting the elk through lesions.

"After a winter of living with the wapiti through their dark days," he recalled, "watching them die, examining them, working in snow and blizzard and below-zero cold, trudging home across the fields night after night with cold and bloody hands and a few more unpleasant data in my notebook—you can imagine my joy at the spring release of the survivors out onto the greening hillsides, up through the aspen groves, and on north to first verdure and new smooth red-brown coats and the endless freedom of the summer world."

Mardy, meanwhile, mothered two more children, Joanna and Donald, tended to home chores, helped Olaus as his secretary, and, when necessary, stayed out of his way.

"Since he was so dedicated to his work," she said in *Wapiti Wilderness*, "that every project or experiment he thought important was bound to go on despite anything or anybody, it was far better just to relax and take it all as it came."

The results of Murie's research were eventually published as *The Elk of North America*. Not only was the book a definitive study of elk, with suggestions for elk management, but it was given the Wildlife Society Award for being an outstanding ecological publication.

By 1935, when Murie's *Alaska-Yukon Caribou* became No. 54 of the North American Fauna Series, and with his elk fieldwork coming to a close, his stature as a field biologist was beyond question. The U.S. Biological Survey liked what he was doing and wanted to keep him busy. Murie was in his late forties when, in 1936, the Survey gave him a new assignment: check out the wildlife of Alaska' Aleutian Islands.

The motor ship *Brown Bear* was placed at Murie's disposal so he could move around the islands stretching a thousand miles west of the Alaska Peninsula into the Bering Sea. With Murie were scientists Cecil S. Williams of the Biological Survey, H. Douglas Gray and Homer Jewell, both of the Alaska Game Commission, and, the next summer, Victor B. Scheffer and John H. Steenis. They found the volcanic Aleutians treeless and, often, fog-bound. Except for the islets, the expedition visited every island clear out to Attu, almost in Siberia.

Olaus, given a choice, walked around the islands even though his assistants often went around by motor dory.

"I know," Mardy wrote me, "he felt that that was the only way he could get the feel of a place, and see all the little creatures, plants, every aspect of the life of a place...He was probably the only man who ever walked around practically every one of those islands."

Another expedition, another report. *Fauna of the Aleutian Islands and Alaska Peninsula* would reach print in 1959.

The Aleutian Islands expedition was one of the few expeditions on which Mardy didn't accompany Olaus. Instead, she and the three children hopped the *Brown Bear* to Seward, Alaska, then headed north overland to Fairbanks where they spent summer with the Rusts. The following summer, while Olaus was back in the Aleutians, Mardy was given a small faculty bungalow at the University of Alaska campus where she worked on Otto Geist's material for the book *Island Between*. The rest of the time, when it came to expeditions, Olaus's bottom line was clear.

"Olaus," Mardy said, "simply told his superiors that he was taking the family with him, and I suppose they knew they would have to allow it, or fire him!"

IV

During Murie's wildlife studies, he nurtured a belief that wildlife and wild country had values needing protection. It was a conviction, in 1945, given opportunity for direct expression when he was asked to become director of the Wilderness Society. Murie had been a member of the Society's Council since its founding in 1935, and was one of the five trustees of the Robert Marshall Wilderness Fund to promote wilderness preservation, but still the request came as a surprise.

At first Olaus hesitated. He didn't want to live in Washington, D.C., where directorship would land him. Mardy agreed. But she also wanted Olaus to leave government work. When Robert Griggs suggested over the phone that Howard Zahniser become executive secretary in Washington, and that Olaus become director in Wyoming at half time and half pay, both Olaus and Mardy bit the hook.

So began a new work, a new job.

"But not only that," Mardy remembered in *Wapiti Wilderness*, "a new home too, a whole new life, a whole new career."

They celebrated Olaus's new work with the Wilderness Society by buying, together with Adolph who had married Mardy's half-sister, Louise, a seventy-seven acre ranch a mile downriver from Moose. "If a man is to appreciate wilderness and its problems," Olaus thought, "he should live with it." The ranch, with eight cabins and three houses, had, at first, no electricity or phone. Olaus and Mardy chose a favorite log cabin and moved in. The road leading to the ranch was snowed-in from December to April, requiring a mile ski in and out.

They loved it.

Murie: On Peace

"I know that when I have stood in Nature's domain, rapt in wonder, in the presence of some manifestation of her charm, perhaps a sunset, a mighty unfolding of mountain ranges to the horizon, or the soft hooting of an owl in the dusk, at such times I have had my greatest peace. At such times I can harbor no ill will toward my fellow man. I do not understand it. But I feel it is God-given."

—Olaus Murie, *Wapiti Wilderness*

It was a demanding, albeit rich, life: a sequestering of body and mind for the sake of America's wilderness preservation movement.

"We had become immersed in the conservation battle," Mardy explained, "and enthralled and stimulated by it and by the interesting people we met in connection with it, and we both knew that life was blooming, expanding, growing because of the new work Olaus had undertaken. It demanded a great deal of us both. Correspondence was never quite caught up with; there were articles Olaus must write, lectures he must prepare, trips here and there and everywhere, to lecture, to meet, to confer, to testify, to teach, to persuade, to urge, to decide, to stand firm. To all of these he brought not only ability and talent but strength, and the desire, the involvement, the dedication."

As director of the Wilderness Society, then president from 1950 to 1957, Murie's stance was characteristically straightforward: save what wilderness you can. Wilderness was a place for exploration, hunting, photography, esthetic experience and scientific study, all valuable to people. National parks could have their motor roads; unspoiled wild areas should be visited by hiking over trails or canoeing.

He put it this way at the Twelfth Alaskan Science Conference:

"A wilderness area should be reserved for those who crave a true wilderness experience, those who can stand weather, who have the stamina to deal with the vicissitudes of camp life, and still enjoy the experience. We surely need this element in our American civilization. It should not be lowered to a common denominator to accommodate great numbers. Those who want wilderness should have the privileges to go there and find it undisturbed. Those who desire other kinds of recreation should be provided with such facilities. We are not all alike. Let us, by all means, have diversity in our culture, a freedom to choose."

Over the years, Murie continued to build both a verbal and literary defense of wild country, whether it was the Chesapeake and Ohio Canal, Washington's Olympic Mountains, the Quetico-Superior, or Jackson Hole National Monument in his backyard. The twenty-five year index, in 1961, to the Wilderness Society's magazine, *The Living Wilderness*, alone listed 32 articles and editorials, 38 book reviews, 88 drawings and comments on 52 subjects by Murie.

Despite all the writing, lecturing and his accelerated artwork (he had begun illustrating his *A Field Guide to Animal Tracks*), or perhaps *because* of such an exhausting schedule, Murie took a break in 1949 to lead a scientific expedition into New Zealand's Fiordland country on invitation from the government of New Zealand. The purpose of the expedition was to study introduced elk and make recommendations for their management. Olaus, working under a Fullbright grant from the U.S. Government, accompanied two dozen scientists and other personnel, together with Mardy and son Donald, into Fiordland National Park. They visited the Caswell area, Stillwater River, Leslie Clearing, George Sound, Hankinson Hut, and the Glaisnock region. A report emerged from the expedition, of course, but most encouraging to Murie was the zeal he discovered in New Zealanders to protect their new elk, the country's forests of kauri pines, and the resolve they showed when designating new wilderness areas.

Murie returned home from New Zealand to accolades.

His Oregon alma mater, Pacific University, awarded him an honorary doctorate degree citing him as "a man of the world terrestrial, authority on its animal life, interpreter of nature's art, student of her design, and exponent of the wilderness in terms of the human spirit." A few years later he was given the Aldo Leopold Memorial Award "in recognition of his inspired contribution to the cause of wildlife conservation, as scientist, counselor, author, artist, and leading champion of the wilderness unspoiled." In a kind of cultural congealing of Murie appreciation, two more awards landed in his hands in 1954: the Cornelius Amory Pugsley Bronze Medal of the American Scenic and Historic Preservation Society, for "effective and outstanding service in the defense of national parks and...wise counsel toward the shaping of national park conservation policies," and the Conservation Award of the American Forestry Association. Murie later received the Audubon Medal (1959), the Izaak Walton League Honor Roll in Conservation (1961), and the John Muir Award from the Sierra Club (1963).

Awards were nice. Saving Alaskan wilderness was better.

Ever since studying Alaska-Yukon caribou in the 1920s, Murie had cherished memories of them sweeping across subarctic taiga and arctic tundra, shearing lichens, nibbling mosses, always moving in migratory harmony with the wild pulse of life. They seemed to represent far northern Alaska and pristine wilderness, a kind of *noumenon*, ala Leopold, without which Alaska and all of America would be impoverished. The possibility of such loss, however, was becoming clear in the late 1940s when studies by the National Park Service and the Arctic Institute of North America indicated that if the wilderness caribou needed to survive was going to be preserved, in effect protecting wild Alaska, it was critical to mobilize political forces.

Murie, now in his fifties, agreed.

He had noticed how historical events, political shenanigans, and agency policy were carving up northern Alaska. Five million acres had been set aside in 1923 as a National Petroleum Reserve. Twenty years later another eighteen million acres were reserved for wartime minerals. By 1949, the National Park Service had initiated an Alaska Recreational Survey under George L. Collins to develop a possible park and recreation plan for Alaska's northern territory. According to Debbie Miller in *Midnight Wilderness*, Murie, representing the Wilderness Society, was then advised to contract Collins and express the Society's thoughts on what wilderness area, if any, should be protected. They agreed to direct attention to the northeastern corner of the state.

Soon Murie and Sigurd Olson were flying above the eastern Brooks Range on reconnaissance. Taking a look. Pondering the possible.

The next year, Collins, field biologist Lowell Sumner, and A. Starker Leopold (Aldo Leopold's son), set up camp along Schrader Lake in the eastern Brooks Range to take a closer look around. With the area's high glaciated peaks, its wide spectrum of wildlife habitats, its caribou, and its vast, incomparable wild reaches, the group could see the region deserved protection. But what kind?

"From the time I first saw it," Collins later said, "it was the finest national park prospect I had ever seen."

The group drew up rough wilderness boundaries and, in 1953, recommended that Canada and the United States work together for an Arctic International Park.

"The conversations, the letters," Mardy said, "the gathering of information, went on. It was agreed The Wilderness Society should take up the challenge. The Sierra Club, the Tanana Valley Sportsmen's Association, and many others would cooperate. But where was the money?"

More field work, too, was needed.

One day Olaus, in New York City, called Fairfield Osborn, president of the New York Zoological Society and the Conservation Foundation, and said he thought he and Mardy should lead an expedition into the Brooks Range.

"Well," Osborn answered, "isn't that something *we* ought to be interested in?"

Thus, in 1956, Olaus and Mardy, together with Dr. Brina Kessel, Bob Krear, and George Schaller spent the summer hunkered down in the Sheenjek Valley of northeastern Alaska's caribou country. Base camp was along a small lake they named Lobo, from the Latin *lupus*, the scientific name for a wolf that appeared to them. As day melded into day, everyone tackled their respective tasks studying arctic plants and flowers, mosses, wolves, grizzly bears, trees, even permafrost. Day hikes and backpacking trips were taken in all directions. There was a mix of rough tussock hiking and clean alpine walking, twenty-four hour sunlight, evening campfires, private moments for Murie to read about Arctic explorer Nansen, and a visit by Supreme Court Justice William O. Douglas and his wife, Merci.

In the back of everyone's mind, meanwhile, were the land's caribou which they watched, heard, tracked, and photographed, hoping to understand the fragile ecological pyramid on which they depended. One day they watched

1,600 caribou pass by.

"This was the culmination of all the good things," Mardy recalled. "Here was the living, moving, warm-blooded life of the Arctic—out of some far valley to the west of this region, into some far valley to the east—with the wisdom of the ages, moving always, not depleting their food supply, needing all these valleys and mountains in which to live."

When Murie's Sheenjek expedition came to an end August 6, the information they had gathered, together with reports from other scientists, covered an area from the Canadian boundary 215 miles westward to Canning River, and from the Arctic Ocean 100 miles south to Lobo Lake. Consensus grew for an American Arctic Wildlife Range. For the rest of the summer, and again in 1957, Murie traveled throughout Alaska promoting the range as a wild place without roads, hence inaccessible to mass recreation, where people craving "a true wilderness experience" could still have the opportunity. What little hunting had gone on in the proposed range could continue. Soon Murie won firm support from the Tanana Valley Sportsmen's Association, the Anchorage chapter of the Isaac Walton League, the Alaska Federation of Women's Clubs, various garden clubs, and even the chamber of commerce and *Daily News-Miner* of Fairbanks.

Victory for Murie and Alaskan wilderness came on December 7, 1960, when Secretary of the Interior Fred A. Seaton, acting by executive proclamation, signed Public Land Order #2214 creating the Arctic National Wildlife Range. At nine million acres (later enlarged to 18 million acres), it became the largest wilderness and wildlife refuge in the U.S.

Olaus and Mardy were in Idaho Falls, attending hearings on a proposed Snake River dam, when they heard the news.

They both wept.

———

With the pinnacle of Murie's career behind him, he and Mardy turned their attention to other wilderness work, a return trip to the Sheenjek Valley in 1961, and to four major writing projects.

Together they wrote complementary chapters for *Wapiti Wilderness*, an account of their experiences in and around Jackson Hole. Individually, Mardy worked on *Two in the Far North*, a memoir of her life with Olaus in Alaska. Olaus, now also sprinting as a writer, kept a journal (divided into Birds, Mammals, and General), completed *Jackson Hole With a Naturalist*, a guidebook to the natural history of Wyoming's Teton country, and he put the final touches on his *Journeys to the Far North*. It was a labor of love recalling his Hudson Bay days, the canoe trip in Labrador, and some of his best adventures in the Yukon and Alaska.

"He seemed able to close off his surroundings," Mardy said of Olaus's use of every spare moment to write, "and concentrate whenever a thought struck. I have memories of his sitting at a table under the back windows of the big living room at Moose, writing away while four, five, seven children, grandchildren, and guest were conversing, playing cards, arguing over a crossword puzzle or a game of Scrabble. He could have gone into his study and closed the doors, but he seemed to find harmony and warmth in the midst of the people he loved."

Inevitably, the life and personality of Olaus Murie—which Howard Zahniser found to be a compelling expression of the concept of wilderness—came to an end. After a long illness, he died quietly on October 21, 1963, in St. John's Hospital of Jackson Hole. He was cremated and his ashes were spread in the backcountry.

"Sun and moon and stars," Murie had written shortly before death, remembering the past, recalling the embrace, "the northern lights, the rising and the setting, day and night, summer and winter—the pageant of the North. All this and its precious wild creatures, I have known.

"And I now also know how greatly privileged I have been."

7

CALVIN RUTSTRUM:
ROLLING STONE OF WATERWAYS

"Can it be... that someday the only inspiration we will have from the wilds will be in the graphic and written form? I doubt it, but I am inclined to believe that past and present wilderness writers will have had a better opportunity to depict the true wilderness than future writers, if most of our natural environment comes to be developed out of its pristine state and much of it developed entirely out of existence."

—Calvin Rutstrum, *Chips From a Wilderness Log*

When spring rains pelted Calvin Rutstrum's sailcoth tent in the 1950s, probably no one was better able to cope comfortably with bad weather than he. Almost half of Rutstrum's life was spent camping in the canoe country of northern Minnesota, northwestern Ontario and Manitoba. He learned woodsman skills from Ojibway and Cree Indians. He picked up other outdoor living techniques from white canoeing partners. And he learned some skills the hard way, alone and by mistake, on both canoe and backpack trips. Whether baking bannock around a campfire or beaching a canoe at the end of a long, wind-tossed lake, Rutstrum evolved into a woodsman of consummate skill. Inevitably, half of his 15 books—including *North American Canoe Country* and *Paradise Below Zero*—focused on living comfortably under wilderness conditions. A simple spring rain was no problem.

While the "how-to" of wilderness life was becoming second nature, however, and eventually Rutstrum's literary tour de force, he was nevertheless developing a philosophy of wilderness life indigenous to his experience and vision. The how-to books, the nuts-and-bolts stuff, were outward manifestations of a much deeper interior life. He was a man of little formal education but great thought. And historians of wilderness literature, few as they might be, will continue to discover that Rutstrum's ideas—as with those wilderness visionaries before him—grew out of much backcountry travel.

And rightfully so.

"Only intimate and prolonged contact with the wilds," Rutstrum was convinced, "seems to allow any significant revelation of its inner secrets."

Hence, by combining reflections with skill, intellectuality with ability, Rutstrum bridged old wilderness ways with new, more environmentally aware, wilderness ways. He was a living synapse in the nerve of wilderness thought.

Cal, of course, never became as influential in North America's wilderness preservation movement as Muir, Marshall or others of their kind. Yet he was nevertheless unique, if not radiant, in an inimitable manner. He was never a bureaucrat. Never an ideological mogul. His dreams were geared to and rooted in the simple joys of backcountry living and travel. In time he touched the lives of thousands of outdoors people, including such notable paddlers and authors as Minnesotan Cliff Jacobson and Canadian Bill Mason.

"Rutstrum totally influenced me," Mason, author of the book *Path of the Paddle* and producer of the film *Waterwalker*, told me of Rutstrum's campcraft legacy. "He became my hero. When someone gave me Calvin Rutstrum's [first] book, I just freaked out. I said, 'This is what I've been looking for.'"

As a hero, Rutstrum was no literary dilettante working from a New England garret replete with laced curtains and expensive Audubon prints on the wall. Nor was he a connoisseur of the growing genre of wilderness literature while working in an Ivy League college library and living in a $200,000 house. At least not young Rutstrum. Young Rutstrum was happiest living out of a trapper's or logger's shack on a wild riverbank or lakeshore; there on sub-zero nights as a fire in his barrel stove roared, he dove into books ranging from Mencken to Thoreau, always striving to understand the knot binding nature and man. Nothing excited him more at other times than to be on the way to a wilderness jumping-off point. With him, perhaps stuck back in a train's baggage car, would be a Peterborough or birchbark canoe, a camp outfit for backcountry travel, and a supply of provisions—flour, bacon and ham, dried apples, prunes, apricots, sugar, coffee and tea. His clothes? An Indian-tanned moosehide shirt, wool stroud pants, a felt hat banded with leather, and moccasins. This was everything he needed to survive in the wealthiest way he knew: leisure under natural conditions. Only this way could he soak up nature. Only this way could he come to know what he was writing about, what he was in love with and what he journeyed north to absorb year after year.

Whether he paddled into the backcountry in the summer only to toboggan out in winter, or traveled into the backcountry by dogsled in winter then canoed out in spring, Rutstrum wanted to become so intimately aware of wilderness that his psyche would blossom into a natural manifestation of it.

Didn't he, late in life, change the title of his autobiography, *Challenge of the Wilderness*, to *A Wilderness Autobiography*? As if he were wilderness per se, clothed and civilized, its voice printed between book covers? He sometimes wrote of being wild country's "indigene." Didn't it need writers willing to explore the limits of natural phenomena intriguing to both laymen and scientists? By being a writer, was he not, as Thoreau once said, a "scribe of all nature"?

This then—this marriage of consciousness and twentieth-century backcountry—is what Calvin Rutstrum's long life was all about. This is what he referred to on Valentine's Day, 1981, when he told me:

"I must have fallen out of the cradle into the woods. And enjoyed it."

I

Exactly when Rutstrum's enjoyment of woods peaked will probably always remain an enigma, but his boyhood, he confessed in retrospect, "signed and sealed" his mind to wilderness. He was born in Hobart, Indiana, on October 26, 1895, 33 years after Thoreau died and four years before Sigurd F. Olson was born. He was the baby of Tiofel and Emma (Carlson) Rutstrum, Swedish immigrants, although Emma's black hair and brown eyes made her look "more like an Italian than a Swede." Cal remembered her as a "very extraordinary woman." An intelligent woman but a religious fanatic. "All she thought morning to night was religion," Cal said. Father Tiofel, doomed never to know his son, was a craftsman hired to apply fabric to streetcar interiors, first in Hobart an hour from downtown Chicago, then in St. Paul's Midway district.

"Both he and I had pneumonia at the same time, lying in the same room," Rutstrum told me. "He died and I recovered. I was about three."

Three. With a son that age mother Emma had to make a living wherever and whenever she could. She married a second time, and bore Cal half-sisters and half-brothers, but a large family didn't stave off the high cost of living. Cal had to work as soon as he knew what a dime was. Working as a lad wasn't, he thought, "an imposing responsibility." It was a fact of life. He shined shoes on city streets, cleaned a bakery's greasy pans, walked from house to house sharpening kitchen knives and scissors, helped on delivery trucks and peddled newspapers. Dinners were often oatmeal and milk; meals with meat were rare.

Public relief? Or, as he put it, mooching? Out of the question.

What Rutstrum *did* question was how he could spend as much time as possible in the neighborhood's hardwood forest. There he played in summer's "green hillside verdure" and slid down the white slopes of winter. A nearby marsh had pollywogs and frogs, cattails and cackling birds, the wonder of sunlight reflecting off water pancaked with lily pads. Strongest of all that sucked at Rutstrum's attention was the Mississippi River. A giant waterway it was, "jammed with floating logs from northern pine forests not yet wholly denuded." And there he was, Rutstrum recalled, "a healthy young animal with less than a dozen years from birth, alive to the early summer sunshine, barefooted, youthfully entranced, eager as spring for life, as intrinsically a part of the river, I believed, as the waterthrush that foraged at the mouth of Minnehaha Creek, where the rippling current joined the mighty Mississippi... To be free as a wild creature, not having to shoulder human cares, able to climb, run, jump, swim, lie on an embankment in the sunshine—these gave a release to the young spirit that may perhaps be described as primitive, but nevertheless exquisite in the most elemental sense."

Rutstrum and pals spent weeks traveling down the Mississippi. They sometimes rode logs and booms:

"Now and then we slipped and fell into the river, sometimes between the logs, but these were merely routine, negligible inconveniences—a chance for the rest of us to laugh at an awkward move. As victim and butt of the joke, we soon climbed back on to the logs if an opening allowed. If the log boom closed over our heads, trapping us beneath, we swam underwater, holding our breath until daylight appeared through another opening. Here we would bring our noses for a breath of air as a seal would in a breather hole under the ice, or a companion would pry logs apart to help cheat death in the morning of life."

Huckleberry Rutstrum and friends ate fish (catching extra to trade for other food and matches), used a sharp-edged stone as a knife, and slept under sandstone cornices along the river, occasionally blanketing themselves with leaves.

When Rutstrum dropped out of school at age 13 to earn a living as a delivery boy for a dry-cleaning business, six 10-hour days a week, he understandably began to miss summers on the river. "The city," he remembered, "began to pall until it was a daily dread. My escape to the wilderness seemed highly imminent. It dominated my consciousness with a compelling, almost it seemed, instinctive force."

Rutstrum cached $25 by the time he was 16, besides acquiring a complete survival outfit: bedroll, sailcoth tent, belt knife, .30-.30 Winchester carbine, cruiser's ax, cook kit, .22 single-shot pistol, ammunition, and fishing tackle, all kept in a Poirer shoulder packsack (Duluth pack).

His intentions were clear.

Twenty-four dollars bought passage to Montana's Mussellshell River Valley, where he rode fence for a cattle ranch. He spent two summers there. During the intervening winter he lived in an abandoned log cabin in the mountains. A mountain winter meant time out for things like reading, particularly when snow depths surpassed anything Rutstrum's southern Minnesota mind was used to. His squat log cabin became like a "smokestack coming out of a snowdrift," the path to the door a snow-walled corridor. Woodchuck Rutstrum read about various wilderness regions, and as his research skated along it slid to a stop on Canada's Precambrian Shield.

The "Shield" was a vast rock tableland of north-central Canada surrounding Hudson Bay, stretching southwest into then-wild northern Minnesota. There ranching and farming hadn't developed the land. Mining was limited by access and scattered ore grades. Virgin forest could still be found. And in the forest on the Shield were lakes and rivers, waterfalls, wildlife—a mosaic of wildness connected by paddle and portage. A lust for the region took root in Rutstrum's heart. He knew—by the time spring sun melted Mussellshell snowdrifts—he was going to leave cattle country for canoe country.

He got off the train in Minneapolis-St. Paul. He took odd jobs as he waited throughout the bug season of May and June for specialized camping equipment he had ordered. Soon his investments were so oriented to wilderness travel that he realized a sudden return to conventional life would have led to bankruptcy. Then Rutstrum, 18, began his all-time favorite canoe trip: a 3½-month, 100-day camping binge on Deer, Pickerel and Battle lakes in north-central Minnesota.

The location was fitting for novice Rutstrum. Deer, Pickerel and Battle lakes were, and still are, strung together by streams and wetlands up a tributary of the Big Fork River. The Big Fork is 170 miles long and gets its name from being the biggest tributary of the Rainy River, into which it flows on the Minnesota-Ontario border west of International Falls-Fort Frances. The Big Fork drops 250 feet throughout its course. Wild rice feathers its headwaters. Pine and birch, alder and poplar bank the river as it drops into the eastern edge of ancient glacial Lake Agassiz. At river's end are enigmatic Indian burial mounds. Instead of canoeing all the way to the burial mounds, however, Rutstrum and friend turned up a creek about 20 miles downstream from the logging village of Big Fork.

The creek was shallow and ribbed with shoal rapids, forcing them to get out of their canoe to push it ahead of them. The virgin country was rich with wildlife and wonder. Rutstrum wasn't quite on the Precambrian Shield that captured his imagination, for only on Rice Rapids and a few others had he actually seen the Shield's granite, outcropping character. But he was enthralled nevertheless. He heard loons call as his canoe cut the waters of calm Deer Lake. Ducks, in flocks, whistled by. On shore were big pines, virgin Norways, abundant back then throughout the region, pine big enough for a person to ride horseback through, their underlying brush so thin in patches of rust-colored needle duff that a man could pitch a tent almost anywhere. Cal stayed in Deer Lake country throughout autumn. He fished and caught northern pike, some weighing 25 pounds. He ate ducks, rabbits, grouse, venison and berries. Staples like flour, sugar, and tea were fetched by a round-trip canoe jaunt of 55 miles. After frosts, October's gold poplar leaves, those from quaking aspen and balm-of-Gilead, fell to the earth in eddies of wind and when wet with rain. The Big Fork froze. So did the lakes. Rutstrum tobogganed out when the ice was safe beneath deepening snow. He left the birchbark canoe behind.

For Calvin Rutstrum, the Big Fork River wilderness was just a beginning.

His trips into northern Minnesota's backcountry and across the border lakes into Ontario became as regular as migrating geese. No matter what job he held, no matter that weight of obligation employers tried to lay on him, he left every August for parts little known. He came to view cities as "large trading posts," and jobs at those posts as a means to get grubstaked for the next adventure. Never was work an end in itself. Never could jobs preempt a canoe trip. This was religion for Rutstrum, as close to religion as he ever got. It was also a religion that some employers simply didn't appreciate. One boss told Rutstrum that, because of his "reckless leisure," he would blackball him so he could never get a job in that city again. Cal looked the guy in the eye and asked him if, in planning to cut off his chances for subsistence survival, he—Mr. employer—expected to remain alive.

Such grit, perhaps, was picked up in dark woods as a kid, on city streets, in scary rapids and eventually in the Navy. No matter. Rutstrum was never easily intimidated, a personality characteristic that came in handy when he became a criminal investigator for the American Banking Association. It was a job he had for 10 years, and one that required him to write daily reports. Here began his writing career.

"Very early," he explained, "when I was in school [prior to dropping out in the seventh grade], "I used to write what they called Journal junior stories. I was a lousy student in school when it came to mathematics. But I could sit down and write a story and get it published in the Journal Junior. I don't remember what I wrote those under. My name was Fred Carlson for a number of years when my stepfather was living. I might have written them under that."

Some stories were probably written anonymously for the hell of it, he said. But what really got him involved with the written word was his work as an investigator of crime.

"I had to write every day. I wrote those reports well enough so that I had quite a few compliments from the head office that I didn't leave anything to anyone's imagination. For instance, if I'd go to a door and ring the bell, and some lady came to the door and answered the door, I wouldn't presume who she was... If there was occasion to ask her who she was, that was all right. But I would describe her in detail. Now, many reporters make the mistake of saying, I went to 1529 Orchard Avenue, and there I talked to Mrs. Brook Jones, you know. Well, that's meaningless. Because how the hell did you know it was Mrs. Jones? It might have been somebody scrubbing the front floor. So, the thing is, I was very careful about all these details. And as I got along, I got very well."

Rutstrum's detective work and writing got an upward push following a bank robbery in Eden, South Dakota. The robbers had bought about a hundred pounds of roofing nails, which they threw out the rear window of a Buick onto the dirt road which was their escape. Rutstrum identified the hardware store where the nails were bought by studying the drop-forging on the nail heads. He also followed the escape route out about nine miles, to where some men were putting a new roof on a barn with nails matching those used during the robbery. The bank thieves were in an Iowa jail within 10 days. A detective magazine got wind of the story and contacted Rutstrum; they wanted to piece together the robbery and investigation into an article, and have Cal sign his name to it. Nothing doing, he said. He would write the story. The magazine "could edit the hell out of it as long as it was my original copy." He wrote the story, the magazine liked it, they phoned him to say they weren't changing a word, and they wanted him to sign a contract to write about all his bank robbery cases.

"It looked like a pretty good deal," he said, "and they paid me a pretty generous check for that. I never wrote a detective story after that."

As a detective, Rutstrum did well in running down hoodlums during the Dillinger era, but when August 15 rolled around he gave the Burns International Detective Agency a week's notice. Which they didn't like. Late summer and early fall was the time, Rutstrum said, when "hoodlums were trying to get in their winter grubstake."

Once, when the agency was peeved with Rutstrum's annual 10-week vacation, a chief head of the firm journeyed from New York to talk with him for two hours. He offered Rutstrum a chance to become one of the agency's district managers.

"Does that mean sitting in an office?" Rutstrum asked. "I wouldn't take the job if you gave me *a million dollars a week*!"

When Rutstrum, a medical corpsman, was released from the Navy after World War I, he immediately started looking for "the release that a rising sun over a stretch of wilderness water would bring." He sailed on the *America* from Duluth up the north shore of Lake Superior, to the fishing village of Hovland, Minnesota, where he hiked north up the Old Trail to Tom Lake. He wanted to walk now, not canoe; the Navy had given him enough water, and he wanted the feel of solid ground beneath his boots. Besides, he realized then that the inland lakes of Superior National Forest were seldom—if ever—visited by man, unlike the region's canoe routes. Most interior wildlife had probably never seen a human being. Inland backcountry, his reasoning continued, was thus more truly inviolate wilderness, and travel by foot with a pack (as he was hell-bent to do) demanded more wilderness skills, particularly better navigation, than canoe travel. He wanted the most wilderness had to offer, a passion which this time nearly cost him his life.

The trouble was ptomaine poisoning from a small can of meat spread.

While hiking along a connecting stream on an east-west canoe route north of Pine Lake, Rutstrum got weaker by the hour until he lacked the strength to put up his tent. He lost track of time. Then consciousness. He lay on the ground for three days... a sick animal... periodically awaking to rain and 35-degree temperatures. His greatest need, he recalled in *A Wilderness Autobiography*, was warmth to prevent hypothermia or pneumonia:

"What a simple matter it had been for me to make a fire after days of rain when I had my strength, simply by splitting out the dry center of any dead piece of wood. Now I could not even rise to my feet, nor, as I tried, swing an ax while on my knees."

Luck was with him. As he lay on the ground he heard brush breaking nearby. He needed food. First he found his single-shot Stevens .22 caliber pistol, then his Winchester carbine. A 200-pound black bear shuffled into view on a game trail. Rutstrum shot it when it was 25 feet away. A bullet in the brain.

Rutstrum was never a man to take life lightly. Particularly his own. He crawled over to the dead bear, skinned open its shoulder, cut off a piece of meat and began to suck it. Raw bloody meat. It made him sicker, but the juices stayed down. He leaned against the bear to absorb its warmth. Soon he felt better. He didn't have strength to cut tent stakes, but he managed to set up his tent anyhow by tying its base to branches. His life was coming from the bear's death, a truth not lost upon him as he recuperated the following week. He ate cooked bear meat, bathed, washed his clothes and sat in the sun. Canada jays picked at bear scraps. So did a weasel. Before Rutstrum packed up and headed onward, he butchered what bear remained so the critters could get at it. The head he mounted on a pole; it was the symbol of the bear as life-giver: also an eventual skull that he might someday take home with him, for the fireplace mantel, should he pass this way again.

He headed west to Mountain and Watap lakes, where he met some Indians and joined them on a canoe trip west to Rainy Lake near International Falls. There he hopped the Canadian National Railway. He traveled east to begin another backpacking trip, this one of 70 miles. He ate fish and grouse. He crossed water barriers by rigging rafts from dead shore-line trees. If he became bored with the wilderness south of the CNR tracks, he went north.

Rutstrum—a rolling stone of waterways—was gathering no moss.

Trip followed trip in no set pattern. Season overlapped season. Rutstrum developed his winter camping skills so he could spend more time outdoors during the subzero months. Sometimes canoes were hauled into the back-country by dogsled or toboggan to be used for traveling after the ice thawed and went out in April or May; at other times, toboggans were hauled into the backcountry by canoe. Perhaps Rutstrum had glimpsed something deep and beyond-the-ranges in the eyes of the dying bear, something he now wanted to explore. Perhaps the whole death/life cycle was a blank spot on his personal map. On the other hand, he might simply have heard Service's "whisper on the night wind." Now he had a star agleam to guide him, and the wild was calling, calling... "let us go."

Rutstrum *kept on* going. On one early canoe trip, he spent seven weeks in Ontario as an assistant to a crew drill-testing mining claims. From three Indians and two whites on the crew, he learned tricks of axmanship, where to catch certain fish and how to preserve them for the trail, how to make jerky and pemmican, and he learned how Indians handled a canoe in whitewater and on big waves.

On other wilderness canoe trips, he:

—Tracked down a member of a British family who had become heir apparent to a lot of money; the only clue Cal was given was that the heir was "somewhere" in Canada's wilderness.

—Spent six weeks in the vicinity of Ontario's McCrea, Pushkokogan and Greenbush lakes looking for two lost boys, finding them alive. Afterwards, he paddled north on the Winnipeg, English and Longlegged rivers to rough-in a temporary, cold-weather cabin.

—Brought Jerry, a nine-year-old kid from a city's inner slums, into Ontario's backcountry for half a summer. There Jerry became friends with Indians, resort owners and surrounding wilderness, around which his adult life would revolve.

—And joined up with a Scotsman for a two-month canoe trip out of Sioux-Lookout, Ontario. In late September they found an Indian couple whose baby had deformed legs. Rutstrum and "Scotty" made arrangements for the baby to get medical help in Winnipeg and Toronto. Years later, when that Indian boy was 19 years old on strong legs, he carried Scotty's canoe over many portages. In thanks and friendship.

"I had a commitment to happiness," Rutstrum said of why he pursued a litany of wilderness canoe trips. "We need the joy of living optimally, where every natural force is playing on one's being, as multi-colored spotlights play on the actor who is exuberant with the joy of assuming his role. That exquisite pleasure of being an integral part of the natural universe, of being in its spotlight, makes one ecstatic about just living."

II

Perhaps it's ironic that Rutstrum, who saw fit to become an integral part of what wilderness remained in his state's backyard, made a nest egg by subdividing and selling land. It happened in the early 1920s, while he was looking for a job whereby, as he put it, he could increase his leisure in a natural environment and spend less time in "Smogopolis." He saw an ad seeking a lakeshore lot salesman. The position required no experience. He answered the ad, got the job and started looking for people who wanted land. Soon he had an "unusually substantial" checking account. He even won a large money award for most sales on the staff.

Rutstrum made his greatest leap toward leisure in real estate, but it didn't happen until he bought three 40-acre tracts of land and a cabin on the Flute Reed River near Hovland. This was the northwest shore of Lake Superior, and it was trout country. The land cost Cal an uncanny price: his fancy bolt-action sporting rifle given to him by a rich Chicago manufacturer in exchange for a favor on a wilderness trip; a five-inch cruiser's compass with tripod; the Colt single-action pistol he had carried on Montana's Mussellshell range; and a clip of cash to clinch the deal. Rutstrum, in turn, divided some of his Flute Reed riverbank into five-acre tracts and sold them to trout fishermen from

Duluth and Minneapolis-St. Paul. The price of his land depended on who he was dealing with. From a clothing store owner he got all the outdoor clothes he required for years to come. A grocery store owner provided him food. Ditto with owners of hardware stores and book stores. By the time Rutstrum settled down in his cabin, he had everything he needed to live a wilderness life indefinitely. Jobs became superfluous.

Although Rutstrum bought more waterfront tracts later in life, and sub-divided them on a substantial investment basis, at no time was subdividing and sales a full-time, routine business. His heart was elsewhere.

Time stood still on the Flute Reed. Especially in winter as cabin-bound Cal read books by scientists, philosophers, poets, musicians and various other writers. He wanted, he said, to see how other men through the ages viewed life. Thoreau's *Walden* was "a real find." Stewart Edward White's chapter, "On Lying Awake at Night," in *The Woods* made such an impression that he read it over and over again. But it was H.L. Mencken's style Rutstrum liked most. He described it as "pungent, very right to the point, no wild extractions, no fooling around." Mencken, known as the "Sage of Baltimore," had written a scholarly work on the origin of the American language; he also wrote two other book series and started *American Mercury* Magazine. Rutstrum said Mencken called "a spade a spade." Perhaps such literary frankness rubbed off on Cal, although later when he was a successful writer, he insisted he hadn't tried to copy anybody:

"Because you can't do that... You're yourself. Your style is you, you know?"

Rutstrum, who said he read everything, was being himself in his Flute Reed cabin. Books there carried him into "strange realms with a depth of feeling and insight that became hourly revelations." At the same time he was reading other people's writings, he was polishing his own, answering the knock on the door of his own literary odyssey. At first he wrote for *American Forest* magazine on such subjects as "Has Man a Sense of Direction? Has Wildlife a Sense of Direction?" and he wrote about amateur photography for *American Photography*. He broke into book publishing in a roundabout way. He was hired by Camp Lincoln, "a rich man's set up" near Brainerd, Minnesota, to give a wilderness program; this shortly after his marriage to Florence in 1929. The camp offered him a good salary each year plus the added incentive of giving him its canoe base if he directed it for five years. He stayed 10 years. The camp wanted a wilderness manual for the kids. Rutstrum wrote it. When Minneapolis bookstores began hunting for copies of the man-ual, then titled *Way of the Wilderness*, Rutstrum talked Chuck Hutchinson, editor of Burgess Publishing Company which had published the manual sole-ly for the camp, into releasing all rights. Cal then made a deal with Macmillan Publishing Company in New York to write "something parallel" to the man-ual. This Rutstrum did, making it more comprehensive, and soon Macmillan published it as a hardcover in a large edition because they suspected it would be a good seller. The Outdoor Book Club wanted 52,000 copies right from the start.

"I said, 'Well, hell!',", Cal recalled. " 'This beats working.' So everything I wrote since then seemed to *turn to gold*. I'm like anybody else. I found a niche and filled it."

The New Way of the Wilderness (1958, illustrated by Les Kouba) wedged open Rutstrum's niche in the field of outdoor techniques: how to camp, travel by canoe, equip and dress for winter, and how to eat well on the trail. *The Wilderness Cabin* (1961, illustrated by Kouba) described how to build log cabins and fireplaces. *North American Canoe Country* (1964, illustrated by Kouba) covered most aspects of wilderness canoe tripping: selecting routes, paddling strokes, solo travel, youth camp canoeing and outfitters. *The Wilderness Route Finder* (1967), again illustrated by Kouba, as were all his books until 1978, focused on orienteering with compass, sextant and natural route finders. *Paradise Below Zero* (1968) described winter camping.

As recreational use of American national forests and wilderness areas doubled, then tripled, Rutstrum was on top of it, guiding it, giving novice hikers and canoeists fundamental information on coping with climate and technical competence. He was a genre brother to Bradford Angier, apostle of wilderness living. In a sense he became a high priest of an emerging camping cult. While other outdoor writers leaned toward prose about cabin life, such as author Helen Hoover who lived a romantic North Woods life at the end of northeastern Minnesota's Gunflint Trail, Cal stuck to the how-to. The nuts-and-bolt stuff. Inevitably, Rutstrum became identified with technical competency, both practiced and professed. It was hard to live down.

Rutstrum's prolific writing enjoyed a groundswell of popularity by the late 1960s, so perhaps it was also inevitable that he would write an autobiography. It was originally published as *Challenge of the Wilderness* in 1970, then reprinted by Nodin Press as *A Wilderness Autobiography* in 1979. Even more than his subsequent *Once Upon a Wilderness* (1973) and *The Wilderness Life* (1975), *A Wilderness Autobiography* went beyond camping techniques to reveal Rutstrum himself: the man wilderness whittled out of an Indiana-born Swede.

But Rutstrum wasn't finished writing. He wrote four more books.

Chips From a Wilderness Log (1978, illustrated by Gary Jones) was a collection of "clippings, scribbling, and notes of a half century accumulated in a wooden soapbox stored in the cache cabin," culled for those "who truly love the wilderness and to those whose inclinations may lead them in that direction." *Hiking Back to Health* (1980) was a 112-page paperback about walking and backpacking's good effects on one's physical and psychic well-being. *A Columnist Looks at Life* (1980) collected 46 columns of Cal's that had appeared in Wisconsin's *Osceola Sun*. Nodin Press, the book's publisher, described it as "Americana at its best, free-swinging and exuberantly in touch with the nation's root feelings." Column subjects included "The Open Mind," "The Conformist," "The Illusion of Plethora," "Nature Indispensable," and over 40 other subjects flippant, timely or rattling Rutstrum's cage.

Finally, *Back Country* (1981, illustrated by Kouba) reaffirmed Rutstrum as a polished storyteller. In what he told me was "just the romance of wilderness," *Back Country* introduces readers to Lars, an old-timer who lived on a raft on the St. Croix River; to Wanda, a young Cree woman of great beauty and intelligence he helped track down by canoe for her lover; to Tom, a six-foot, athletically built Cree in his early twenties who paddled the Upper Berens River system with Rutstrum for most of an autumn; to Charlie, a one-armed paddler who traveled with Cal for seven weeks; and to an abandoned Indian mother of two, for whom he shoots and butchers a moose.

These chapters—each a slice of life in the Canadian bush—color what Rutstrum called his extraordinary standard of living. He was always interested in knowing how to *live* life, not just how to make a living. And during his natural and human encounters in North America's backcountry, he realized over and over again that the poverty which his family faced when his father died never deprived him of life's true wealth.

"The sun rose and set in all its glory ever anew each day without financial or material aid," he explained in *The Wilderness Life*. "The rain fell on the forest bloom to keep me ceaselessly contemplating its magnificence though no hand cultivated it nor turned any watering spigots. Trails through the wilds, which I had no part in blazing, had been provided by the treading of its forest creatures for ages. I was given twelve breaths of pure, invigorating air every minute at no cost, by the miraculous conversion forces inherent in vegetation. The fuel needed for my tea pail and bannock-baking fire was supplied merely by reaching for it and using an ax to render it fit for my immediate use. The stage for my entertainment was set in the most dramatic style wherever I turned: vast waterfalls fell in spellbinding, thunderous spectacles to amaze, while along the river wildlife played their repertorial parts, though I paid not a single penny for admission."

Here is Rutstrum back-patting himself for his good fortune as only he was most fit to see. His writing style, however, was not always so eloquent. For someone endeared to Mencken and Thoreau, he was capable of using outlandish words that would have raised the hackles of E.B. White and William Strunk, Jr., both experts on writing style and conciseness.

Where else does one find in wilderness literature words such as *supererogation, ensconced, prodigiousness,* and *avoirdupois?* Game wardens were "disposed," not busy. And who but self-educated Rutstrum could come up with this chapter's opening sentence: "While it can be said that some kind of motorized transportation equipment makes accessible all areas of the world, no matter how remote, this premise is so contingent upon a number of inhibiting factors, the possibility of reaching many of them in this manner is highly theoretical, often near impossible."

If, as Rutstrum said, writing style is inseparable from oneself, he was occasionally unable to simplify his subtlest intellectual discoveries. He never misused hundred-pound words, as sophomoric writers might, but neither was he always sensitive to his reader's occasional inability to tote such weight.

However, Rutstrum the writer was also Rutstrum the thinker. He was never merely content to resurrect old friends in his books, nor to unclothe himself historically. In his four most autobiographical books, and in places throughout the others, the boy who had camped along Minnehaha Creek between Minneapolis and Lake Minnetonka emerges a wilderness philosopher.

"Broadly speaking," he once aptly asked, "what widely disseminated philosophic understanding... do we have at all about wilderness as it pertains to life in general?"

Rutstrum tried to answer that question, or at least contribute to an answer in a cultural effort which began in earnest during Thoreau's time. Rutstrum defined *wilderness philosophy* as "a love of wisdom derived from natural phenomena." A wilderness philosopher, moreover, "tends to deal more with the profound abstraction of natural phenomena along with a utilitarian moderation and sanity... He sees a resource-finite world where happiness needs to be sought in economic wisdom (seeing in complement a green, fresh world)... Material needs? Yes, but when brought to insatiable greed, he knows that it dulls the spirit of life and lays waste a tenable world."

What is most apparent to a wilderness philosopher, Rutstrum believed, is once he has made the natural transition to a healthy body and mind in a situation providing ample leisure, he discovers it can be an opportunity to reduce one's "philistinism," leading to a broadened understanding and appreciation of art, literature, science and music. A natural setting is the key, together with a receptive mind. Urban life, he thought, is often too stressful to allow study and intellectual enjoyment. Culture comes when one pauses long enough from industrial obsession to realize that beyond normal needs we begin, as puppets of materialism, to harvest diminishing returns.

The portage to Rutstrum's tenable world was outlined in *A Columnist Looks at Life*:

"1. Get off the industrial treadmill of planned obsolescence and produce only high-quality long-lasting goods. Subvert the machine to man's welfare, not man to the machine.

2. Lay most of the emphasis on individual worth for infinite possibilities of life. Especially decry mass-mind psychology in any form and regard the totalitarian slave states as a menace.

3. Restore our environment to a healthful state at any cost, for without such action all will eventually be lost.

4. Vastly increase man's leisure, through automation and computerization (if these were intended to have benefits) for his physical and mental welfare."

Rutstrum felt true welfare and wealth lay in aligning oneself with the integrating forces of nature and their potential. Wilderness as a way of life meant functioning subject to these forces, these "continually amending" elements. Fulfillment was to "awake in the freshness of morning and know that one is a part of the rising sun, the orange-tinted fog, the vibrant earth" and the magnificence of growth.

Pretty? Yes. Outward-bound and optimistic? Definitely. But one thing Rutstrum *wasn't* was an incurable romantic.

"Poetry," he once wrote, "frequently perverts and handles illusion quite well... It metaphorically often lies horribly."

He tried, when writing, to be rational. Factual. And to avoid the levity of a style summed up simplistically by a reader as "the birds sing in the trees, tra la la la." He was disgusted by writers who gave nature supernatural significance which "gild(ed) the lily and obscure(d) the flower."

When I asked Rutstrum how he felt in the woods, he said he didn't get "into the superlative realm... What isn't apparent, I don't conjecture." He said he wasn't a religious or spiritual person. His great-grandfather was jailed in Sweden for trying to separate church and state; afterwards he migrated to the U.S., where he founded the town of Sugar Grove, Pennsylvania. Now Cal, his great-grandson, hoed a similar row. He rejected the Bible's human image of God as "a little ridiculous." How, he asked, could the Bible be literally true when one rendering of it claims the world was created in 4004 B.C.? Yet science, with its carbon 14 measurement of decay, proves earth has existed for billions of years? Hadn't there been, over time, about 5,000 religions in the world? Hadn't the Bible's gospels and epistles been rewritten and tampered with? Rutstrum thought it all fiction. He believed in what he saw.

Was he a pantheist?

"I don't attach any labels to myself at all."

What, then, of an afterlife?

Rutstrum said, in *Chips From a Wilderness Log*, that he liked to think his body was partly composed of the chemistry of a feather that fell from a bird in flight a thousand years ago, from a sunbeam, from a shaft of lightning, and an arrow that fell when primordial man roamed the earth.

"I'm convinced beyond any question or doubt," he told me, "that when this life is gone you are a forgotten entity. I don't think there is any afterlife. The same biological process that occurs when a cockroach dies is when you die. Exactly... Man has no concern for the hundreds of billions of years that occurred before he got here; that doesn't bother him at all. He wants to be considered as living forever. The only promise you got of living forever is that you'll be taken up into the ether to a platform somewhere and you're going to be allowed to strum on a harp all day long.

"I don't like music that well."

Should we, he asked in *Back Country*, deny conspicuous natural evidence on superstitious grounds? On guesses of those wishing not to see what they see? Should we burn those people at the stake who earlier didn't agree with obvious invalidated concepts? Should we make the intellectually honest drink poison hemlock, or should we put them in dungeons and stretch them on the rack? This for refusing what Cal described as "obscurantists"?

"There before our eyes," he concluded, "we see on the wilderness floor the eagle and the human animal assimilated into earth exactly the same way."

Regardless, Rutstrum felt it legitimate to ask questions about the significance of life. Was it merely a packrat existence of accumulation, or was it a noble life of admirable conduct, intellect or of some other worthy contribution sending out "small or great waves of magnanimity"?

Rutstrum: On Immortality

"Wilderness enough to be the preservation of the world still exists. We can enjoy it today and save it for coming generations. Invite them to a clean, unspoiled world. If we do, they will want to know about us. That is real immortality. But if we don 't leave our descendants a habitable life-affirming world, we'll deserve to be forgotten, and their willingness to forget would be our eternal death."

—Rutstrum,
Chips From a Wilderness Log, 1978

Rutstrum sometimes knew sociological despair when wrestling with life's great questions, including environmental ones. Asked about the earth's current acid rain crisis, he said he didn't know how it would come out.

"People have more interest in the dollar than anything else," he said. "They fight for (material gain) until they become the richest man in the graveyard, and they die. No one remembers them. They're a lost entity... But they still keep doing it over and over again. I don't know just how you're going to convince people [of the need for clean air and water] when they're not educable."

Whoa.

Rutstrum's voice—in the dining room of his fieldstone house on the outskirts of Marine-on-St. Croix, Minnesota—drops silent. He could see with the vision of 86 years one of the most enduring problems of civilization: education and cultural transmission of life-sustaining values. It is a slow process, sometimes leading into a swamp of negativity. There in Rutstrum's house one could see the edge of that swamp. Yet Rutstrum refused to go—hadn't gone—further. He was essentially an optimist, as found repeatedly in what he called his "brain children": his books.

"From the vibrant earth," he had written in *The Wilderness Life*, "will come great and beautiful people, domestic and wild life, forests and bloom. The silent life of earth, if we could hear it stirring in the elements beneath our feet, in the air, and in the chemistry of light, would be an almost frightening potential to contemplate, most likely greater than anything we have conceived in the past or that exists at present."

Rutstrum was talking about nature's regenerative forces, those which integrate rather than disintegrate. He knew we are nature. In every plant, raindrop and person was nature's illimitable disintegrating and integrating forces, but the dominant one was integrative. It used the substance of disintegrating physical and chemical processes to achieve again and timelessly again natural reproduction. This was evolution. This was *ascending* nature at work. The atomic waters of life flow upward, fountainlike, to recirculate forever. Breakdown feeds buildup. The process—according to the world of Calvin Rutstrum—is most pure and apparent in wilderness with which North America was, and remains, rich.

But what is it behind the regenerating cycles of nature that keeps everything moving? I asked Rutstrum this, for I was eager to press a point one more time. What keeps everything evolving, alive, ascending?

"If you can answer that question," he said, "you're going to do very well."

III

As Rutstrum's education, fame and relative fortune grew, so did the sequence of cabins housing his vision. He abandoned his Flute Reed cabin when the gravel road along Lake Superior's northwest shore between Duluth and Grand Marais became an asphalt highway. There were also other reasons for Rutstrum's departure. The area's moose and deer "were being slaughtered by a vast horde of invading hunters who came in fast cars and hurried in nervous panic out of the forest with their kill, scarcely glancing at the grand spectacle of nature." He complained of fly rods being whipped on the banks of the Flute Reed like alders snapping in the wind; unlike before, he could no longer catch a mess of trout for dinner from favorite pools below rapids. Car exhaust replaced balsam fir fragrances. Hovland's community atmosphere changed into "little more than a filling station stop for cars with restless drivers." Progress had reached the North Shore. Although Rutstrum never admitted it, certainly he knew that by subdividing his Flute Reed property he had ironically contributed to the changes he now escaped from.

His next cabin was on Three-Mile Island in Sea Gull Lake, at the end of the Gunflint Trail north of Grand Marais and at the east end of today's Boundary Waters Canoe Area Wilderness. He first visited the site in winter by snowshoeing in and pulling a toboggan of camping supplies. He barged in cabin lumber the following spring when lake ice thawed. There Rutstrum lived for much of 10 years. Canoe trails led in every direction, particularly to the north into Canada and northwest into Quetico Provincial Park. People from surrounding wilderness cabins visited him regularly, yet it was a great hideout for the likes of Cal. But time would not stand still. He became squeezed on two sides. To the southeast by development along the Gunflint Trail (soon to become a 50 miles-per-hour asphalt highway), and to the west by increasing restrictions in the Boundary Waters Canoe Area.

Unlike many other residents on the perimeter of the BWCA, however, Rutstrum didn't resent the growing network of U.S. Forest Service regulations seeking to re-create wilderness conditions along part of the Minnesota-Ontario border. He approved of the airplane ban of 1949 which forbade planes below an altitude of 4,000 feet over three designated roadless areas, not because he didn't sympathize with owners of private property in these areas but because he had witnessed and heard of too much plane-related abuse.

Prior to the airplane ban, he had often found "vast quantities" of empty beer bottles, beer carton cases and garbage litter either right in the camping areas or on the edge in the brush "until every camp was a fly-infested rubbish heap." He heard environmental horror stories of pilots and their clients jettisoning garbage over Superior National Forest. Wealthy fly-in fishermen landed on remote lakes, where they fished off plane pontoons and flew out with their catch. The airplane ban, which naturalist and wilderness philosopher Sigurd F. Olson fought relentlessly for, put a stop to this. The backcountry immediately became cleaner. This Rutstrum liked.

He also got a glimpse of other environmental controversies while living on Sea Gull Lake. The border lakes had always been a hotbed of issues revolving around consumptive uses like mining and logging versus ecosystem preservation. A businessman in International Falls to the west had tried to dam the region's major waterways to produce electricity. Loggers had fought for the right to cut trees clear to water's edge and lost. Uncontrolled growth on private land within much larger chunks of public land was debated in the courts. Throughout many of the battles the forestry phrase of *multiple use*, Pinchot's greatest linguistic legacy, was the key term used by consumptive groups to defend their interests. Yet Rutstrum, sitting on the east edge of the BWCA, distrusted such catch phrases. *Multiple use*, he said, carried strong democratic and red-blooded American connotations, but in actual practice often meant squeezing "every last industrial dollar out of a region, the ravaged area left to those who sought to preserve a natural environment." When it came to wilderness, Rutstrum figured development was synonymous with vandalism.

Perhaps if Rutstrum had stayed on Sea Gull Lake long enough, he would have been asked to leave by the Forest Service as it tried to possess and consolidate private lands within the boundaries of the expanding BWCA. His response would have been interesting.

Woodsman Rutstrum, however, had other concerns. He was beginning to see again what an asphalt highway does to wilderness. As the Gunflint Trail was upgraded, fishermen swarmed in over the new highway until Cal's fishing went to hell. Loons and Canada jays, the latter known as camp robbers because of their playful camp thievery, were shot at. The clincher for Rutstrum came on a Sunday morning, when two motorboats pulling water skiers raced pass his door and around the islands beyond.

Time to move.

His third move, to what he thought was the perimeter of wilderness, led to Marchington Lake 30 miles east of Sioux Lookout, Ontario. The "perimeter" for Rutstrum was a compromise between urbanity and the primordial, a jumping-off place to both wilderness and city with the former often the favored end of the spectrum. Such was Marchington Lake at 50 degrees north latitude, where he built two cabins with lumber salvaged from an old school in the village of Ghost River. His guest cabin functioned as a writing shack when he and Florence were alone. Around the cabins was what

Canadians call "the bush." To the east were 28 miles of wilderness water ending at a twin waterfall cutting through a granite canyon. To the northeast was Howling Wolf River. Windigo Falls, Kimmewan Lake and giant Lac Seul lay to the northwest. Other waterways led to Lake St. Joseph, Savant Lake and Wabakimi country. The closest road was 25 miles away.

Here Rutstrum—when it came to wilderness cabins—made his last stand.

It was a stand compromised by outer-suburbia living. He had bought five acres of land in 1927 within the limits of Minnesota's oldest village, Marine-on-St. Croix. There, overlooking the St. Croix River Valley on what once was an island when the water was higher, Rutstrum built a stone house. He hand-cut and masoned each quarry stone, and meticulously fit each wood beam into place. This building, not the Marchington cabin, became Rutstrum's main residence replete with modern conveniences.

There were other residences. While carrying a Duluth pack between Grand Portage, Minnesota, and Thunder Bay, Ontario, Rutstrum found a cabin site on Cloud Bay along Lake Superior's north shore. He had been searching for a cool place to go during hot weather ever since he got rid of his Flute Reed property; he and Florence wanted someplace breezy and bug-less during Marchington's June-July bug season. They found nothing suitable on the U.S. side of the border because Highway 61 was too close to the lake. Rutstrum bought a piece of Cloud Bay shoreline. What was going to be "a simple little cabin" became a substantial home due to zoning regulations. The Rutstrums had $120,000 tied up in their Cloud Bay property by 1981, the land itself worth $90,000.

The nest on Cloud Bay was more collateral for another residential adventure, this time in the arid Southwest. Florence used to go with her aunt to Mexico every year, and she kept coaxing Cal, who had usually headed off in the opposite direction on a tundra dogsled trip, to go with her. He finally agreed. They got as far as New Mexico's Pecos River and desert country, where they bought an adobe house which they remodeled and modernized. They stayed there parts of seven years in the early 1960s until it lost its charm.

"There were too many hoodlums around there," Rutstrum said. "Whenever we left they would break in and take everything that was in the place. Albuquerque had more break-ins per capita than any other town in the United States. And, I didn't get along very well with sandstorms and dust storms, so we finally sold the property to the original owners. They were sorry they sold it so they didn't have to be sorry any more. We were glad to get rid of it."

No wonder Rutstrum's book, *Greenhorns in the Southwest*, sold poorly.

Something else had nagged at Rutstrum's nerves besides sand, wind and the monotony of constant sunny weather. He kept having visions of rushing rivers, tumultuous rapids and windblown rain on whitecapped lakes. He recalled the fragrance of crushed fir needles, of cedar brushing his shoulders on portages, and of delicate twinflowers vibrating pink in the breezes following summer thundershowers. He missed canoe country's shin-deep mosses, its twisted white pines on rocky islands, and the banksides of white bunch-berry blossoms sprinkled among aromatic spikes of Canada mayflowers. He had experienced North America's desert, prairie, mountain and lake country, and he knew now what held for him the most compelling lure.

This at age 65.

Yet there was something more to owning a home and three "second-homes" than mere discovery of climatological preference. He had begun to explore the psychological effects places have on inhabitants. He sensed the *magic* of place, what he described as the almost inscrutable shiftings of char-acter and attitude responding to a region's daylight, vegetation, soil, wildlife, altitude and human occupants.

"What effect," he asked, "does change of geography actually have upon thinking? Can we assume the same mental outlook about matters pertinent to our daily existence in a lush mountain canyon with a wilderness waterfall tumbling at our feet, as we might on the Arctic prairie, the desert, or open sea? It is doubtful. We are too much the product of environment, reflecting the influences that are constantly impinging upon us."

We might, he concluded, be chameleon-like. More than our common reaction suggests.

Here, then, is the rub.

By migrating among residences, and by regularly visiting wilderness areas, Rutstrum sought to expose himself to the widest array of natural influences possible. This he knew would be his education. This would give him ground on which to stand and speak about nature, yet not only nature but North American culture rooted in it. He centered himself on this quest between society and wilderness, between the silences of solitude under open sky and the grinding of book presses—first those commissioned by Macmillan then Stein and Day's, Nodin's, and that of ICS Books. Rutstrum had always been hooked into the North American system of doing things, but only by being flooded with the "multi-colored spotlights" of natural forces did he experi-ence the exquisite pleasure of being "an integral part of the natural universe."

Although we are urbanized to the point of possible catastrophe, he wrote in *Back Country*, perhaps our route to survival is to keep one steadying hand on backcountry so there is less dependence on the other hand of the city.

Rutstrum wrote elsewhere that if we become aware of origin, of basics, of natural phenomena, of wilderness in essence, it will probably be because our understanding of ecological interdependence is telling us human survival is hopeless without it. Wilderness, he said, together with city, countryside, ocean, lake, river, people, flora and fauna—"all are now bound up in one interrelated ecology where, if wilderness is ravaged, the whole will suffer, city-life no less than natural phenomena." This was—for a rolling stone of waterways—deep vision.

It stayed with him to the end.

Rutstrum died on February 5, 1982 after a half-year illness at the L.O. Simensted Nursing Care Unit at Ladd Memorial Hospital in Osceola, Wisconsin. His death was not announced for two weeks at the request of

Florence. Yet, four years earlier, Cal had made his own request: a chip from a wilderness log.

"If you want to do something for me after I'm gone," he quipped, a bit like Mencken, "live so as not to defile the precious earth."

8

SIGURD F. OLSON: VISIONARY VOYAGEUR

"All of us are dreamers. Dreams are what started everything. Dreams are the most realistic way of looking at life. Dreamers are not shadowy ephemeral-thinking people. The dreamers are the realists. They are the ones who look through all the facade to all the things that we're doing to our environment and see the end result as it affects humanity. We are asking ourselves a great question... and all of us interested in wilderness preservation are asking it all the time, and that is: What kind of a world do we want?"

> — Sigurd F. Olson
> Ninth Biennial Wilderness Conference
> San Francisco, 1965

You always began at the beginning with visionary voyageur Sigurd F. Olson of northeastern Minnesota's Quetico-Superior canoe country. As a wilderness consultant for the Izaak Walton League of America, and as a president of both the Wilderness Society and the National Parks Association, Olson discovered long ago that new adventures were always coming up, always beginning and ending sacred circles. For Olson—like Thoreau before him on Mt. Katahdin, Muir on Taylor Glacier and Marshall in Koyukuk country—those adventures meant keeping his feet on the ground and his paddle in the water. Especially the latter. For it was the canoe that carried Olson to open horizons and the far waterways of the North. It was the canoe, timeless in origin, graceful in design, that inevitably brought Olson to the heart of what he came to call the *singing wilderness.*

Olson's singing wilderness had to do, he said, with the calling of loons, the northern lights, and the great silences of the Quetico-Superior country lying northwest of Lake Superior. It was concerned with simple joys, and "the timelessness and perspective found in a way of life that is close to the past." But most of all, it had to do with awakening and realization: the constant search for understanding which, for Olson, became a naturalist's way of life.

It wasn't surprising, therefore, that at mid-life Olson found himself threading his way along the boundary waters of the Quetico-Superior in northeastern Minnesota and northwestern Ontario by canoe. He had begun at Lac la Croix, worked his way through the labyrinth of islands and channels of Crooked Lake, then portaged up the rapids of Basswood River. Soon Basswood Lake drifted behind him as did the full sweep of Knife Lake and cliff-ringed Ottertrack. He reached Saganaga on the fifth day. As he put his canoe in the water, he watched sunlight strike a stand of dark pine on an opposite shore and brush the trunks with flame. A distant rock point stood out bright as a ray of sun struck it, making it, he later said, look luminous and spearlike against the dark background.

Saganaga was calm as loons called. Here was Olson's dream come true.

But Olson, despite the beauty around him, was struck with nostalgia for an almost forgotten time. A time, years earlier, when he had searched for the perfect wilderness lake.

"Always before me was the ideal," he wrote of that time in *The Singing Wilderness*, "a place not only remote, not only of great beauty, but possessed of an intangible quality and spirit that typified to me all of the unbroken north beyond all roads."

He had looked for the perfect lake for years on many canoe trips, yet always there was something wrong, some *something*, he wrote, which kept each lake from being the one of his dreams. Sometimes it was shape, or size, or possibility of accessibility. Or the lake wasn't quite perfect because of an intuition, "an unsettled state of mind," or some other reason beyond the ken of consciousness. In time he began to doubt his own search, began to wonder if he even knew what he was looking for.

But then he found it. Saganaga.

"My first glimpse from the western narrows was enough," he recalled, "and as I stood there and looked out across the broad blue reaches to the east with their fleets of rocky islands, the hazy blue hills toward the hinterlands of the Northern Light Country, I knew I had reached my goal. How I knew without having explored the lake, I cannot say, but the instant I saw the lake, I realized it was the end of my search, and that there was nothing more beyond the hills. I shall never forget the sense of peace and joy which was mine at the discovery. Perhaps I was ready for Saganaga; perhaps all the searching that had gone before had prepared me. Whatever it was, I was content at last, knowing that I would find in this lonely solitude the realization of all my dreams."

It was on Saganaga, ironically, that Olson witnessed what a road could do to wilderness.

At first his Saganaga experience was a euphoric one. The air was crystalline. Each campsite was better than the one before. There was a hill from which coyotes called on moonlit nights. There were moose in swampy bays, friendly birds, busy beavers and playful otters. The place felt right as Olson came to know every island and channel. He knew where pine, oak and maple trees were, and which were most colorful in autumn. He knew where arbutus bloomed in spring, and where water lilies made shallows look swept with white. Saganaga became home.

Then he read the news.

While on a trip away from the Quetico-Superior, he read a newspaper clipping about a road to Saganaga. He could hardly believe it. He ripped the clipping into shreds and clenched the shreds in his fist. Something deep inside began to burn, and he vowed someday he would return.

It took years, but Olson at mid-life found himself back. The same islands rode at anchor in the distance. The same lichen-covered cliffs and gnarled pines made it seem like he had never left. Even the loons still called as he pitched his tent at an old favorite site. In him, he recalled in *The Singing Wilderness*, grew the old sensation of immensity.

But he was apprehensive.

He paddled south at dusk, weaving his way through channel after channel until he reached the mouth of a long bay where he had heard the road had come. As he rounded a final point, he saw it: the flow of light from a lodge window "like the rising of a full moon." It was a rising of sorts, and he glided down its path of light toward the window until he heard slow, seductive music coming from the lodge. Dancers came outside to smoke cigarettes in the dark. Bodies drifted back and forth behind the window. A car arrived, its beam of light knifing through the surrounding darkness.

"In a way it was very pleasant," he remembered, "listening and watching from the canoe. Light and music and laughter were good after days in the bush. The warmth and gaiety invited me, and suddenly in the darkness and solitude from which I had come there seemed to be a great loneliness. At that moment I doubted myself. Perhaps I had been wrong about silence and solitude, about places where time meant nothing and where a man might stand aloof and alone and listen to his dreams. Perhaps this was what it should be, this the real goal.

"But then like a flood I remembered the nights I had waited and listened in this same little bay when the only sounds were sloshing of moose in the shallows, the whack of beaver tails, the eternal song of the swamp, music that for ages past had never changed, and I knew that for me there was no question."

Suddenly the whine of an outboard motor shook Sig from his daydreaming. The boat's light leapt forward, and in a roar of sound and light it burst past Olson, leaving him bobbing in its wake. He swung his canoe around in the dark, headed for his camp, but turned for one last look. A pinpoint of light and melody meandered across the water. He touched, he said, his paddle to water, and the old Saganaga was gone.

———————

Saganaga was one of several turning points for Olson, an about-face in both innocence and romance at the end of the Gunflint Trail on the northeastern corner of today's Boundary Waters Canoe Area Wilderness (BWCAW). For the rest of Olson's life—and he would live to be 83—he did everything in his power not only to preserve the ecological and wild integrity of the Quetico-Superior, of which the BWCAW is part, but also to understand what wilderness means. En route he was at once both preservationist and philosopher. He was a canoe trip guide. He was the author of nine books and at least 100 magazine articles. He was a wilderness consultant for the Izaak Walton League of America, a friend to men like Bob Marshall and Justice William O. Douglas, and an advisor to the President's Quetico-Superior Committee. He was, moreover, a teacher and college dean. He gave generously of his time to the young and questioning, answering their letters promptly when lesser men would never take the time. And because Olson's life spanned the end of Muir's, Service's, Marshall's and Rutstrum's, it was like an advancing wave, an embodiment of the wilderness ideal as it evolved through the twentieth-century.

Two wilderness themes were dominant in Olson's thought and writings, and they alone make his life's work stand out.

He was, on the one hand, fascinated by the incessant search of people for the primordial in their lives, their hunger for things natural and wild, their craving for experiences bringing them close to the earth. We must, Olson was convinced, feel the ground under our feet, use our muscles to move through forests, and sit next to wood fires in places sheltered from storms. Our subconscious is aswarm with racial memories, he said, and they root us in those millions of years when we shared "ancient ecological balances and relationships with other creatures in a common environment." Thus we are physiologically and psychically attuned to a primeval past, and we are never perfectly happy when we are removed from it completely. For modern people, there was—and is—a hunger and craving going on.

Yet when Olson spoke of the real significance of wilderness, he insisted it was a cultural matter. It wasn't just hiking, canoeing, hunting and fishing. Wilderness had to do with the human spirit. What we are trying to preserve, he said, is not scenery as much as the human spirit itself.

"Not only has wilderness been a force in molding our character as a people," he wrote, "but its influence continues, and will, if we are wise enough to preserve it on this continent, be a stabilizing power as well as a spiritual reserve for the future. The intangible values of wilderness are what really matter, the opportunity of knowing again what simplicity really means, the importance of the natural and the sense of oneness with the earth that inevitably comes within it.

"These are spiritual values. They, in the last analysis, are the reasons for its preservation."

Inevitably, Olson—like those wilderness visionaries before and during his time—bridged the gulf between wilderness life and city living. He knew well that going to either extreme left a person short of wholeness. Wilderness wasn't an escape for him. He wasn't playing Daniel Boone. He knew the old frontiers, the true wildernesses of the past—the places without regulations and firegrates, and with grizzlies—were largely gone except in much of Alaska and far northern Canada. For Olson, nevertheless, wild areas, even if not perfectly wild, offered people opportunities to connect with their past in ways helping them move confidently and more wholly into their future. Wilderness was not merely the first home of people. It still was. Yet today, perhaps more so than ever, it promised balanced vision and ecological insight. Wilderness, with its sunsets and rainbows, rising mists and howling wolves, starry black expanses and bottomless silences, was a doorway to awe and wonder. Here was a jumping-off place for the spirit, a gateway to consciousness and oneness as people searched over the eons for echelons of insight.

I

Sigurd Ferdinand Olson was born on April 4, 1899, the second son of Lawrence J. and Ida Mae (Cedarholm) Olson. His father was pastor of the Humboldt Park Baptist Church on the north side of Chicago, where at the turn of the century there was still much open country. Streetcars were drawn by horses, their manure piled between the tracks. Olson saw his first automobile when a rich parishioner brought his car to the church on a Sunday afternoon to give everyone rides. When his parents installed a telephone, his mother let him listen to the first call; he didn't understand the conversation but long remembered envisioning little girls dancing along the wire.

Another indelible memory of Olson's youth was running with his mother through colored leaves when he was four or five years old, running and twirling through yellows, golds and reds, and running some more until they sank to the ground amid a hurricane of color. There and then, he recalled in his autobiography, *Open Horizons*, beauty and color became a permanent part of his life.

Olson's family moved to Sister Bay, Wisconsin, when he was five; Sister Bay was a small town south of Porte des Mortes ("Death's Door"), a small channel noted for its shipwrecks at the end of Door Peninsula. The Olsons moved from there to Prentice, Wisconsin, then Ashland on the southwest shore of Lake Superior. Sig's boyhood days were filled with trout fishing, spring's yellow cowslips, and the pungent smell of balm of Gilead. Sometimes young Sig would curl up among the roots of a large pine, where he felt like a part of the tree as it swayed in the wind. The experience seeded in Olson a lifelong love for virgin growth trees.

At other times, when not reading history, travel or poetry books from his father's library, books about Kit Carson, Daniel Boone, Natty Bumppo and tales of Canadian Mounted Police, Sig would take shelter in a hut he built of sticks and boughs. In front of it was a fireplace with blackened pot where he cooked rabbits, crayfish, clams and other food that came his way, including a Canadian jay. There he saw deer. At times he hunted partridge almost every morning before school. Logging roads became his paths, while beyond—shimmering blue on calm days, frothy with ocean-sized waves on stormy days—lay the great waterways of lakes Michigan and Superior.

"Nobody in the family understood why on earth I had to be running off in the woods all the time," Olson told Terry Wolkerstorfer of the *Minneapolis Star*. "I'd take off for the boondocks and be gone all day."

Olson didn't think of himself as a "serious" student in high school, although he claimed to know more about plants and animals than his biology teacher. Nor was he a stranger to pranks. One Halloween he came up with the idea of getting an old lumber wagon to haul up the high school's front steps and park against the door. Just as he and friends were finishing, the night watchman caught them in the glare of his flashlight. They let go of the wagon. It rumbled down the school steps taking two chips out of each step on the way down. They all stood in front of the principal the next morning as each was fined $2 apiece, more money than young Sig had ever seen.

Olson enrolled in Ashland's Northland College, where he studied all the natural sciences he could. He was a member of the glee club, and was drafted by the drama club to play the lead roll in Henrik Ibsen's "A Doll's House." He also played football. Left end. He later claimed he had been fast on his feet, could block, and could make good flying tackles.

His dedication to football, however, couldn't match his love for duck hunting and the outdoors.

"We had a big game coming up," he explained. "It was November, cold, snow on the ground. All of a sudden I heard the bluebills coming down and I just took off. The team left without me and I was in absolute disgrace. And rightfully so, rightfully so. They should have kicked me out of school."

It was through Northland College that Sig began a lifelong romance with Elizabeth Uhrenholdt. He had become friends with Andrew Uhrenholdt, the son of a farmer from Seeley, Wisconsin, and Sig had noticed a picture of a young woman on Andrew's desk. It was Elizabeth, Andrew's sister, daughter of Soren and Kristine Uhrenholdt, natives of Denmark who were homesteading along the Namekagon River. There were four girls and four boys in the Uhrenholdt family, but it was Elizabeth Sig wanted to meet. They eventually became friends and married in 1921.

Education, meanwhile, hounded Olson's mind. The time came during his last year at Northland College when he had to choose a career, some nugget of direction to which he hadn't, he suddenly realized, given much thought. On the one hand, his father felt there were only three valid career choices for any good man: ministry, teaching or farming. Lawrence hadn't been forceful about this, but over the years Sig's father had slipped it into his sons' minds. Spiritual values were what was important. Sig had been too busy working on "Dad" Uhrenholdt's farm—clearing tamarack and spruce out of a swamp hole, getting a worker's feel for the land—to dwell much on the future. All he knew was "unless some part of each day were spent under open skies I was unhappy."

He decided for the moment to take up farming. He wanted to own some land, live close to the soil, and get the same pioneering feel for seasonal rhythms as his future father-in-law had. He enrolled at the University of Wisconsin in Madison, felt his heart break when he took the train south, and dove into agricultural studies.

"Through this initial period," he recalled, "I must have been numb with loneliness and longing, for all I could think of was the woods. Gradually, however, new vistas opened up on field trips taken in soils, botany, and geology. Listening to instructors explaining natural phenomena, rock formations, or vegetational types outside the classroom awakened something within me and I began to see the vague outlines of work I could enjoy. Until then I had not pictured what graduation might bring in its wake, but now it seemed that teaching somewhere in the north and near the woods was the answer."

He eventually began to see how he might perhaps apply his education and woods experience to interpreting the country, how, while feeding his mind, senses and spirit, he could pass it on to others. The ticket was to get back in the north, so when the mining town of Nashwauk in northeastern Minnesota offered him a job to teach agriculture and related sciences, he accepted immediately.

One look at a map of the region's iron range, with its blue lakes and unpeopled forests, cemented his decision.

No sooner was Olson in Nashwauk than he headed into the surrounding woods. Sometimes he took trips by himself, like when he met woodsman Al Kennedy and, later, began hunkering down at one of Kennedy's cabins on McCarty Lake. At other times he took classes on field trips to surrounding mine pits, meadows and various forest types. He and his students practically deserted the classroom. Olson had decided field observations were just as important as laboratory experiments. Then one day Kennedy told Sig if he *really* liked the woods, he should check out the lake country east of the Vermilion Range. There a person could put a canoe in anywhere and paddle to Hudson Bay or northwest to fabled Flin Flon.

Kennedy bet if Sig ever visited that country, he'd never come back.

Sig went. He had heard other intriguing rumors about the Quetico-Superior, that land mass encompassing Minnesota's Superior National Forest and Ontario's Quetico Provincial Park. The time had come to go. In June following his first year at Nashwauk, he and three friends headed out on a three-week canoe trip, beginning on Fall Lake east of Ely. He later mentioned the trip in his book, *Open Horizons,* and described it at length in his chapter, "The Explorers," in *Runes of the North.*

And how exciting this first trip was. The foursome paddled north and northeast to Knife Lake, Ottertrack and Saganaga Lake. Granite slopes slanted down to the edges of lakes, making perfect canoe landings. Pine stands with their rust-colored needle duff offered smooth, fragrant tent sites. Cliffs rose up from deep water, veined sometimes with white quartz or wet with thin streaks of falling water. Large lake trout were caught with big Skinner spoons. Stars splashed night skies. Sig wanted to run and shout with excitement but held back his feelings. At Saganaga they turned north to Saganagons, then down the falls chain to Kawnipi, Sturgeon Lake, down the Maligne River, then up into Beaverhouse and Quetico lakes. They saw no one.

Here, however, their romantic bubble burst.

They found a tent near a beach, a big motorized bateau, a stove, and fallen trees. *Cut* trees. It was a logging camp. Three loggers came down to meet them at water's edge and invited them in for coffee. Sig and friends learned the large pines they had seen were scheduled to be cut, that all the surrounding country—as far as the loggers were concerned—was already leveled. Young Olson wanted to tell the loggers how he felt, how the sunlight had brushed the big white and red pines with flame, how their boughs had danced in his campfire's gold light... but he couldn't get the words out. Like his friends, he spoke of prospecting, rock, and timber stands, although he knew little about them. The very image of the country strewn with slash and other logging debris seemed unreal. Olson laughed when the loggers saw them off, kidding them not to get lost, but inside his heart was heavy.

Fortunately for Olson, the logging camp itself seemed to become unreal as he and friends finished their canoe trip, they to paddle waterways home, Sig to hike out and get married. The camp became dreamlike, a nightmare of the past, and soon it was forgotten.

Al Kennedy, meanwhile, was right. Young Sig—with his first Quetico-Superior canoe trip behind him—now wanted to paddle Quetico-Superior waterways forever.

But how could he do this? How could he keep his life orbiting around the northern part of Minnesota? He mulled the possibility of getting a job with the mines in the Ely area. Perhaps he could join a survey team in the backcountry. What about a mink farm? Maybe he could get a teaching position at Ely's high school. Olson seemed to cover all the angles as he returned to the University of Wisconsin for postgraduate geology and botany studies. Finally, in 1923 he moved to Ely when offered a teaching position at the high school. Soon he taught at both the high school and Ely's new junior college en route to becoming head of the college's biology department.

Olson had answered, he later wrote, the "song of the north."

It was a strong song, and it immediately lured him into guiding canoe parties throughout the Quetico-Superior. He started by exploring the lakes and rivers within 20 to 30 miles of Ely, finding the smoothest glaciated granite shores for campsites, finding spots with adequate firewood, learning where various species of fish were, and discovering where moose and deer were most abundant. He also developed camp cooking techniques: how to make bannock, breads and pies in a reflector oven, and how to steak and broil fish. He studied local guides. Men like Buck Sletton, a big, burly ex-Marine who believed loafing and having fun were more important than traveling and fishing, a philosophy Sletton's clients loved.

There was Arne, a squint-eyed Finn, Matt Heikkila, the epitome of all northern woodsmen, the Mizera brothers, who looked like the area's traditional French-Canadian voyageurs, and Gunder Graves, a lumberjack-turned-guide. There was Big Bill Wenstrom who taught Olson how to best throw a canoe on his shoulders. There was Johnny Sansted who showed him how to flour fish with a paper bag. There was Joe Chosa, Frank Santineau, friend John Dahl, and other skilled canoemen like Johnny, Alex and Waino Peura. Good guides could do little wrong in Olson's eyes. In their blood were the trees and rocks and an ancient knowledge being passed from canoeist-to-canoeist. Sig wanted to know and work with them. To learn their skills. He hung around Wilderness Outfitters in Ely his first spring there, hoping to get a guiding job, to become part of an unspoken brotherhood who could never get enough of the magic that, as Kipling had poeticized, lay beyond the ranges.

Olson began guiding on June 23, 1923, first with a fishing trip down the Basswood River into Crooked Lake, then north into Quetico. He later guided all over the region. He was given a Canadian guiding license, replete with the seal of the Province of Ontario across the top, by Walt Hurn at King's Point on Basswood Lake. He also had a guide's license from the state of Minnesota. Olson continued to guide summers and weekends throughout the 1920s. Some summers he was gone from home practically every day. Despite the pay—$6 to $8 a day—he loved it.

"The guide not only did all the cooking and all the routine around the camp," he told Ben Kern of the *Minneapolis Tribune*, "but he had to know how to take care of people... had to watch them like a hawk. Start early morning. Work until 10 at night. So much to do. So much to get ready. But I thought... it's a shame to take my guide's wages, I enjoyed myself so much."

Some of the country Olson guided in was unmapped. Few people knew where many of the smaller lakes were.

"I would take out a party," he once said, "climb a hill, see a spot of blue through the trees, and cut a portage through to it. Then I'd climb another hill to find the next lake. I made some rough maps for my own use."

As Olson's reputation slowly grew, so did a subtle change in his guiding clientele. His geology and botany background, together with some studies at the University of Illinois from 1930-31 (where he did a master's thesis on the eastern timber wolf), enabled him to interpret the Quetico-Superior in ways that went beyond fishing holes and hunting sloughs. He began to understand the wide scope of the region's history, including the enigmatic red ochre Indian pictographs on rock cliffs along waterways, and the intriguing era of fur-trading and fur transportation along the boundary waters in the 1700s and 1800s. He noticed, as he shared his knowledge, a shift in what people were visiting wilderness for. People like Grace Lee Nute, author of *The Voyageur* and *The Voyageur's Highway*, whom he and Elizabeth guided into the Quetico's Maligne River region in 1953. Like Will Dilg, founder of the Izaak Walton League of America, and writer Don

Hough of the *Saturday Evening Post*. Like forester and wilderness preser-
vationist Bob Marshall, whom he guided on a five-day canoe trip in 1937
(see chapter four, section IV). And Supreme Court Justice William O.
Douglas, whom he guided on a 100-mile loop from Basswood Lake, down
Basswood River, then to Quetico's Robinson Lake, Sarah, McIntyre, Brent,
Elk and Crooked lakes before returning to Ely via Basswood.

Such people—businessmen, doctors, lawyers, legislators and newspaper
editors—were, Olson detected, searching for something far more important
then walleyes and bluebills. They wanted simplicity, silence, a sense of space
and contact with the past.

II

Perhaps Olson wouldn't have been aware of such poetic notions as simplicity, silence and contact with the past if he hadn't been such a voracious
reader. In *Open Horizons*, he talks of how he once was thrilled by reading
Henry Van Dyke's description of rapids in moonlight, particularly the phrase
"like an enchantment of tranquillity." He read American and English poets,
the writing of John Muir, John Burroughs, Hudson and Thoreau.

In his chapter, "No Place Between," in *The Singing Wilderness*, Olson
talks of spending a day in a backwoods cabin, hunkered down reading
Thoreau while making friends with resident Canadian jays and red squirrels.
It was Thoreau, Olson later wrote, who was "the arch philosopher of the
stay-at-homes. By long association and developed familiarity in his immediate environment, he was able to give us a new viewpoint, and philosophy of
intimacy with simple things."

Sig also read Lao Tzu, Robert Service, Loren Eiseley, Henry Beston, Pierre
Teilhard de Chardin, Einstein, Owen Barfield and Stanley Diamond. Often on
canoe trips he carried small slips of paper with quotes from great thinkers
which, when winds were calm, he placed on a pack in front of him to read and
mull as he paddled. In this way he made contact with other minds. He kept
driving, as he put it, a wedge into a rift "that would widen and make me think
more like the poets and philosophers than a hunter and a woodsman."

Olson had wanted to know as a young man what it was like to work in the
woods "with constant searching for the same down-to-earth authenticity I
had found on the homestead in Wisconsin." How to handle an ax with power
and precision. How to paddle without effort. And how to slice fillets neatly
with a feel for flesh and blade. Inevitably, however, his reading and days spent
in wilderness led him to what he called intangibles.

Intangibles like *silence*. More than a temporary release from noise, silence
was "a primordial thing that seeped into the deepest recesses of the mind
until mechanical intrusions were intolerable."

Intangibles like *timelessness*: "the actual comprehension of time being endless and relative with all life flowing into its stream."

And intangibles like the sensation of *space*, together with the freedom of
coming and going, of being wrapped in water, woods and wildlife, of being

caught up in a sea of horizons both distant and near, each one steeped in its own mystery and magic.

All this became a part of Olson's consciousness, framed his search, and filled him with a love for the Quetico-Superior and waterways further north that couldn't be stilled.

Great geologists, meanwhile, such as Drs. N.H. Winchell and C.K. Leith, opened Olson's eyes to earth's evolving crust. Another geologist, Dr. Wallace Atwood, left in Olson an indelible impression of how ice-age glaciers had plowed down from the Hudson Bay country southwestward across the Canadian Shield and Quetico-Superior: their ice two miles thick, their bases embedded with boulders, the entire mass gouging out lakes, damming ravines, forming the same rivers, waterfalls and rapids Olson found on his canoe trips.

Still other studies widened Olson's questing vision. His tracking and study of wolves in the Quetico-Superior, together with a summer spent with a scientific expedition studying various creatures in relation to their Quetico-Superior habitat, deepened his dawning grasp of ecology. He came to understand how all life is interdependent, how any change—no matter how small—could upset the balance of the whole. Olson eventually viewed ecology as a science so vast no mind had yet fathomed its secrets. It affected his entire understanding.

"More than knowledge," he said of ecology, "it was deeply involved with my own attitude and emotional reaction to the wilderness. A visceral sort of thing beyond mind and factual information, it was an inherent feeling that went down into that vast primordial well of consciousness, the source of man's original sense of oneness with all creation, a perspective reinforced with logic and reason, cause and effect, and scientific method."

Ecological perspective accentuated Olson's appreciation of what lay around him.

The granite cliffs, the stands of birch and balsam fir making way for pines, the incessant lapping of water among shoreline rubble, the realization that at one time a mountain range comparable in height to India's Himalayas had loomed over the Quetico-Superior, only to be eroded to its present granitic peneplain—all this flooded Olson with a sense of nature's dynamism. To recall this, and to know how Indians and canoemen of eastern America once streamed across the land, gave him a rich sense of not only the Quetico-Superior's past but his own as well. With this feeling, so often charged by beauty under wilderness conditions, Olson felt whole and complete.

He called it, at times, *oneness*. And *oneness* became the basis not only of his emerging land ethic but of his philosophy of wilderness preservation as well.

Perhaps it was only natural for Olson to attribute his own gropings for wholeness to people in general. He had seen changes come over many of the men and women he guided. They would go in to hook lake trout or smallmouth bass and come out hooked on sunsets and rhythms attuned to wind and weather. Stone-faced businessmen would come out laughing. The weak and pale would come back stronger and burnished brown by sun. Olson had hardly been guiding a half-dozen years when he became convinced that, although people said they were entering wilderness to fish, hunt, take photos or conduct scientific investigations, their true motives were entirely different.

"What [one] is really looking for," he wrote in 1932 at age 33, "is that intangible something he calls 'the Wild,' and if he hunts or fishes hard enough, he will find it in the close contact with nature those pursuits entail."

To most people, Olson added in "Search for the Wild," wilderness contact is a necessary part of existence. The contact meant more to some people than others, "all depending upon the potency of their primitive inheritance." As far as Olson was concerned—and this is a theme found throughout much of his later writings—modern man was barely removed from his woodsman and pioneer roots. Forty years maybe. Perhaps a hundred. "It is a long jump from the life of those days to the concentrated civilization of our cities and larger towns," he said, "and it is rather hopeless to believe that in the short space of a generation or two, we can completely root out of our system the love of the simple life and the primitive. It is still deeply rooted and it will be hundreds or thousands of years before we lose very much of it."

Wilderness contact was an inheritance so deeply ingrained in man's nature, Sig added, so taprooted in the million years of his wild evolutionary past, that his recognition of it and desire for it—like seeing home from a distance—could never be stifled.

And how did one touch one's wild, simple past?

By getting down to bare essentials in the outdoors. By hauling and drinking wild water. By burning wood for heat and staring into coals. By flexing muscles against wind and weight, and traveling light and sleeping beneath the stars.

All these things people had done for thousands of years. By going back and doing them again, by leaving their cars, city homes, indoor plumbing, and electricity to touch the basics again, people became aware of the long road down which their kind had come. True, this was a poetic notion, like silence and timelessness, but it offered satisfactions to the human body, and therefore the spirit, that in Olson's opinion appeared to be on the cutting edge of cultural extinction.

III

Certainly it's not surprising, given Olson's background, that he turned his attention in the 1920s and 1930s to preserving what today is Quetico Provincial Park and the Boundary Waters Canoe Area Wilderness. Sig was aware of Thoreau's remark that "In wildness is the preservation of the world," but not until he came face-to-face with threats to the wilderness integrity of his Quetico-Superior did the force of Henry David's words strike home.

As R. Newell Searle tells the story in *Saving Quetico-Superior: A Land Set Apart*, there were plans in the early 1920s to build roads between Ely and the Gunflint Trail north of Grand Marais, between Ely and Buyck, and to run spurs off the new roads to remote lakes like Lac la Croix and Trout Lake. This might have aided the Forest Service's fire fighters, as planned, but conservationists felt the roads would break up a large wilderness area already praised as prime canoe country. As early as 1922, the Forest Service hired Arthur Carhart, a young landscape architect, to study the "human resources" of the national forests. After visiting Superior National Forest in northeastern Minnesota, he reported that it was "purely a boat or canoe forest," that it was already superb canoe country and should be developed accordingly. Roads were inconsistent with such sentiment, and so it wasn't surprising that the first of many environmental battles over how the Quetico-Superior should be designed and managed broke out over the subject of roads. "A Road to Every Lake" became the slogan of developers. Yet the opposition, led by Paul B. Riis, an Illinois landscape architect and member of the American Institute of Park Executives (and a friend of Carhart's), together with Will Dilg of the Izaak Walton League, was victorious. Most of the proposed roads were canned.

"We had learned much during this initial skirmish," Olson recalled, "experience we would need in the years ahead, and found to our surprise that if people felt strongly enough, if they were truly sincere and believed in the rightness of their cause, they would be heard. The wilderness group had won its first victory and had made friends everywhere."

They would need those friends. Edward Backus of International Falls, a large, financially shrewd man who had millions of dollars invested in the pulpwood industry, proposed damming a long chain of boundary water lakes to generate electricity. The chain of lakes lay right in the heart of the Quetico-Superior. Seven proposed dams would have raised the level of such lakes as Little Vermilion 80 feet, Saganaga and Crooked 15 feet, and Loon Lake 33 feet. Waterways would have been backed up for miles— flooding trees, killing them, and at low water leaving rings of gray, dead trees around lakeshores.

Backus had a large following for what seems now like a preposterous plan, but it was only because of Ernest Oberholtzer, the Quetico-Superior Council, and council supporters that the scheme was finally killed.

Olson viewed the Backus-Oberholtzer years-long battle from the side, but not without concern. At stake was the canoe country he guided in, and the waterways north of the town in which he taught. He therefore took heart when he learned of a plan drawn up by Oberholtzer to protect much of the border country, a plan for a place that would combine the best of both a national park and national forest. As Oberholtzer envisioned it, the "park" would stretch from Rainy Lake east of International Falls to Grand Portage on Lake Superior. The Rainy River and Pigeon River watersheds on both sides of the international border would be kept inviolate. The region would be administered by an international organization.

Oberholtzer, who was known for taking frequent canoe trips (once for six months), felt like Carhart that the region should be preserved for water travel recreation. Preferably with canoes.

"The public knows the region in no other way," he wrote. "Destroy the beauty of the visible shores and islands of these lakes and rivers and you destroy the whole charm and pleasurable utility of the region for the public."

Oberholtzer and the Quetico-Superior Council, of which he was president, heeded a request by both American and Canadian legions to designate the proposed wilderness park an "international peace memorial forest." As such it was known and fought over for 25 years.

"For a long time," Olson wrote Oberholtzer in 1930, "I have been following your work with more than passing interest and believe sincerely that what you are doing is a great thing. For the past ten years I have been trying to do what little I could to stem the tide of exploitation that seems to be continually on the verge of wiping out our last wilderness, but as you know it has been an uphill fight....

"I think the move to make an international park of the two areas concerned is the only solution to the problem. In that way only will it be possible to keep the Superior National and the Quetico from private development and subsequent ruin."

Olson explained to Oberholtzer how in 1927 while canoeing he "worked up the Quetico River against a million feet of logs coming down from the Beaverhouse, Quetico, Batchewaung and Pickerel, logs that I had seen as trees and growing timber just a few short years before, then coming down as saw logs to the mills." Olson saw the destruction left in the wake of logging: "shorelines stripped, islands denuded, backwaters from their driving dams flooding and killing everything, all rapids sluiced and portages made into unsightly tote roads," and worst of all cruisers and camp builders working into the heart of the Quetico Preserve itself. He realized then the only thing that could save the country would be to make it into a park. Action would have to be taken quickly "or the last remnant would be gone."

Olson told Oberholtzer about his guiding experiences, and how with no exception all his clients felt the Quetico-Superior should be set aside as a recreational preserve.

"They know," he added, "that the wilderness with its growing timber has a value that cannot be computed in dollars and cents, something that perhaps they cannot explain, an intangible spiritual value that they can find nowhere else but in the wilds. With them it is a religion."

Sigurd ended his introductory letter to Oberholtzer by giving him his unqualified support and the support of every guide in his outfit. He had acquired part ownership (one-third) of Border Lakes Outfitting Company in Winton on Fall Lake.

The Quetico-Superior Council's battle for an international peace memorial forest went on for decades, and Olson's role in the struggle increased over the years. The Council's first victory came in the form of the Shipstead-Nolan Act in 1930; it withdrew public lands along the border from entry or appropriation, and forbade logging within 400 feet of the natural water line of waterways. The Act also forbid alteration of natural water levels including those of rapids, shores and waterfalls in the border region, thus ending the Backus dam plan unless Congress dictated otherwise. According to historian Searle, the Shipstead-Nolan Act "was the first statute in which Congress explicitly ordered federal land to be retained in its wilderness state...." It also gave legislative sanction to new land-service conceptions. The size of the area affected in northeastern Minnesota? About 4,000 square miles, an area almost as large as Connecticut.

The Shipstead-Nolan Act was just the beginning. In time, as the Quetico-Superior Council and the President's Committee for the Quetico-Superior sought to consolidate a wilderness region under one guiding plan, there were battles over everything from enlarging Superior National Forest to consolidating its roadless areas; from the acquisition of private property threatening wilderness values to financial compensation to counties for lands taken off tax rolls.

The worst fight, however, was in the mid-1940s over an airplane ban.

Planes were as thick as blackflies as pilots flew fishermen into remote lakes, where they quickly caught their limits. Some planes circled canoe parties, or even landed to offer paddlers rides at $2.50 a person. Frank B. Hubacheck, who had bought land on Basswood Lake to keep it from being logged, and who subsequently teamed up with the Quetico-Superior Council to defend the area's wilderness values, once counted 38 planes fly over his place in *one day*. Olson, while on a canoe trip down the NinaMoose River to Agnes Lake south of Lac la Croix, watched seven planes land and take off while he paddled across Agnes.

Building supplies, meanwhile, were being flown into remote parcels of private property along the border. By 1946, there were almost 20 resorts built or being built on major canoe route lakes like Basswood, Crooked and Knife. Ely had become the largest inland seaplane base in the world.

Olson was aware of what airplane traffic and resorts nestled in public areas could do to the old Quetico-Superior wilderness and its aura of spaciousness, isolation and inaccessibility. In a 1948 article titled "Voyageur's Return," he described visiting three Quetico-Superior areas in 1947 that he had first visited almost three decades earlier.

The changes shocked him.

"When I first came to the Minnesota-Ontario border country," he wrote, "it was wild and unknown, and all roads stopped long before they reached its borders. It was possible to put in with a canoe at some little frontier town and travel for weeks without seeing a soul... The opportunity of exploration, of camping where men had never camped before, of being on my own in a great wilderness was a tremendous experience."

What appealed most to Olson in those early days was the region's unspoiled condition, its clean campsites, short portages, winding and broken lakes—what appeared overall to be the finest canoeing terrain between Lake Superior and Hudson Bay.

What he found in 1947 was disconcerting. Litter peppered the pines and needle duff of "Paradise Harbor" between Knife and Ottertrack lakes. Olson attributed the problem to a new fly-in fishing camp on Knife. Glorious Bart Lake northeast of Crooked Lake, where Olson had once caught four- and five-pound bass, was now relatively fishless. Why? "Minnows and plugs, and baits of all kinds, and the shipping out of great catches by plane." He found three stashed flat-bottomed boats while portaging into Bart. Empty oil drums were strewn along the shore, and the faint trace of a woods trail he had known in 1922 was "a muddy morass of tracks." At the other end of the portage were more boats, a big dock, a live box and a minnow trap. Olson blamed the new fly-in resort on Crooked Lake's Friday Bay for the changes.

The third place Olson revisited was Curtain Falls, outlet of Crooked Lake, which he portaged around while on a swift cruise of 200 miles. (He was canoeing around Hunter's Island, a large chunk of the Quetico-Superior separated from mainland by lakes and rivers.) The last time Sig had seen Curtain Falls was before World War II. It had been ripe with a feeling of the past's voyageurs, and the pounding of their moccasined feet. This time at the upper end of the portage Olson found boats with shiny motors, and a party of fishermen taking pictures; each man was dressed for dinner at the new resort nearby.

"Grand spot," one of them said to Olson. "Can you imagine all this power going to waste out here?"

Sig could see the new varnished buildings, swimmers lolling in the sun, and a red and silver plane tied to one of the docks.

"Flying is great stuff," the fisherman said to Olson. "Just think, we made it in here in just 27 minutes. It will take you a good three days to get out."

Olson didn't linger. He loaded his canoe and pushed off. He wanted to remember Curtain Falls as it had been the first day he saw it and again later when he brought his sons there.

"I wanted desperately," he explained, "to keep the old wilderness tradition intact and forget that now it was just a scenic showplace littered with film packs."

It wasn't that Olson didn't have an appreciation for aircraft. He knew what they could do militarily in defense of a country. He had once even written an article encouraging their use by the Forest Service for fire protection, rather than developing roads. The problem was the impact planes had on intangible values. Beyond the flown-in fishermen, beyond the flown-in lumber, it was the sight and buzz of planes that anchored consciousness to modern times in what otherwise might be the natural timelessness of wilderness. The resort owners and their guests no doubt meant well, but the impact air traffic was having on the region's growing number of canoeists—particularly in a place where for 30 years preservationists had struggled to protect silence, scenery and other natural values—was intolerable.

So Olson fought for an air ban. In what amounted to a quantum leap in his career as a wilderness preservationist, he joined a mushrooming movement to keep private planes from flying below an altitude of 4,000 feet over the Superior National Forest's roadless areas.

Around Ely the battle aroused hard feelings among neighbors, partly because the Ely Rod and Gun Club favored the air ban. A homemade bomb was thrown against the house of ban supporter and Ely outfitter Bill Rom after a volatile meeting; the bomb exploded but did little damage. A judge's signature was forged on a letter protesting the ban. And environmentalist Hubacheck was threatened with a beating and told to stay out of some Ely businesses.

At stake, of course, were not only wilderness values but also the Ely region's tourism income. Owners of fly-in resorts realized an air ban would force them to shut-up shop.

Supporters of the ban grew in number as the issue raged. They included area chambers of commerce, Jaycees, the St. Louis County Farm Bureau, the Izaak Walton League, Friends of the Wilderness, American Legion posts, Frank Robertson who showed the film "Wilderness Canoe Country" over 500 times, Chester S. Wilson, Commissioner of Conservation in Minnesota, Bill Magie, the President's Quetico-Superior Committee, and many other organizations and individuals. Olson spent the entire summer of 1949 in Washington, D.C. promoting the air ban among politicians and government agencies. Such tidal dedication couldn't be stemmed. On December 17, 1949, President Truman signed Executive Order 10092 establishing an air reservation over Superior National Forest. It was the first time in American history air traffic had been controlled for reasons other than public safety or national defense.

Olson was pleased.

"Faith in the ideals of wilderness preservation," he noted in a 1950 magazine article, had "triumphed."

IV

Olson had good reason to feel a sense of triumph in the wake of President Truman's air ban, because the publicity and momentum behind the air ban was due in large part to his emerging career as a writer. While falling in love with the Quetico-Superior as a young man he had searched for a way to express his evolving ideas and feelings.

Pen and typewriter were the answer.

"As time went on," he explained of his early Quetico-Superior days, "there was a certain fullness within me, more than mere pleasure or memory, a sort of welling up of powerful emotions that somehow must be used and directed. And so began a groping for a way of satisfying the urge to do something with what I had felt and seen, a medium of expression beyond teaching, not only of students, but of those who had been my companions in the wilderness, some medium, I hoped, that would give life and substance to thoughts and memories, a way of recapturing and sharing again the experiences that were mine."

He figured there must be something more than watching animals on his trips into the backcountry, some reason beyond merely acquiring more knowledge and experience, "some aim," as he put it, "that would give purpose to what I had seen, learned, and thought about." Explaining the wilderness in all its infinite shades seemed like an impossible task, yet he began to see how he must discover his own particular wilderness world with a new understanding. He must portray it with whatever comprehension he could summon. When Sig realized his task was to become a writer—to capture the campsites, vistas and sensations of sparkling waters and calling loons—a new horizon opened up to him. He thought the very act of wrestling with words and sentences helped him perceive more accurately. Writing generated an energy that tapped new awareness and knowledge.

Sig's first appearance in print (once he had taught himself how to type with a guidebook in three 20-hour days of practice) was due to his brother Ken. Ken Olson was a reporter in the early 1920s for the *Milwaukee Journal*. He wrote Sig asking him to write an article about one of his canoeing adventures, and he promised to get it published in the *Journal*. Sig agreed, wrote and rewrote "Wilderness Canoe Trip" for days between trips, then dropped it in the mail. The story was in print when he got back from his next canoe trip. Although he later found the story filled with "more clichés and horrible stuff than you can imagine," he was thrilled to see his name and words in black-and-white.

A quick look at a draft of that story reveals Olson's preservation and spiritual inclinations.

Wilderness, he claimed, was set aside by God for those "who would deeply love and truly understand nature in all its moods... a little bit of Paradise, inaccessible for those who would despoil it." While smoking pipes in front of their tent, he and three friends watch "a thin rim of silver, then slowly, majestically, golden mellow, a glorious summer moon dripping out of the dark placid water of Ottertrack." Though they were "poor in worldly goods, can anyone else," he asks, "love the forests, lakes and streams any more than we do? Our bodies are strong and full of the vigor of life... We do not ever hope to accumulate worldly wealth but shall gather instead something far more valuable, a store of memories."

They will not fear death, he adds, "because we will have drunk to the full the cup of happiness and contentment that only close communion with nature can give." Day after day goes by beneath their paddles as they "drink in the beauties of countless water falls, rapids and virgin forests, see naked grandeur as God intended it to be, unscathed by the hand of man."

Such romantic rapture was tempered by the time Olson sold his first magazine story in 1925. Titled "Fishing Jewelry," the piece garnered Olson $25 and helped pay for the hospitalization and delivery charges of their second son, Robert K. (Their first son, Sigurd T., was born the opening day of duck hunting season, September 15, 1923.) After that first sale Sigurd and

Elizabeth celebrated. Sigurd felt he had it made, that "from now on nobody can turn me down."

Yet publications *kept on* turning him down.

Not until 1928 did "Snow Wings" sell to Boy's Life and "Reflections of a Guide" to *Field and Stream*. The next year only one Olson manuscript reached print, when "A Wilderness Canoe Trip" was published in *Sports Afield and Trails of the Northwoods*. In 1930, the same year Olson wrote Oberholtzer approving of the international peace memorial forest plan, he published four manuscripts, three in *Sports Afield and Trails of the Northwoods*: "Confessions of a Duck Hunter," "Stag Pants Galahads" and "The Poison Trail."

Such success was welcome, yet Olson noticed a growing gap between what editors wanted and what he felt like writing.

"Editors wanted action," he explained, "and whenever I injected the slightest bit of philosophy or personal conviction, it was usually deleted. At first I accepted the editing with good grace; happy to have them take my stories at any price, but as time went on I began to feel as though I had entered a sort of cul-de-sac from which there was no escape, a grinding out of more and more adventure yarns with nothing in them of my own ideas or knowledge of the country."

Olson was encouraged in 1932 when *Sports Afield and Trails of the Northwoods* published his "Search for the Wild," in which he explored why people visit wilderness areas. Soon he was writing regularly about conservation subjects pertinent to the Quetico-Superior. Some articles, like "Roads or Planes in the Superior" (1934), were published in the *Minnesota Waltonian*, while others, like "The Evolution of a Canoe Country" (1935), found a home in *Minnesota Conservationist*. While hunting, guiding and fishing stories represent the bulk of his literary output prior to World War II, Olson—by 1938—was happily making a transition to subjects closer to his heart.

It was, in fact, September 1938 that Olson published "Why Wilderness?" in *American Forests*. Eight drafts of the manuscript are in Olson's files, and when one studies the published result it is apparent why he took care to make his case clear. The subject is like the one in "Search for the Wild" of six years before, but this time Olson is writing with more conviction. More force. His words are urgent, and they recognize—and identify with—a new kind of wilderness visitor.

"I have seen them come from the cities down below," Olson wrote of the people he guided, "worried and sick at heart, and have watched them change under the stimulus of wilderness living into happy, carefree, joyous men, to whom the successful taking of a trout or the running of a rapids meant far more than the rise and fall of stocks and bonds. Ask these men what it is they have found and it would be difficult for them to say. This they do know, that hidden back there in the country beyond the steel and the traffic of towns is something real, something as definite as life itself, that for some reason or another is an answer and a challenge to civilization."

Olson saw hunger in the eyes of the men he spoke of, a "torturing hunger for action, distance and solitude, and a chance to live as they will." Only two kinds of experience, he said, could put the minds of such men at peace: war, or the way of the wilderness.

As for wilderness enjoyment, it was nothing new. He pointed out that there are many references in historical literature to the healing powers of solitude, the joys of contemplation and communion with nature. Thoreau was an example. But Thoreau, despite his genuine philosophy, didn't begin to touch the feelings—"the fierce, unquenchable desire"—of Sigurd's men. The outdoors and delights of meditation weren't enough. Men needed the "sense of a actual struggle and accomplishment, where the odds are real and where they know that they are no longer playing make-believe. These men need more than picnics, purling streams, or fields of daffodils to stifle their discontent, more than mere solitude and contemplation to give them peace."

Sig cited the sense of oneness with life that people in almost any wilderness sometimes experience. With it is consciousness of unity with the primal forces of creation—a consciousness which annihilates feelings of frustration, unreality and futility. Backcountry comradeship was also important; men missed it in civilized living as much as they missed contact with the wild. Sig had seen a bond among men "that could only be forged in the wilds, something deep and fine, something based on loyalty to open skies and distance and a way of life men need."

"Why Wilderness?" was one of Olson's strongest magazine pieces in the first half of his writing career. It evinced a macho bravado on Olson's part that, although genuine, eventually subsided in favor of more contemplative journalism.

By 1941, he was writing short, interpretive vignettes for the *Minneapolis Star Journal*, which subsequently became syndicated columns published throughout the Midwest. Eventually, however, Olson's chronic literary bane—lack of action—led to his column's demise.

The important thing for Olson was he was beginning to find his own literary voice. He wasn't merely writing in the rhythms and ideological wake of W.H. Hudson, Aldo Leopold, Burroughs or Thoreau. He became, in fact, critical of his predecessors.

In an undated, penciled note to himself in his files, perhaps written for a future article, Olson mentioned the desire of writing well enough "so that anyone reading any article or story of yours cannot help but feel uplifted and happy." The great American nature writers, he said, hadn't yet touched "the joy in doing anything out-of-doors, love of the soil, of travel, of hunting, of fishing, of everything—no dried melancholy philosophy but something new and alive." A philosophy of happiness in action was what was needed. "The joy of doing things for their own sake."

"Strike a note and hold it," Olson added. "The world is sick of tragedy, tears, broken hearts. What it wants is light heartedness—happiness, a chance to enjoy....

"Stop regretting what is going on—No one loves a reformer—necessary as they are. Be an interpreter of the happy life—."

Human feelings and emotions, he scribbled on his manifesto, are the only worthwhile things in life: "Nothing else matters, just that—love—understanding, sympathy."

Olson became an interpreter of the happy life as he expanded his vignettes into longer, more comprehensive essays. The idea, he later said, was to crystallize a thought and develop it. To actually become a successful writer was a long, difficult process. It wasn't just a case of sitting down and pounding on a typewriter. It was "a case of having an idea, a dream, that's got to come out... The ideas come from something that's been simmering in the back of your mind for a long, long time."

The important thing was *desire*.

"You've got to want very much to write," he said late in life. "Writing must become the most important thing in the world to you. I know, in my own case, success in writing was a long time in coming, as it always is. But I felt I must write, I *must* keep at it, I must forget my rejection slips of which I have millions. *You've got to want to write badly enough to keep on in spite of anything else.*"

As Bernadette Pyter explains in "A Bio-Bibliography of Sigurd F. Olson," Olson continued to hone his interpretive vignettes until they became characteristic of his literary style. His subject matter remained his personal experiences in the Quetico-Superior, but by 1950, Pyter says, Olson was seeing through the eyes of a self- proclaimed wilderness lover, "not just through the eyes of a sportsman enjoying the wilderness." His vignettes were usually personal perspectives of the wilderness revolving around a single incident. The incidents—be they the year's first snow, digging a well, building a sauna, finding pine knots or watching eelpouts spawn in winter moonlight—were embellished with tales of the region's voyageurs, recollections of past experiences, narratives about Indians and pioneers, and insightful explanations of the Quetico-Superior's ecology, botany and geology. Many of the vignettes were published in *Gopher Historian, Sports Illustrated* and *National Parks Magazine,* but all along Olson sought a more lasting home for his work.

"What I had in mind," he wrote Harold Latham of MacMillan Publishing Company as early as January 1943, "was a book of short sketches, possibly fifty or sixty thousand words all told with the material grouped seasonally."

Olson wanted to call his first book *Hours Afield*. He admitted the material represented "a personal, rather interpretive slant."

Latham wasn't interested in *Hours Afield* at the time, nor was any other publisher. Not until the early 1950's did Olson's book writing get a surprising break. Olson was a friend of Rachel Carson, author of *The Sea Around Us* and *Silent Spring,* and she—like one or two friends earlier—advised Sig to send his sample chapters to agent Marie Rodell. Olson did. Rodell circulated the manuscript. After eight rejections she confessed to Sig he should put a little more action into his prose.

Olson thought not. Which proved wise.

In 1956, after Rodell placed *Hours Afield* with publisher Alfred A. Knopf, it was published with the improved title of *The Singing Wilderness*. It was a great moment for Olson as both he and Knopf approached the pinnacles of their careers. When Knopf died at 91 in August, 1984, author John Hersey, writing in *Publishers Weekly*, called Knopf "the greatest publisher this country ever had." Knopf's roster of writers included D.H. Lawrence, Willa Cather, T.S. Eliot, Franz Kafka, Jean-Paul Sarte, John Updike, Somerset Maugham and Hersey. Olson joined this prestigious guild with satisfaction. All but one of his nine subsequent books were published by Knopf.

The Singing Wilderness, illustrated with black and white scratchboard drawings by Francis Lee Jaques, is a collection of Olson's essays honed and polished since his early Quetico-Superior years. The title, of course, refers to the Quetico-Superior, while the text describes Olson's experiences in the north and his search for insight and geo-psychic meaning. Some chapters are reprinted magazine pieces. Titles include "The Loons of Lac la Croix," "Silence," "Northern Lights" and "Timber Wolves." Friend Frank B. Hubacheck, reviewing the book for *Journal of Forestry*, claimed its 33 "prose poems" should be "rationed like water to a desert traveler." Hubacheck said Olson had caught the "serene soul of the country as well as its beauty." Elizabeth M. Cole in *Library Journal* felt the book was most moving "because of the indirect and personal presentation of the importance of the wilderness area." Jack Durham, reviewing for *American Forests*, devoted over an entire page to *The Singing Wilderness*. After praising the book's style, content and author, Durham said the book was "a rewarding adventure in revelation," a book for the young in spirit with the "day-light view all over it." He admired Olson's fearlessness in communicating his love for the outdoors.

There was at least a dozen reviews of *The Singing Wilderness* in North American press. Most were favorable. The American Library Association named it The Notable Book of 1956.

Olson—with reviewers' praise in his literary sails—tackled his second book immediately. Knopf published *Listening Point* in 1958.

Here again, Sigurd gathered together his best interpretive vignettes, this time those focusing on and orbiting around "a bare glaciated spit of rock in the Quetico-Superior country" where he had a log lake cabin.

"From it," he wrote at his poetic best, "I have seen the immensity of space and glimpsed at times the grandeur of creation. I have sensed the open span of uncounted centuries and looked down the path all life has come. I have explored on this rocky bit of shore the great concept that nothing stands alone and everything, no matter how small, is part of a greater whole."

Listening Point was also illustrated by Jaques, who had become a wildlife artist and museum dioramist of international reknown. Chapters included "The Cabin," "Laughing Loon," "Painted Rocks," and "The Portage," each a crystallization around a subject tied loosely to the book's main theme. Olson's lakeshore and primitive cabin epitomized for him wilderness everywhere. It spoke to him of belonging, wonder and beauty. Everyone has a listening point somewhere, he said; his functioned as a place of both insight and departure.

Listening Point received predominantly favorable reviews. Yet no sooner had it been named the Minnesota Centennial Book than Olson was busy on a third. *The Lonely Land,* however, departed from the vignette format in favor of narrative. Voyageur Olson stood revealed.

V

Sig had always had an affinity with historic French-Canadian voyageurs, those short but brawny paddlers from Montreal country who traveled the Quetico-Superior's boundary waters during the heyday of the fur trade in the 1700s and 1800s. They were, in a sense, canoe country's version of Himalayan sherpas. Olson had read about them while studying Quetico-Superior history, and had even canoed with some of their descendants during his early guiding days. Not only did voyageurs symbolize canoe country's historic past—when paddles flashed in the sunlight and French chansons echoed off rock cliffs in narrow waterways—but they also represented fading eras of adventure, exploration and romance, all of which appealed to Olson's spirit.

"These wiry little men," he wrote, "seldom more than five feet four or five—dressed in breech cloth, moccasins and leather leggings reaching to thighs, a belted shirt with its inevitable colored pouch for tobacco and pipe, topped off with a red cap and feather. They were a breed apart. From dawn until dark they paddle their great canoes and packed enormous loads, facing storms, wild uncharted rivers, hostile Indians and ruthless rivals with a joy and abandon that has possibly never been equaled in man's conquest and exploitation of any new country."

Sig was also intrigued with voyageur canoe routes. He knew wilderness shaped those who passed through it, who steeped themselves in it, and hence to get to know the voyageurs he would have to become acquainted with their highways. It was a simple prescription.

Not until 1954, however, when Olson joined a group of distinguished Canadian canoemen to retrace the old Pierre de la Verendrye route from Grand Portage on Lake Superior to Fort Frances on Rainy River, did the lure of ancient canoe trails in the far Northwest grip him with vengeance.

"The urge began," he explained, "the moment we pitched our tents near the rebuilt North West Company stockade on the north shore of Lake Superior. Gagnon's Island lay like a watchdog off the entrance to Grand Portage Bay. Hat Point with the gnarled old Witches Tree at its tip was waiting as always for the brigades to come by. In the blue distance was the shadowy outline of Isle Royale. It was the same as the day in 1731 when La Verendrye and his voyageurs made the terrible nine-mile carry around the rapids of the Pigeon River toward the unknown country beyond for the first time. That night those men were with us and when the haze of our campfire drifted along the beach, it seemed to join with the smoke of long forgotten fires and lay like a wraith over the canoes, tepees, and tents along the shore."

With Olson on that memorable Verendrye trip of the "new voyageurs" were Canadian paddlers who had begun retracing voyageur routes a year or so earlier: Dr. Omand Solandt, chairman of Canada's Defense Research Board, and Eric Morse, national director of the Association of Canadian Clubs. Also with the group was Blair Fraser, editor of *Maclean's Magazine*, and Anthony J. Lovink, the Netherlands Ambassador to Canada. Nineteen fifty-one had found the group paddling down Canada's Gatineau Valley, and in 1953 they had canoed part of Quetico Park. Morse, aware of Olson's background, had asked him to join the group on their trips. Sig agreed. He was soon recognized as the group's most valuable member.

"We called him 'Bourgeois'," Tyler Thompson, a former U.S. Ambassador to Finland (and the only other American on one of the trips) said of Sig in *Audubon*. "In the old days, bourgeois was the chief trader and the leader of the expedition. The big difference was that in those days the bourgeois let the voyageurs do the paddling and most of the work. In our case, Sig was the best woodsman, and he did more than anybody else on the trip."

The group's 1954 trip covered 266 miles—242 by canoe, 24 on foot over portages—between Grand Portage and Fort Frances. Sig, as became customary, did all the cooking. Morse, the trip historian, read passages from old journals at night as the group sat around the fire sipping their daily ration of 3½ ounces of rye each. Lovink, who complained of being too old for the trip, carried the biggest canoe (an 83-pound aluminum one) and the heaviest pack. The first part of the trip was the worst. After the first portage of nine miles going uphill with full food packs, the group had to wade up a series of rapids on the Pigeon River before hacking a route around a high dam in a gorge blocking the way to South Fowl Lake. There had been a portage, but they missed it.

The trip eased in misery as they crossed Mountain Lake, the Laurentian Divide, Gunflint Lake, then paddled down Granite River to Saganaga. Continuing westward, they crossed Ottertrack, Knife and Prairie Portage before reprovisioning at a friend's summer place on Basswood Lake.

Rather than going west at this point, however, the group veered north to Quetico Park's Maligne River via Lake Kahshahpiwi to look for remnants of the Dawson Road. The "road" had been a water and log corduroy route pieced together in the 1860s and 1870s to connect Thunder Bay, Ontario, with Fort Garry (now Winnipeg). It took the new voyageurs four hours to paddle the trip's last nine miles on Rainy Lake against a 30 mile-per-hour wind. They arrived at Fort Frances with peeling noses, dirty fingernails and the natural informality that wilderness life brings.

"We hadn't more than set foot on the dock," Blair Fraser recalled, "before civilization caught up with us. The Netherlands had been waiting to shake hands with Ambassador Lovink. Tony had been paddling bow and glistened with water all over. He had nothing on but a pair of spun-glass swimming trunks and a peaked cap with a gull's feather in it. He stepped ashore and greeted his compatriots with as much aplomb as if he were wearing striped pants and morning coat."

The trip was a tough one, especially for guest paddler John Endemann, Deputy High Commissioner for South Africa, who had never been in a canoe. Most of the group were nevertheless hooked on voyaging. They had, Fraser said, accomplished what they had set out to do: make fresh contact with their cumulative historical roots. Their past.

Two years later, as documented in *The Lonely Land*, many of the same group—with Olson as leader—paddled part of Saskatchewan's Churchill River. Along were Ambassador Lovink, historian Morse, Dr. Solandt with rationed rum, Denis Coolican, president of the Canadian Bank Note Company, Ltd. and Major General Elliot Rodger of the Canadian Army, who had been on at least one previous voyageur trip but couldn't make the 1954 Verendrye expedition. They began at Ile a la Crosse near the headwaters of the Churchill, traveled east on the lake-necklaced river, then portaged into the Sturgeon-Weir watershed for a take-out at Cumberland House 500 miles from their start.

Editors might have formerly complained about lack of action in Olson's writing, but that was not a concern when Sig wrote of this trip. Something happened around every bend. There were windstorms and rapids, old Indian camps and grueling portages. One night they even lost a canoe.

Olson had, of course, developed a special feeling for canoes. Of all kinds of transportation he had tried, the canoe had provided the most pleasure. He had known the canoe on solo trips close to home, had known the wood-canvas craft—a Morse-Vezie and a White brothers model from Maine's Penobscot country—on many guiding trips. Now on the Churchill he paddled a 16-foot Peterborough Prospector.

Surely the canoe sang to him on lakes Primeau and Sandfly, Trout and Otter, Keg and Amisk. Perhaps as he passed through Pelican Narrows he recalled how he had described the canoe, now an inseparable part of his life, in *The Singing Wilderness:*

"The movement of a canoe is like a reed in the wind. Silence is part of it and the sounds of lapping water, bird songs, and wind in the trees. It is part of the medium through which it floats, the sky, the water, the shores... A man is part of his canoe and therefore part of all it knows. The instant he dips a paddle, he flows as it flows, the canoe yielding to his slightest touch, responsive to his every whim and thought."

The canoe, he had said, gave a "sense of unbounded range and freedom, unlimited movement and exploration such as larger craft never know."

A man felt at home with a paddle in his hand "as natural and indigenous as with a bow or spear." Paddling a canoe, moreover the actual swinging through a stroke—set in motion forgotten reflexes and stirred "ancient sensations deep within his subconscious." The way of a canoe was the way of the wilderness; it led to profound and abiding satisfactions, to freedoms that were almost forgotten, and to waterways—such as the Pigeon and Churchill—of ages past.

There were more canoe trips for Olson and his Canadian co-voyageurs after they paddled through the lonely land. There was the jaunt into

Reindeer-Athabasca lakes country in 1957. A trip down the Camsell River from Great Slave Lake to Great Bear Lake in 1959. There was the Rat River. The Mackenzie River. There was the God's Lake-Hayes River route to Hudson Bay in 1964. Each trip began as a name which became a dream, and each dream swept into Olson's past. The canoe trips, moreover, were like footsteps across what Olson came to call *pays d'en haut*, French for "the upper country." There his heart grew rich.

"They were very rugged trips," Tyler Thompson told Frank Graham, Jr. "Each one lasted about three weeks and covered about five hundred miles. Just before I joined the group there was one man who almost didn't make it. The canoeing and the carrying were so arduous that he was sure he was going to die before they got him out."

Graham, writing in *Audubon*, cited how on the Hayes River one of the Olson expedition's canoes swamped in rapids and the group lost its food and cooking utensils. Olson and companions each lost about 15 pounds in the next two weeks as everyone ate fish and moldy flour with whittled spoons and forks.

On another trip, Olson slipped on a portage and gashed his mouth; two front teeth were later pegged by a Japanese dentist at Fort Churchill.

Hardships. Dreams. Voyages. A feel for the land. A successful book-writing career. The warmth of human associations. All began to fuse together for Olson by the 1960s and 1970s. Unlike many outdoors people, however, who never go beyond the sensual high of wilderness adventures, Olson now wanted to explore more deeply what became the next step in the natural progression of his lifelong quest: the fruition of mind and spirit.

VI

Olson's quest could not—and would not—come at the expense of his social obligations, for Olson believed good citizenship meant responsibility not only toward countryside and home but toward community as well.

His own roles in community affairs advanced rapidly from the late 1930s through the 1960s. After 12 years of teaching botany, biology and zoology at Ely Junior College, he became the college's dean from 1935 to 1946. His friend Bill Langen, principle of Ely Memorial High School for 30 years and husband of Ann Langen (who helped edit some of Sig's books), remembered Olson as being a democratic teacher and dean. Langen said Sig had good rapport with the college's 185-200 students. He also had a sweet tooth, and sometimes held informal gatherings of students and instructors around a box of chocolates. Field trips, as in Nashwauk, were commonplace for Olson, and he was known as a good classroom speaker.

"Sig could think on his feet," Langen said. "But he wasn't the easiest guy to get next to. It took a little time."

Olson spent almost two years with the U.S. Army in 1946 and 1947. At first he was stationed in England as head of the University of Shrivenham's zoology department, then he lectured in the U.S. while working for the

Army's Information and Education Division. He decided to write full-time in 1947 when he returned to Ely. He also wanted to dedicate his energies to wilderness preservation.

"I was scared stiff to make the break," he said later. "But I just couldn't stand to have walls around me anymore."

His first full-time wilderness work was local. According to Searle in *Saving Quetico-Superior*, Olson formally joined the Oberholtzer team to establish an international peace memorial forest in the Quetico-Superior in 1947. It was a pivotal point in his life. Apparently Olson was hunting deer on Basswood Lake north of Winton when he fell on the ice and injured his hip. He limped to Frank Hubacheck's nearby lodge for help. There the two men sat next to a fire talking about local wilderness preservation efforts. Hubacheck complained he and his friends didn't have time to advance the Quetico-Superior cause as fast as they would like. Hubacheck, together with his friend Charles Kelly, invited Olson to accept a permanent assignment as a consultant to the Quetico-Superior Council. Olson agreed. By late November, Searle wrote, Olson was determined to, in his own words, "go into the fight with everything I've got and stay with it until we are through."

He would never be free from Quetico-Superior battles again.

His star was rising on other horizons in the meantime. It was in 1947 that Olson became a wilderness ecologist for the Izaak Walton League of America. A year later he became a regular contributor to *The Living Wilderness*, house publication of the Wilderness Society. In March 1948, he was writing to the Society's Howard Zahniser of how pleased he was with the Society's letterhead and type.

"Of all the organizations in the United States," he added, "[the Wilderness Society] is one whose ideals are the closest to my heart."

Throughout 1949, Olson traveled, corresponded and spoke in favor of the air reservation over Superior National Forest. His writing appeared in *Sports Afield, Conservation Volunteer, Forest and Outdoors* and *National Parks Magazine*. Continuing media publicity and experience with wilderness legislation led to more environmental group positions in the 1950s, such as presidency of the National Parks Association for five years. He became a member of the governing council of the Wilderness Society in 1956, served on its Executive Committee from 1958 to 1959 and from 1962 to 1964, then became the Society's president in 1968. In the 1960s he was also a member of the Secretary of the Interior's Advisory Committee, and a consultant on wilderness preservation to the Director of the National Park Service.

At one time or another, Olson was active in almost every major American environmental organization as well as several in Ontario. En route he became involved in a litany of wilderness battles; some were over the Indiana Dunes National Lakeshore at Lake Michigan's lower end, Florida's Everglades, Point Reyes National Seashore north of San Francisco, northern Minnesota's Voyageurs National Park, Washington's Cascades National Park and Olympic National Park.

"There was a proposal at the time," Olson told me of the Olympic Park battle, "for a highway to be built along the west coast of Washington where Olympic National Park's preserved beach is now. The area would have been developed for real estate, too. Justice William Douglas and I [together with 20 or more others] hiked from Lake Ozette to LaPush in three days. When we got to LaPush, some protesters—protesting against us!—met us. They had a huge sign, four feet high, twenty feet long, saying 'Bird Lovers Go Home.' We were outraged. As soon as we read the sign, we said to each other, 'Okay, if that's how they feel, and if the land can't fight for itself, we'll go back to Washington, D.C., and muster all the influence and support we can get.' We won, too."

There were other battles over California's redwood trees, the same ones Muir had fought to preserve. Over Grand Canyon's free-flowing water. Over the Chesapeake and Ohio Canal's towpath. There seemed to be a battle around every bend as Olson and friends tried to keep the flame of wilderness preservation alive.

———— ▬ ————

The evolution of Olson's spiritual thought parallels the development of his wilderness work and concepts. Not until the late 1940s, however, did he readily and frequently admit wilderness preservation was a matter of cultural, humanitarian and spiritual values.

In a 1946 article titled "We Need Wilderness," Olson debunked Webster's definition of wilderness as a "trackless waste uninhabited by man." He claimed, based upon the men who had been with him on a recent canoe trip, that wilderness was so tied up with mankind's cultural background and traditions, philosophies and emotions, it simply couldn't be ignored any longer. "*Wilderness to the people of America,*" he emphasized by writing in italics, "*is a spiritual necessity, an antidote to the high pressure of modern life, a means of regaining serenity and equilibrium.*" The most important reasons people visited wilderness, he said, were for perspective and the good of their souls:

"Then when the old philosophy of earth-oneness begins to return to them, they slowly realize that once again they are in tune with sun and stars and all natural things."

Wilderness, he added, was difficult to evaluate because of its emotional appeal. Its real worth depended on how people felt about it. And what it did for them. "If it contributes to spiritual welfare, if it gives them... a sense of oneness with mountains, forests, or waters, or in any way at all enriches their lives, then the area is beyond price." Because wilderness rejuvenated the emotional lives of people, and because it stimulated the noncorporeal side of their characters, its most important function would always be "as a spiritual backlog in the high speed mechanical world in which we live."

Olson expanded this same theme two years later in a feature essay for *The Living Wilderness.* His essay, titled "The Preservation of Wilderness," explored some of the intangible values of wild country but also argued that wilderness preservation was far more than preserving recreational areas for athletic or aesthetic types. Wilderness was important *economically* because some communities were becoming dependent on wilderness-based tourism. *Educationally*, it offered people "living pictures of the America... our forefathers knew." And wilderness acted *scientifically* as a control for study and research, a norm against which ecological change could be evaluated by scientists; this function of wilderness was particularly appropriate to forestry and agriculture. It was the emotional importance of wilderness, however, that Sig insisted on threading through his 1948 essay. Emotional values led to spiritual values interwoven in man's quest for meaning.

Olson's "spirituality of wilderness" reached a climax of sorts in 1961. He was, by then, recognized coast-to-coast as a spokesman on wilderness subjects ranging from the Quetico-Superior and national parks to people's primordial hungers. He spoke in April at the Sierra Club's 7th Wilderness Conference in San Francisco, and what he had to say summarized thoughts he had mulled for years. Now he hammered them into characteristic conviction.

"Henry David Thoreau said many wise things," he began, "but perhaps the wisest and most prophetic was his well-known 'In wildness is the preservation of the world.' He said this over a century ago during our pioneer era when the continent was still uncrowded and largely undeveloped. Even then he could see what was going to happen."

Olson cited the mechanical changes that had swept across North America. The dive into industrialism. The reshaping of the land into farms and cities, suburbs and freeways. All this within a hundred years or less. People were shocked, he said. They might not realize this consciously but deep inside was an insecurity—"a gnawing unrest that somehow the age of gadgetry and science cannot still." Olson reiterated his long-held belief of how people were rooted physiologically and psychologically to their wild past. Because the age of mechanization had dawned suddenly, he said, people hadn't had enough time to adjust.

Sig referred to Richard Garrington's *A Guide to Earth History*, and how in it Garrington broke down the four-billion-year history of earth into a single year. The first eight months would lack life. The next two months would consist of primitive creatures like viruses, single-celled bacteria and jellyfish. Mammals would appear the middle of December. Man as we know him: 11:45 p.m. on December 31. Written history: barely 60 seconds on the clock. Man's machine age would fit within the final second of earth's compressed year.

As a result, Olson explained, people couldn't forget their organic past. Without some kind of contact with it they felt a lack of completion. Something was amiss despite the advance in comforts technology brought, despite longer and healthier lives, despite increased security and what appeared to be progress in community welfare. Signs of man's hunger for his past were everywhere: split rail fences, historical knick-knacks, pine-paneled walls of rooms with smoke-stained timbers, fieldstone fireplaces, TV shows depicting cowboys and pioneer life, and vicarious fascinations with contemporary explorers and wilderness expeditions.

Sigurd reminded his audience of how he had seen people change in wilderness. How during his guiding years he had watched people shed city habits and settle down to the hard work and simplicity of primitive living. They seemed to laugh more, enjoy little things, take time to watch sunsets, birds and to look at flowers. Deep and abiding friendships were made. Men and women pawed mementos between trips, pored over maps, talked to old paddling partners with the excitement of reminiscence in their eyes.

And what did these people remember?

"Not the fishing, or the miles they had traveled, nor the game they had killed. What stayed with them was the good feeling after a day of tough portages or fighting some gale, the joy of warmth and food after exposure and reaching an objective under their own power. They remembered ghostly mornings when the mists were rolling out of the river mouths, days when the lakes were gay with whitecaps, evenings when the hermit thrushes sang and the west was flaming above the ridges. Theirs were visions of wilderness lakes when the islands lay like battleships before them, but most of all was the silence and sense of removal. These were spiritual dividends, hard to explain, impossible to evaluate, that brought them back time and again."

Identification with terrain during wilderness travel is one of its spiritual aspects, Sig said. The land is touched and known in ways cars and planes never share. He found it good to know the spirit of such travel and wild adventure was alive in American youth. What they would find in the continent's outback would nourish them for the rest of their lives.

Nourishment was what mattered. The real significance of wild country was cultural.

The time had arrived to enter a new era in thinking about wilderness. To see, as a mature people, beyond purely economic factors. "To bridge the gap between our old racial wisdom, our old primeval consciousness, the old verities, and the strange conflicting ideologies and beliefs of the new era of technology." This was our mandate.

Wilderness's greatest role, Olson concluded, was to offer our age "a familiar base for explorations of the soul and the universe itself. By affording opportunities for the contemplation of beauty and naturalness as well as further understanding of the mysteries of life in an ecologically stable environment, it will inculcate reverence and love and show the way to a humanism in which man becomes at last an understanding and appreciative partner with nature in the long evolution of mind and spirit."

Culminating words, these. A zenith in wilderness thought.

Olson's speech, "The Spiritual Aspects of Wilderness," was first published in the proceedings of the Sierra Club's 1961 conference, *Wilderness: America's Living Heritage*, edited by David Brower, then again in *Voices for the Wilderness* (1969), edited by William Schwartz. It was a stirring call to everyone who hungered for nature and wildness, a call—Olson noted—broached by Thoreau before him. A call not for wilderness exclusive of modern civilization, but for wilderness as bedrock of, and a necessary complement to, contemporary culture.

The important thing for wilderness preservation, Olson later explained, was to build a broad base of values for wilderness protection—"a base of sufficient depth and solidity to counter the charge that [wilderness] exists for only a privileged and hardy few."

By responding to this challenge, everyone interested in wilderness—the Sierra Club, the Wilderness Society, the Audubon Society, other great conservation and preservation organizations, and all state and federal government agencies—would inevitably discover and illumine the all-encompassing humanitarian values of wild country. This Sigurd had tried to do by speaking out on spiritual aspects of wilderness. Such values, he believed, would, above and beyond the human need for outdoor physical recreation, save wilderness.

This was Olson's message. This his meaning. This the gospel he carried into his last years.

VII

Olson was a writer to the end. The keys of his old Royal typewriter in the small cabin of his Ely home's yard could be heard clacking in the stillness of East Wilson Street's alley, day after day, book after book.

In 1963, two years after *The Lonely Land*, Knopf published Olson's *Runes of the North*. It was an intricately designed book of two parts filled with adventures, legends and reflections of Sig's expanding life in the North. Part One, *Le Beau Pays*, focused like his other books on the Quetico-Superior: its deer, cranberry bogs, spring sensations, his first trip into canoe country in the early 1920s, the Ross light, and hunting moons, among other subjects. Part Two, *Pays D'en Haut*, encompassed many of Sig's most delightful canoeing essays based on trips in northwestern Canada.

Six years later, following a mild heart attack, Olson saw two more of his books reach print.

Open Horizons, his autobiography, describes his youth in northern Wisconsin, his university studies, his move to Nashwauk then Ely, his years as a guide, his emergence as a writer and the evolution of his work as a wilderness preservationist. Edward Weeks, writing in *Atlantic*, called the book a "paean to the all-engulfing silence of wilderness, to the glory of the stars, and to the sheer delight of making one's way by canoe and portage through new and unmapped country." The book's greatest weakness is its lack of dates and related historical specifics. Its strength lies in Olson's remarkable facility to portray his perspective and share with his growing audience his interpretation of the past. *Open Horizons* was reprinted annually for at least five years.

In *Hidden Forest*, also published in 1969, Olson collaborated with Minnesota photographer Les Blacklock in a coffee-table book format fusing photos with text in a seasonally arranged description of forest life.

Knopf published *Sigurd F. Olson's Wilderness Days* in 1972, which was in its fifth printing by July 1980. As Olson explained in his "Author's Note," the book is an anthology of his and readers' favorite chapters from his previous books. Chapters are arranged seasonally. Brown type on heavy paper makes this book one of Olson's most handsome accomplishments. *Wilderness Days* received the Burroughs Medal in 1974 from the John Burroughs Memorial Association.

Olson's most successful book, however, was probably *Reflections from the North Country*, published in 1976. Olson thought its success was due to its universal appeal. It describes, in his own words, "the long view of a naturalist and wanderer through wild country and all he has written and thought about over the years." The 28 essays (ranging from "Intuition" and "Evolution of Mind" to "The Emergent God") and epilogue are a partial summing up of his personal beliefs, a climax to the philosophical and spiritual themes touched on in earlier articles and books.

"When a man has traveled the wilderness most of his life," Olson said at the onset of *Reflections*, "his earliest memories steeped in beauty and the joys such experience gives, when he has watched the changes that have come not only to the land itself but to the people, their attitudes, and the world, now entirely different from the one he first knew, it is only natural to reflect on countless explorations and interpret them in the light of the slow filtrations into consciousness of an almost forgotten way of life. It becomes, in a sense, a distillation of how he feels and looks at things, the development of a point of view that encompasses his understanding of man's long relationship to nature, all living things, and the universe itself."

Olson's final book, *Of Time and Place*, was published in 1982.

"It will be similar to *Reflections*," he told me in July 1979, "but on different philosophical subjects. Never on the same ones. The major theme is, as the title suggests, that everything has its time and place. Things come together causing change, giving meaning."

Sig hoped *Of Time and Place* would be a "guide to knowing." He returned to his vignette style as his 36 chapters, some rewritten three to eight times, examined mementos, mavericks, droughts, campsites, favorite rivers and night sounds. The chapters are anecdotal memoirs without dates, bound together between covers. Here is not the wholeness of Sig's earlier books, nor the deep thinking of *Reflections*, although at times, and in places, he is characteristically philosophical, almost forcefully so. *Of Time and Place* is basically biographical chinking in the poetic cabin his other eight books had built.

While building that literary cabin, however, Olson never wearied as a writer.

"Even at the tender age of eighty," he once said, "my greatest happiness is sitting down and working on this next book. It's a great source of happiness to me. I think I'm just as thrilled working now on this new book as I was working on my first one. And if I live to be a hundred, and

I write another dozen books, it won't change. Each one is a challenge and a joy."

———

Perhaps Olson needed all the joy he could summon from 1950 to the late 1970s, as he continued to fight relentlessly in defense of wilderness values in the Quetico-Superior. It was fitting that his career as a wilderness preservationist—ranging as it had from Florida to Alaska—should inevitably come careening home. It was the Quetico-Superior that had sparked his original vision. And it was *upon* the Quetico-Superior, as H.S. Salt once remarked about great nature-lovers, that Olson had stamped the impress of his character; thus, in a sense, it belonged to him "by supreme and indisputable right" for he had made it peculiarly and perpetually his own.

Once the air ban was established over Superior National Forest in 1949, Oberholtzer and Olson resumed work on the international treaty to set aside the Quetico-Superior as a peace memorial forest. Olson, by this time, did not believe in being too cautious. "Nothing is ever gained except by courage and action," he had written Fred Winston.

It was important to be realistic, however, and as Sig helped Oberholtzer rewrite the Quetico-Superior Council's proposed treaty he inserted ideas subtly different than those of Oberholtzer's.

Oberholtzer, historian Searle explained, persisted in regarding the Quetico-Superior region as he had found it in his youth: unmapped, unsurveyed, immeasurable and extending wildly northward to Hudson Bay and the Arctic barrens. He wanted to preserve the entire Rainy River and Pigeon River watersheds. Olson, meanwhile, was aware of Atikokan's growing mines north of Quetico, adjacent pulpwood logging, and other developments on the perimeter of what was becoming large wilderness islands. There were railroads, a new highway connecting Thunder Bay with Fort Frances, and electric lines. Hence, when Olson rewrote treaty drafts, he emphasized preserving the "wilderness character *of the interior*" of the Quetico-Superior. This irked Oberholtzer. He warned Olson to bear in mind that Quetico Park and Superior's roadless area was not necessarily the region's best wilderness—that they were, in fact, prototypes for a larger preservation program applied to the region's two watersheds.

The greatest opportunity for wilderness preservation, Oberholtzer insisted, lay in Ontario.

Olson, however, was advised by Ontario legislators and conservationists that the Quetico-Superior Council had to be practical. Ontario would only match U.S. involvement in the proposed peace memorial forest acre for acre. As a result, perimeter areas were slowly eliminated from wilderness consideration. By 1960, Ontario and the U.S. had made a decision. The core of Quetico would be kept in its natural state, as would Superior National Forest's roadless areas (renamed the Boundary Waters Canoe Area in 1958), but they would not be governed under international jurisdiction. Instead, Ontario's premier, Leslie M. Frost, and the U.S. exchanged letters promising to collaborate with one another in joint management of the Quetico-Superior as a wilderness area. The letters also established the Quetico-Superior International Advisory Committee to watchdog Quetico-Superior affairs and recommend mutually acceptable policies.

This wasn't, of course, what Oberholtzer and Olson had dreamt about and fought for, but it was a great step forward from the rampant logging and lack of management Olson witnessed on Quetico River in the 1920s. Now, in 1960, clear legal precedent was recognized and set. With it came victory for lovers of wilderness.

For Olson, there would be little peace. While he worked on his last two books there were constant attempts to change the legal status of the BWCA. There was fighting over logging, motorboats, snowmobiles, silence and group quotas. Hard feelings reached a crescendo in the mid-1970s when legislators from northern Minnesota submitted a bill to Congress seeking to open part of the BWCA to development in a plan establishing a new interior wilderness zone and a perimeter development zone. Preservationists fought the proposal by submitting their own bill banning logging, restricting motorboats, forbidding snowmobiles and enlarging the BWCA's boundaries to 1.1 million acres.

As the pro-wilderness bill gained momentum, tourists were stopped at road blockades in northeastern Minnesota and asked to sign antiwilderness petitions. Cars at BWCA access point parking lots were vandalized. And when bill hearings were held in Ely, resident Olson—who had always favored complete wilderness protection for the BWCA—was booed at the podium.

This could not, and did not, discourage Olson who believed in what Finnish people called *sisu*, an inner strength of vision and purpose which refuses defeat. Olson, by the late 1970s, was identified with the ecological integrity of the Quetico-Superior and with the preservation of wilderness values throughout North America. This image he accepted; from it he refused to back down. When the 1978 pro-wilderness BWCA bill passed Congress, Sig knew it preserved for today's 160,000 annual BWCA users a vestige of wild America. The BWCA wasn't *pristine* wilderness, for man's impact was found throughout the area, but the BWCA had the *potential* to be recreated and managed in ways approximating wild conditions. This made all the difference in the world to Olson; it represented a saving by preservationists of a wonderful country just in the nick of time. The 1978 BWCA bill was a small victory on a continental scale but for Olson it was a vision materialized. It was a victory, moreover, which functioned like a prism by symbolizing and reflecting wilderness battles everywhere.

Here, on the American side of the Quetico-Superior, wilderness trials had resulted in important wilderness management precedents. Here policy had been debated, agonized over and established. Such policy, Olson hoped, would fuel the decisions in favor of what little wilderness remained in the decades ahead.

The end came suddenly for visionary Olson on January 13, 1982. He and Elizabeth had gone snowshoeing together on a beautiful winter afternoon to try out new snowshoes they had just bought. Elizabeth's snowshoes didn't fit well so she decided to return to the house. Sig kept going, exploring a little wooded valley a few blocks from his Ely home. There he was found unconscious in midafternoon. Cardiopulmonary resuscitation failed. Death was attributed to heart attack.

Yet Olson had not gone snowshoeing that Wednesday without sitting at his typewriter. Without speaking for his kind one last time.

He had walked, as he had done countless times, to his writing cabin, closed the door, and put a piece of paper into his typewriter. Perhaps he paused for a moment to glance outside at the sparkling snow. Or perhaps he struck and held a match to his pipe's Irish Mead tobacco. Alone, separated from his family and friends, he typed one line:

"A new adventure is coming up and I know it will be a good one"

EPILOGUE

THE WILDEST EDGE

"We need a civilization that can live fully and creatively together with wildness. We must start growing it right here, in the New World."

—Gary Snyder, *The Practice of the Wild*

Sigurd Olson was right when he slipped that sheet of paper in his Royal typewriter on January 13, 1982, and typed one line. A new adventure *is* coming up.

For all of wild nature, we hope it will be a good one.

There are positive signs as we head toward the end of the century. The United States, for starters, has a Wilderness Preservation System that was enacted in 1964 by President Lyndon Johnson when he signed Public Law 88-577: the Wilderness Act. He was, one might say, forced to do it. Movement for such an Act, designed to put federal protection around chunks of wild country, had been brewing for over thirty years, but it was the 1950 Dinosaur National Monument battle that put full political pressure up at the top.

The battle revolved around a dam that the Bureau of Reclamation proposed to build on the Colorado-Utah border in Dinosaur National Monument. Millions of Americans, having sought solace and beauty in the outdoors after World War II, weren't going to stand for it. Conservationists pitted themselves against developers. Pamphlets, books, and features in *Life*, *Reader's Digest*, and *Newsweek* highlighted the controversy. Visionaries like Sigurd Olson, Olaus Murie, Wallace Stegner, Chief Justice

231

William O. Douglas, and the Wilderness Society's Howard Zahniser appealed to America's need for natural beauty and the inspiration of untamed lands. Statistical data was slammed around. Politicking intensified. Hundreds of state and national conservation and preservation organizations banded together. And the dam was stopped.

Wilderness preservationists immediately took the offensive.

They prevailed upon Minnesota senator Hubert Humphrey and Pennsylvania representative John Saylor in 1956 to introduce bills "to secure for the American people of present and future generations the benefits of an enduring reservoir of wilderness." For the next eight years, as the echoes of Thoreau, Muir, Marshall, Leopold, Murie, and Olson ricocheted in corridors, chambers, and committee meetings, debate over a wilderness bill was incessant. There were eighteen public hearings, sixty-five drafts of a bill, and thousands of pages of testimony.

"We are not slowing down a force that inevitably will destroy all the wilderness there is," Zahniser told wilderness activists. "We are generating another force, never to be wholly spent, that, renewed generation after generation, will be always effective in preserving wilderness. We are not fighting progress. We are making it."

When President Johnson finally signed the Wilderness Act, fifty-four areas totaling over nine million acres became the core of the nation's (and world's) unprecedented Wilderness Preservation System. The System continued to grow over the next thirty years until today, due largely to the 1980 Alaska National Interest Lands Conservation Act, it includes approximately 477 units totaling 91 million acres. Thirty-two million of these acres are in the lower forty-eight states. Impressive. Yet even counting Alaska, less than 4% of the entire American landscape has been given legal protection.

Along the way, as one wilderness area was fought over after another, no word was more important nor, ironically, more subjective, hence ambiguous and confusing, than *wilderness* itself. The word generated more debate than any other aspect of the Wilderness Act, and is still under fire. The old etymological Teutonic and Norse roots of *wilderness*, referring to a place of wild beasts and forests uninhabited by man, have slowly given way to all manner of meanings. They vary from a geographical place to a *quality* of a place produced by a feeling (freedom? the power of natural forces? physical challenge? isolation? the elements of risk and adventure?) rooted in a mix of place and human subjective response. As Roderick Nash says in *Wilderness and the American Mind*, the word *wilderness* is "so heavily freighted with meaning of a personal, symbolic and changing kind as to resist easy definition."

Still, good lawyers that they were, legislators of the Wilderness Act had to come up with a working definition:

"A wilderness, in contrast with those areas where man and his own works dominate the landscape, is hereby recognized as an area where the earth and its community of life are untrammeled by man, where man himself is a visitor who does not remain. An area of wilderness is further defined to mean... an area of undeveloped Federal land retaining its primeval character and influence, without permanent improvements of human habitation, which is protected and managed so as to preserve its natural conditions and which (1) generally appears to have been affected primarily by the forces of nature, with the imprint of man's work substantially unnoticeable; (2) has outstanding opportunities for solitude or a primitive and unconfined type of recreation; [and] (3) has at least five thousand acres of land and is of sufficient size as to make practicable its preservation and use in an unimpaired condition..."

There is more wild country, of course, than there is *designated* wilderness. Designation is a legal application of status with attendant management philosophy and practice. Wildness itself blooms from the earth and exists, to various degrees, in many places outside the Wilderness Preservation System. Hence the many, scattered, ongoing wilderness battles as American culture determines how to best use its remaining natural lands.

Howie Wolke, in *Wilderness on the Rocks*, estimates there are about 80 million American acres (excluding Alaska) outside the Wilderness Preservation System that *could* fit the criteria of the Wilderness Act. This land, together with designated wilderness, comprises a total wilderness resource base of 167 million acres in the contiguous forty-eight states.

And what is the statistical status of wilderness worldwide?

Who, really, knows?

In 1987, however, on behalf of the fourth World Wilderness Congress, the Sierra Club did a world wilderness inventory of areas of a million acres or more showing no development. A third of the earth, it turns out, is still relatively wild. About 42% of the earth's remaining wilderness is in the high Arctic and Antarctica, with Antarctica and Greenland nearly all wilderness. Twenty percent of the world's wild country consists of warm deserts, mostly in Africa, while 38% (13% of earth's total landmass) exists in temperate regions, the tropics, and in a few mixed mountain regions.

This doesn't mean that the inventoried areas, showing no development, are pristine in the prehistorical sense of the word. As Bill McKibben says in *The End of Nature*, gases and other outflowages of human civilization are spreading all over the globe. Riding wind and water. Interesting chemicals, in other words, are falling on the fragile mosses and lichens of the high Arctic. What those chemicals are doing to plants and ecological food chains is anyone's guess, but they are—like industrial humanity's effect on global climate—leaving human signature.

Pristine or not, wilderness and its cultural defense has taken an interesting turn since the days of John Muir and Bob Marshall who, one suspects, would barely recognize today's debate. Preserving wild country is no longer simply a matter of putting a boundary line around a natural area and setting it aside for hunting, hiking, canoeing, or shooting photos. The significance of wilderness, and the issues surrounding that significance, are changing, and we should have all seen it coming when Leopold began pointing out wild country's scientific and ecological values.

"One could argue," Dave Foreman remarked in his 1991 essay, "The New

Conservation Movement," "that the evolution of the conservation movement's arguments form the '70s to the '90s recapitulated the personal evolution of Aldo Leopold."

Like Leopold, who moved from a recreational appreciation of wild country to a scientific one, today's wilderness preservationists are moving toward a centralizing recognition that wild country is critically important to global biodiversity. Thus, as Foreman says, wilderness protection is being reframed from an aesthetic and utilitarian issue to an ecological one. In short, wilderness areas are important because of their diverse species. The larger the wilderness, the more diverse the species. The more biodiversity, the healthier the earth's ecological pyramids.

This is good for people. It might also be an innate, biocentric right of nature itself. Worth compassionately defending. Worth fighting for.

"Our job is to argue for the natural world," Foreman says of preservationists who share such a view. "We speak for Wolf."

Biologists, meanwhile, are discovering that *islands* of biodiversity are not sufficient. It is not enough to just have parks, refuges and isolated wilderness areas as piecemeal units in an overall land protection system. For the greatest flow, or interchange, of biodiversity, it will be necessary in the future to establish biological corridors, or linkage zones, between the units that will permit full species movement throughout biogeographical regions. This will involve many ongoing land management battles, based on hard science, and a cultural acknowledgment that wilderness areas and parks are essentially core preserves in an *unfinished* North American system of linked ecological preserves.

Just as science has begun to change the dynamic of land designation and management, there has been an equally significant change in how people are using park and wilderness resources. We are, it seems, bringing our technology with us. In doing so, we are altering the wilderness "experience" as Muir and Marshall et al. knew it, and we need to ask ourselves how and why.

One of the most interesting analyses, and profoundly important statements, in this regard is Guy and Laura Waterman's 1993 book, *Wilderness Ethics: Preserving the Spirit of Wildness*. The Watermans, who live on a twenty-seven acre homestead in Vermont, have long been associated with hiking, mountain climbing, and outdoor writing. They've covered the miles: they are not spring chickens: and they've watched as technology has begun to infiltrate the boundaries of wilderness areas.

"Without underestimating for a moment the importance of physical preservation [of wilderness]," they say, "we venture the opinion that the intangible or spiritual side of wilderness is also important—and even more in jeopardy."

In the past, for example, one of the intangible values of a wilderness experience was the sense of remoteness and isolation, the "barrier of silence," that surrounded the adventure and accentuated its risk, heightening the challenge. "Getting away from it all," gaining psychological space, counted. So did the chance of *no rescue*. Such being-out-of-touch, Watermans add, was not "a small added spice, but a vital ingredient, an essential condition to adventure, a *sine qua non* for the spirit of wildness."

This is changing with communications technology. Radios are being used for daily contact on expeditions, and cellular phones and battery-powered TVs are turning outdoor adventures into techno-romp-arounds.

What happens to the sense of solitude when, with a button, you can tie yourself back to technological civilization? or when you can call 911?

Watermans tell of a lost hiker with a battery-powered TV who, for several days, watched reports of rescuers looking for him. There was also a lost hiker in California who used a cellular phone to call his wife who, in turn, notified the U.S. Forest Service which sent a helicopter to find him. The rescue, we suppose, was good for the man and his wife, but was a *helicopter* rescue necessary? What about the backcountry hikers who had to see and hear the helicopter chop by, anchoring them back to time? What did the man, with his cellular phone, learn about risk and wild space? And who should pay for all of this technological rescue ruckus anyway?

"Cellular phones," Watermans are convinced, "pose a threat to wildness that should be taken seriously right now."

The real issue: What forms of technology are compatible with the backcountry experience we want to preserve?

There are global positioning systems (GPSs) to think about: Do they add to, or subtract from, the timeless challenge of wilderness navigation? What about bicycles? Do they belong in wild country? And what will we have to say about the inevitable one person flying machines?

Watermans raise many other questions in their examination of wilderness ethics, yet none, not even communications technology, is as critical or timely as aircraft. Wilderness is *sonic* as well as visual and tactile. What happens to the feeling or spirit of a wild place, no matter how remote, when a military bomber on a training mission passes overhead at treetop level, shaking the ground with its rumbling power? or when a fighter jet splits the sound barrier in a mock dogfight with another jet at 10,000 feet?

The eyes leave the flower or ice crystal and see the Gulf War.

This is exactly what is happening in many parts of alleged wild America. Small planes, too, whether buzzing Devil's Tower, touring the Grand Canyon, or setting one of us down in the Brooks Range, are part of a growing wilderness dilemma. According to a *New York Times* survey, ninety national parks and monuments, or a quarter of all the units in the national park system, report problems with aircraft. For good reason the National Park Service and Forest Service are doing a study.

If wilderness is more than a boundaried natural place, as Roderick Nash and Watermans claim, and if it has, in fact, several dimensions of experience loosely termed "intangible" or "spiritual," then we must also implicate our wilderness managers and biologists. At what point do boardwalks, developed trails, and regulations impose on the experience of wildness visitors aspire toward? To what extent should the hand of well-meaning agency people reach? What is gained in wildness by withholding that hand? As for biological studies of wilderness wildlife, do they go too far when they result in brightly ribboned trails and enclosures, radio-collared wolves and bears, spray-numbered animals, blood tests, tranquilizations, and the pulling of teeth?

"Is there left any cold far waste," Watermans ask in exasperated but singing prose, "where no motor drones and no scientific progress is made, where man is not doing any beast any favors, where some great white animal pads silently its solitary way under a sky full of stars, alone?"

Yes, we can fortunately assure Watermans and ourselves. Despite all the questions and challenges, and the new ones to come, and thanks to our wilderness visionaries, there are still such places.

Out there.

On the wildest edge.

OF TIME AND SPACE:
A CHRONOLOGICAL VIEW

1817—Henry David Thoreau born

1834—Ralph Waldo Emerson moves to Concord, Massachusetts

1837—John Burroughs born

1838—John Muir born

1841—Thoreau begins studying Oriental books

1845—Thoreau moves to Walden Pond

1846—Thoreau climbs Mt. Katahdin

1847—Thoreau leaves Walden Pond

1849—Thoreau's *A Week on the Concord and Merrimack Rivers* published

1849—Muir emigrates to U.S. with his father

1851—Thoreau lectures on "The Wild" in Concord

1853—Thoreau's Chesuncook canoe trip

1854—Thoreau's *Walden* published

1857—Thoreau explores Penobscot River's East Branch by canoe

1859—Muir begins his fascination with machinery

1861—Thoreau visits Minnesota

1862—Thoreau dies

1864—Muir roams Ontario's woods and bogs, finds *Calypso borealis*

1867—Muir injures eye, then hikes 1,000 miles to Gulf of Mexico

1868—Muir embraces California's Sierra-Nevadas

1869—Muir begins writing for publication

1871—Muir and Emerson meet in Yosemite

1879—Muir canoes to Glacier Bay, Alaska

1887—Aldo Leopold born

1889—Olaus Johan Murie born

1889—Muir meets *Century's* Robert Underwood Johnson

1889—Muir makes 10-day solo trip on Alaskan glaciers

1892—Muir and others found Sierra Club

1893—Muir meets Burroughs, visits Thoreau's grave

1894—Muir's *Mountains of California* published

1895—Calvin Rutstrum born in Indiana

1896—National Forestry Commission appointed to survey U.S. forest reserves

1896—Robert Service emigrates from Scotland to Canada

1899—Sigurd F. Olson born

1901—Muir publishes *Our National Parks*

1902—Bob Marshall born in New York City

1903—Muir and Pres. Theodore Roosevelt camp together in Yosemite

1908—Muir begins fighting Hetch Hetchy dam

1911—Service canoes McKenzie River to Yukon River and Dawson City

1913—Rutstrum canoes Minnesota's Big Fork River en route to Deer Lake

1914—Muir dies

1914—Murie explores James Bay of Hudson Bay

1916—National Park Service established

1919—Leopold and Arthur Carhart meet in Denver

1920—Murie begins Alaska-Yukon caribou studies

1921—Leopold publishes "The Wilderness and Its Place in Forest Recreation Policy"

1923—Olson begins guiding in Quetico-Superior

1925—Leopold publishes "Wilderness as a Form of Land Use"

1927—Murie begins elk studies

1929—Marshall visits Wiseman, Alaska, and Brooks Range for first time

1930—Marshall's "The Problem of the Wilderness" is published

1930—Olson writes Oberholtzer approving Quetico-Superior park plan

1930—Marshall lives in Wiseman and explores Brooks Range

1932—Olson publishes "Search for the Wild"

1933—Marshall's *Arctic Village* and *The People's Forests* published

1933—Leopold publishes "The Conservation Ethic"

1935—Marshall and friends start the Wilderness Society

1937—Marshall publishes "The Universe of the Wilderness is Vanishing"

1937—Marshall appointed head of Forest Service's Div. of Recreation & Lands

1937—Marshall canoes in Quetico-Superior with Sig Olson

1938—Marshall explores headwaters of Koyukuk River in Brooks Range

1939—Marshall dies

1941—Leopold publishes "Wilderness as a Land Laboratory"

1945—Murie becomes director of The Wilderness Society

1946—Olson publishes "We Need Wilderness"

1947—Olson becomes consultant to the Quetico-Superior Council

1947—Olson becomes wilderness ecologist for Izaak Walton League

1948—Olson publishes "The Preservation of Wilderness"

1948—Leopold dies fighting a grass fire

1949—Air ban established over Superior National Forest's roadless areas

1949—Leopold's *A Sand County Almanac and Sketches Here and There* published

1953—Olson guides Grace Lee Nute in Quetico Park

1956—Olson publishes *The Singing Wilderness* and canoes Churchill River

1956—Murie leads scientific expedition into eastern Brooks Range

1956—Humphrey/Saylor introduce wilderness bill

1960—Arctic National Wildlife Range established

1961—Olson presents "The Spiritual Aspects of Wilderness" to Sierra Club's
          7th Wilderness Conference

1963—Murie dies

1964—U.S. Congress passes Wilderness Act

1969—Olson publishes *Open Horizons*

1975—Rutstrum publishes *The Wilderness Life*

1976—Olson publishes *Reflections From the North Country*

1979—Rutstrum publishes *A Wilderness Autobiography*

1980—Alaska National Interest Lands Conservation Act

1982—Olson and Rutstrum die

SELECTED BIBLIOGRAPHIES

CHAPTER ONE
HENRY DAVID THOREAU: ILLUMINATIONS OF A WALKER

Bode, Carl, Ed., *The Best of Thoreau's Journals,* Carbondale, Southern Illinois University Press, 1967, 1971.

Canby, Henry Selidel, *Thoreau, Boston*, Houghton Mifflin Co., 1939.

Channing, William Ellery, Thoreau: *The Poet-Naturalist*, New York, Biblo and Tanner, first published 1902.

Flanagan, John T., "Thoreau in Minnesota," *Minnesota History*, Vol. 16, March 1935.

Friesen, Victor Carl, *The Spirit of the Huckleberry: Sensuosness in Henry Thoreau*, University of Alberta Press, 1984.

Harding, Walter, *The Days of Henry Thoreau*, New York, Alfred A. Knopf, 1966; revised and updated hardcover edition: Princeton University Press, 1983; revised and updated paperback edition: New York, Dover Books.

—, *Henry David Thoreau: A Profile*, Hill and Wang, 1971.

—, ed., *In the Woods and Fields of Concord, Selections From the Journals of Henry David Thoreau*, Salt Lake City, Gibbs M. Smith, Inc., 1982.

—, *A Thoreau Handbook*, New York University Press, 1959, 1961.

—, and Carl Bode, *The Correspondence of Henry David Thoreau*, New York University Press, 1958.

—, and Michael Meyer, *The New Thoreau Handbook*, New York University Press, 1980.

Huber, J. Parker, *The Wildest Country: A Guide to Thoreau's Maine*, Boston, Appalachian Mountain Club, 1981.

Krutch, Joseph Wood, *Henry David Thoreau*, New York, William Sloane, 1948.

Lebeaux, Richard, *Young Man Thoreau*, University of Massachusetts Press, 1977.

McIntosh, James, *Thoreau as Romantic Naturalist; His Shifting Stance Toward Nature*, Ithaca, Cornell University Press, 1974.

Meltzer, Milton and Walter Harding, *A Thoreau Profile*, The Thoreau Foundation, Inc., 1962.

Paul, Sherman, *The Shores of America: Thoreau's Inward Exploration*, Urbana, The University of Illinois Press, 1958.

Salt, Henry S., *Life of Henry David Thoreau*, Archon Books, 1968; first published, 1890.

Sanborn, Franklin B., *The Life of Henry David Thoreau,* Houghton Mifflin Co., 1917; republished by Gale Research Co., Book Tower, Detroit, 1968.

—, *The Personality of Thoreau*, Folcraft Press, Inc., 1901.

Selected Bibliographies

Stowall, Robert F., *A Thoreau Gazetteer,* ed. by William L. Howarth, Princeton University Press, 1970.

Swanson, E.B., "The Manuscript Journal of Thoreau's Last Journey," Minnesota History, vol 20, June 1939.

Thoreau, Henry David, *Cape Cod*, Thomas Y. Crowell Co., 1961.

—, *Excursions*, New York, Corinth Books, 1962.

—, *Journal*, ed. Bradford Torrey and Francis H. Allen, New York, Dover Publications, 14 vols. in 2 books, 1962.

—, *The Journal of Henry David Thoreau*, intro. by Walter Harding, Salt Lake City, Gibbs M. Smith, Inc., 15 vols. pb., 1984.

—, *The Maine Woods*, ed. by Joseph J. Moldenhauer, New Jersey, Princeton University Press, 1972.

—, *Natural History Essays*, Salt Lake City, Gibbs M. Smith, Inc., 1980.

—, *Walden*, with intro. essay, "Down the River with Henry Thoreau by Edward Abbey", Salt Lake City, Gibbs M. Smith, Inc., 1981.

—, *Walden and Other Writings*, New York, Garden City, International Collectors Library, 1970.

—, *A Week on the Concord and Merrimack Rivers*, Thomas Y. Crowell Co., 1961.

—, *The Writings of Henry David Thoreau*, New York, AMS Press, 20 vols., 1968.

Van Doren, Mark, *The Portable Emerson*, New York, The Viking Press, 1946.

Wagenknecht, Edward, *Henry David Thoreau*, What Manner of Man?, Amherst, University of Massachusetts Press, 1981.

Wolf, William J., *Thoreau: Mystic, Prophet, Ecologist*, Philadelphia, United Church Press, 1974.

CHAPTER TWO
JOHN MUIR: FOOTLOOSE IN RANGES OF LIGHT

Bade, William Frederic, *The Life and Letters of John Muir*, 2 vols., Houghton Mifflin, 1924.

Barrus, CIara, *The Life and Letters of John Burroughs,* Houghton Mifflin, 1925.

Brooks, Paul, *Speaking For Nature*, Houghton Mifflin, 1980.

Clarke, James Mitchell, *The Life and Adventures of John Muir*, San Diego, The Word Shop, 1979.

Cohen, Michael P., *The Pathless Way: John Muir and American Wilderness*, University of Wisconsin Press, 1984.

Davis, Millard C., "The Influence of Emerson, Thoreau, and Whitman on the Early American Naturalists—John Muir and John Burroughs," The Living Wilderness, Vol . 39, 1966-67, p. 18-23.

Foerster, Norman, *Nature in American Literature*, Macmillan Co., 1923.

Fox, Stephen, *John Muir and His Legacy*, Little, Brown and Co., 1981.

Kimes, Maymie B. and William F., *John Muir: A Reading Bibliography*, Palo Alto, William P. Wrendon, 1978.

Muir, John, *Mountaineering Essays*, Gibbs M. Smith, Inc., 1984.

—, *My First Summer in the Sierra*, Houghton Mifflin, 1911.

—, *Our National Parks*, Houghton Mifflin, 1901.

—, *Steep Trails*, ed. William Frederic Bade, Houghton Mifflin, 1918.

—, *The Story of My Boyhood and Youth*, Houghton Mifflin, 1912.

—, *A Thousand-Mile Walk to the Gulf*, Houghton Mifflin, 1916.

—, *Travels in Alaska*, Houghton Mifflin, 1915.

—, "The Wild Parks and Forest Reservations of the West," Atlantic Monthly, vol. 81. 1898.

—, *Wilderness Essays*, Peregrine Smith Books, Inc., 1980.

Peck, Robert McCracken, "A Cruise for Rest and Recreation," (about the Harriman Expedition to Alaska) *Audubon*, Sept., 1982, p. 86-99.

Seaborg, Eric, "The Battle for Hetch Hetchy," Sierra, Nov.-Dec. 1981, p. 61-65.

Teale, Edwin Way, *The Wilderness World of John Muir*, excerpts with commentary, Houghton Mifflin, 1954.

Watkins, T.H., with photos by Dewitt Jones, *John Muir's America*, New York, Crown Publishers, 1976.

Wolfe, Linnie Marsh, *John of the Mountains; The Unpublished Journals of John Muir*, Houghton Mifflin, 1938; reprinted by University of Wisconsin Press, 1979.

Wolfe, Linnie Marsh, *Son of the Wilderness: The Life of John Muir*, New York, Alfred A. Knopf, Inc., 1945; reprinted by University of Wisconsin Press, 1978.

CHAPTER THREE
ROBERT W. SERVICE: THE WILD TRANSFORMATION

Klinck, Carl F., *Robert Service: A Biography*, New York, Dodd, Mead and Company, Inc. (DMCo.), 1976.

Service, Robert W., *Ballads of a Cheechako*, DMCo., 1917.

—, *The Collected Poems of Robert Service*, DMCo., 1940.

—, *Harper of Heaven*, DMCo., 1948.

—, *Ploughman of the Moon: An Adventure Into Memory*, DMCo., 1945.

—, *Rhymes of a Rolling Stone*, DMCo., 1912.

—, *The Spell of the Yukon*, DMCo., 1915.

CHAPTER FOUR
BOB MARSHALL: FROM KNOLLWOOD TO ALASKA'S KOYUKUK

Bach, Orville E., "Elder of the Tribe: Bob Marshall," *Backpacker*, Summer 1974, p. 94-101.

Edwards, Mike, "A Short Hike with Bob Marshall," *National Geographic*, May 1985, p. 664-689.

Fox, Stephen, *John Muir and His Legacy: The American Conservation Movement*, 1981. Boston-Toronto, Little Brown & Co., 206-212.

—, "We Want No Straddlers," *Wilderness*, Winter 1984, 4-19.

Glover, James and Regina, "Robert Marshall: Portrait of a Liberal Forester," *Journal of Forest History*, July 1986, p. 112-19.

Glover, Jim, "The First Forty-Sixers," Adirondack Life, Jan./Feb. 1985, p. 17-23.

A Wilderness Original: The Life of Bob Marshall, 1986, Seattle, The Mountaineers Press.

Marshall, George, "Bibliography of Robert Marshall: A Supplement," *Living Wilderness*, Summer 1954, 31-35.

SELECTED BIBLIOGRAPHIES

—, "Bob Marshall and the Alaska Arctic Wilderness," *Living Wilderness*, Autumn 1970, p. 29-32.

—, "On Bob Marshall's Landmark Article," *Living Wilderness*, Oct./Dec. 1976, p. 28-30 (followed by a reprint of Bob's "The Problem of the Wilderness").

—, "Robert Marshall as a Writer," *Living Wilderness*, Autumn 1951, 14-23 (includes an extensive bibliography of Bob's books, articles, booklets, letters, reviews of Bob's books, and biographical sources about Bob).

Marshall, Robert, *Alaska Wilderness: Exploring the Central Brooks Range*, ed. with introductions by George Marshall, second edition, Berkeley, (the first edition was published as *Arctic Wilderness*) University of Calfornia Press, 1970.

—, *Arctic Village*, New York, Harrison Smith and Robert Haas, 1933.

—, "Impressions From the Wilderness," Living Wilderness, Autumn 1951, p. 10-13.

—, *The People's Forests*, New York, Harrison Smith and Robert Haas, 1933.

—, "The Problem of the Wilderness," Scientific Monthly, Feb. 1930, p. 141-148.

—, "The Universe of the Wilderness is Vanishing," *Nature Magazine*, April 1937, p. 235-240.

Mitchell, John G., "In Wildness Was the Preservation of a Smile," *Wilderness*, Summer 1985, p. 10-21.

Nash, Roderick, "The Strenuous Life of Bob Marshall," *Forest History*, Oct. 1966, p. 18-25.

—, *Wilderness and the American Mind*, New Haven and London, Yale University Press, p. 200-208.

Olson, Sigurd, "Quetico-Superior Elegy," *Living Wilderness*, Spring 1948, p. 5-12.

CHAPTER FIVE
ALDO LEOPOLD: WITNESS AT THE BREAK OF DAY

Bailey, Liberty Hyde, *The Holy Earth*, New York, 1915.

Bradley, Harold C., "Aldo Leopold: Champion of the Wilderness," *Sierra Club Bulletin*, May 1951, p. 14-18.

Brown, David E. and Neil B. Carmony, *Aldo Leopold's Wilderness: Selected Early Writings by the Author of A Sand County Almanac*, Stackpole Books, 1990.

Callicott, J. Baird, *Companion to A Sand County Almanac: Interpretive and Critical Essays*, University of Wisconsin Press, 1987.

Elder, John, "Hunting in Sand County," Orion, Autumn 1986, p. 46-53.

Errington, Paul L., "In Appreciation of Aldo Leopold," Journal of Wildlife Management, October 1948, p. 341-50.

Flader, Susan L., "Aldo Leopold and the Wilderness Idea," Living Wilderness, December 1979, p. 4-8.

— and J. Baird Callicott, eds., *The River of the Mother of God and Other Essays by Aldo Leopold*, University of Wisconsin Press, 1991.

— and Charles Steinhacker, *The Sand County of Aldo Leopold*, Sierra Club Books, 1973.

—, Thinking Like a Mountain: *Aldo Leopold and the Evolution of an Ecological Attitude Toward Deer, Wolves, and Forests*, Columbia: University of Missouri Press, 1974.

Fox, Stephen, *John Muir and His Legacy: The American Conservation Movement*, Little, Brown & Co., 1981. (Reprinted in 1986 as *The American Conservation Movement: John Muir and His Legacy*, (University of Wisconsin Press.)

Gibbons, Boyd, "Aldo Leopold: A Durable Scale of Values," *National Geographic*, November 1981, p. 682-708.

Hendee, John C. with Robert C. Lucas and George H. Stankey, *Wilderness Management*, U.S. Forest

Service, Misc. Publication No. 1365, 1978.

Leopold, Aldo, *A Sand County Almanac and Sketches Here and There*, Oxford University Press, 1949; original edition in paperback, OUP, 1968; enlarged paperback edition, *A Sand County Almanac: With Essays on Conservation from Round River*, Sierra Club and Ballantine Books, 1970.

—, "A Biotic View of Land," *Journal of Forestry*, September 1939, p. 727-30.

—, "Conservation Esthetic," *Bird-Lore*, March 1938.

—, "The Conservation Ethic," *Journal of Forestry*, October 1933, p. 634-43.

—, "Conservationist in Mexico," *American Forests*, March 1937.

—, "Conserving the Covered Wagon," *Sunset Magazine,* March 1925, p. 21, 56.

—, "The Ecological Conscience," *Bulletin of the Garden Club of America*, September 1947, p. 45-53.

—, "Forestry and Game Conservation," *Journal of Forestry*, April 1918.

—, *Game Management*, Charles Scribner's Sons, 1933.

—, "Game Management in the National Forests," *American Forests*, July 1930.

—, "The Last Stand of the Wilderness," *American Forests and Forest Life*, October 1925, p. 599-604.

—, "Naturschutz in Germany," *Bird-Lore*, March-April 1936.

—, "Origins and Ideals of Wilderness Areas," *Living Wilderness,* July 1940, p. 7.

—, "A Plea for Wilderness Hunting Grounds," *Outdoor Life*, November 1925.

—, "Some Fundamentals of Conservation in the Southwest," *Environmental Ethics*, Summer 1979, p. 131-41.

—, "Threatened Species," *American Forests*, March 1936.

—, "Why the Wilderness Society," *Living Wilderness*, I, 1935, p. 6.

—, and Olaus Murie, "Wilderness and Aircraft," *Living Wilderness*, Autumn 1947, p. 1-6.

—, "The Wilderness and Its Place in Forest Recreation Policy," *Journal of Forestry*, November 1921, p. 718-21.

—, "Wilderness as a Form of Land Use," *Journal of Land and Public Utility Economics*, October 1925, p. 398-404.

—, "Wilderness as a Land Laboratory," *Living Wilderness*, July 1941, p. 3.

—, "Wilderness Values," *Living Wilderness*, March 1942, p. 24-25.

Leopold, Luna B., ed., *Round River: From the Journals of Aldo Leopold*, Oxford University Press, 1953. Paperback, 1972.

Lime, Dave, ed., *Managing America's Enduring Wilderness Resource*, St. Paul: Minnesota Extension Service, 1990. (See "Let the Fire Devil Have His Due: Aldo Leopold and the Conundrum of Wilderness Management," 88-95.)

Meine, Curt, *Aldo Leopold: His Life and Work*, University of Wisconsin Press, 1988. (The definitive biography of Leopold, circa 1994; includes extensive bibliography.)

Nash, Roderick, *Wilderness and the American Mind,* Yale University Press, 1973. Reprinted 1982.

Oelschlaeger, Max, ed., The *Wilderness Condition: Essays in Environment and Civilization*, Sierra Club Books, 1991. (See especially Curt Meine's "The Utility of Preservation and the Preservation of Utility.")

Ouspensky, Pyotr D., *Tertium Organum: The Third Canon of Thought, A Key to the Enigma of the World*, Knopf, 1925, 1981.

Schoenfeld, Clay, "Aldo Leopold Remembered," *Audubon*, May 1978, p. 28-37.

SELECTED BIBLIOGRAPHIES

Stegner, Wallace, "Living On Our Principal," *Wilderness*, Spring, 1985, p. 5-21.

Tanner, Thomas, ed., *Aldo Leopold: The Man and His Legacy*, Ankeny, Iowa: Soil Conservation Society of America, 1987.

Wild, Peter, *Pioneer Conservationists of Western America*, Mountain Press, 1979.

FILM

Meyer, Ronald C., *Aldo Leopold: A Prophet for All Seasons*, videotape, 56 min., a Metabases Production, distributed by NorthWord Press, Inc., Box 1360, Minocqua, Wisconsin 54548.

CHAPTER SIX
OLAUS JOHAN MURIE: EMBRACING THE WILD PULSE OF LIFE

Clepper, Henry, ed., *Leaders of American Conservation*, New York, The Ronald Press Co., 1971.

Curry, Peggy Simson, "Portrait of a Naturalist," *Audubon*, Nov.-Dec., 1963.

Glover, James and Regina, "The Natural Magic of Olaus Murie," Sierra, Sept.-Oct., 1987, p. 69-73. (James Glover, as of 1994, was working on a book-length biography of Murie.)

Miller, Debbie S., *Midnight Wilderness: Journeys in Alaska's Arctic National Wildlife Refuge*, San Francisco, Sierra Club Books, 1990.

Murie, Adolph, *A Naturalist in Alaska*, New York, Devin-Adair Co., 1961.

Murie, Margaret E., "Return to the Sheenjek," *The Living Wilderness*, Vol., 41, No. 138, July-Sept. 1977, 4-12.

—, *Two in the Far North*, New York, Alfred A. Knopf, 1963. Second edition: Alaska Northwest Publishing Company.

—, and Olaus, *Wapiti Wilderness*, New York, Alfred A. Knopf, 1966.

Murie, Olaus J., *Alaska-Yukon Caribou*, U.S. Department of Agriculture, Bureau of Biological Survey, 1935.

—, *The Elk of North America*, The Stackpole Company and the Wildlife Management Institute, 1951.

—, *Fauna of the Aleutian Islands and Alaska Peninsula*, and Victor B. Scheffer, *Invertebrates and Fishes Collected in the Aleutians*, U.S. Fish and Wildlife Service, Washington, D.C., 1959.

—, *A Field Guide to Animal Tracks*, Boston, Houghton Mifflin, second edition, 1975.

—, "A Good Life," address before the Annual Convention of the American Association for Health, Physical Education and Recreation, at Missoula, Montana, April 30, 1963.

—, *Jackson Hole With a Naturalist*, Jackson Hole, Frontier Press, 1963.

—, *Journeys to the Far North*, The Wilderness Society and American West Publishing Company, 1973.

—, "Our Wilderness," *Atlantic Naturalist*, Vol. 8, No. 1, Sept.-Oct., 1952.

—, "Scientific and Esthetic Values of Wilderness," Fifth World Forestry Conference, Seattle, Washington, Aug. 29-Sept. 10, 1960

—, "Wilderness Philosophy, Science, and the Arctic National Wildlife Range," an address presented at the Twelfth Alaskan Science Conference as part of the Symposium: Science and the Arctic National Wildlife Range.

—, Untitled address before the Arizona-Sonora Section, American Society of Range Management, at Nogales, Arizona, January 17, 1963.

Poole, A.L., ed., *Preliminary Reports of the New Zealand-American Fiordland Expedition*, New Zealand Department of Scientific and Industrial Research, Bulletin 103, Wellington, N.Z., R. E. Owen, Government Printer, 1951.

Wild, Peter, *Pioneer Conservationists of Western America*, Mountain Press, 1979.

Zahniser, Howard, "Olaus J. Murie, 1889-1963," *The Living Wilderness*, Summer-Fall 1963, p. 3-14.

CHAPTER SEVEN
CALVIN RUTSTRUM: ROLLING STONE OF WATERWAYS

Rutstrum, Calvin, *Back Country*, Pittsboro, Indiana, ICS Books, Inc., 1981.

—, *Chips From a Wilderness Log*, New York, Stein and Day, 1978.

—, *A Columnist Looks at Life*, Minneapolis, Nodin Press, 1981.

—, *Hiking Back to Health*, Pittsboro, Indiana, ICS Books, Inc., 1980.

—, *The New Way of the Wilderness*, New York, Macmillan Co., 1958.

—, *North American Canoe Country*, New York, Macmillan Co., 1964.

—, *Once Upon a Wilderness*, New York, Macmillan Co..1973.

—, *Paradise Below Zero*, New York, Macmillan Co., 1968.

—, A *Wilderness Autobiography*, Minneapolis, Nodin Press, 1979. (Originally published as *Challenge of the Wilderness*, T.S. Dennison and Co., 1970).

—, *The Wilderness Cabin*, New York, Macmillan Co., 1961.

—, *The Wilderness Life*, New York, Macmillan Co.. 1975.

—, *The Wilderness Route Finder*, New York, Macmillan Co., 1967.

CHAPTER EIGHT
SIGURD F. OLSON: VISIONARY VOYAGEUR

Frome, Michael, *Promised Land; Adventures and Encounters in Wild America*, New York, William Morrow and Company, Inc., 1985, p. 139-154.

Graham, Frank, "Leave it to the Bourgeois," *Audubon*, Nov. 1980, p. 35f.

Huyck, D.B.. "Sig Olson: Wilderness Philosopher," *American Forests,* May 1965, p. 46f.

Link, Mike, ed., *The Collected Works of Sigurd F. Olson: The Early Writing: 1921-1934*, Voyageur Press, 1988.

Olson, Sigurd F, with photos by Les Blacklock, Hidden Forest, New York, Viking Press, 1969.

—, "The Intangible Values of Wilderness," *National Parks Magazine*, July-Sept. 1954, p. 99f.

—, *Listening Point*, New York. Alfred A. Knopf, Inc., 1980.

—, *The Lonely Land,* New York, Alfred A. Knopf, Inc., 1961.

—, *Of Time and Place*. New York, Alfred A. Knopf, Inc.. 1982.

—, *Open Horizons*, New York, Alfred A. Knopf, Inc., 1969.

—, "The Preservation of Wilderness," *The Living Wilderness*, Autumn 1948, p. 1-8.

—, *Reflections From the North Country*, New York, Alfred A. Knopf, Inc., 1976.

—, *Runes of the North*, New York, Alfred A. Knopf, Inc., 1963.

—, *Sigurd F Olson's Wilderness Days*, New York, Alfred A. Knopf. Inc., 1972.

Selected Bibliographies

__, *The Singing Wilderness*, New York, Alfred A. Knopf, Inc., 1979.

__, "The Spiritual Aspects of Wilderness," in *Voices for the Wilderness,* ed. William Schwarz, New York, Ballantine Books, 1969.

__, "We Need Wilderness," *National Parks Magazine,* Jan.-Mar. 1946, p. 18f.

__, "Why Wilderness?" *American Forests,* Sept. 1938.

Pyter, Bernadette, "A Bio-Bibliography of Sigurd F Olson," Master's thesis, University of Minnesota, 1972.

Searle, R. Newell, *Saving Quetico-Superior: A Land Set Apart*, Minnesota Historical Society, 1977.

Vickery, Jim dale, "A Bluejay Calling: A Conversation With Sigurd F. Olson," *Canoe,* Jan.-Feb. 1980, p. 16f.

FILM

Christenson, Ray and Steve Kahlenbeck, *The Wilderness World of Sigurd F. Olson*, 16mm or videotape, 28 min., Filmedia, Inc., 10740 Lyndale Ave. South, Minneapolis, MN 55420.967.

EPILOGUE
THE WILDEST EDGE

Allin, Craig W., *The Politics of Wilderness Preservation*, Greenwood Press, 1982

Berry, Thomas, *The Dream of the Earth*, Sierra Club Books, 1988.

Devall, Bill, and George Sessions, *Deep Ecology: Living as if Nature Mattered*, Peregrine Smith, 1985.

Foreman, Dave, and Howie Wolke, *The Big Outside: A Descriptive Inventory of the Big Wilderness Areas of the United States*, New York, Harmony Books, 1989.

Foreman, Dave, *Books of the Big Outside*, seasonal catalogue, Ned Ludd Books, P.O. Box 85190, Tucson, Arizona 85754.

—, "The New Conservation Movement," *Wild Earth*, Summer, 1991, p. 6-12.

Martel, Ned, and Blan Holman, "Inside the Environmental Groups, 1994," *Outside*, March 1994, p. 65-73.

McCloskey, J. Michael, and Heather Spalding, *A Reconnaissance-Level Inventory of the Wilderness Remaining in the World*, prepared for the Fourth World Wilderness Congress, Sierra Club, Washington, D.C., 1987.

McKibben, Bill, *The End of Nature*, New York, Random House, 1989.

Oelschlaeger, Max, *The Idea of Wilderness: From Prehistory to the Present*, Yale University Press, 1991.

Skutch, Alexander, *Life Ascending*, University of Texas Press, 1985.

Snyder, Gary, *The Practice of the Wild*, North Point Press, 1990.

Waterman, Guy, and Laura Waterman, *Wilderness Ethics: Preserving the Spirit of Wildness*, Woodstock, Vermont, Countryman Press, 1993.

Wolkie, Howie, *Wilderness on the Rocks*, Arizona, Ned Ludd Books, 1991.

SOURCE NOTES

CHAPTER ONE
HENRY DAVID THOREAU: ILLUMINATIONS OF A WALKER

PAGE

15 "I make it my": HDT, *The Journal of Henry David Thoreau*, eds. Bradford Torrey and Francis H. Allen, New York. Dover Publications, Inc.. (1962), vol. V, p. 478.

15 "Perhaps, I most": HDT, *The Maine Woods*, ed. Joseph J. Moldenhauer, New Jersey, Princeton University Press (1972), p. 69.

16 "In wildness": HDT, *Excursions*, New York, Corinth Books (1962), p. 185; originally Ticknor and Fields (1863).

16 "led the intellectual": Roderick Nash, *Wilderness and The American Mind*, New Haven and London, Yale University Press (1973), p. 95.

16 "came to grips": Ibid., p. 84.

16 "Thoreau lived when": William O. Douglas, in Walter Harding's *The Days of Henry Thoreau*, New York, Alfred A. Knopf (1966), p. Vll.

17 "My life was": HDT, *Selected Journals of Henry David Thoreau*, ed. Carl Bode, New York, New American Library (1967), p. 117-18.

19 "Let men": HDT, *Writings*, Boston, Houghton Mifflin (1906), 20 vols., vol. vi. p. 8-9; also Harding, *The Days of Henry Thoreau*, op. cit, p. 50.

20 "I see nothing": Ellery Channing, *The Correspondence*, op. cit, p. 161.

21 "crystallization" etc.: HDT, *Walden and Other Writings*, New York, International Collectors Library, Nelson Doubleday, Inc. (1970), p. 67-71.

21 "For the first week": HDT, Ibid., p. 71.

21 "a broad margin": HDT, The Journal, op. cit . IV. p. 433.

21 "I went to": HDT, *Walden and Other Writings*, op. cit, p. 75.

22 "Let us settle": HDT, Ibid., p. 80.

22 "In any weather": HDT, *The Writings of Henry David Thoreau*, Walden Edition, Boston and New York, 20 vols. (1906). II, p. 17-18.

23 "The belief that": Nash, op. cit., p. 85.

23 "in a single" etc.: Emerson, Nature, in *The Complete Essays and Other Writings of Ralph Waldo Emerson*, ed. Brooks Atkinson, New York. Random House—The Modern Library (1940), p. 14f.

23 "had a definite": Nash, op. cit, p. 85.

23 "For whether": John Madson. "Grandfather Country," *Audubon*, May, 1982, p. 51.

24 "Be fruitful": Genesis. *Bible*, 1:28.

24 "terrific drama in": Turner, *Beyond Geography: The Western Spirit Against The Wilderness*, New York, Viking Press (1980), p. 207.

25 "Like the Hindu": Christy, *The Orient in American Transcendentalism, A Study of Emerson, Thoreau, and Alcott*, New York, Octogan Books, 1969, p. 207.

25 "to transact some": HDT, quoted in Christy, Ibid., p. 203.

25 "Sometimes, in a summer": HDT, *Walden and Other Writings*, op. cit., p. 92-3.

26 "stupendous and cosmogonal": HDT, Ibid., p. 246.

26 "like a fragrance": HDT, quoted in Christy, op. cit., p. 189.

26 "To be in company": HDT, *Walden and Other Writings*, op. cit., p. 113.

26 "What sort of space": HD, Ibid., p. 110.

26 "at very short": HDT, Ibid., p. 113.

26 "such sweet" etc.: HDT, Ibid., p. 109-10.

27 "ready enough to": HDT, Ibid., p. 116f.

27 "was not trying" Harding, quoted in *Henry David Thoreau, What Manner of Man?*, by Edward Wagenknecht, Amherst, University of Massachusetts Press (1981), p. 99.

27 "with their bodies": HDT, *Walden and Other Writings*, op. cit., p. 116f.

27 "into which the rivers": HDT, Ibid., p. 119.

27 "sanitive... poetic" etc.: HDT, The Journal, op. cit., IX, p. 208-9 (1104).

28 "Before he set out": Channing, *Thoreau: The Poet-Naturalist*, New York, Biblo & Tanner (1966): first published 1902, p. 41-2.

28 "as if I had": HDT, The Journal, II, p. 404-5.

29 "During many years": Sanborn, *The Personality of Thoreau*, Folcraft Press, Inc. (1901), p. 4.

29 "There goes a": HDT, Ibid., p. 161f.

29 "In his trips": Burroughs, *The Last Harvest*, Houghton Mifflin Co. (1923), p. 160-61.

30 "a lumberer's drink" etc.: HDT, *The Maine Woods*, op. cit.. p. 28.

31 "Sometimes it seemed": HDT, Ibid., p. 63.

31 "It was vast": HDT, Ibid.. p. 64.

32 "What is this Titan": HDT, Ibid., p. 71.

32 "dinging... ever there is no": HDT, *The Journal*, op. cit., I, p. 54.

32 "but its own": Garber, quoted in Wagenknecht, op. cit., p. 150.

33 "a star on": HDT, *The Maine Woods*, op. cit., p. 83.

34 "an exploration by river": Wolf, *Thoreau—Mystic, Prophet, Ecologist*, Philadelphia, United Church Press (1974), p. 49.

34 "highly poetic": Ibid., p. 52.

34 "should contain": HDT, *A Week on the Concord and Merrimack Rivers*, New York, Thomas Y. Crowell (1961), p. 11-12.

34 "In my Pantheon": HDT, Ibid., p. 74-5.

35 "It is necessary": HDT, Ibid., p. 78.

35 "The wisest man": HDT, Ibid., p. 81.

35 "The perfect God": HDT, Ibid.. p. 81-2.

35 "He really thought": HDT, Ibid., p. 88.

35 "One of the most": Harding, *The New Thoreau Handbook*, with Michael Meyer, New York University Press. (1980), p. 11.

35 "The wares are": HDT, *The Journal*, op. cit.. V, p. 459.

36 "round which" etc.: HDT, *A Week*, op cit, p. 474f.

36 "Let us not": HDT, *The Writings of Henry David Thoreau*, Riverside Edition, Boston (1893), 11 vols., vol. 9, p. 160.

36 "a rural fragrance": Fields, "Our Poet-Naturalist," *Baldwin's Monthly*, April, 1877, also Harding, *The Days of Henry Thoreau*, op cit., p. 331.

37 "the stamp of": Ricketson, *The Correspondence*, op cit., p. 332.

37 "to a large extent": Porte, *Emerson and Thoreau: Transcendentalists in Conflict*, Wesleyan University Press (1965), p. 151.

37 "it is instead": Wagenknecht, op. cit., p. 56.

38-40 "Both Indians" etc.: HDT, "Chesuncook," in *The Maine Woods*, op cit., p. 90f

40 "Let me live" etc.: HDT, "Walking," in Excursions, op cit., p. 160f.

41 "the tonics and barks": HDT. Ibid., p. 185f.

42-43 "Our baggage" etc.: HDT, "The Allegash and East Branch," in *The Maine Woods*, op cit., p. 185f.

46 "One world": HDT, in *Thoreau*, by Henry Seidel Canby, Boston, Houghton Mifflin Co., 1939, p. 434.

SOURCE NOTES

CHAPTER TWO
JOHN MUIR: FOOTLOOSE IN RANGES OF LIGHT

PAGE

47 "I only went": John Muir (JM), *John of the Mountains; The Unpublished Journals of John Muir*, by Linnie Marsh Wolfe, Boston—Houghton Mifflin Co.,1938; reprinted by University of Wisconsin Press, 1979, p. 439.

49 "Climb the mountains": JM, quoted in *The Wilderness World of John Muir*, ed. Edwin Way Teale, Boston, Houghton Mifflin Co.,1954, p. 311; also in The Life and Letters of John Muir, by William Frederic Bade, Boston, Houghton Mifflin Co., 1924, 2 vols., 1:363.

49 "Do not thus": JM, in *John Muir and His Legacy*, by Stephen Fox, Boston, Little, Brown & Co., 1981, p. 5.

50 "The shadows were" etc.: *The Life and Letters of John Muir*, op cit., 1:253f.

51 "with red-blooded": JM, *The Story of My Boyhood and Youth*, Boston, Houghton Mifflin Co., 1913, p. 1-2; see also Teale, op. cit., p. 4.

51 "true on its": Teale, op. cit., p. 4.

52 "the grand, simple": JM, *Story of My Boyhood*, op cit., p. 32-33; also Teale, ibid., p. 18.

52 "Bairns... you needna" etc.: Daniel Muir, in JM, *The Story of My Boyhood*, ibid., p. 53; Teale, ibid., p. 27.

52 "Wooingly teaching her": JM, Ibid., p. 63-4; Teale, ibid., p. 32.

53 "I want you": Daniel Muir, in *The Life and Letters*, op cit., 1:62.

54 "began to relish": JM, in *The Story of My Boyhood*, op cit., p. 245.

54 "ever heard of": Daniel Muir, Ibid., p. 258.

56 "to whirl... like": JM, *Son of the Wilderness: The Life of John Muir*, by Linnie Marsh Wolfe, New York, Alfred A. Knopf (1945); reprinted by University of Wisconsin Press, 1978, p. 92.

56 "They were alone": JM, in Fox, op. cit., p. 43; also Boston Recorder, 12-21-1866.

56 "I am captive": JM, *The Life and Letters*, op cit., 1:204.

57 "My right eye" & "study the things": JM, *Son of the Wilderness*, op cit., p. 104f.

57 "Oftentimes...": JM, *A Thousand-Mile Walk to the Gulf*, Houghton Mifflin Co., 1916, x.

58 "delirious bewilderment": JM, Ibid., p. 127.

58 "on no subject": JM, Ibid., p. 70-1.

58 "The world... was": JM, Ibid., p. 136-37.

59 "Now, it never": JM, Ibid., p. 138-9.

59 "the philosophical basis": Fox, op. cit., p. 53.

60 "Now we are": JM, *My First Summer in the Sierra*, Houghton Mifflin Co., 1911, p. 20-21.

61 "I took off": JM, Ibid., p. 157-59; see also Teale, op. cit., p. 127.

62 "There is no": Whitney, in *The Life and Letters*, op. cit., 1:277.

62 "that the Valley": Le Conte, Ibid., 1:285.

62 "You would not": JM, Ibid., 1:299.

62 "grandeur of forces": JM, Ibid., 1:294.

63 "the first man": Agassiz, in *Son of the Wilderness*, op. cit., p. 160.

63 "No scientific book": JM, *The Life and Letters*, op. cit., p. 300.

63 "When I discovered": JM, quoted in *The Pathless Way; John Muir and American Wilderness*, by Michael Cohen, Madison, University of Wisconsin Press, 1984, p. 41.

64 "and we can": JM, quoted in Fox, op. cit., p. II.

64 "coupled with": JM, *The Life and Letters*, op. cit., II:85.

65 "When tired with": JM, *Steep Trails*, ed. William Frederic Bade, Boston and New York, Houghton Mifflin Co., 1918, p. 62f; also Teale, op. cit., p. 254f.

66 "When the heat": JM, Ibid.

67 "dulse and tangle": JM, *A Thousand-Mile Walk*, op. cit., p. 123.

67 "one great song": JM, Ibid., p. 162.

67 "Some of my": JM, *The Life and Letters*, op. cit., 1:296.

67 "give some of": JM, Ibid.

67 "My life work": JM, in Fox, op. cit., p. 23.

67 "Can't get a": JM, *Son of the Wilderness*, op. cit., p. 171.

68 "while those invented": JM, *The Life and Letters*, op. cit., II:7.

SOURCE NOTES

68 "only to entice": JM, Ibid., II:28.

68 "he was like": Watkins, *John Muir's America*, New York, Crown Publishers, 1976, p. 98.

68 "flesh and bone": JM, *My First Summer*, op. cit., p. 20-1.

69 "This grand show": JM, *John of the Mountains*, op. cit., p. 438.

69 "The great wilds": JM, *Steep Trails*, op. cit., p. 104.

70 "for the welfare": JM, Ibid., p. 104.

70 "Well, yes": JM, *Son of the Wilderness*, op. cit., p. 196.

70 "How I should": Mrs. John Strentzel, Ibid., p. 175.

70 "the most charming": JM, *Steep Trails*, op. cit., p. 101.

71 "All's well, Mother": Louie Strentzel, *Son of the Wilderness*, op. cit., p. 204.

71 "the happiest man": JM, *The Life and Letters*, op. cit., II:134.

72 "lost and choked": JM, *John Muir and His Legacy*, op. cit., p. 72.

73 "Go across": JM, *Son of the Wilderness*, op. cit., p. 212.

73 "The Storm King": JM, *The Life and Letters*, op. cit., II:167-8.

74 "A ranch": Louie Muir, *Son of the Wilderness*, op. cit., p. 243-4.

75 "Johnson, Johnson" etc.: JM, in *Remembered Yesterdays*, by Robert Underwood Johnson, Boston, Little, Brown & Co., 1923, p. 279-80.

75 "John the Baptist": Johnson, Ibid., p. 283.

75 "No weather": Johnson, Ibid., p. 284.

77 "should be thrown": JM, *John of the Mountains*, op. cit., p. 350-51.

77 "Any fool can": JM, Our National Parks, Houghton Mifflin Co., 1901, p. 364-65.

78 "Forestry seemed so": Nash, *Wilderness and the American Mind*, New Haven, Yale University Press, 1973, p. 134.

79 "bright dark eye": JM, The Life and Letters, op. cit., II:266f.

80 "I'm not worthy": Burroughs, *The Life and Letters of John Burroughs*, by Clara Barrus, Houghton Mifflin Co., 1925, 2 vols., II:297.

80 "A very interesting": Burroughs, Ibid., I:340 and 360.

81 "I puttered around" etc.: Muir, Ibid., p. 126-27.

81 "liked to get": Burroughs, quoted in "The Two Johns—Burroughs and Muir," by Paul Brooks, *Sierra*, Sept.-Oct., 1980, p. 56-7.

81 "Thrash the ground" etc.: *Burroughs, The Life and Letters of John Burroughs*, op. cit., II: 138.

81 "joy in the universe": Burroughs, Ibid., p. 139.

81 "Oh, get a": JM, Ibid., p. 119.

81 "just to see": Burroughs, Ibid., p. 118.

82 "rallied and solidified": Wolfe, *Son of the Wilderness*, op. cit., p. 268.

82 "and get them": JM, *Our National Parks*, op. cit., pref.

82 "keeping out destructive": JM, Ibid., p. 360.

82 "The wonderful advance": JM, Ibid., p. 362.

83 "that even nature": JM, *The Life and Letters*, op. cit., II:237.

83 "in the midst": JM, Ibid.. II:341f.

83 "I do not": Roosevelt, in *Son of the Wilderness*, op. cit., p. 290.

84 "As regards some": Roosevelt, in *The Life and Letters of John Muir*, op. cit., II:412-13.

84 "No nation": Roosevelt, "Wilderness Reserves: The Yellowstone Park," in *The Winning of the West, The Works of Theodore Roosevelt*, New York, Memorial edition (1924-26), 23 vols., III:311-12.

85 "It was a land": Roosevelt, *The Life and Times of Theodore Roosevelt*, by Stefan Lorant, Doubleday and Co., Inc., 1959. p. 206-7.

86 "in love with": JM, Muir Papers, May 19/1903, cited in Fox, op. cit., p. 126.

87 "to sacrifice his": Phelan, in *Son of the Wilderness*, op. cit., p. 316.

87 "for water tanks": JM, quoted in "The Battle for Hetch Hetchy," by Eric Seaborg, Sierra, Nov.-Dec. 1981, p. 64.

87 "They will see": JM, *Son of the Wilderness*, op. cit., p. 342.

87 "Its currents pour": JM, *John of the Mountains*, op. cit., p. 67.

87 "The richest sun-gold": JM, *The Life and Letters*, op. cit., II:215-16.

88 "in bright prismatic" etc.: JM, *Travels in Alaska*, Boston and New York, Houghton Mifflin Co., 1915, p. 300f; see also Teale, op. cit., p. 304-7.

88 "The sense of: JM, *The Life and Letters*, op. cit., II:333-34.

CHAPTER THREE
ROBERT W. SERVICE: THE WILD TRANSFORMATION
PAGE

91-92 "The Call of the Wild": Robert Service, *The Collected Poems of Robert W Service*, Dodd, Mead & Co. (1940).

92 "Seems to me": Skilly, for this quote, and those by Service while on his Slave-Mackenzie-Rat-Porcupine-Yukon rivers canoe trip, see Service's Book Ten, "The Spell of the Yukon," in *Ploughman of the Moon: An Adventure Into Memory*, New York, Dodd, Mead & Co, 1945, p. 407-458.

94 "My great-grandfather": RS, Ibid., p. 15

94 "I'm sorry to say": RS, Ibid., p. 66.

95 "Another gold rush": RS, Ibid., p. 260.

95 "Why don't you": White, Ibid.. p. 323.

96 "Vice seemed to": RS, quoted in *Robert Service: A Biography*, by Carl F Klinck, New York, Dodd, Mead & Co. (1976), p. 36f.

96 "Verse, not poetry": RS, *Ploughman*, op. cit.. p. 458.

97 "I envied no one": RS, Ibid.. p. 355.

98 "The only exciting" etc.: RS, Ibid., p. *407f.*

102 "dreaming to-night": RS, for this and other poetry quotes, see *The Collected Poems,* op. cit.

104 "Of all my life": RS, *Ploughman*, op. cit., p. 339.

CHAPTER FOUR
BOB MARSHALL: FROM KNOLLWOOD TO ALASKA'S KOYUKUK
PAGE

105 "To countless people": Bob Marshall (BM), "The Universe of the Wilderness is Vanishing," *Nature Magazine*, April, 1937, p. 236.

106 "All at once": BM, *Alaska Wilderness: Exploring the Central Brooks Range*, edited by George Marshall. Second edition. Berkeley, University of California Press, 1970, p. 133-35.

107 "the most efficient": Yard, in Nash, Roderick, "The Strenuous Life of Bob Marshall," *Forest History*, Oct. 1966, p. 23.

107 "did as much": Douglas, "For Every Man and Woman Who Loves the Wilderness," *Living Wilderness*, Fall/Winter 1956-57, p. 23-24.

108 "definitely formed on": BM, *Alaska Wilderness*, op. cit., p. 1-2.

108 "He was the fastest": BM, in Glover, Jim, "The First Forty-Sixers," *Adirondack Life*, Jan./Feb. 1985, p. 21.

109 "vague notions of": BM, *Alaska Wilderness*, op. cit., p. 2.

109 "They never felt": BM, "Impressions From the Wilderness," *Living Wilderness*, Autumn 1951, p. 10f.

111 "a region which contains": BM, "The Problem of the Wilderness." reprinted in *Living Wilderness*, Oct./Dec. 1976. p. 28f: see also Scientific Monthly, Feb. 1930.

113 "the absolutely unassessable": BM, Alaska *Wilderness*, op. cit., p. 11.

114 "But it was": BM, Ibid., p. 51-2.

114 "the supreme exultation": BM, Ibid., p. 74.

115 "We didn't say": BM, Ibid., p. 109.

116 "The fact that": BM, *Arctic Village*, New York, Harrison Smith and Robert Haas, 1933, p. 289.

116 "would rather eat": BM, Ibid., p. 379.

116 "an unusually interesting": *Forum*, June, 1933, v-vi,

116 "There can be": BM, *The People's Forests*, New York, Harrison Smith and Robert Haas, 1933, p. 62.

117 "is not to make": BM, Ibid., p. 172f.

118 "to reorient themselves": BM, Quetico Superior Papers, Minnesota Historical Society Archives, P34, Box 40.

118 "is the "preservation": BM, Ibid.

118 "His eyes reflected": Schaefer. "Mount Marcy, and—the Wilderness," in *Living Wilderness*,

Summer 1966, p. 8-9.

119 "natural mental resource" QSP, op. cit.

119 "for in the past": BM, Ibid.

120 "He was so": Broome, in Fox, Stephen, "We Want No Straddlers," *Wilderness*, Winter 1984, p. 10.

120 "Instead of the": Yard, Ibid.

120 "Right here I": Leopold, "The Last Stand of the Wilderness," *American Forests and Forest Life*, Oct. 1925. p. 602.

120 "To me": BM, QSP, op. cit.

121 "To countless people": BM, "The Universe of the Wilderness is Vanishing," *Nature Magazine*, April 1937, p. 235-240.

123 "making some short": Oberholtzer, QSP, op. cit.

123 "No launches" etc.: BM, in Olson, Sigurd, "Quetico-Superior Elegy," *Living Wilderness*, Spring 1948, p. 5f.

125 "I keep thinking": BM, *Alaska Wilderness*, op. cit. p. 63.

125 "Of course, Bob": Eaton, Ibid., p. 115.

125 "unpleasant remarks": BM. Ibid., p. 114.

125 "Everything we looked": BM, Ibid., p. 126.

126 "Bob probably": George Marshall, "Bob Marshall and the Alaska Arctic Wilderness," *Living Wilderness*, Autumn 1970, p. 30-32.

126-27 "Because the unique": BM. U.S. Congress, House Doc. No. 485, 75th Congress

128 "No man in the country": Oberholtzer, QSP. op. cit.

128 "one of its greatest": Olson, "Quetico-Superior Elegy": op. cit.. p. 12.

CHAPTER FIVE
ALDO LEOPOLD: WITNESS AT THE BREAK OF DAY
PAGE

129 "It is only": Aldo Leopold (AL), *A Sand County Almanac*, Oxford University Press (1966); paperback, *ASCA: With Essays on Conservation from Round River*, (source for *WV*) New York, Sierra Club/Ballantine (1970), 279.

131 "From the beginning": Curt Meine, *Aldo Leopold: His Life and Work*, University of Wisconsin Press (1988), 40.

132 "Dressed in his": Meine, "Aldo Leopold's Early Years," in *Companion to A Sand County Almanac: interpretive and Critical Essays*, ed. J. Baird Callicott, University of Wisconsin Press (1987), 24.

132 "but who can": Meine, op. cit., 43.

133 "We were eating": AL, op. cit., 138.

133 "I realized": AL, Ibid., 138.

135 "the protection": AL, quoted in Roderick Nash, *Wilderness and the American Mind*, Yale University Press (1973), p. 183; or Leopold's Papers, Box 5.

136 "not as meat": AL, "Wildlifers vs. Game Farmers: A Plea for Democracy in Sport," *Bulletin of the AGPA*, April 1919; reprinted in *Aldo Leopold's Wilderness: Selected Early Writings by the Author of A Sand County Almanac*, eds. David E. Brown and Neil B. Carmony, Stackpole Books (1990), p. 55-60.

137 "The problem spoken": quoted in Meine, *Aldo Leopold: His Life and Work*, op. cit., p. 177f.

138 "fulcrum point": Meine, Ibid., 194.

138 "a guiding principle": AL, "The Wilderness and its Place in Forest Recreation Policy," Journal of Forestry, November 1921. p. 718-21.

139 "Here was a": Meine, op. cit., p. 227-28.

140 "which have carried": AL, "The River of the Mother of God," in *The River of the Mother of God and Other Essays by Aldo Leopold*, eds., Susan L. Flader and J. Baird Callicott, University of Wisconsin Press (1991), p. 123-127.

142 "cutting off": AL, "Conserving the Covered Wagon," *Sunset Magazine*, March 1925, 21f.

142 "in a distinctly": Flader, op. cit., p. 26.

143 "I do not": AL, "The Pig in the Parlor," reprinted in Flader and Callicott, op. cit., p. 133.

143 "From the earliest": AL, "Wilderness as a Form of Land Use," *The Journal of Land and Public*

Utility Economics, October 1925, 398-404; reprinted in Flader/Callicott, op. cit., p. 134-42.

147 "a federal bureau:" AL, in Meine, op. cit., p. 257.

148 "by which": AL, *Almanac*, op. cit., p. 290.

148 "Possibly": AL, "Some Fundamentals of Conservation in the Southwest," *Environmental Ethics*, Summer, 1979, 131-41; also in Meine, op. cit., p. 214.

149 "Is a wolfless": AL, in *Round River: From the Journals of Aldo Leopold*, ed., Luna B. Leopold, Oxford University Press (1953), p. 150.

149 "lies not in": AL, *Game Management*, Charles Scribner's Sons (1933), p. 21.

150 "He was one": Joe Hickey, in *Aldo Leopold: A Prophet for All Seasons*, Ronald C. Meyer, video-tape, Metabases Production.

150 "We want no": Bob Marshall, see Meine, op. cit., p. 343.

151 "[Leopold] has done": Marshall, in Stephen Fox, *John Muir and His Legacy: The American Conservation Movement*, Little, Brown and Company (1981), p. 210.

151 "We do not": AL, "Why the Wilderness Society," The Living Wilderness, I, 1935, p. 6.

152 "These possible reasons": AL, Almanac, op. cit., p. 74.

153 "We Americans": AL, "Naturschutz in Germany," Bird-Lore, M/April 1936; also quoted in Meine, op. cit., p. 356.

153 "only sick land": AL, quoted in Companion to *A Sand County Almanac*, ed. Callicott, op. cit., see appendix; also in Meine, op. cit., p. 368.

154 "derangement in": AL, "Wilderness as a Land Laboratory," The Living Wilderness, July 1941, p. 3.

154 "There are some": AL, Almanac, op. cit., p. xvii.

155 "the thread": see Ribbens in Companion, ed. Callicott, op. cit., p. 101.

155 "a kind of": AL, Almanac, op. cit., p. 239f.

156 "Every living": AL, in a 1941 lecture, see Meine, op. cit., p. 413-14.

156 "We seek": AL, Almanac, op. cit., p. 280f.

157 "And when the": AL, Ibid., p. 233.

158 "lilac shoots": AL, in Ribbens/Callicott ed., op. cit., p. 106.

CHAPTER SIX
OLAUS JOHAN MURIE: EMBRACING THE WILD PULSE OF LIFE
PAGE

159 "Whether it": Olaus Murie (OM), "A Good Life," address, Annual Convention of the American Association for Health, Physical Education and Recreation, Missoula, Montana, April 30, 1963.

160 "He was the": Howard Zahniser, "Olaus J. Murie, 1889-1963," *The Living Wilderness*, Summer-Fall, 1963, p. 3.

160 "As I look": OM, untitled address to the Arizona-Sonora Section, American Society of Range Management, at Nogales, Arizona, January 17, 1963.

161 "Another man": OM, in Curry, Peggy Simson, "Portrait of a Naturalist," *Audubon*, Nov.-Dec., 1963, p. 17.

161 "the north had": OM, *Journeys to the Far North* (JFN), The Wilderness Society and American West Publishing Company, 1973, p. 33.

161 "I went along": OM, Ibid., p. 43.

163 "It was still": OM, Ibid., p. 126.

163 "blue and gray": OM, Ibid., p. 131.

163 "I seemed to": OM, Ibid., p. 132.

164 "All I can": Margaret E. (Mardy) Murie, *Two in the Far North* (TFN), New York, Alfred A. Knopf, 1963, p. 95-96.

164 "We really came": Margaret E. Murie, henceforth MM, correspondence with author, Dec. 15, 1978.

165 "What are you": in correspondence with author, Nov. 21, 1978.

165 "Each mouse label": MM, TFN, op. cit., p. 166.

165-66 "It was a": MM, Ibid., p. 181.

167 "After a winter": OM, and MM, *Wapiti Wilderness* (WW), New York, Alfred A. Knopf, 1966, p. 139.

167 "Since he was": MM, Ibid., p. 146.

168 "I know": MM, correspondence with author, Nov. 21, 1978.

168 "Olaus simply": MM, correspondence with author, Dec. 15, 1978.

168 "But not only": MM, *WW*, op. cit., p. 267.

168 "If a man": in Curry, op. cit., p. 16.

169 "I know that": OM, *WW*, op. cit., p. 189.

169 "We had become": MM, Ibid., p. 275.

169 "A wilderness area": OM, "Wilderness Philosophy, Science, and the Arctic National Wildlife Range," address, Twelfth Alaskan Science Conference as part of the Symposium: Science and the Arctic National Wildlife Range.

170 "a man of": for notes on OM awards, see Zahniser, op. cit.

171 "From the time": Collins, in Miller, Debbie S., *Midnight Wilderness: Journeys in Alaska's Arctic National Wildlife Refuge*, San Francisco, Sierra Club Books, 1990, p. 166.

171 "The conversations": MM, *TFN*, op. cit., p. 326.

171 "Well...isn't": in MM, Ibid., p. 326.

172 "This was the": MM, Ibid., p. 401.

172 "He seemed able": MM, preface, *JFN*, op. cit., p. 12.

173 "Sun and moon": OM, Ibid., p. 245.

CHAPTER SEVEN
CALVIN RUTSTRUM: ROLLING STONE OF WATERWAYS

PAGE

175 "Can it be": Calvin Rutstrum (CR), *Chips From a Wilderness Log*, New York, Stein and Day Publishers, 1978, p. 80.

176 "Only intimate": CR, *The Wilderness Life*, New York, Macmillan Publishing Co., 1975, p. 87.

176 "Rutstrum totally influenced": Mason, author interview, March 1985.

177 "I must have": CR, author interview, Feb. 1981.

177 "more like an": CR, Ibid.

177 "Both he and I": CR, Ibid.

178 "a healthy young" etc,: CR, *A Wilderness Autobiography*, Minneapolis, Nodin Press, 1979, p. 11f; originally published as *Challenge of The Wilderness*, T.S. Dennison & Co., 1970.

178 "The city": CR, Ibid., p. 18.

180 "very early": CR, author interview, Feb. 1981.

180 "had to write": CR, Ibid.

181 "It looked like": CR, Ibid.

181 "Does that mean": CR, Ibid.

181 "the release that": CR, *A Wilderness Autobiography*, op cit., p. 54.

181 "What a simple matter": CR, Ibid., p. 63f.

183 "We need the joy": CR, *The Wilderness Life*, op. cit., p. 237.

184 "pungent, very right": CR, author interview, Feb. 1981.

184 "Because you can't": CR, Ibid.

184 "strange realms": CR, *A Wilderness Autobiography*, op. cit., p. 103.

184 "a rich man's": CR, author interview, Feb. 1981.

185 "I said, 'Well'": Ibid.

185 "clippings, scribblings": CR, *Chips*, op. cit., intro.

186 "The sun rose": CR, *The Wilderness Life*, op. cit., p. 9f.

186 "While it can": CR, *Back Country*, Indiana Camp Supply Books, Inc. , 1981, p. 70.

187 "Broadly speaking": CR, Ibid., p. 237-38.

187 "a love of wisdom": CR, Ibid., p. 242.

187 "1. Get off": CR, A *Columnist Looks at Life*, Minneapolis, Nodin Press, 1981, p. 121-22.

187 "awake in the": CR, *The Wilderness Life*, op. cit., p. 26.

188 "Poetry frequently perverts": CR, *Back Country*, op cit., p. 20.

188 "into the superlative": CR. author interview, Feb. 1981.

188 "I don't attach": CR, Ibid.

188 "I'm convinced beyond": CR, Ibid.

188 "There before our": CR, *Back Country*, op. cit., p. 25.

189 "People have more": CR. author interview, Feb. 1981.

189 "From the vibrant": CR, *The Wilderness Life*, op. cit., p. 215.

190 "If you can": CR, author interview, Feb. 1981.

190 "were being slaughtered" etc.: CR, *A Wilderness Autobiography*, op. cit. p. 104.

191 "until every camp": CR, Ibid., p. 117.

191 "every last industrial": CR, Ibid., p. 118.

192 "There were too": CR, author interview, Feb. 1981.

193 "What effect does": CR, *A Wilderness Autobiography*, op. cit., p. 160.

193 "all are now": CR, Ibid., p. 197.

194 "If you want": CR, Chips, op. cit., p. 150.

CHAPTER EIGHT
SIGURD F. OLSON: VISIONARY VOYAGEUR
PAGE

196 "Always before me", Sigurd F Olson (SO). *The Singing Wilderness*, New York, Alfred A. Knopf, 1979, p. 99.

196 "My first glimpse": SO, Ibid.. p. 100.

197 "In a way": SO, Ibid., p. 104.

198 "Not only has": SO, "The Spiritual Aspects of Wilderness," in *Voices for the Wildeness*, ed. William Schwarz, New York, Ballantine Books, 1969, p. 140.

200 "Nobody in the family": SO, quoted in "His Lifetime Spent in Love With Nature," Terry Wolkerstorfer, *Minneapolis Star*, Sept. 13, 1976, p. IB.

200 "We had a": SO, Ibid.

201 "Unless some part": SO, *Open Horizons*, New York, Alfred A. Knopf (1969), p. 64.

201 "Through this initial": SO, Ibid., p. 65.

203 "The guide not only": SO, quoted in "Sigurd Olson's Continuing Love Affair With Nature," *Minneapolis Tribune*, July 15, 1979, p. 13C.

203 "I would take out": SO, quoted in "Leave it to the Bourgeois," by Frank Graham. Jr., *Audubon*, Nov. 1980, p. 35.

204 "that would widen": SO, *Open Horizons*, op. cit., p. 37.

204 "with constant searching": SO, Ibid., p. 82.

204 "a primordial thing": SO, Ibid., p. 102.

204 "the actual": SO, Ibid., p. 105.

205 "More than knowledge": SO, Ibid., p. 164.

206 "What [one] is": SO, "Search for the Wild," *Sports Afield and Trails of the Northwoods*, May-June 1932, p. 33.

206 "It is a": SO, Ibid., p. 51.

207 "purely a boat": Carhart, quoted in R. Newell Searle, *Saving Quetico-Superior, A Land Set Apart*, Minnesota Historical Society Press, 1977. p. 23.

207 "We had learned": SO, *Open Horizons*, op. cit., p. 198.

208 "The public knows": Oberholtzer, in *Saving Quetico-Superior*, op. cit.. p. 65.

208 "For a long time": SO, Quetico Superior Papers, Minnesota Historical Society Archives, Box 47, Olson letters.

209 "was the first": Searle, *Saving Quetico-Superior*, op. cit., p. 89.

209 "When I first" etc.: SO, "Voyaguer's Return," *Nature Magazine*, June-July 1948, p. 289f.

211 "Faith in the ideals": SO, "Wilderness Victory," *National Parks Magazine*, April-June1950, p. 51.

211 "As time went on" etc.: SO, *Open Horizons*, op. cit., p. 174.

212 "who would deeply" etc.: SO, Ms. in Sigurd F. Olson Papers, Minnesota Historical Society Archives, 32.B.3.4F.

213 "Editors wanted action": SO, *Open Horizons*, op. cit., p. 184-85.

213 "I have seen" etc.: SO, "Why Wilderness?," *American Forests*, Sept. 1938.

214 "so that anyone": SO, Olson Papers, op. cit.

215 "A case of" etc.: SO, "The Wilderness World of Sigurd F. Olson," 16mm film or videotape, by Ray Christensen and Steve Kahlenbeck, Filmedia, Inc.

SOURCE NOTES

215 "You've got to": SO, Ibid.

215 "not just through": Pyter, "A Bio-Bibliography of Sigurd F. Olson," thesis for partial fulfillment of Master of Arts Degree in Library Science, Jan. 1972, University of Minnesota, p. 15.

215 "What I had": SO, Olson Papers, op. cit.

216 "rationed like water": Frank B. Hubacheck, Journal of Forestry, July 1956, p. 474-75.

216 "because of the": Cole, *Library Journal*, March 15, 1956. p. 711.

216 "a rewarding": Durham, *American Forests*, Dec. 1956, p. 59f.

216 "From it": SO, *Listening Point*, New York. Alfred A. Knopf, 1980, p. 3-4.

217 "These wiry little": SO, The Lonely Land, New York, Alfred A. Knopf, 1961, p. 7.

217 "The urge began": SO, Ibid., p. 12.

218 "We called him": quoted in Graham, "Leave it to the Bourgeois," op. cit., p. 31, 228 "We hadn't more": Fraser, "We Went La Verendrye's Way," *Maclean's Magazine*, October 1, 1955.

219 "The movement of a canoe" etc.: SO. *The Singing Wilderness*, op. cit., p. 72f.

220 "They were very": Graham, op. cit., p. 37.

220 "Sig could think": Langen, author interview, 1985.

221 "I was scared": SO, in Graham, op. cit., p. 36.

221 "go into the": Searle, *Saving Quetico-Superior*, op. cit., p. 150-1.

221 "Of all the organizations": SO, Olson Papers, op. cit.

221 "There was a": SO, author interview, 1977.

222 "Wilderness to the people" etc.: SO, "We Need Wilderness." *National Parks Magazine*, Jan.-March 1946, p. 19f.

223 "Henry David Thoreau said" etc.: SO, "The Spiritual Aspects of Wilderness," op. cit., p. 131f.

224 "Not the fishing": SO, Ibid.

225 "a base of": SO, "The Spiritual Need for Wilderness," speech at the April, 1965, Ninth Biennial Sierra Club Wilderness Conference.

225 "paean to the": Weeks. Atlantic, June 1969, p. 113.

226 "the long view": SO, *Reflections From the North Country*, New York, Alfred A. Knopf, (1976), xii.

226 "When a man": SO, Ibid. p. xi.

226 "It will be": SO, author interview, 1979, see Vickery, Jim dale, "A Bluejay Calling: A Conversation with Sigurd F. Olson," *Canoe*, Jan.-Feb. 1980, p. 16f.

226-27 "Even at the tender": SO, film, Christensen and Kahlenbeck, op. cit.

227 "Nothing is ever": SO, Olson Papers, op. cit.

227 "wilderness character of": see Searle, Saving Quetico-Superior, op. cit., p. 204.

229 "A new adventure": SO, quoted by Malcolm Mclean, president of Northland College, at Olson's funeral in Ely, MN.

INDEX

Index